THE TEXTUAL TOWNSMAN

The Textual Townsman

WRITING URBAN IDENTITY IN EARLY MODERN JAPAN

Thomas Gaubatz

Columbia University Press
New York

Columbia University Press wishes to express its appreciation for assistance given by the Wm. Theodore de Bary Fund in the publication of this book.

Columbia University Press
Publishers Since 1893
New York   Chichester, West Sussex

Copyright © 2026 Columbia University Press
All rights reserved

Library of Congress Cataloging-in-Publication Data
Names: Gaubatz, Thomas author
Title: The textual townsman : writing urban identity in early modern Japan / Thomas Gaubatz.
Description: New York : Columbia University Press, 2026. | Includes bibliographical references and index.
Identifiers: LCCN 2025023627 (print) | LCCN 2025023628 (ebook) | ISBN 9780231221306 hardback | ISBN 9780231221313 trade paperback | ISBN 9780231563666 ebook
Subjects: LCSH: Japanese fiction—Edo period, 1600–1868—History and criticism | Cities and towns in literature | Group identity in literature | National characteristics, Japanese, in literature | Literature and society—Japan | LCGFT: Literary criticism
Classification: LCC PL747.37.C5 G38 2026 (print) | LCC PL747.37.C5 (ebook) | DDC 895.63/32093552—dc23/eng/20250626

Cover design: Melania Shipton
Cover image: Adapted from Santō Kyōden, *Grilled and Basted Edo Playboy* (*Edo umare uwaki no kabayaki*, 1785), first fascicle, 10. Courtesy of the Tokyo Metropolitan Library.

GPSR Authorized Representative: Easy Access System Europe, Mustamäe tee 50, 10621 Tallinn, Estonia, gpsr.requests@easproject.com

CONTENTS

Introduction
Writing Urban Identity   1

Part I. Reimagining Urban Community

Chapter One
The Community of the Marketplace   49

Chapter Two
The Poetics and Politics of Townsman Property   91

Chapter Three
From Townsman Culture to Townsman Narrative   132

Part II. Copying Characters

Chapter Four
The Misfortune of Being Saved by One's Arts   171

Chapter Five
Representing Normality   213

CONTENTS

Epilogue
From the Textual Townsman to Edo Urbanism 255

ACKNOWLEDGMENTS 271

NOTES 277

BIBLIOGRAPHY 303

INDEX 319

THE TEXTUAL TOWNSMAN

INTRODUCTION

Writing Urban Identity

> Someone once said: If you are born a townsman and wish to take pleasure in that path, you must first grasp the rank and standing of the townsman, and then, having learned the principles that make a townsman a townsman, correct your heart and govern yourself accordingly.
>
> —NISHIKAWA JOKEN, *THE TOWNSMAN'S SATCHEL*

In 1719, the Nagasaki-based merchant-intellectual Nishikawa Joken (1648–1724) released *The Townsman's Satchel* (*Chōnin bukuro*), a collection of didactic reflections directed at readers of the urban, commercial classes: the "townsmen" (*chōnin*) of the title. Joken was best known for his wide-ranging writings on astronomy and geography and for his flirtations with Western learning, but in *The Townsman's Satchel* he assumed the role of popular educator, drawing equally on his training in Confucian thought and his lived experience as a merchant in the great port of Nagasaki. His publisher, the enterprising Kyoto bookseller Ibarakiya Ryūshiken, was one of the premier printers of works of popular instruction, having met with great success with the didactic tracts of the Confucian educator Kaibara Ekiken (1630–1714). But Joken's works were of a slightly different and, at the time, quite novel character. Ekiken was a humanistic thinker who in many ways rejected the moral rigorism of some of his warrior peers and aimed to educate a wide audience that crossed class grounds, but his work was still structured by a consciousness of social hierarchy and shot through with the paternalistic concern of a member of the social elite. In contrast, Joken blended the language and values of the Confucian tradition more richly with the lifeworlds of his townsman readership.

INTRODUCTION

The Townsman's Satchel is striking for its eclecticism. Joken's work unfolds as an open-ended grab bag of anecdotes, aphorisms, didactic admonitions, philosophical musings, erudite etymologies, and diverse textual references both to the Chinese classics and to the Japanese vernacular tradition. As Joken writes in his preface—which assumes less the pedantic seriousness of an educator than the tongue-in-cheek self-deprecation of a popular humorist—snippets of conversations heard here and there have piled up in his ears, and, because he is too foolish and incompetent to judge which to heed or how to put them into practice, he has thrown them all into this "townsman's satchel" in the hope that someone might make use of them, even if only for passing amusement. In keeping with Joken's sardonic posture, the work is equivocal to the point of near contradiction. Rarely does Joken state any principle outright: He begins with an anecdote or adage that he has heard somewhere; ruminates on its implications, sometimes affirming it and sometimes questioning it; and eventually comes to a tentative conclusion, only to seemingly contradict himself with a contrasting anecdote a few pages later. He makes virtuosic use of the aphorism: the nugget of folk wisdom that seems to mean more than it says, but that never exhausts the possibility of exceptions and even competing truths. The true merchant is the one who engages in commerce for social good rather than individual profit—but "a folding screen must be kept crooked to stand up," and the merchant whose morals are too straight will soon see his business fold.[1] The townsman cannot do without learning, but excessive attention to study can threaten the integrity of one's business. The text is one of moderation, of provisional truths, and of an always only conditional embrace of didactic principles.

The irony of *The Townsman's Satchel* is that it addressed an imagined readership of self-identified townsmen who nevertheless had to be told, and told in writing, "the principles that make a townsman a townsman" (*chōnin no chōnin taru kotowari*).[2] The text is structured by a certain aporia of meaning at the heart of the identity of the early modern townsman: Townsman status was a "way" (*michi*) one was born into and lived within before it was articulated in language and understood as part of a larger social or urban imaginary. The eclectic, unbounded, and contradictory nature of the text—its very form as a "satchel" of fragmentary truths—evokes the complexity of the social world behind this textual process of normalization, the diversity of social positions and values and worldviews that were just barely contained within the seemingly straightforward category of townsman. Urban identity was less a stable category of social being than an ongoing process of social becoming, one that would be mediated through textual practices of reading and writing. The nature of this textual becoming is the subject of this book.

Although the earliest complete edition of *The Townsman's Satchel* dates to 1719, the work seems to have been composed over a decade or two: its preface bears the date of 1692, at the height of the late seventeenth-century urban zeitgeist of the Genroku era (1688–1704). When Jōken was writing, Japan's urban centers were sites of unprecedented social diversity, where disparate status communities were set into mutual relation through spatial proximity and economic interdependence and integrated into larger social and spatial imaginaries. Early in the seventeenth century, shogunal policies of peacetime social and economic administration had led to the formation of castle towns throughout the realm; the rise of a robust domestic money economy in the middle decades of the century spurred the explosive growth of these emerging cities as rural entrepreneurs rushed to participate in the urban marketplace and impoverished peasants absconded from the countryside in the hope of finding work and social advancement amid the city's tantalizing opportunities. First among the realm's burgeoning cities were Kyoto, Osaka, and Edo, but with the rapid development of transportation, trade, and communication networks in the latter half of the century, these central hubs were steadily integrated into an interregional economic system that reached to provincial castle towns, post stations, market towns, and hot springs as the countryside was progressively woven into a porous and heterogeneous urban fabric. The late seventeenth-century cultural efflorescence known as "Genroku culture" (*Genroku bunka*) was a product of this complex, multivalent, diverse, dynamic, and urbanizing society.

The rapid urbanization of the seventeenth century went hand in hand with another historic development that would have profound and lasting effects on Japanese culture and society during the centuries that followed: the commercialization of the woodblock print.[3] Following a brief period of experimentation with movable type in the early decades of the Tokugawa peace, the middle years of the seventeenth century saw the formation of a commercial publishing industry based on the technology of the woodblock print, which was better attuned to the orthographic complexities and aesthetic principles of the Japanese script, the technological capabilities of a handicraft culture, and the capital limitations of the early marketplace.[4] This early woodblock-print culture had a strong didactic orientation. Informed by the textual traditions of the social and cultural elite (court aristocrats, high-ranking warriors, old Kyoto merchant families, and the Buddhist clergy), seventeenth-century print initially centered on scholarly work in the Confucian and Buddhist traditions or on the reproduction of the classical literary canon—or else, when addressing wider audiences, transmitting elite literacies and values in a top-down fashion. However, as the reading public grew and intellectuals of different social backgrounds found opportunities to put their voices into print, this culture came to assume diverse forms, articulating and lending fixity to the values and worldviews of Tokugawa Japan's diverse status communities. Though the print culture of seventeenth-century Japan was initially based in the old cultural center of Kyoto, the latter half of the century would see the growth of semi-autonomous publishing fields in Edo and Osaka, built on the unique literacies and sensibilities of the urban demographics of those cities—and, as the seventeenth century gave way to the eighteenth, the progressive integration of these disparate communities into an interregional print marketplace.[5] The result of this proliferation and diversification of published expression was a complex and highly differentiated field of print genres, each tailored to a different readership through its unique material forms and textual strategies: Tokugawa print culture was one expression of a stratified status polity, projected into textual form.[6] But just as the space of the city could integrate diverse status communities into a provisional (if always heterogeneous) unity, woodblock-print culture could likewise act as a unifying force, crossing boundaries of locality or class or status to produce a shared sense of identity in the face of difference. Jōken's text is a case in point: the didactic musings of a Nagasaki merchant-intellectual published by a Kyoto bookseller and addressing the townsmen of the realm at large. The townsman's processes of textual self-formation were defined by this push and pull between the constitutive particularism of a diverse and stratified urban world and the normalizing force of a didactic print culture.

During the decades in which Jōken was composing his eclectic work, other writers were also experimenting with attempts to render in writing the complex and dynamic social realities of the urban world. The date of

INTRODUCTION

Joken's preface places it shortly before the death of Ihara Saikaku (1642–1693), the experimental linked-verse poet turned fiction writer. Saikaku's early fiction had consisted of heavily allusive, ironic, and ribald explorations of the hedonistic world of erotic leisure, but in his late works he turned his attention to the everyday economic affairs of the urban townspeople, producing a series of works that modern scholars have dubbed his "townsman pieces" (*chōnin-mono*): *Japan's Eternal Storehouse* (*Nippon eitaigura*, 1688), *Worldly Mental Calculations* (*Seken munezan'yō*, 1692), and the posthumously compiled *Saikaku's Loose Threads Tied Off* (*Saikaku oridome*, 1694). Like Joken's work, Saikaku's depictions of the townsman's lifeworlds consist of eclectic, meandering, and often contradictory collections of narrative anecdotes, descriptive sketches, and didactic admonitions—a flexible and formless form suited to the complexities and contradictions of contemporary urban life. A master of citation, Saikaku drew on a diverse range of textual structures, print genres, and literary forms to capture the complexity and dynamism of the townsman's social and economic existence, developing new kinds of narrative form and narrative voice that would be used and adapted by later writers to capture the shifting topoi of the urban world. In so doing, he pioneered a set of conventions and representations that would repeatedly be used and adapted to write urban identity.

If Joken began *The Townsman's Satchel* amid the urban zeitgeist of the Genroku era, the publication of the completed work by Ryūshiken came in a slightly different cultural moment: the rising climate of conservative moralism and economic austerity of the Kyōhō era (1716–1736). As the explosive economic growth of the seventeenth century gave way to a period of social stasis, the early eighteenth century saw the gradual articulation of a set of stable norms, structured around the institution of the townsman household (*ie* 家), that became the orthodox, orienting ideology of urban society. These standards were produced within and disseminated through new forms of didactic and informational print material that circulated through an increasingly unified, interregional publishing marketplace. Just as the social dynamism of the late seventeenth century was reflected in Saikaku's narratives of mobility, the popular fiction of the Kyōhō era was deeply colored by a consciousness of fixed roles and a stultifying sense of everyday normality. The writer to best capture this normalizing zeitgeist was Ejima Kiseki (1666–1735), whose "character pieces" (*katagi-mono*) depict eccentric and deviant characters who are desperate to transgress the rapidly ossifying norms of polite townsman society. Kiseki's character pieces, which drew on and transformed the narrative forms Saikaku developed, would in turn become the basis of one of the most productive genres of eighteenth-century popular fiction, acting as a framework for humorous reflection, sometimes transgressive and sometimes deeply normative, on the possibilities of individual expression within the social roles that the townsman had carved out for himself.

This book explores how old identities were transformed and new ones constructed in the space of the early modern city and in the medium of the woodblock print. It begins from the premise that, even and especially within a society that was segmented into distinct status groups (*mibun*), identity was not a given but a problem. In particular, the heterogeneous, stratified, and conflictual space of the city demanded new articulations of identity and community that would allow diverse urban dwellers to make sense of their place and social prospects within a larger world. The urban community contained ambiguities and tensions that demanded explanation, driving the production of voluminous bodies of printed matter. I argue that urban identity was predicated on textual practice: articulated in writing, mediated by commercial print, and in many cases given narrative form and imagined through literary tropes and metaphors. I focus on the figure of the townsman, but attend equally and especially to the margins of townsman identity, both inner and outer: the internal hierarchies and tensions that a unified sense of townsman identity served to resolve or conceal, as well as the other status groups that the townsman defined himself against but that were never fully excised from the urban community and from the townsman's sense of self. My analysis focuses on the complex interplay between the literary and the social—the ways in which emerging categories of social subjectivity were reflected in new print genres and explored through new narrative forms. I show how the identity of the townsman was shaped by the circulation of printed texts, and how forms of literary narrative played important roles in imagining and orienting his place in the urban world: making sense of the diversity of urban society, policing the boundaries of urban identity, and offering a space for the symbolic exploration of modes of social becoming and self-expression that were excluded from what became an oppressively normalized set of orthodox townsman values.

INTRODUCTION

My central contention is that the narratives of townsman identity offered by popular prose fiction symbolically contained the tensions within a heterogeneous and stratified urban society. Here I mean *contain* in two senses. On the one hand, any vision of urban identity and community had to be capacious and inclusive enough that it could address readers of diverse backgrounds and what were in practice very disparate and even oppositional life prospects. On the other, any such sense of identity was inevitably predicated on contradictions, hierarchies, and exclusions that threatened the sense of an urban community unified by shared values and lifestyles; those internal tensions had to be either addressed and accounted for or otherwise effaced. One of the key ideological functions of popular fiction at this moment was to offer symbolic resolution to these tensions. In a word, popular fiction offered a vision of urban identity that was simultaneously normative and diverse: a set of flexible sociocultural norms that could include and set into meaningful relation disparate social positions.

THE POLITICS OF TOWNSMAN LITERATURE

This book addresses one of the oldest debates surrounding Tokugawa popular fiction: What was the political significance of cultural production by commoners? To date, the popular culture of Tokugawa Japan has often been viewed as a site of symbolic subversion of shogunal ideologies. In such a schema, the townsman has generally played a heroic role, whether as a proto-bourgeois figure bracing against the strictures of a feudal regime or as a proxy for the common people at large, and "townsman literature" (*chōnin bungaku*) appears as a voice of popular resistance (though usually only symbolic or implicit) to warrior authority. The precise nature of this assumed subversion varies depending in part on the genre and moment: The works of Saikaku and Kiseki are of a different form and spirit than, say, the popular fiction of nineteenth-century Edo. It also reflects the methodological inclinations of the modern critic: Ideological subversion may take the form of parody of classical texts, satire of contemporary society and politics, inventive circumvention of governmental censorship, or simply the uninhibited expression of commoner worldviews, often centered on money (social mobility, conspicuous consumption, leisure), that seem to defy the moral rigorism and hierarchical consciousness of the ruling warrior class.[7] Regardless of the particular form, such interpretations generally have relied on a rubric of realism, wherein the townsman's literary expression exposes a complex and vibrant reality obscured or distorted by official ideology, while also (in literary historical terms) anticipating the rise of modern forms of realist representation. In the background of these interpretations is the premise of the Tokugawa shogunate as a feudal and authoritarian regime that enforced its hegemony through the "status group system" (*mibun-sei*): the administrative division of society into a rigid hierarchy of hereditary status groups, with all but the elite ranks of the warrior class excluded from political power. If the townsmen were the politically alienated victims of social control, then townsman literature was the heroic voice that emerged in the sphere of culture in response to its suppression in the sphere of politics, a voice that therefore could not help but carry an implicit import of political subversion. Recent treatments in the field of cultural history have shown significant nuance in treating these premises, emphasizing the ideological ambivalence of popular culture and its relationship to the status group system, but the ultimate horizon of political interpretation remains one of a binary opposition between dominant and dominated classes.[8] Even when not called out by name, the townsmen continue to reemerge as the authentic source of a vibrant urban and commercial culture that carries the potential of relativizing, if not outright subverting, the hegemonic ideology of the ruling (warrior) class.

Such approaches have not gone uncontested. One of the most vocal critics of the narratives of townsman literature was Nakano Mitsutoshi, who argued that Tokugawa popular fiction was devoid of original ideological content (*shisō-sei*). To Nakano, popular fiction had two aspects: On the one hand, it served to disseminate the values of the ruling class, and on the other it incorporated elements of formalistic literary play that served primarily to entertain. Nakano would stress that these two functions, manifest in the dual modes of didacticism (*kyōkun*) and amusement (*kokkei*), were complementary, that the forms of literary play carried out under the banner of amusement were not at all subversive, merely in service of a larger didactic purpose—the proverbial spoonful of sugar—and that the dominant values disseminated in these ways were enthusiastically embraced and reproduced by the populace.[9] Nakano's highly polemical revision to Tokugawa literary history did not so much do away with the premises of townsman literature as reproduce them in an inverted form: Here the rigid social hierarchies of the status group system exist not to be resisted or subverted but simply to be embraced as a harmonious social totality. "It goes without saying that upper-class culture was considered superior. Certainly there was a lively townsmen's culture, but it was always in an inferior position vis à vis the upper-class culture, which it constantly sought to imitate."[10] Needless to say, this vision of an apolitical literature is not without its own politics. It posits that the purpose of literary production is to reaffirm the legitimacy of political authority and the social status quo. In practice, however, critiques such as Nakano's have not succeeded in establishing an alternative interpretive paradigm as much as they have done away with interpretation altogether: Scholarship has in recent decades moved away from literary interpretation and ideological critique and toward empirically oriented modes of literary and book history. One is tempted to conclude that this turn away from interpretation by the literary field is to a degree complicit in the persistent returns to the politics of townsman literature. Interpretation can of course not be done away with entirely, and when empiricist forms of literary history attempt to do so, older paradigms will continue to reproduce themselves, especially in the form of larger narrative histories that, to one degree or another, must consider the politics of cultural production and the macroscopic questions of who has a voice and what that voice says. In the absence of a substantive alternative, the politics of townsman literature continue to haunt Edo studies as a sort of perennial return of the repressed, the kind of methodological straw man that specialist scholars delight in polemicizing against and in doing so endlessly reproduce.

My aim, in contrast, is to properly revive the specter of townsman literature, and in so doing to offer an alternative paradigm for interpreting the politics of Tokugawa popular culture. I do so by shifting focus from self-expression to self-fashioning. I approach townsman literature not as a passive and representational medium through which the townsman gives expression to forms of subjectivity rendered invisible by official ideology, but as an active and generative medium that produces new kinds of identity and community by giving form to the shared sensibility of its readers. In this regard, I approach townsman literature as one example of what David Atherton has referred to as "the politics of form" in early modern Japanese literature. Highlighting the homology between a literature structured by genre form and the formal distinctions of the status group system, Atherton sketches a literary politics in which popular fiction functions as symbolic reflection on a society structured by formal categories of status. Drawing on Jacques Rancière's theorization of the politics of aesthetics, Atherton argues that "the formal mutations of commercial fiction possessed the power to rework the relationship among present, past, and future; to defamiliarize social conventions; to make latent social, economic, and affective forces apprehensible; to mold the contours of different forms of community; and to authorize the voices that could be heard within those communities—voices that might otherwise be inaudible beyond the page."[11] I take inspiration from this method insofar as I am concerned with the capacity of literature to aid in the reimagining and ordering of society, and that I do so with particular attention to the logic of status group as a structuring principle and to the formal conventions of certain genres of narrative. However, my feeling is that the level of conceptual generality opened up by such a broad interpretive paradigm transcends the properly political and points toward the epistemological: It describes the modes of knowledge and representation of the early modern moment but resists generalization concerning how such modes may reflect consistently and concretely on the structures of the social and political fields. If, following Rancière, we take the politics of aesthetics (or literature) to be in the "distribution of the sensible," then the context of early modern status society demands attention to the possibility of different and competing sensibilities, rooted in if not strictly bound by the values and orientations of different status communities.[12] In this sense, my grasp of politics is narrower and perhaps more conventional. It concerns the question of power relations between status communities or social classes, power relations within status communities (hierarchies of prestige or wealth that may be mitigated or amplified, effaced or revealed), and, most critically, where the boundary of a status community is drawn—who gets to be a townsman, how, and why.

I explore these questions through the lens of print culture: I see popular print as addressing a public and thus giving shape to a community, disseminating norms and producing new kinds of identity.[13] In this context, literature gave shape to the sensibilities of communities of readers. Understanding this generative function requires taking seriously the didacticism of Tokugawa popular fiction, but with the caveat that the ruling class and its ideologues did not have a monopoly on didacticism. Literature could transmit the worldviews of different social classes. In particular, commercial print culture was from the late seventeenth century onward often aligned with the social and economic agency of the urban commoner classes. By giving didactic expression to the values and worldviews of those social strata, popular fiction contributed to the normalization of urban society, producing new identities and giving shape to new communities oriented by those identities. This media-centric perspective demands a shift away from the assumption of realism—revealing realities obscured by ideology—toward a framework of performativity, wherein the circulation of print is part of the dialogic process through which social identities are perpetually produced and renegotiated from generation to generation. In other words, I see popular fiction as an ideologically productive medium: not merely a negation of dominant ideologies, nor an unequivocal reproduction of the same, but as a medium for the bottom-up articulation of the worldviews of emergent communities within the dominated classes. I argue that these communities came to possess and exert new forms of social power that were ultimately symbiotic with warrior authority but constituted through their own systems of domination: the internal economic hierarchies of urban commoner society and the systematic marginalization of the rural periphery and the urban underclass. In my reading, the politics of townsman literature was the symbolic production of the townsman subject through the ideological legitimation of these emergent forms of social power.

These literary arguments, however, are built on a more basic historical contention that, in the late seventeenth century, the forms of identity and community represented by the term *chōnin* were less clear, unified, and coherent than has been assumed to date, whether in literary or cultural history. Prior treatments of townsman literature have taken the term *chōnin* to refer to an a priori category of subjectivity, a social given that awaits literary expression; these assumptions, in turn, are built on the outdated premise that the Tokugawa status group system was an arbitrary and artificial construction imposed by the warrior authorities in a top-down fashion as a technique of social control. According to such an understanding, Genroku culture represents the triumphal moment in which the urban commercial classes achieved confident and implicitly subversive self-expression in the fields of popular cultural production. To the contrary, my study begins from the observation that the seventeenth century was a time of radical shifts in the nature of urban identity and community: a moment in which the nature of urban community was thrown into question

INTRODUCTION

because of the integration of disparate geographic communities into an interregional commercial network and the subsequent commodification of urban property. These social and spatial transformations were coeval with new textual practices: They were inextricably intertwined with the circulation of woodblock-printed texts through an increasingly integrated trans-urban publishing industry, the development of which went hand in hand with the formation of new and larger visions of urban community and identity. My interest is in the roles played by printed texts in making sense of such shifts and, in particular, in the forms of social meaning made possible through literary narrative. The remainder of this introductory chapter presents the grounds for and stakes of this historical contention. In so doing, I also offer a preliminary sketch of the method that orients the readings that follow.

FROM TOWNSMAN TO URBAN COMMONER

The first commonplace that must be overturned in order to grasp the dynamism of the Tokugawa urban world is the notion that the status group system consisted of a rigid hierarchy of "four estates" (*shimin*): the social taxonomy, borrowed from Song Confucianism, of warrior/administrators, peasants, artisans, and merchants (*shinōkōshō*). According to this framework, it is often said that the category of *chōnin* comprised artisans and merchants, the merchants being the lowest on the social totem pole based on a stigmatization of commercial enterprise as lacking in social value. Although the taxonomy of the four estates was sometimes used by social thinkers to describe the social functions carried out by different populations, this was a theoretical construction rather than an administrative one. Moreover, the social functions described by the four estates—administration (warriors), agricultural cultivation (peasants), production of craft goods (artisans), and distribution of resources (merchants)—were generally taken in a nonhierarchical sense: The idea was that each class had an important role to play. In any case, the populace of Tokugawa Japan was not divided into four estates in any formal sense.[14]

Nor were distinctions of status simply imposed on the populace from above. Revisionist social and urban histories of the past few decades, still undigested by the literary field, have sketched a more complex and nuanced image of this system, its social logics, and its political dynamics.[15] Informed by an attention to social marginality and to the autonomy of dominated classes within the Tokugawa polity, this work approaches the status group system as a reflection of the bottom-up organization of local communities, their multivalent modes of interface with one another, and their always imperfect integration into the structures of shogunal administration. One of the methods brought to understand these status communities is an attention to space: what Yoshida Nobuyuki terms "socio-spatial structure" (*shakai-kūkan kōzō*) and David Howell glosses as the "geography of status."[16] The premise is that distinctions of status reflected the organization of local communities and were inscribed in the spatial matrix of the Tokugawa polity in the boundaries of and relationships between communities. This homology between the social and the spatial operated at various levels, ranging from the macroscopic administrative distinctions between different districts (urban versus rural) to the division of such districts into smaller units (warrior households, townsman blocks), and further down to the spatial structure of individual lots, houses, and tenements. Even at the lower end of the unpropertied urban margins, status subjectivity was defined by less concrete but still socially constitutive spatialities such as the itinerary of the street peddler, the commercial network of the trade organization, or the territory of the outcast headman.[17] Moreover, these distinct valences of socio-spatial structure intersected and overlapped in complex ways given that individuals might carry some obligations to the community of their residence and others to their trade organizations. The result was a complex and multivalent system of spatialized status distinctions that Tsukada Takashi has dubbed "stratified and composite" (*jūsō to fukugō*).[18] When such multivalent constructions of status are taken into account, Tokugawa urban society appears less as a stable and static matrix of discrete containers than as a complex fabric of intersecting and competing forms of social power, one in which conflicts among communities (or between local communities and administrative authority) often played out through competing claims to and appropriations of space.[19] These methods bear some resemblance to Henri Lefebvre's iconic dictum that "(social) space is a (social) product," but the methods of socio-spatial structure apprehend the production of space on a more microscopic level: not the large-scale, phenomenological spatial schemas that define a society and a historical moment (and that, to one degree or another, reflect the ideologies of the ruling class) but the intricate lived spaces that define everyday social existence and that, at least in the early modern moment, were never fully assimilated into a uniform and top-down spatial imaginary.[20] Moreover, and in contrast to earlier approaches that viewed the early modern city largely in terms of warrior authority over the dominated commoner classes, the perspective of socio-spatial structure tends to foreground the differentiated forms of authority exerted at various levels and by distinct communities, all with their own hierarchies of dominant and dominated strata.

The identity of the townsman was rooted in the socio-spatial structure of the urban block or ward (*chō* 町). Though the precise form of the *chō* was subject to variation in relation to local topography and other concerns of urban planning, in its most archetypal form, what is now called the "two-sided *chō*" (*ryōgawa-chō*), it consisted of several dozen shopfronts arranged in two rows, facing one another across a shared thoroughfare of roughly one hundred yards. At each end of the *chō* were manned sentry posts and gates that were closed to enforce curfew. In theory, property within the *chō* was divided into lots of roughly equal size, and each was owned by the (typically male) head of a commoner household; these propertied household heads collectively made up the formal community of the *chō*, sometimes referred to as the *chōjū*. Membership in this local community dictated much of the social lives of individual townspeople given that it entailed and was reproduced through participation in collective rituals—marriage, funerals, annual celebrations as for the New Year, and so on. It also frequently shaped the economic activities of its members, given that many *chō* were organized by trade, acting as local guilds or informal cartels. Individual members of the *chō* community of course had spheres of social exchange that reached beyond the borders of the *chō*, whether in the form of extended family networks, commercial and professional connections, or circles of artistic and cultural exchange. These broader networks would increasingly shape the social and spatial practices of townsmen as the early modern era progressed but, at least in the seventeenth century, the local community of the *chō* played an outsized role in the daily lives of its members. Just as the status of the warrior was linked to his affiliation with his lord's household (*ie*) and the status of the peasant reflected his residence in a rural village (*mura*), the townsman was defined by his membership in the local community of the ward: A *chōnin* was not a man of the city at large as much as a man of his own *chō*.[21]

Historically, the institution of the *chō* as the basic unit of urban community had roots in the war-torn chaos of medieval Kyoto. Such neighborhoods had emerged from the collapse of the urban grid of the Heian capital, and, amid the turmoil of the medieval period, had formed close-knit communities, assembled for collective self-protection.[22] Although the autonomy of these communities would be forcefully broken by the unifying hegemons of the late sixteenth century, the *chō* as a self-governing community remained the paradigm of socio-spatial structure in the urban centers of early seventeenth-century Japan, providing (with some regional variation) the template for development in Edo and other castle towns.[23] The community of the *chō* was also incorporated seamlessly into the Tokugawa polity as the terminal unit of administration for urban districts. In the eyes of the state, townsman status was linked to membership in a *chō* community for the purpose of administration as well as for the extraction of formal duties, which might include maintenance of thoroughfares and open spaces, various forms of corvée labor, and taxes levied both in money and in kind. This was merely one expression of a larger social system in which local communities were bound by certain obligations to the warrior administration and were in turn granted certain privileges and protections; as long as the obligations were fulfilled without disruptions to the public order, communities remained largely autonomous.[24] This interface between local community and warrior authority, mediated through the system of mandatory population registration (*ninbetsuchō*), served to integrate the self-organizing and particularistic forms of local community into the rational administrative structure of the Tokugawa state.[25] Thus the community of the *chō* was the framework through which the individual townsman became a part of the polity by fulfilling his designated duties to the realm.[26] Despite this incorporation, however, the *chō* continued to be organized and regulated from the bottom up, by and in the interest of its members.

This local sense of townsman identity—the *chōnin* as man of his *chō*—was quite narrow. First, it was gendered. In most accounts, the townsman was a man, and although women occasionally assumed full public stature as household heads, these cases were rare. One of the nearly universal characteristics of the Tokugawa status system in all of its valences was that it treated women as dependents of the male household head and compartmentalized women's activity and labor within the literal space of the home.

Second, the local sense of townsman identity was marked by class. Because membership in the *chō* community was limited to those who held property, it excluded anyone who resided in the *chō* but did not own property there—dependents (children, but also servants, apprentices, and clerks) and, more important, renters. Although the class of renters was likely small at the dawn of the Tokugawa period, the explosive growth of cities during the seventeenth century largely took the form of a rapidly expanding population of renters, many of whom came from rural origins and most of whom resided in small, densely packed tenements (*nagaya*). The renter class became an enormous substratum of urban society, above the underclass of beggars and outcasts, but nevertheless alienated from urban property and thus from participation in local self-government. (This class stratification within the *chō* intersected in unexpected ways with hierarchies of gender, for the norms of gender tended to be much looser among the lower ranks, where the distinction between public and private was less strict and women as well as men were often expected or simply required to work to survive.)

Despite this stratification, and in contrast to the narrow sense of the townsman as the propertied household head, another, looser use of the term *chōnin* became increasingly operative as the centuries of the Tokugawa period progressed. In short, the word *chōnin* came to be used with little distinction among the various ranks within urban commoner society, in a capacious sense that could include the wealthy and propertied alongside the desperately poor. This loose usage is perhaps most common in official sources, or broadly those written by warriors: Although the difference between the property-owning townsman and the renter was a matter of great concern for the residents of the *chō*, the warrior authorities did not always make such distinctions. Shogunal officials would sometimes distinguish between the propertied and unpropertied classes of urban commoners, referring to the latter with informal and largely pejorative terms such as "lower ranks" (*shimojimo*) and "persons of trifling stature" (*karoki monodomo*), but such distinctions usually were made in the case of conflicts between the different urban strata, like the periodic urban riots that occurred in moments of famine and economic crisis. Excepting such moments of crisis, official sources like shogunal edicts would often use the term *chōnin* loosely as one of address and interpellation of the nonwarrior urban classes broadly speaking. This usage was also based in broader distinctions of socio-spatial structure: not the particularistic locality of the individual *chō*, but the broad and schematic distinction between urban districts (*machikata*) and rural districts (*zaikata*). The more general interpretation of the word *chōnin*, however, was not just a matter of warrior observers painting urban society in broad strokes. Indeed, it was a natural reflection of an inherent ambiguity and porousness within the category of *chōnin* itself, one that emerged into clear relief during moments of relative social mobility—when the lower ranks alienated from rural society might abscond from their villages to make a commercial livelihood in the growing cities, when the urban poor might find a way to work their way up into property ownership, and when, conversely, the wealthy and established might decline and fall into obscurity. Even though the distinction between the propertied and the unpropertied was important and would remain operative throughout the era, it was one of the more porous of the social distinctions that defined Tokugawa society.

Incidentally, the ambiguities inherent in the category of *chōnin* in its seventeenth-century context—between a particularistic sense of the term and a generic one, between a sense that is strictly gendered and one that is not—are reflected roughly in the two common English translations: *townsman* and *urban commoner*. Although the latter is the more common in recent scholarship, I favor the former for its specificity, for how it evokes a historical link to local forms of community (the *chōnin* as man of the *chō*), and for how it makes explicit the implicit gendering of proper *chōnin* status as fundamentally a form of masculinity. Throughout this book, I for the most part use *townsman*, even when such specificities are being thrown into question, to retain a focus on what is at stake in the loss of specificity, but on occasion use *urban commoner* when referring to populations that are clearly marked as outside the milieu of propertied *chōnin* society but still fall within larger articulations of urban community.

These divergent meanings mark a space not just of discursive tension but of social contestation that would play out in practice from the seventeenth century into the eighteenth. In a word, the proper sense of *townsman* gave way to the more capacious *urban commoner*: *Chōnin* identity shifted from a function of membership in local communities to a flexible sense of shared values, social and economic practices, lifestyles, and sartorial and aesthetic expressions. This shift was precipitated by the historic transformation of the domestic economy in the latter half of the seventeenth century: the development of robust and interregional networks of transportation, communication, and trade; the rapid growth of the domestic consumer economy; the emergence of cities as hubs of consumption and marketplaces orienting the production of goods in the rural hinterland; the concomitant explosion of urban populations; and the commodification of urban property in the face of the circulation of merchant capital across geographical boundaries. Large numbers of peasants migrated from the rural periphery into cities to become part of an urban underclass of renters, part of the urban community in practice if not necessarily in name. Some of their descendants, over the course of a generation or two, were able to literally make names for themselves, working their way up into property ownership. Many more, though, languished as day laborers or street peddlers at the margins of urban society. Even the ranks of propertied townspeople became increasingly stratified. Some old households withdrew from active business, sustaining themselves through strategic lending of capital reserves. Others faded into obscurity or ruin (whether because of the whims of economic fortune or the immodest spending of household heads and heirs), and others succeeded in meteoric rises to the heights of the merchant elite. The *chō*, of course, remained present as an institution throughout the Tokugawa period and, certainly to a greater degree than in the modern era, shaped the lives of its residents. But the late seventeenth century saw the gradual and relative waning of the *chō* community as an institution that defined the social and economic practices of its members. It became a framework to work with or within or even against but not to be defined and thus constrained by.

One might describe this shift as the formation of townsman culture, or, more precisely, *the townsman as constituted through the formation of a shared culture*. This transformation, in which the defining parameters of townsman identity shift away from particularistic and local socio-spatial structures toward larger and looser formations of shared values, includes dimensions that cannot be fully accounted for by the empiricist methods of social history, and that demand attention both to the social imaginary as expressed in cultural production (literature and theater) and to the material ways such a cultural imaginary circulated and was standardized: the emerging communicative networks of woodblock-print culture.[27]

It is in the context of a shift from the community of the *chō* to the formation of a diverse and deeply stratified urban society that I situate the popular fiction of Saikaku and Kiseki as a series of discursive and narrative attempts to make sense of townsman identity. At a point when a local and particularistic sense of identity was being eroded by historic demographic shifts brought about by the evolution of the domestic marketplace, what did it mean to be a townsman? What did it mean for the propertied elites whose communities were gradually being hollowed out and rendered porous by the commodification of urban property? What did it mean for the generations of interregional merchant capitalists whose social influence and economic clout flowed smoothly across the geography of status? What did it mean for the fluid and mobile but highly economically insecure lower stratum of renters and unpropertied working poor who, without being proper members of any local community, came to make up the majority of the urban population? How could these disparate strata make sense of their respective prospects and mutual relations? Were they, after all, part of a shared community—a society of townsmen unified by values and lifestyles—and if so, what forms of social agency did that sense of shared identity enable, and what did it preclude or obscure? My grasp of the politics of townsman literature, if we would call it that, is not in the confrontation between townsman and warrior subjectivities within a framework of resistance or subversion, but in the question of how the textual practices of the slowly congealing townsman community structured, made visible (or invisible), and made sense of the emerging hierarchies, boundaries, and power structures of urban society. In other words, the question is what was at stake in the formation of a shared sense of townsman identity.

Let me clarify what I mean by identity. For this study, I understand identity largely in relation to status group: The identity in question is that of the *chōnin*, and his identity was with others who identified or were identified as such. To the extent that status group is understood in relation to community membership, I understand identity and community as two sides of the same coin, and my perspective throughout this book shifts frequently from one side to the other. This parallelism is most concrete in the bottom-up articulations of identity rooted in socio-spatial structure—the *chōnin* as member of the *chō*—but more broadly I attend to the ways in which the question of what it meant to be a townsman is inextricably intertwined with questions of who that category included, who it excluded, who was allowed to enter into or assume it, how and to what degree, and so on. Although these questions are not precisely those of community in the concrete sense of the *chō*—as it were, a Weberian *Gemeinschaft*—they are oriented around distinctions between an *us* and a *them* (or multiple *thems*) and around a felt and lived sense of equivalence among the *us*, a belief that whatever circumstances of geography or occupation or birth that might separate the *us*, "*we* townsmen" are still ultimately in the same situation, faced with similar prospects of how to navigate it and to what possible ends, and a comparable set of values, attitudes, and practices that guide that navigation. This sense of identity as a "*we* townsman" is of a different type and order from the formal structures of status group, whether those regulated locally by *chō* membership or those administered from above through population registers and urban edicts. I am concerned precisely with this shift: with the moment at which a particularistic sense of status as membership in local community gives way to and transmogrifies into a looser, more portable, and more capacious sense of (status-based) identity rooted in shared values and practices.[28]

One is tempted to describe this emergent sense of townsman identity as a kind of class consciousness. I avoid this term for a few reasons. First, despite its sometimes porous boundaries, the category of townsman is not one of social class. Although it is true that in practice the term *chōnin* became unmoored from the community of the *chō*, it remained, even at its loosest and most flexible, defined by the categorical and hereditary distinctions of status that structured Tokugawa society. Perhaps more important, the internal stratification of the townsman status group itself resists an attempt to collapse it into a single class. It would be more accurate to say that the townsman status group had its own internal class structure—the differentiated strata of tenement renters, shopfront renters, and propertied household heads, each of whom had its own set of interests and opportunities—and that the shared sense of townsman status identity that emerged around the turn of the eighteenth century functioned precisely to efface those differences. Conversely, however, my point is also not to suggest that this was purely a discursive construction, that it was a strategic projection by early modern ideologues or a methodologically prescribed hallucination by modern historians. As a useful example of such a treatment of class, Sarah Maza has argued provocatively that the French bourgeoisie did not exist, in the sense that none of the historical actors who might be identified as such claimed membership in it or claimed to be

INTRODUCTION

acting in its interest: Her intervention is to deconstruct "the myth constructed by modern historians of a hegemonic, self-conscious, and more or less unified bourgeoisie."[29] I share certain sympathies with her approach, in the sense that I consider the image of a unified townsman class, an agent of cultural resistance in lieu of revolutionary politics, to be part of the historiographical myth of townsman literature. But where Maza goes so far as to suggest that the bourgeoisie did not even exist as consciousness, I suggest that the early modern townsman status group, to the degree that it transcended the particularities of locality and the bounds of local community (the *chōnin* without a *chō*), existed primarily as consciousness.[30] This emerging sense of townsman identity, less class consciousness than class-as-consciousness, served not to articulate a position of cultural resistance, but to compensate for and symbolically resolve the latent tensions and ambiguities within an increasingly diverse and stratified urban society. In my reading, the politics of the townsman and his textuality concern the internal hierarchies of urban society, the logics of appropriation and exploitation that structured and enabled urban commoner property, and the drawing of symbolic and social boundaries separating the townsman proper from the urban poor and the outcast classes.

This sense of townsman identity, the townsman's class-as-consciousness, was coeval with the circulation of texts and was structured by textual practices of reading and writing. It was through the narrative articulations of popular fiction circulating in the print marketplace that the townsman imagined his identity as part of a larger urban community. Here I take inspiration from Pierre Bourdieu for his attention to the ways in which the fundamental social categories through which a society imagines itself are produced in discourse and legitimated through publishing: "The capacity for bringing into existence in an explicit state, of publishing, of making public (i.e. objectified, visible, sayable, and even official) that which, not yet having attained objective and collective existence, remained in a state of individual or serial existence—people's disquiet, anxiety, expectation, worry—represents a formidable social power, that of bringing into existence groups by establishing the common sense, the explicit consensus, of the whole group."[31] Per Bourdieu, social classes in the first place are merely probabilistic clusters of social positions; these classes emerge into self-awareness and are thus brought into existence only through discursive and symbolic acts, especially those that project publics through the circulation of media. To a certain degree, this ubiquitous process applied to all status groups in Tokugawa society, which came to be oriented to varying degrees by shared norms (of warrior or peasant identity) that transcended locality and operated across regions and domains, a consequence of a society gradually becoming more interconnected, networked, and mobile. But these processes were especially important, and took unique forms, for the category of *chōnin*. One reason is the innately porous nature of the townsman community, which demanded textual production to aid both in navigating its ambiguities and in policing its boundaries, most notably the problematically unstable boundary between the townspeople and the lower urban margins. More importantly, though, the fundamental nature of the townsman's livelihood, habitus, indeed his very social being, was built on literacy. The townsman's subjectivity was constituted as textual practice.

THE SOCIAL POETICS OF THE WOODBLOCK PRINT

The Tokugawa period was the first time in Japanese history that literacy spread beyond small circles of elites. In the preceding centuries, in keeping with the material and social affordances of a manuscript culture, access to the technology of writing remained the purview of political and religious authorities—court aristocrats, high-ranking warriors, and members of religious institutions. Although the medieval period saw the emergence of new literary traditions among the elite Kyoto commoner stratum (*machi shū*) and some spread of literacy among the common people, it would not be until the seventeenth century and the Pax Tokugawa that the production and consumption of written texts would become a matter of daily life for large segments of the population. Although literacy remained far from universal, the administration of nearly every status community was built on written communication and the production of documentary records and regulations. Within a polity predicated on and structured by the use of textual communication, literacy became an imperative, a highly valued skill that promised concrete benefit and even social mobility to individuals and communities. This historical condition, that of a social world in which the routines of everyday life are inextricable from textual practice, has been referred to by historian Amino Yoshihiko as a "society of writing" (*moji shakai*)—alternatively, a "textual society."[32]

INTRODUCTION

This textual society was inflected differently for different status groups, however. Textual practice was perhaps most common among the ruling warrior class, especially following the shogunate's endorsement of the "two paths of martial and literary arts" (*bunbu ryōdō*), which aimed to effectively refashion the warrior class into a stratum of cognitive laborers dedicated to the everyday tasks of social administration. Literacy—especially facility with the scriptural language of classical Chinese and, through it, the Chinese classics—had always been highly valued in the upper ranks of warrior society; under the new demands of peacetime and fostered by the Tokugawa shogunate's promotion of education, literacy now spread throughout warrior society through the near-universal institution of domain academies. For the warrior, the technologies of writing and reading were prerogatives of status; they were also practical necessities for anyone who held (or wished to hold) a bureaucratic position within an administrative class. Conversely, literacy was relatively slow to develop among peasants, especially those on the lower rungs of the village hierarchy. This is not to suggest that literacy was not seen as having great value in rural society, that it was not supported by local schoolhouses and addressed by vast quantities of agricultural texts, or that it did not spread steadily across the centuries of the Tokugawa peace.[33] But the peasant, to the degree that they remained a peasant, was bound to the village of their birth, and the primary way the status community of the village reproduced itself was through a combination of oral transmission of folk knowledge and practical transmission of manual skills. Amid the strenuous daily and seasonal cycles that structured the peasant's everyday life, textual practice, though carrying the promise of great benefit, was a luxury to be pursued in moments of leisure. Despite the proliferation of local schoolhouses to the point of near ubiquity by the nineteenth century, rural literacy rates remained inconsistent, showing great regional variation even when first surveyed systematically in the Meiji period.[34]

The circumstances were different for the townsman, for the very livelihood of the urban and mercantile classes depended on a facility with textual communication. Bookkeeping and calculation. Contracts. Lawsuits. Deeds for the purchase, sale, or rental of urban property. Correspondence, for coordination with family branches and communication with business partners. The higher ranks of the townsman class also pursued textual practice as a kind of leisure, in the myriad forms of cultural play through which elite merchants rubbed elbows with high-ranking warriors and court aristocrats—linked verse, mad verse, *nō* chanting, all the forms of classical cultural training that marked a shared pedigree across status groups within the upper strata of urban society. In the words of social historian Nakai Nobuhiko, "In contrast to the peasant, who was raised amid the community of a household or a village and who was educated through processes of oral and bodily transmission, the townsman's distinctive process of self-formation was rooted in the acquisition of literacy."[35]

Traces of such textual processes of self-formation can be seen in the earliest years of the Tokugawa period. Among the most famous documents of early merchant culture is the seventeen-article testament of the Hakata merchant Shimai Sōshitsu, intended to define the proper conduct of his heir through principles of personal economy, hard work, humility, and caution in business ventures; similar documents, like that of the Kōnoike house, would be produced later in the seventeenth century.[36] However, although such early house codes were at some level related to the townsman's self-formation, these texts remained local in scope. Shimai Sōshitsu's famous testament was, after all, intended as a private document for his heir, and perhaps for the small circle of relatives who he envisioned managing the affairs of the household in his heir's stead. Moreover, although such house codes have often been used in historical ethnographies of Tokugawa merchant culture, they remained quite rare in the seventeenth century. They would not become common until the eighteenth century, when the household had been established as the near-universal unit of townsman society, and even then likely existed in only a small number of relatively elite families.

The same could be said for one of the other textual foundations of seventeenth-century townsman identity: ward documents and regulations. These regulations took a number of forms. Some promoted goodwill among members by mandating collective decision making, regular meetings, and shared participation in community celebrations and rituals. Others policed the exclusion of outsiders by placing restrictions on the status or occupation of houseguests, renters, or buyers of urban property. Still others aimed to smooth over tensions and promote an image of equality by regulating architectural appearances and limiting the frontage occupied by a single household. The social logic running through such regulations is that of a nominally egalitarian local community invested in social rituals and material practices that prioritize collective over individual interest.³⁷ They also give a clear articulation of the identity of the *chōnin* as townsman: In early ward regulations, the term *chōnin* often referred exclusively to householding members of the *chō* in question. For example, a set of regulations from the Kyoto ward of Honnōjimae-chō, dated to the ninth month of 1620, dictates, "When a house is to be bought or sold, the seller must be guaranteed by a *chōnin*, and the buyer must be guaranteed by someone of another *chō*."³⁸ Here, the term *chōnin* refers specifically to a member of Honnōjimae-chō itself: The fundamentally local, limited range of the community (and of the audience for such regulations) gave the word an almost deictic quality, the reference of which was only fixed by the social affiliations of the people who used it. And this highly local sense of townsman identity was rooted in and reproduced through the social and material affordances of a manuscript-based textual culture. The limited circulation of handwritten documents—house codes, ward regulations—naturally defined the scope of the status communities and social identities that they could aid in articulating and reproducing.

Such manuscript culture persisted through the Tokugawa period, but its influence in mediating status-based identity (the particularism of local manuscript circulation) would be increasingly counterbalanced by the normalizing influence of woodblock-printed texts. My interest in this book is in how the new constructions of townsman identity—and the formation of townsman identity as such—were intertwined with the new textual practices of commercial woodblock-print culture. In this regard, I am in dialogue with a growing body of work on the social impact of woodblock print capitalism on early modern Japan. Mary Elizabeth Berry has shown how the medium of commercial woodblock print, informed by and built on the taxonomic rationalism of the shogunate's systems of social administration, functioned to produce a "library of public information" that gave early modern readers a shared image of themselves and their world. In mapping out its forms and functions, Berry suggests also that the books of this library integrated (new) readers into a new kind of public, defined by its access to and participation in the community of print: "Making society visible to itself, they conspired in the making of society."³⁹ Similarly, Eiko Ikegami has situated the emergence of woodblock-print capitalism amid what she refers to as a "network revolution" in which—due to the increasing density of communicative, economic, and associational connections throughout society—early modern Japan saw the formation of new modes of sociality, community, and identity as "emergent properties in networks."[40] Although this work has tended toward the empirical rather than the theoretical, much of it resonates with a media-theoretic perspective—whether that of McLuhan, Eisenstein, Ong—on the ways in which new media technologies and modes of inscription emerge in tandem with new communicative circuits and produce new forms of consciousness, community, and subjectivity. I share this interest in the capacity of print media to bring communities into being, what might be called the social poetics of the woodblock print.

I remain wary, however, of any direct analogy between the widely documented (if variously interpreted) historical impact of movable type in Europe and that of xylographic printing in Japan, which might, under the guise of an expansive comparativist vision, all too easily collapse the particularities of Tokugawa Japan (and of the xylographic regime) into familiar historical narratives of modernization. With respect to the historiographical frameworks embraced by print culture studies such as those of Berry and Ikegami, I am skeptical of how readily they point, despite various hedges, to the horizon of modernity. Conversely, such studies also tend to posit the Tokugawa status group system as an implicitly oppressive one that must be overcome, in this case by the circulation of texts across boundaries both social and geographic—and the community formed by such circulation is none other than the modern nation, or something resembling it. Thus, with regard to print, the narrative that emerges is one of an emerging print culture, driven by the commercial demands of the marketplace and centered on the sensibilities of a commoner readership, that increasingly circulates across boundaries of status to throw existing social hierarchies and distinctions into question. Certainly, books can and do cross boundaries, but this does not necessarily mean that they suspend, subvert, or dissolve those boundaries: As the revisionist urban history has shown, the boundaries themselves were equally a reflection of the bottom-up social organization of local status communities. One of the unique qualities of the Tokugawa polity, especially in the microcosm of the city, was that it placed such disparate communities in proximity, established relations between them, and made them mutually intelligible without collapsing the distinctions between them. I suggest that the urban medium of the woodblock print did the same. Although I agree that early modern identity might be understood as an emergent property that took form through interaction and was shaped by cultural practices, including and especially the powerful mediation of print media, my readings suggest that such practices have no obligation to liberate or to subvert. They are equally likely to reproduce and reify norms of status by projecting them into the realm of culture, or produce new norms with their own logics of hierarchy and exclusion—or simply engage in a subtle renegotiation of existing identities and social boundaries.

My interest is in the social poetics of woodblock-printed media as a space for the articulation and negotiation of forms of identity and community: not just those that defy the logic of status (whether in a top-down or bottom-up sense), but also and especially those forms of identity and community at the very heart of the status system, which themselves were emergent properties of the socio-spatial networks of a society in flux. If the commercial woodblock-print industry served the function of producing new publics, it did not simply do away with distinctions of status. The category of *chōnin*, which had originally existed only through the particularistic structures of local communities or as a heuristic administrative abstraction, emerged as a coherent form of subjective identification through the operation of woodblock-print capitalism in constituting new publics. Such status publics were, of course, not always clearly and precisely differentiated: They evolved in tandem with the publishing field. This process must be traced both through the material circulation of printed texts and through the interpretation of the contents of printed works—whom they address, how, and how those modes of address may draw or collapse social distinctions. In both regards, the late seventeenth century saw the formation of new forms of commercial print that addressed and thus gave form to a townsman reading public.

For most of the seventeenth century, the emerging field of commercial print made few firm distinctions of status. Regarding the corpus of popular print known to posterity as *kana-zōshi* (vernacular booklets), Laura Moretti has argued convincingly that seventeenth-century print culture was centered on the didactic production of a "community of fully-fledged human beings."[41] To do so, these texts often reproduced, adapted, and popularized the ideologies of the dominant social class, but they only rarely worked to police distinctions between warrior, townsman, peasant, and outcast: They projected the values of the ruling class as the basis of universal norms. This was probably a reflection, at least in part, of an early and exploratory stage in the development of the publishing field, which was putting out material in a haphazard fashion and only heuristically developing a grasp of the particular demographics of its readership. Of course, in some very loose sense, the imagined reader of seventeenth-century vernacular print was an urban reader. To a large degree, it was specifically a Kyoto reader, given that Kyoto was overwhelmingly the center of print production until the later decades of the seventeenth century. But Kyoto was also uncommonly diverse in its demographics. In addition to the burgeoning commoner populations, the city boasted a social and cultural elite drawn from the old court aristocracy, the old townspeople of late medieval Kyoto, the Buddhist clergy, and the elite warrior class, as well as the lower-ranking warriors, *rōnin*, and lesser priests who were likely behind much of the city's popular textual production.

The situation was different in Osaka, however, and the emergence of textual genres written by, for, and about the townsman was driven by the entrepreneurial development of the publishing field in that city. Osaka was a community of merchants. Although the city grew rapidly as an economic hub given its status as the central marketplace for rice and agricultural goods from the provinces, it was slow to develop a textual culture of its own; the earliest independent publications of Osaka booksellers appeared only in the early 1670s. The Osaka publishing industry, which emerged even later than that of Edo, initially consisted primarily of small booksellers dedicated to linked verse, reflecting the rising popularity of the Osaka-based Danrin school of Nishiyama Sōin. These booksellers operated at a much smaller scale than did the established publishing houses of Kyoto, existing primarily to produce and circulate materials among small and relatively closed circles of linked-verse practitioners. Another portion of the early Osaka publishing field produced local guidebooks, business directories, and gazetteers—a clear reflection of the commercial orientation of the merchant metropolis. In addition, a small but rapidly growing number of booksellers devoted their energies to producing didactic and informational texts for a newly literate commoner readership—an entrepreneurial faction of the publishing field that both cultivated and was cultivated by the entrepreneurialism of Osaka's merchant residents. Yet another segment, slightly later to develop, was dedicated to the publication of *jōruri* librettos, responding to the growing popular interest in the puppet theater as it evolved toward the depiction of everyday commoner lives in the domestic tragedies of Chikamatsu Monzaemon and his contemporaries.[42] In all these subsections of Osaka publishing, one can observe a divergence from the textual culture of seventeenth-century Kyoto, which, despite the innovations within the *kana-zōshi* corpus, remained strongly linked to the classical tradition and thus rooted in the literacies and norms of the military and aristocratic classes. In Osaka, we see the emergence of a textual culture produced by and for commoners.[43]

This commoner-centric textual culture slowly took root during the 1670s, but it was only with the sensational popularity of Ihara Saikaku's early works of erotic prose fiction that the Osaka publishing field grew to a scale that could equal or compete with that of peers in Kyoto and Edo.[44] One of the first known writers of townsman stock, Saikaku was born into a wealthy Osaka merchant household in 1642, and by the age of fifteen had begun composing linked verse.[45] When he was twenty-five, following the untimely death of his wife, he retired from the affairs of his household, took the tonsure, and dedicated himself to a literary career as an experimental linked-verse poet on the cutting edge of the Danrin school, achieving significant local fame through extraordinary performances of extemporaneous solo composition (*yakazu haikai*). Perhaps inspired by the capacity of such media spectacles to reach an audience beyond the small circles of linked-verse practitioners, the author shifted his focus to fiction with the sensational *The Life of an Amorous Man* (*Kōshoku ichidai otoko*, 1682), infusing the vernacular prose narrative of the *kana-zōshi* with the urbane wit and sophisticated wordplay cultivated through his poetic practice. Saikaku's shift to prose narrative and his embrace of the emerging systems of commercial print would allow him to reach a wider urban audience, both in Osaka and beyond; within a decade, the popularity of his fiction would transform the Osaka community of boutique booksellers into one of the driving forces in the interregional integration of commercial publishing.[46] Indeed, the publishing history of Saikaku's work marks a narrative of the progressive cultivation and normalization of multicity publishing agreements and systems of distribution. Following the publication of *The Life of an Amorous Man* by the otherwise anonymous and likely amateur publisher Aratoya Magobei (Kashin), the sensational work saw repeated reprintings, including a high-profile pirate edition released in Edo with illustrations by the popular woodblock artist Hishikawa Moronobu, suggesting an emerging awareness of Edo as a ready market for print fiction. Some of the works that followed entailed joint publishing agreements with Edo booksellers acting as exclusive distributors, but *Japan's Eternal Storehouse* (*Nippon eitaigura*, 1688) was the first to be published as a "three-city edition" (*santoban*), printed by the Osaka publisher Morita Shōtarō in collaboration with Kaneya Chōhei in Kyoto and Nishimura Baifūken (more commonly known as Hanbei) in Edo.[47] The phenomenon of three-city editions, which gradually became more common after this text, indicates how Saikaku's distinctive voice and vision were coeval with the progressive development of an interregional urban fabric of trade, transportation, and communication systems, through which printed texts circulated along with other goods. The townsman's processes of self-formation played out within the socio-spatial affordances of these evolving systems of material distribution and textual communication, as print disseminated norms and narratives that told the entrepreneurial classes who and how they should be.

Ihara Saikaku may have been singularly influential in driving the development of the Osaka publishing field, but he was not alone in writing to address the rapidly increasing readership of the late seventeenth century.[48] Saikaku's fiction, beginning with *The Life of an Amorous Man*, quickly became the template for a new field of witty, aesthetically sophisticated, entertainment-focused, popular prose: the body of vernacular short fiction known to posterity as the *ukiyo-zōshi* (floating world booklets).[49] Although Saikaku would generally be recognized (if sometimes contested) as the pioneer and paragon of the form, other emerging writers would follow in his footsteps to carve out a new market for popular fiction. Some of the authors to find success in Saikaku's wake were, like him, linked-verse poets by training, but many were also author-publishers—enterprising booksellers who undertook the task of filling out their product lines with their own pens. Some were based in Osaka, such as Nishizawa Tahei, a purveyor of *jōruri* playscripts that transitioned to popular fiction through the efforts of the second household head under the penname of Ippū. Kyoto came to have its share of writers as well, beginning with Nishimura Ichirōemon, Saikaku's most immediate epigone and primary rival in the field of prose fiction; with the rise of Hachimonjiya Jishō and Ejima Kiseki in the early eighteenth century, Kyoto would gain ascendancy over the field of popular fiction. Less common were Edo-based writers. A few, such as Ishikawa Tomonobu, followed in Saikaku's footsteps, but it would not be until the rise of Edo *gesaku* in the mid-eighteenth century that that city would become a driving force in the interregional print marketplace. Although the new currents of commoner-centric print culture that flowed out of Osaka would largely integrate (notwithstanding some local rivalries) with the Kyoto bookselling establishment, the dynamics of print culture would, at least for a generation or two, continue to be defined by the cultural authority of the Kamigata region. The townsman textual culture and the normative images of townsman identity disseminated through print at this moment would overwhelmingly be centered on Kyoto and Osaka. Even when authors like Saikaku and his various followers depict the townsmen of Edo (or of provincial castle towns), it is very much through a Kamigata brush.

In most histories of Tokugawa period literature, Saikaku's fiction is taken to mark a pivotal break from the generally didactic textual culture that defined the seventeenth-century *kana-zōshi*: The birth of the *ukiyo-zōshi* represents a new tradition of popular fiction, one largely unconcerned with the transmission of matters of moral import or practical value. In contrast, I follow Laura Moretti's suggestion that the *kana-zōshi* and *ukiyo-zōshi* have more in common than previous scholarship may have acknowledged.[50] In particular, I maintain that the works I take up in this book in many ways extend the didacticism of seventeenth-century print culture, that many early modern readers looked to the works of Saikaku and his followers not just for entertainment but also for didactic messages and practical value. Nevertheless, while acknowledging these continuities and stressing the didactic functions of more recognizably literary texts, I would like to observe a subtle but substantive shift in the nature of literary textuality, precipitated in large part by the entrepreneurial environment of the Osaka publishing field. The late seventeenth century saw an increasing distinction between texts that aimed to instruct and those that aimed to entertain. In this regard, the emergence of new forms of prose fiction was only half of the equation: The birth of the *ukiyo-zōshi* went hand in hand with the formation of newly specialized print genres dedicated to didactic instruction and informational transmission.

To give one example, the loose genre of "courtesan review" (*yūjo hyōbanki*), which had been a perennially successful category of popular print throughout the seventeenth century, was, like most popular print of its time, remarkably eclectic in both form and content: It comprised material ranging from detailed and sexually explicit review books to instructional conduct guides to collections of supposedly true anecdotes to evocative and allusive narratives of urban pleasure. In all these forms, the genre is known to have richly informed and in many ways overlapped with Saikaku's early erotic works.[51] As Saikaku and his contemporaries took this inspiration to develop new forms of aesthetically sophisticated comic narrative, the genre of courtesan review gradually faded in popularity, replaced by simple informational guidebooks or "detailed views" (*saiken*), consisting of maps to the brothel districts with names of women working there and prices for their services.[52] Similarly, the period from the late seventeenth century through the first few decades of the eighteenth saw the birth of a panoply of informational and instructional genres—ranging from the highly popular *chōhōki* (records of great treasures; see chapter 4) to the moral tracts of Kaibara Ekiken. Fiction of this period—in the hands of writers such as Saikaku, Nishimura, Miyako no Nishiki, Yashoku Jibun, Nishizawa Ippū, and Ejima Kiseki—moved steadily away from the eclectic and heterogeneous textuality of the *kana-zōshi* and toward the more formally consistent forms of fictional prose narrative that aimed explicitly to entertain.

Despite this general shift, however, the *ukiyo-zōshi* in its mature form still incorporated strong elements of didacticism. Many works written well into the eighteenth century continued to express moral premises, in their prefaces, in their narratorial voices, and even in the didactic implications, whether practical or ethical, that may be read between the lines of their stories. This was the case even for Saikaku's early erotic works. Although they eschew explicit instruction in favor of presenting a complex and multivalent grasp of contemporary social realities, works such as *The Life of an Amorous Man* and *The Great Mirror of Myriad Elegance* (*Shoen ōkagami*, 1684) act as inductive explorations of the ethos of refined libertinism known by the term *sui* (elegance, connoisseurship), revealing both practical and ethical dimensions of the cult of romantic sophistication and interpersonal savoir-faire that had over the seventeenth century emerged in the context of the licensed sex trade. These are not works that sought to strictly prescribe a concrete set of principles, certainly not moral principles in any conventional sense, but they still express the instructive functions of the earlier generation of courtesan reviews, presenting a vision of erotic sophistication that was ideologically powerful precisely to the degree that it was embedded in vividly realized and often ambivalent narrative forms.

INTRODUCTION

This tendency is even more pronounced in the author's townsman pieces, beginning with *Japan's Eternal Storehouse*. Just as Saikaku's early erotic works were shaped by earlier courtesan reviews and pleasure guides, these works drew from a textual genealogy of entrepreneurial manuals and get-rich guides that claimed to instruct enterprising readers on the path to wealth. Saikaku problematized and complicated some of the claims made in that corpus—work hard, be honest, exercise personal thrift—but he also fleshed out those principles, made them concrete, and wove them through narratives that have almost always been read, both by Saikaku's contemporaries and by modern scholars, as didactic tales of a different order. In other words, Saikaku took the blunter and more direct didacticism of seventeenth-century print culture and sublimated it into more complex forms of narrative that demand active interpretation to unpack but that nevertheless extend the didactic function of offering examples of conduct and probing them as potential models for emulation.

More fundamentally, it was the very nature of the medium of the woodblock print to exert a normalizing force. Print fiction presented images of townsman identity that became norms simply by virtue of their circulation, and disseminated narratives of the townsman's social trajectories, both upward and downward, that created a shared social imaginary in increasingly integrated communities of urban readers. Even when not explicitly didactic, such narratives acted as a model, showing the entrepreneurial townspeople what they should look like and who they should aspire to be. However complex, ambivalent, unpredictable, or even satirical and self-critical this body of fiction might be, it is the nature of print to lend a fixity to the images and stories that circulate in its pages. These stories were idiosyncratic, surely, but readers throughout urban Japan encountered the same idiosyncrasies, through which they became less eccentricities and more norms in and of themselves: elements of a shared print culture, a collection of "mirrors" (*kagami*) and "primers" (*tehon*), as the titles of so many works suggest, that members of the entrepreneurial classes could use to imagine and fashion themselves.

INTERPRETING THE "SPACE OF THE COLLECTION"

The chapters of this book center on two bodies of work: part 1 on Ihara Saikaku's townsman pieces and part 2 on Ejima Kiseki's character pieces.

My focus on these writers is to a degree strategic, less concerned with their significance from the perspective of literary history and more with the lenses they offer into the townsman's processes of textual self-fashioning. Saikaku, the great pioneer of townsman prose, is the one writer in perhaps all of Japanese literature who is most thoroughly and consistently seen as the spokesman for a single social group or class; his work thus offers an ideal staging ground for a revision to the politics of townsman literature.[53] Kiseki, though long dismissed as merely a formal stylist and competent popularizer of townsman prose, likewise interests me for how his writing extends and reflects critically on the same processes—not as an epigone of Saikaku, but as a highly original writer and deceptively observant satirist, one who creatively adapted Saikaku's prose into new symbolic forms that allowed him to comment on the increasing conservatism of townsman society in the early eighteenth century. More generally, these writers orient my study because they exemplify the sublimated didacticism of the *ukiyo-zōshi*, which they use to explore the question of what kinds of conduct define the proper (or improper) townsman.

The works of Saikaku and Kiseki are rarely unambiguous or unequivocal in their didactic import: Principles are posed and then questioned, sometimes tacitly subverted by the plots that unfold within and despite their didactic framing, sometimes reaffirmed or sometimes displaced by new principles that set new narrative arcs into motion. The fiction of Saikaku is distinguished by a nimble and mercurial style of narrative, informed by the imaginative leaps of Danrin linked verse, that jumps unpredictably from one topic to the next, often accompanied by a tonal inversion (as from the elevated to the vulgar or the tragic to the comic) and a subversion or reevaluation of claims that the narrator has just made.[54] Most *ukiyo-zōshi* writers would follow this model to one degree or another; Ejima Kiseki, who learned the craft of writing through self-conscious emulation of Saikaku's prose, would take this style of tonal shift and narrative pivot and adapt it in new forms to his own purposes. In a compelling study of this "undermined voice of didacticism," David Gundry has argued that Saikaku's unique narrative style works in service of the "establishment of new hierarchies based on wealth and personal cultivation," giving expression to the sensibility of "the ambitious and assertive bourgeois who is concerned with social self-advancement rather than with leveling social distinctions."[55] I agree with Gundry's diagnosis of the guiding sensibility of Saikaku's work, and my readings seek to extend this diagnosis to an understanding of the functions of print generally in articulating a townsman sensibility. However, it seems to me that this analysis does not go far enough in grasping the radical heterogeneity of Saikaku's writing, which does not consistently aim to subvert the didactic voice, but just as often seems to deploy an affirmative and unironic didacticism: The tension is not merely between narrative voice and content, but also between inconsistent and contradictory orientations toward the didactic voice itself.

This is in part a product of the paratextual structure of the *ukiyo-zōshi*. The works of Saikaku and Kiseki consist of collections of short narratives—typically three to five stories per volume in works of five or six volumes (sometimes more and occasionally fewer)—in which the tone and didactic import of a work might vary significantly from story to story, with some seeming to unironically manifest didactic principles and others throwing them into question. Even though any given work is nominally unified under a title and central theme, the form itself is at every level characterized by a heterogeneity of content that no unifying frame can perfectly contain. Indeed, the radical internal heterogeneity of the *ukiyo-zōshi* as a literary form poses a profound challenge for interpretation or even convincing description because a reading of any given story is rarely enough to stand in for the collection as a whole. How should we understand the internal contradictions of this genre—the ambivalent tension between didactic frame or voice and unpredictable diversity of narrative content?

To make sense of this tension, the literary scholar Hirosue Tamotsu proposed the term "space of the collection" (*shū no kūkan*). In Hirosue's theorization, this form was inherent in the seventeenth-century *kana-zōshi*—it was the very form of the *kana-zōshi*—but only with the work of Saikaku was this paratextual form transmuted into a textual form, structuring the narrative logic and ideological content of individual stories. Saikaku's stories manifest this space of the collection in microcosm—in diffuse narratives with more lateral than forward motion, shaped by often random or unexpected encounters that occasion radical shifts in perspective and even voice. Saikaku's stories resist narrative and ideological closure because each perspective is relativized in turn by the possibility (even if left unrealized) of further twists and inversions: Each story is its own collection of micronarratives that resist resolution into a single coherent plot or worldview. In Marxian fashion, Hirosue gives particular attention to how this form may serve to decenter the dominant worldview of the ruling warrior class, expressed in moralistic discourse.[56] In this regard, the space of the collection resonates with Mikhail Bakhtin's theorization of heteroglossia and its literary manifestation in the polyglot novel. To Bakhtin, the power of the novel as literary form lies in its capacity to represent the sociolinguistic diversity of the contemporary world, thus constructing novelistic style as a dialogic space of confrontation between different languages and, through them, different worldviews or ideologies. Indeed, Bakhtinian analyses of Tokugawa popular literature have, like Hirosue's, tended to foreground the functions of literary heteroglossia as a way of decentering, if not explicitly subverting, official (shogunal) ideologies and the hegemonic worldview of the ruling (warrior) class.[57]

I take inspiration from Hirosue's space of the collection, which becomes an orienting metaphor in the chapters of this book. However, I am concerned not with the decentering of classical language and the subversion of warrior hegemony, but with the construction of a hegemonic textuality of the townsman class. My interest is in how the *ukiyo-zōshi* gave birth to new forms of language and narrative that were able to exert symbolic authority despite the ideological contradictions that they palpably manifest: They were able to exert symbolic authority precisely by their capacity to contain such contradictions. Toward that end, I believe that an alternative possibility remains, in the work of both Hirosue and Bakhtin, of reinterpreting the dialogic form of the space of the collection. For example, Bakhtin's treatment of heteroglossia in the novel offers a more complex and ambivalent grasp of the ways in which novelistic form places the centrifugal forces of heteroglossia in tension with the centripetal forces of unitary language: "A unitary language is not something given but is always in essence posited—and at every moment of its linguistic life it is opposed to the realities of heteroglossia. But at the same time it makes its real presence felt as a force for overcoming this heteroglossia, imposing specific limits to it, guaranteeing a certain maximum of mutual understanding and crystalizing into a real, although still relative, unity."[58] To Bakhtin, this "maximum of mutual understanding" is the literary reflection of the sociolinguistic community of the nation, unified through national language. But one need not focus on the community of the nation (and the historical horizon of modernity) to acknowledge the ways in which a dialogic literary form can, paradoxically, assert an ideological vision of the world. Similarly, my adaptation of Hirosue's space of the collection focuses on the ways in which this textual space—though ambivalent, multidimensional, and often contradictory—ultimately may assert a central set of norms, a hegemonic set of social positions, and the worldview of an emergent class (class-as-consciousness): in short, a sense of identity in the face of a plurality of subjectivities.

My argument, in a word, is that the space of the collection—a compilation of diverse and divergent narratives, loosely unified under a nominal didactic frame—functioned as a device of ideological consolidation. The *ukiyo-zōshi*, in the quasi-didactic genealogy running from the townsman piece to the character piece, served to sketch certain central norms of urban identity while charting the range of individual expression and particular manifestation that such norms could admit: how different forms of conduct (as for different trades or geographic regions or economic strata or genders) could or could not manifest, through and despite their particularities, the shared norms that defined the urban community. By giving representation to diverse cases but still setting that diversity in relation to unifying principles, the collection sets the diversity of the urban world into mutual relation as part of a community of shared values. These works also limn the boundaries of that community, marking its limits with cases that diverge too far from the norm—but also, and more subtly, mark a range of transgression that may be tolerated as merely a quirk or unique case, or a moral lapse that may situationally be overlooked. Perhaps most fundamentally, the form allows for the representation of contradictions, of cases that seem to defy the central didactic premises of the collection, but that by their very inclusion are domesticated and rendered harmless—as it were, the exceptions that prove the rule. Through these functions—the inductive exploration of didactic principle, the charting of diverse forms of expression, the marking of limits of the community, the registering and containment of contradiction and exception—the *ukiyo-zōshi* modeled how a diverse urban community could, despite that diversity and indeed despite palpable stratification and tension within that community, nevertheless be unified by a shared sense of townsman identity. Indeed, the ultimately ideological import of the space of the collection was, I argue, to contain the tensions within the urban community.

The framework of the space of the collection is particularly apt in light of the spatial dimensions of identity and community in early modern Japan.

Whereas Hirosue understood the space of the collection in a largely figurative (ideological) sense, my deployment of this concept focuses more literally on the ways in which the *ukiyo-zōshi* depicts, contains, and maps out a set of social positions that are also spatial positions, situated within the local geographies of urban landscapes (both real and imagined) and within the larger geography of status that was the Tokugawa polity. Even to the degree that townsman identity was understood in spatial terms, this was a spatiality that cannot be reduced to the fundamentally local units of socio-spatial structure, whether the *chō*, the tenement, the trade association, or even the city; it was a spatiality that comprised the intersection of all these, as a cognitive map of social relations in which certain trajectories were possible, others just barely imaginable, and still others utterly outside the townsman's socio-spatial imaginary. The townsman of early modern Japan had to make sense of his place in a world that profoundly transcended the local, to grasp economic opportunities that existed precisely in the intersections and collisions between status communities and in the networks of trade and transportation running between cities and into the surrounding countryside. To extend the spatial metaphor, to imagine townsman identity writ large was to imagine the city writ large—not even the individual city of Kyoto, Osaka, or Edo, but the interregional urban network that existed as much as a set of dynamic urbanizing processes as it did as a stable urban space. The early modern city, like all cities, was not just an empirical space, but also and more so an imagined one. The townsman was defined by his capacity to imagine it and by the ways in which he did. The space of the collection manifest in the *ukiyo-zōshi* was none other than this urban spatial imaginary: a transregional urban community that included vastly disparate social and geographic positions, their differences maintained and tensions between them acknowledged, nonetheless integrated into a coherent vision of urban commoner identity centered on certain hegemonic positions and certain dominant values.

The exemplary figure for this space of the collection is Saikaku's *Japan's Eternal Storehouse*. In this text, Saikaku presents a wide-ranging exploration of the urban economy through a set of ambivalently didactic narratives of rags to riches and riches to rags. The work consists of six volumes and thirty stories, each of which depicts the economic opportunities available to different social positions, and the possibilities and pitfalls of different trades and modes of commerce: street peddlers, wholesale merchants,

INTRODUCTION

clothiers, working craftsmen, moneylenders, fishermen, and so on, covering the whole socioeconomic span from the working poor to the fabulously wealthy. It also gives an acute attention to geographic locale, every story framed around the commercial practices of a particular place: many stories focus on the major urban hubs of Kyoto, Osaka, and Edo, but others range widely to provincial castle towns, post towns, temple towns, ports, and even into the countryside, to fishing towns and rural villages that were steadily being incorporated into the interregional consumer economy. Yet, despite the particularities of place and occupation that inform Saikaku's stories, the image to emerge from the text is one of a larger urban community, one that includes a vast range of local variation but is still unified by a set of shared values and lifestyles. The text's didactic voice, which persistently though never completely seeks to extract general economic principles (do's and don'ts of the market economy) from each story, functions to impose a modicum of coherence to the space of the collection that was the interregional urban community of the late seventeenth century.

Part 1 of this book uses a series of readings of *Japan's Eternal Storehouse*, and the other texts and discourses surrounding it, to explore the formation of the townsman subject. I argue that Saikaku's work attempts to make sense of a fundamental shift in the nature of urban identity and community: from a highly particularistic and exclusivistic sense of propertied membership in local communities (the *chō*) to a capacious and flexible form of identity—the *chōnin* writ large—based on a set of shared urban values, lifestyles, commercial practices, and ultimately on a set of shared stories and forms of narration. The irony of this new sense of identity was that it existed in the face of significant diversity, tension, stratification, potential conflict, and contradiction within the newly imagined urban community. The three chapters of this section use distinct methods of analysis, built on dialogue with different fields, to illuminate both the tensions within townsman society and the textual strategies by which Saikaku's work contains those tensions.

In chapter 1, I map out the social and geographical positions contained within this text, asking how Saikaku integrates them into a complex but normative image of urban society. Through careful dialogue with social history, the chapter describes a shift in the spatial locus of *chōnin* identity: from the community of the city block or ward (*chō*) to the atomic unit of the individual merchant household (*ie*) and its relationship to an expansive, interregional urban marketplace. I argue that Saikaku imagines the marketplace itself as a kind of community, one defined not by locality and personal relationships but instead by a shared entrepreneurial ethos: a set of urban values, lifestyles, and commercial practices, a vision in which anyone can become a townsman simply by choosing to act like one. Central to this ethos was the premise that the individual entrepreneur could build name, wealth, and property out of nothing. Chapter 2 asks how Saikaku envisions the poetics of wealth, and how he rationalizes such mobility in a world where, according to official ideology, everyone had a prescribed place. I argue that Saikaku envisions commerce as an amoral, spatial practice in which various forms of appropriation and exploitation are justified by a perceived condition of existential insecurity, figured through tropes of drifting through the floating world. This chapter also suggests a new interpretation of the politics of townsman literature, which I argue to be symbiotic with rather than oppositional toward shogunal authority, marked by its own systems of power and appropriation, and predicated on a series of symbolic and social exclusions: of the rural periphery, of the working poor, and of the outcast class. Chapter 3 examines the formal elements of Saikaku's work: narrative structure and voice. I argue that the narrative form of *Eternal Storehouse* presents a series of strategies for containing certain fundamental tensions and contradictions: the emerging socioeconomic hierarchies within the townsman community and the historical contingency of the distribution of wealth, which threatened any promise of entrepreneurial mobility through individual effort. Tracing elements of Saikaku's prose style to the economic rhetoric of earlier seventeenth-century get-rich guides and their medieval antecedents, I show that Saikaku's writing contains these tensions by relativizing the authority of didactic principle and acknowledging its situational failures without fundamentally throwing its legitimacy into question.

As the explosive economic growth of the seventeenth century slowed, the cultural dynamism of the Genroku era gave way to a moment of cultural conservatism that would peak with the Kyōhō Reforms of the 1720s. In townsman society, the turn to the eighteenth century saw Saikaku's mercurial ideal of the self-made entrepreneur displaced by a sense that the lower ranks should emulate the urban elite and that children should emulate their parents. In short, the conduct of the townsman came to be defined by copying one's social betters or forebears, and such imitation quickly congealed into a set of stable social forms, roles, and patterns of conduct. For the most part, these norms were oriented around the institution of the household, which was organized for the preservation and transmission of wealth and property in perpetuity; the energies of each member came to be subordinate to the corporate needs of the household. Individual households had, of course, existed for some time among the more elite ranks of urban society, but it was with the turn of the eighteenth century that the household became a nearly universal institution, its norms disseminated in a productive but deeply derivative body of commercial printed matter: New genres of didactic tracts and conduct guides digested the cultural literacies and manners of the elite, adapting and repurposing them for the newly literate entrepreneurial classes. The character pieces of Ejima Kiseki were the iconic literary expression of this moment. Centered squarely on social roles conceived within the confines of the wealthy townsman household, Kiseki's works captured the lingering tensions and contradictions within a rapidly normalizing townsman society. On the one hand, they seem to rebel almost compulsively against that normalization, depicting eccentric characters who transgress the norms of the household in innumerable and gratuitously deviant ways. On the other, even through the depiction of such transgressions, these works would progressively distill a set of highly conventionalized and generic images of townsman life, the imagination of transgression constrained within an ever more limited horizon of harmless, everyday normality. The chapters of part 2 trace the dialectical interplay of these tensions in Kiseki's work, revealing how the normalizing function of the space of the collection was given its most pure expression in the character piece.

One of the developments of townsman culture in the early eighteenth century was an increasing focus on the role played by leisure in the townsman's sense of self. In chapter 4, I use a reading of Kiseki's *Characters of Worldly Young Men* (*Seken musuko katagi*, 1715) and *Characters of Worldly Young Women* (*Seken musume katagi*, 1717) to illuminate the contradictions within the ideology of the townsman household. On the one hand, townsman ideologues had always expressed a deep anxiety about the addictive appeal of the "leisure arts" (*yūgei*)—forms of amateur training in a range of artistic practices like poetic composition, calligraphy, and flower arrangement—and their potential to distract undisciplined household heads from dedication to their "house trade" (*kagyō*). On the other hand, at least among the more elite ranks of urban society, certain forms of leisure practice, especially training in the polite leisure arts, came to be seen as near-obligatory signifiers of social standing and indispensable means of elite socialization. By exploiting these contradictions for humor, Kiseki's works present a withering critique of the alienated consciousness produced by the ideology of the household. Chapter 5 then zooms out to trace the development of the character piece as a genre. Here I argue that Kiseki's focus on eccentricity was one reflection of the formation of a townsman habitus—a sense of normative speech, dress, conduct, taste—and a concomitant concern with behaving appropriately to one's social position. This chapter builds on the previous one, but here I trace how the author's sense of critique mellowed over time to produce benign and familiar images of harmless eccentricity, what I refer to as a sense of normality. The ultimate ideological function of this literary form, I argue, was both to represent and to contain the heterogeneity of habitus by imagining alterity only in domesticated forms.

As should be clear from this synopsis, this book presents a detailed and multifaceted interpretation of a small selection of canonical texts rather than a more comprehensive and descriptive survey of the early modern townsman's textual culture. Even with respect to the *ukiyo-zōshi*, although I believe that many of the ideological functions traced in this book might apply in a loose sense to the form as a whole, I have eschewed the monumental undertaking of a larger survey, which might tend more in the direction of the descriptive and literary historical, in favor of a series of interpretive essays that develop my argument from multiple angles while developing multiple readings of a few key texts. I close this introduction by explaining the rationale for this choice.

First, concerning some notable omissions: I have attempted to address, at least in passing, the various other textual genres that defined the townsman's processes of textual self-fashioning—house codes, entrepreneurial guidebooks, didactic tracts, and household almanacs—but some bodies of texts I did not take up in detail. One is the textual culture of the eighteenth-century Shingaku (heart learning) movement of merchant morality headed by Ishida Baigan and Tejima Toan. The rise of the Shingaku movement coincides with the end of my study (the work of Ejima Kiseki), but

Shingaku thought would not have a clear impact on popular fiction until somewhat later, in the Edo-based *gesaku* corpus, so I have chosen to focus on the textual cultures that had more immediate influence on the form and content of the *ukiyo-zōshi*. (That said, many of the ideological functions that I see unfolding in the *ukiyo-zōshi*, especially Saikaku's work, seem to anticipate the Shingaku concern with the morality of commerce and of capital accumulation, as I explore in chapter 2.) The other body of texts I have not taken up is Edo *gesaku*. This is in part out of concerns of scope, but more importantly because *gesaku* was defined by a different and more complex collision of social subjectivities unique to the cultural dynamics of the city of Edo—warrior-intellectuals, cultural professionals, townsman dilettantes, plebeian entertainers—and reflected the formation of larger publics, urban communities, and forms of identity that, indeed, crossed boundaries of status, though not those of locality. These forms of urban subjectivity, in turn, had their own textual forms and their own politics. These are briefly sketched in the epilogue.

However, my choice to focus in depth on a few canonical texts is not merely out of pragmatic concerns of scope or focus. Throughout this book, I have explicitly resisted a descriptive or survey mentality, one built on the assumption that all these works and their genres are merely reflections of an underlying townsman culture assumed to be both stable and coherent. Such an approach may produce a seamless narrative that, to more effectively assert the authority of its narrator (the modern scholar), moves with great agility between genres and discursive domains and felicitously chosen examples, but simultaneously tends to elide the complexities and contradictions, the subtle shifts in identity from one moment to the next, the friction between theoretical models and historical realities. By the very logic of historical narrative, cultural history can often ascribe to its objects an underlying coherence and, in so doing, can run the risk of obscuring both the messy complexity of historical reality and the beautifully heuristic process of historical (and literary) interpretation; it can also gloss over the idiosyncrasies and unique textual strategies of different literary genres, reducing literary texts to more or less transparent documents of values. Although my ultimate concerns are in some sense historical, the extended attention I have given to these select texts is a product of my belief that, to make responsible use of literary texts as historical documents, one must first account for their nature as literature—and that such an account should reveal rather than obscure the challenges of interpretation and the contradictory meanings that may be contained even within the same text. Indeed, the interpretations offered in this book at times contradict one another. I believe that these contradictions should illuminate the nature and ideological power of a literary form such as the *ukiyo-zōshi*, a reflection of the townsman's haphazard and always incomplete process of constructing meaning out of the messy realities of urban existence.

I have resisted, in particular, the impulse to filter the figure of the early modern townsman through a familiar narrative of the rise of a merchant class in the face of feudal authority. I have done so, in part, because such stories have already been told, but more importantly because they tend to efface the particularities—specificities of geographic place, economic rank, occupation, gender; unique qualities of literary textuality and form—that were profoundly significant to the Tokugawa reader, whose lifeworld we must reconstruct to make sense of his literature. The narrative built on that erasure would simply reaffirm so much that we otherwise already believe we know about the emergence of a merchant class, the forms of its literary expression, and the political import of its cultural agency. In a sense, this book is a rebuttal to such narratives. If the formation of the townsman's subjectivity might indeed be seen as a process of effacing, obscuring, or otherwise downplaying the significance of particularities of place, rank, occupation, and so on, and replacing them with universal and portable signifiers of townsmanness, then such a process cannot be understood without first attending to the particular in order to perceive what is at stake when it is displaced by the universal. The approach I have taken to understanding this transformation is an unapologetically paranoid one: Most of my chapters are, in some sense, reading against my authors to reveal and to critique the political stakes of the townsman's processes of textual self-formation. It is my hope, however, that this paranoia should be taken as a form of respect for the particularities of text and context, which both warrant and reward close scrutiny.

Put differently, my aim in this book is not to construct a seamless narrative of the formation of townsman identity, but to trace how the townsman narrated his identity. Both the literary and historical fields have generally treated the social category of townsman as a *signified*, a substance or position that exists a priori in the social space and is given expression through literature and other textual representations, and in turn have used those representations as windows to reconstruct the townsman subject. To the contrary, I contend that the townsman subject was primarily a *signifier*: that the townsman self was produced performatively through signifying acts that were inextricable from the texts the townsman produced and consumed. The pages that follow trace the process by which the diverse signifieds of Tokugawa urban society—the different socioeconomic strata, the various trades, the geographic locales and neighborhoods, the familial roles and individual dispositions—came to be contained within the space of the collection, wherein they could, in all their particularity, be repurposed in service of the literary signifiers of townsmanness.

PART I

Reimagining Urban Community

Chapter One

THE COMMUNITY OF THE MARKETPLACE

The first printing of Ihara Saikaku's *Japan's Eternal Storehouse* (*Nippon eitaigura*), published in the first month of 1688 by the Osaka bookseller Morita Shōtarō, opens with a striking illustration: a series of storefronts lined up one after another (figure 1.1). The image, which continues from the recto to the verso of the first folio, was Saikaku's fanciful interpretation of a table of contents and repeats in each of the text's six volumes. Each shop curtain is decorated with an image evoking the name and trade of the townsperson protagonist of the given story, whether merchant or artisan. The text accompanying the illustration invokes the language of the marketplace. Each story is given a subtitle announcing its protagonist as "renowned throughout" (*kakure naki*) their city of residence and business: "An overnight millionaire renowned throughout Edo!" "A frugal man renowned throughout Kyoto!" "A merchant renowned throughout Izumi!" "A branch shop renowned throughout Edo!" Echoing the extravagant claims of the merchant's sales cry, Saikaku advertises his protagonists and their stories as merchandise on display in a shopping arcade, each calling and inviting the reader to turn the pages of the book, as one might turn the corner of a shop curtain to peer in for a closer look. With this evocative image of an urban landscape, populated by the promotional language of commerce, Saikaku articulates an unprecedented awareness of stories as products: goods made to be sold in a commercial marketplace.

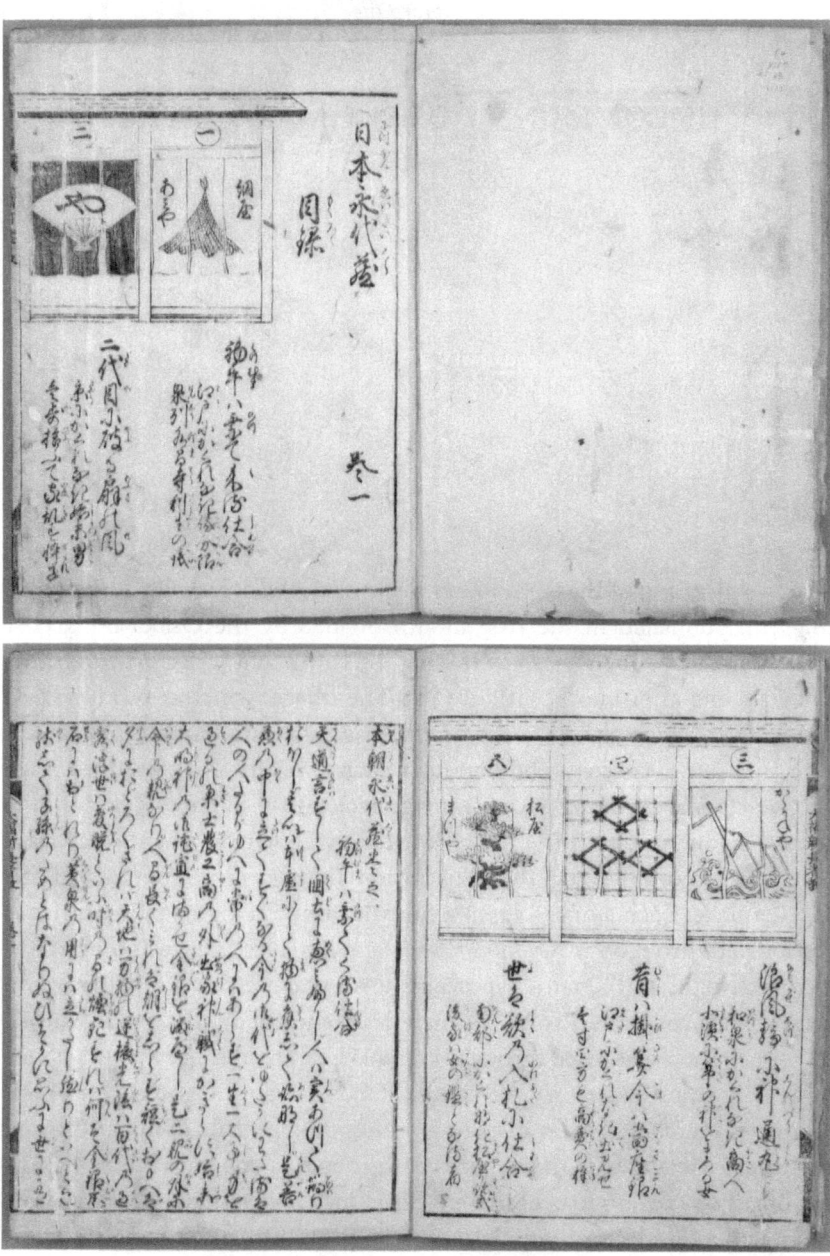

FIGURE 1.1 *Nippon eitaigura*, Morita edition. Table of contents to first volume (1o and 1u–2o). Courtesy of Waseda University Library.

THE COMMUNITY OF THE MARKETPLACE

A Marxian reading in the vein of Mikhail Bakhtin might take this citation of the language of the marketplace as a leveling or subversive force: a triumphal citation of everyday merchant voices that, whether explicitly or implicitly, flies in the face of a feudal social order.[1] But to focus only on the leveling language of the marketplace is to overlook the social implications of the material landscape evoked so precisely in this illustration. To a reader at the time, the everyday spatial environment suggested in this table of contents had both more concrete and more specific social meanings, linked to institutionalized forms of status, community, and commercial practice—indeed, linked in a profound though soon to be repressed way with the very identity of the townsman. This was the socio-spatial landscape of the *chō* 町: a close-knit, local community of several dozen commoner households, typically set in two rows facing each other across a shared roadway, that served as the template for urban development and administration in cities and towns throughout the realm. Saikaku's table of contents not only evokes the world of commerce and the language of the marketplace, but also draws on an embodied, material sense of urban community, and the tension between these two perspectives—the *chō* as local community versus the city and realm as marketplace—shapes the narratives that make up this work.

Japan's Eternal Storehouse is a collection of thirty stories that chart narratives of social mobility—both upward and downward, along with occasional tales of immobility—through the urban economy of the late seventeenth century. It is framed, and was likely marketed, as a set of stories of didactic value: narratives, many based (however loosely) on real-life figures, that exemplify the principles of entrepreneurial success. In this regard, it was the successor to and extension of a long series of entrepreneurial handbooks that had constituted a perennially popular genre of didactic literature since the dawn of commercial publishing in the 1620s (for further discussion, see chapter 3). Compared with earlier works in the genre, many of which consisted of little more than pedantic lectures on the value of thrift and hard work, *Eternal Storehouse* is striking for its narrative richness and for the breadth of the social imaginary it projects. Geographically, the three major cities of Kyoto, Edo, and Osaka receive repeated attention, but Saikaku's vision extends across the realm, examining commercial developments in provincial castle towns, rural market towns, trading posts, ports, and fishing villages—all of which were being steadily incorporated into an increasingly networked economy driven by urban consumption. In terms of social position, *Eternal Storehouse* likewise ranges widely. A young man from Edo borrows a thousand coppers from the Mizuma Temple in Izumi Province (near Osaka) and uses the fund to start a business lending capital to Edo fishermen. In Kyoto, a hardworking fan merchant passes away, leaving his business to his exceedingly stingy and socially maladjusted heir. In Osaka, an outcast sweeper-woman accumulates a small fund of capital by illicitly selling the spilled rice that she sweeps up at the Kitahama rice market. In Edo, an enterprising merchant overcomes the stagnating clothing market by developing a new sales model. In Nara, an elite fabric broker declines because of his personal profligacy, leaving a young widow saddled with debt. A humble soy-sauce peddler in Ōtsu, an innovative whaler-cum-fishing magnate in Kii Province, a dishonest tea dealer in Echizen—the list goes on. Saikaku synthesizes this vast diversity of geographic, social, and economic positions into a new vision of urban community, one unified not by locale, occupation, or social position, but by a shared sense of values: the entrepreneurial ethos of the market economy.

Eternal Storehouse sketches the contours of an imagined urban community: not that of a single *chō*, nor even of a single city, but of the diverse and distant but increasingly connected urban (and urbanizing) spaces of late seventeenth-century Japan. An imagined community akin to Benedict Anderson's nation: a horizontal sense of fellowship among individuals who likely will never meet, but nevertheless possess vivid images of one another as part of a shared (not to say collective) endeavor.[2] Indeed, Mary Elizabeth Berry has offered an evocative reading of *Eternal Storehouse* as a reflection of an early modern sense of the Japanese nation, one based on a shared body of public information mediated by (woodblock) printed texts.[3] In her reading, *Eternal Storehouse* acts much as the novel in Anderson's formulation: the archetypal articulation, enabled by (woodblock) print capitalism, of a shared body of experience that limns the boundaries of a community identified with the people and territory of Japan—there it is in the title, after all—and with the Tokugawa state. In contrast, I wish to highlight the ways in which the community that this text imagines is inflected and structured by status. Warriors are occasionally present, but appear largely as a *them* rather than an *us*, in the background of stories about commoner entrepreneurship; the same goes for the clergy, aristocracy, and intelligentsia. Peasants appear only to the degree that they abandon cultivation to become merchants or reorganize their agricultural production to participate in the interregional economy, driven by consumption in and distribution through urban markets. Unsurprisingly, outcasts are rendered largely invisible, though they can at times be glimpsed in the margins of narratives of the social mobility of urban commoners. It is also a gendered community, centered on the male merchant. Women appear frequently throughout the text, occasionally attributed with economic autonomy, but in nearly every case, that agency is ultimately channeled into the entrepreneurial successes of a husband or son. Saikaku would deal with these populations elsewhere in a sprawling body of work that probed the full reaches of the floating world with insatiable curiosity, but in *Eternal Storehouse*, as in the aptly named townsman pieces generally, he is concerned above all with the urban, commercial classes, with the question of what distinguishes them from other classes, and where the lines of townsman identity are to be drawn.

This chapter argues that *Eternal Storehouse* carries out a fundamental reimagining of the nature of the urban community. The text registers a shift away from a sense of local community, rooted in particularities of geographic place and trade and linked to the socio-spatial structure of the *chō*. Saikaku replaces the *chō* with a universal, portable, and adaptable ethos that transcends those particularities, offering the promise of social mobility and the accumulation of wealth through individual effort. In Saikaku's vision, it is the adoption of this ethos, modeled on the commercial practice of the interregional merchant, that defines the newly imagined urban community: an atomized community of entrepreneurial individuals, each master of his own fate and all on equal footing in the marketplace. I refer to this money-based community of entrepreneurial townsmen as the *community of the marketplace*. As urban identity transforms from a function of local community into one of lifestyle and ethos, the boundaries of the community of the marketplace appear flexible and to a degree porous, but distinctions of status do not disappear. Indeed, Saikaku's text is a careful exploration of what social positions may be incorporated into the urban community and which may be pushed to its boundaries—and, as we will see in chapter 2, of how the formation of the townsman subject was coeval with the marginalization of the townsman's others. Even within the community of the marketplace, Saikaku is concerned with who succeeds and who fails, with using the ethos of the entrepreneurial merchant to construct and to legitimate new hierarchies within urban society.

One way to understand this shift is as a movement away from the constitutive particularism of the townsman (*chōnin*) as a figure of fundamentally local urban community—the geographical and occupational specificity of the *chō*—toward a sense of something resembling a merchant class unified by shared values and lifestyles. Indeed, it was through this shift that the term *townsman* itself came to be strongly associated with commerce and trade rather than artisanal production. Working craftsmen, though always part of the urban community, were pushed to the margins of a dominant construction of townsman identity centered on the ideal of the merchant entrepreneur—an ideal that celebrated the buying and selling of goods above their manufacture. In this sense, Saikaku's vision of urban community suggests a kind of dematerialization, a replacement of material practice (investment in the built environment and in material production) with symbolic practice rooted in the circulation of money—pure exchange of values and quantities—and ultimately in the circulation of texts. To be a townsman was to participate in an economy of signs mediated by texts.

To show how this was a fundamental reimagining, I use a method that is historicist in a very concrete sense, focused on unpacking and explicating the place that Saikaku's protagonists occupy in a shifting social and economic landscape. In many cases, when Saikaku bases his characters on historical figures, this means reconstructing those figures and their social positions in some detail, and comparing those reconstructed social positions with Saikaku's depiction of the same. To understand how Saikaku situates his characters within a social space and in relation to one another, I consider the narratives that he builds with and around them—whether they rise or fall, how, and why—but, to attend more closely to the text's social dimension, this chapter largely brackets questions of narrative form and voice, as well as those of genre and literary history, leaving these to the chapters that follow.

This mode of analysis is bound to strike some readers as exceedingly literal (and not terribly literary), but its purpose is twofold. First, by attending to the structures of the social field that exist both within and behind Saikaku's text, my intention is not to dig through it to reveal an objective narrative of seventeenth-century social history (that is, to recapitulate historical narratives that are better developed elsewhere) or to argue that Saikaku accurately apprehended such a narrative and documented it in realist fashion. Instead, by comparing Saikaku's stories with the historical episodes, figures, and processes that they narrate (and with the narratives that modern historians have made of them), I aim to shed light on what was new and unique about Saikaku's imagined urban community, what other communities and urban imaginaries it may have displaced, and thus what may have been at stake in this literary reimagining. Second, and to that end, I wish to emphasize that minute distinctions in socioeconomic practice—between types of merchants and between subtly but fundamentally distinct modes of commercial exchange—that may seem to the modern reader as technical to the point of pedantry in fact were freighted with symbolic weight. This significance would have been intuitively obvious to Saikaku's readers, but that significance is lost when relegated to a contextualizing introduction or a footnote, something that at some point informs the text but ultimately is judged (by the modern scholar or editor) to be external to it, a bit of historical trivia of interest to only the specialist. In other words, *Eternal Storehouse* is not just a set of stories about merchants and commerce in a universal sense, in service of universal and normative (that is to say, Western) narratives of sociocultural history, but also a set of stories about particular types of merchants situated amid a particular set of shifting commercial regimes. Those particularities are not (social or historical) externalities to the (literary) text, but are fundamental to understanding its project, even when they are present only as traces, hints, and ellipses. Indeed, Saikaku's vision of urban community was precisely one that functioned by rendering details of location, occupation, and social position into externalities, circumstantial differences that may shape one's opportunities but are ultimately subordinate to a performed entrepreneurial ethos and to a narrative logic of social mobility.[4]

TRACES OF LOCAL COMMUNITY

That *Eternal Storehouse* opens by using the architectural symbolism of the *chō* is to a degree ironic, for Saikaku's urban imaginary is predicated on the collapse and hollowing out of the *chō* community, posing in its place a set of commercial values and practices that operate across local boundaries and in the face of local norms. The waning influence of the *chō*, and with it the blurring and broadening of townsman identity, was part of the larger cluster of historic transformations in urban space amid which Saikaku was writing and out of which he sought to extract narrative meaning. Over the course of the seventeenth century, the emergence of mutually amplifying cultures of conspicuous consumption among both warriors and elite commoners encouraged the rapid development of urban consumer markets; the formation of robust transportation and communication networks accelerated the integration of geographically distant cities and distribution hubs into an interregional market economy; the same networks drove the transformation of rural production as cultivators of various stripes began producing for urban markets, while those disenfranchised by the stratification of rural communities frequently absconded to find low-skilled work or entrepreneurial opportunity in the growing cities; the resulting redistribution of wealth and stratification of urban society resulted in the gradual commodification of urban property and, with it, community membership, throwing the boundaries of the *chō* (and those of the city at large) into question. But before exploring how Saikaku makes sense of these historical transformations, we must start by understanding the nature of the *chō* community and the forms of local identity that it represented.

To understand the centrality of the *chō* community to early constructions of townsman identity, we may look to *chō* regulations. Urban historian Yoshida Nobuyuki has surveyed regulations from seventeenth-century neighborhoods to reconstruct the ways in which such communities both enabled and constrained the activities of their individual residents. Such codes served a number of functions. First, they often mandated certain shared architectural standards; most often, these were limitations on the size of total frontage allowed to a single household, presumably as a way of enforcing a uniformity of appearance that would represent a uniformity of status.[5] Second, they promoted goodwill between members by mandating collective decision-making and encouraging regular hosting of neighborhood meetings—both for administration and for collective observance of social rituals such as marriage, retirement, and funerals. To be a member of the *chōjū* (neighborhood collective) was not only to be socially present for such rituals, but also to fund them: Membership entailed a material investment in the community through the lives of one's fellow members. Third, then, regulations often policed membership in the *chō* with restrictions on who could buy or rent property and under what conditions. Such regulations manifest a wariness toward strangers (no doubt a holdover from the medieval roots of the *chō*, reinforced by the still-stringent

THE COMMUNITY OF THE MARKETPLACE

shogunal policies of residential registration) as well as a pragmatic concern with particular trades that were seen as dangerous or simply unpleasant. The image to emerge from these functions is that of a small, local, and egalitarian community organized for the benefit and protection of its members, one that prioritized the well-being of the collective over the advancement of the individual, and that thus carefully regulated who could be a member and how individual members could diverge from the will of the collective. Although such a community may appear to modern sensibilities as restrictive and perhaps overbearing—certainly it was experienced as such by some of its members, at least in Saikaku's stories—it must be kept in mind that the communitarian vision of such local urban communities was the early modern legacy of the self-governing communities of war-torn medieval Kyoto, wherein local solidarity and extreme caution toward outsiders were existential imperatives.

Saikaku's *Eternal Storehouse* opens by visually citing the architectural space of the *chō* in its table of contents and thus evokes an ideal of the seventeenth-century *chō* as a local, collectivist, egalitarian community. This framing, like that of so many of Saikaku's works, turns out to be ironic, for the stories contained in this collection are of individual households bracing against the limits of the *chō* community, operating across its boundaries, or finding ways to appropriate and instrumentalize its collective rituals in service of individual profit. The image of the *chō* in this text is that of a community hollowing out, as membership is liquidated in favor of the liquid flows of capital across local boundaries, and as forms of commercial practice associated with and structured by local community struggle to compete with the new forms of interregional merchant entrepreneurship. But hints of the collective socioeconomic practice of local communities haunt the background of Saikaku's stories of entrepreneurial success; there are moments when the local community and its socioeconomic logics emerge briefly into the foreground, only to be pushed back to the margins and displaced by new commercial regimes. These stories are an illuminating starting point for revealing the nature of the historic shift from the community of the *chō* to that of the marketplace.

In "A Lucky Bid from the World of Greed" (*Yo wa yoku no irefuda ni shiawase*, vol. 1–5), Saikaku narrates the fortunes of a broker of bleached fabric by the name of Matsuya in the city of Nara.[6] Despite having once been numbered among the most prosperous local merchants, Matsuya was decadent in his personal habits and died around the age of fifty, leaving his wife and children saddled with debt. Matsuya's widow is an attractive young woman of twenty-seven or twenty-eight, and the narrative largely concerns her enterprising response to this predicament. A model of industry and feminine virtue, she refuses to remarry and instead adopts a modest appearance and dedicates herself to managing the household alone. Her efforts prove inadequate, however, and she learns "the difficulty of a lone woman making her way in the world" (*onna bakari mo yo o tategataki koto*). As her inherited debts pile up, she offers her house as payment, but her creditors refuse, whether out of pity or of greed, on the grounds that her debts exceed the value of the property: She owes five *kanme* of silver, but the house is worth only three, and selling it would thus leave her homeless and still in debt. From the depths of her despair, the widow then concocts a plan. On consultation with the *chō* council, she decides to dispose of her residence by lottery: She sells tickets for four *monme* of silver apiece, with the winner receiving the house. The lottery is a smashing success because buyers think "at worst it's a mere four *monme*" (*tenpo ni shite gin yon monme*) and she sells three thousand tickets for a twelve-*kanme* profit, pays off her debts, and walks away with seven *kanme* to become independently wealthy once again, while the winner of the lottery, a serving maid, "becomes a householder for a mere four *monme*" (*yon monme nite iemochi to nareri*). In the late seventeenth century, the annual salary for a maid was around one gold *ryō*, or sixty *monme* of silver by the standard calculation, so the investment of four *monme*, though not a trivial sum, was within the reach of the middle and even lower strata of the urban community.[7] The illustration (figure 1.2) emphasizes the cross-status diversity of buyers: samurai, priests, servants, retirees, and others.

    The story, which initially seems to be centered on the widow's feminine virtue, pivots to become a fable of entrepreneurial invention, praising her brilliance in concocting a lottery to escape her debts. But it also allegorizes the renunciation of local community and its displacement by new logics of urban commerce. The widow's spark of entrepreneurial wit turns on an appropriation of the existing practice of the community lottery (*tanomoshi*), which typically acted as a rotating source of capital for community members. The lottery, now more commonly known as a *mujin* (literally, "inexhaustible") association, operated as follows: Each member would contribute a fixed sum, which the winner could dispose of as they saw fit, and the

FIGURE 1.2 *Nippon eitaigura*, Morita edition. Illustration to "A Lucky Bid from the World of Greed" (vol.1, 18u-19o). Courtesy of Waseda University Library.

lottery would repeat at fixed intervals until every member had enjoyed access to the fund.[8] Needless to say, this system only worked if all members were obliged to participate, even after they had won the lottery. Tetsuo Najita has shown how such lotteries functioned essentially as credit and loan associations, occasionally also serving as insurance and welfare systems, based on an ethos of mutual trust and concern that was rooted in the collective mentality of local communities.[9] The Matsuya widow's lottery appropriates this practice and reorients it around a different logic, addressing not the local community of the *chō* but the larger and more amorphous community of the city-as-market, in which individual agents act out of economic self-interest. Such appropriations would become more common later in the Edo period, but were often frowned upon by samurai authorities and intellectual elites, who regarded them as an illicit hijacking of systems of social support, debased by the desire for individual profit; certainly in the seventeenth century, such appropriations were at best rare, and Saikaku's narrative is more imaginative than factual.[10]

In the background of "A Lucky Bid from the World of Greed" are a set of historical shifts surrounding the structure of urban communities. First is the stratification of urban society: On the one hand, we have a large substratum of nonhouseholding but upwardly aspirational urban residents (the ticket buyers, exemplified by the serving maid), and, on the other, a higher stratum of anonymous lenders who, as the owners of the late Matsuya's debts, stand in a position to seize the widow's house and, with it, her now-commodified status as a householding community member. Second, then, is the commodification of urban property and, with it, the hollowing out of the *chō* as an integral social unit. One might observe here that the appropriation and repurposing of the community lottery in this story is highly economically implausible (by the end, the widow could just as well purchase her house back and walk away with a tidy profit), but, more important, flies in the face of even the most rudimentary notion of *chō* self-administration: It is almost unimaginable that the council of *chō* elders would consent to granting householder status and community membership to literally anyone who could pull together the negligible cost of a lottery ticket. Yet the same norms of community self-government were already being broken down by the commodification of property amid the rise of a money-based market economy. If *chō* elders would likely balk at granting householder status to a random serving maid, they would be much less likely to object if the property and status of the Matsuya house were merely absorbed by its anonymous creditors, wealthy townsmen in their own right, though likely belonging to other *chō*. Seen from this perspective, the widow's entrepreneurial solution extends the logic of commodified urban property to (what was at the time) an absurd conclusion: It places the power of that commodification in the hands of the marginal members of the community—in this story, both women. For women to claim legal possession of urban property was not unprecedented. It was generally possible for women to inherit property in the absence of a suitable male heir or to receive a portion of property when the estate was divided among children. However, though such cases would become more common in later decades, they generally remained exceptions to the rule and were in practice usually treated as serving a temporary custodial role until a suitable male head could be found to assume responsibility for the estate.[11] Such assumptions are no doubt behind Saikaku's depiction of the Matsuya widow—but the

THE COMMUNITY OF THE MARKETPLACE

resolution of passing property to a maidservant through a lottery remains highly improbable.

The appeal of this fanciful and almost certainly fictionalized anecdote is in imagining a witty, improvised solution to a particular social and economic predicament, one that occurs amid a set of inexorable changes that threaten to constrain and marginalize the widow. The fantasy that Matsuya's widow manifests is the notion that no predicament cannot be resolved or escaped through a bit of entrepreneurial creativity: by taking stock of one's resources; imagining creative, outside-the-box methods for their disposal; and thereby cashing them in for a better deal. Note that this is not merely an operation of rational quantification, by which measure she is trapped in inescapable debt. The widow does not simply liquidate her assets for an equivalent in cash. More than mere calculation, it is a sleight of hand through which the widow is able to, in the course of that liquidation, multiply the value of her estate, as if pulling value out of thin air. This is the merchant virtue labeled by Saikaku as "wit" (*saikaku*): Saikaku frames the episode in the context of a moralistic discussion of contemporary marriage customs and praises the widow for her wifely loyalty, but ultimately it is the fact that "her wit exceeded that of a man" (*saikaku otoko ni masaredo*) that allows her to improvise a way out of her predicament, earning the narrator's praise as "a mirror for the people of the world" (*yo no hito no kagami*). (The nature of this entrepreneurial wit is discussed in detail in chapter 2.) But the critical trade that she makes in doing so is to renounce her membership in the *chō* community, which was based on householder status, in exchange for individual wealth.

The community of the *chō* was historically linked to specific forms of commerce and particular economic roles. These, too, are in the background of the story of Matsuya's widow. Although the widow is likely Saikaku's fictional invention, the Nara bleached-cloth broker named Matsuya was, like many of the text's protagonists, based on a historical figure of the same name: A real Matsuya was part of a small community of elite textile brokers authorized as shogunal suppliers. Saikaku takes care to note that Matsuya was what was known as a "purchasing broker" (*kai-toiya*), a term that refers to a class of elite marketplace managers. Despite the name, the purchasing broker did not buy and sell goods himself, but rather managed a marketplace and inn for visiting merchants, negotiating deals among buyers, sellers, and middlemen in exchange for commissions. (The term *toiya* is conventionally translated as "wholesaler," but this translation derives largely from the eighteenth century and later, especially from the Edo context, where it was pronounced *tonya*.) Social historian Tsukada Takashi has used the figure of the *toiya* to distinguish between the category of *chōnin* and that of "merchant" (*shōnin* or *akindo*): in essence, a distinction between socioeconomic practices rooted in the *chō* community and those defined by the circulation of merchant capital across social and geographic boundaries. Tsukada takes the *toiya* (in the sense of the purchasing broker) as paradigmatic of the *chōnin*, in that his main form of capital was urban property and his main function was maintenance of that property for markets that would benefit the local community; this is reflected in the fact that his income was largely from rent and transaction fees rather than selling goods for profit, and his tax obligations were calculated in relation to frontage (the size of the property he maintained). This stands in contrast to the (often interregional) merchants who gathered in such marketplaces to procure and dispose of goods, whose resources were in the form of liquid capital, and whose commercial practice was focused on individual profit regardless of concern for individual communities, even if that meant bullying competitors to establish monopoly privileges.[12] In Saikaku's time, the category of *toiya* was still strongly associated with an old guard of elite townsmen, many of whom enjoyed the direct patronage of warrior authorities and the social status that came with that patronage. They were often seen, like Matsuya, as decadent in comportment and ultimately insolvent; the term "broker millionaire" (*toiya chōja*) appears throughout Saikaku's works to describe a formerly elite class of townsmen whose ostentatious displays of wealth and sophistication often belied their troubled finances. From this perspective, the story of the Matsuya widow becomes a fable not only of the hollowing out of the *chō* community, but also of the decadence and historical decline of the modes of commercial practice oriented by and around that community.

A more detailed study of the figure of the broker millionaire appears in "Shippers and Packhorses in the Courtyard of Abumiya" (*Funabito umakata Abumiya no niwa*, vol. 2–5), which depicts the fortunes of the Abumiya house of Sakata, a shipping hub for the northern provinces.[13] Saikaku's description of Abumiya's business emphasizes both the scale of his operations and the ostentatious quality of his provisioning:

THE COMMUNITY OF THE MARKETPLACE

In the town of Sakata, there dwelled a great broker by the name of Abumiya. He had once run a humble inn, but by his wit in recent years the house had come to prosper, and he now drew guests from every province. He was the foremost receiver of rice from the northlands, and there were none who didn't know the name of Sōzaemon. With a frontage of sixty yards and a lot a hundred-thirty yards deep, his warehouses were built up against his lodgings, and the scene of his kitchen was truly a sight to behold. He had an administrator of rice and miso, a receiver for firewood, a director of appetizers, a chef, a supervisor for the lacquerware cupboards, a controller for sweets, a tobacco officer, a tea-room officer, and a dedicated errand runner.[14]

Despite Saikaku's allusion to Abumiya's humble origins, the historical Abumiya line appears in the historical records of Sakata as a rice broker as early as the 1590s; Sōzaemon was the third household head, and achieved the status of town elder, a post that would be held by his descendants until the end of the Edo period.[15] Saikaku's description of Abumiya's origins as a "humble inn" distorts what was likely a privileged pedigree dating back well into the medieval era, but it nevertheless evokes the function of the *toiya* as a physical marketplace that also offered lodging to its clients. Saikaku describes Abumiya explicitly as a "great broker" (*ōdoiya*), a category roughly equivalent to the purchasing broker and contrasted with the "lesser brokers" (*kotoiya*), namely, the merchant middlemen and distributors who used such marketplaces to conduct their transactions. The scale and staffing of Abumiya's business as rendered by Saikaku reflects a role that combined the demands of managing a marketplace with those of offering hospitality. Saikaku stresses Abumiya's modest comportment, but a degree of ostentation is necessitated both by the nature of his trade and by his status within the community. His propensity for visible displays of wealth is shown to overlap with his role as a public functionary, signified by his attire and performatively formal demeanor: "He wore formal overskirts throughout the year and was never seen to slouch" (*nenjū hakama o kite, sukoshi mo koshi o nosazu*). As the story closes, Saikaku's narrator explicitly links the ostentatious comportment of the broker millionaire to the social status and commercial demands of the broker's trade: "All in all, a broker's finances are never what they seem from the outside, for unanticipated expenses crop up all over. But if he were to keep a humbler profile, his businesses would inevitably decline and the house wouldn't last for long."[16]

The further difficulty of Abumiya's business is that, because the broker himself is neither buyer nor seller, his income comes only from fixed transaction fees, and thus seems humble in comparison with both the volume of goods he manages and the variable expenses associated with a role that combines brokering deals, managing a warehouse, and offering lodging and entertainment—all of which depend on a sense of trust built on social prestige, thus ostentation. In light of these challenges, Saikaku's narrator notes, brokers often "find the income from their transaction fees too tepid and set out to do their own business with the goods entrusted to them. These ventures mostly fail, bringing losses to their clients as well."[17] Indeed, many brokers in Saikaku's time had begun to conduct side businesses of speculative trading with the wares that their customers deposited with them. In other words, they had begun to illicitly emulate the commercial practices of the merchants and middlemen who use their marketplaces to conduct their business of buying and selling for profit.

As if to emphasize this comparison, Saikaku interjects a series of observations about the merchants—or, rather, the clerks of merchant houses—who come to the Abumiya on business: "Upon consideration, when someone must be sent to a distant province to do business, an upright clerk is no good. He will be cautious in all things as others jump on opportunities, and will thus bring no profit. But one who is so bold as to incur losses on his master's behalf will also be quick to do good business, and his profits will bury his losses."[18] The clerk who sees an opportunity to do some side business, indeed with the goods entrusted to him by his master, does well to trust his judgment: On the market, money is made by bold investment. But the same conduct—speculative trading for private profit with the goods entrusted to one's care, with the hope that any losses can be won back—is criticized for the "great broker."

As the story concludes, Saikaku describes Abumiya's solution to the dilemma faced by the broker millionaire: He invents an accounting system that aids him in separating costs from gross profits and thus prevents him at least from spending beyond his means. As with Matsuya's widow, Saikaku's imaginative solution momentarily amuses the reader with its inventive wit, but ultimately fails to solve the underlying problem: that Abumiya's business is a difficult one with unpredictable costs, many of which are inevitable because they are linked to the public status of the *toiya* as *chōnin*, and the increasingly precarious position of this business model was a historical problem that could not be solved by something as simple as fastidious accounting. Indeed, the historical resolution to the problem of the broker millionaire was simply that brokers got into the business of buying and selling: The category of *toiya* merged with that of the merchant middleman to become a wholesale merchant (this is the sense that the term *toiya/tonya* had in eighteenth-century Edo, and how it is largely understood today). In contrast, "Shippers and Packhorses in the Courtyard of Abumiya" offers an amusing, imaginative, alternative solution to this historical problem, suggesting that a clever enough broker might avoid the fate of the class of privileged townsmen simply by the merit of individual business sense.

The depiction in *Eternal Storehouse* of the old guard of townsmen brokers such as Matsuya and Abumiya is, in a sense, ambivalent. On the one hand, Saikaku situates both among a declining milieu of old families and local communities, and that affiliation is revealed as a liability that the individual townsman must find a way to escape and transcend. On the other hand, both stories suggest that transcending that milieu is indeed possible through individual diligence and entrepreneurial wit, and that ultimately the fate of the townsman is a matter of his or her individual character. Even if the townsman-broker like Abumiya is able to survive in the evolving economy, his status as a privileged broker, which once vouchsafed his livelihood, is merely one business model competing in a marketplace no longer bound by the concerns of the local community. It is merely personal cleverness that allows the individual townsman to transcend the particularities of their trade or position, along with the bounds of their particular community, to gain standing in the newly imagined community of the urban marketplace.

THE MERCHANT AND THE MARKETPLACE

One common narrative of economic history that is often told through and about *Eternal Storehouse* is that of a shift between two classes of urban commoner: from "privileged townsmen" (*monbatsu chōnin*) of the early to mid-seventeenth century to the "newly emerging townsmen" (*shinkō chōnin*) of the late seventeenth century.[19] In such a narrative, which is premised on a schema that valorizes a movement from feudalistic elites to free-market entrepreneurs, the newly emerging townsmen are those who rise to wealth by their own powers, riding the waves of the domestic consumer economy that saw explosive growth in the latter half of the seventeenth century. Although broadly descriptive of Saikaku's moment, this narrative is in many ways imprecise. The term "newly emerging" (*shinkō*) is a relative one that might be applied equally to any number of new commercial regimes: to the Osaka rice merchants and financiers of the mid-seventeenth century, who rose to prominence in response to the shifting financial demands of *daimyō* houses, or to the wholesale merchants of the late seventeenth and early eighteenth centuries, who came to organize the distribution of goods in the interregional marketplace. The question of relationship to local authority also obscures as much as it reveals, because each such wave in turn developed its own symbiotic relationship with warrior authorities, resulting in different sets of privileges. The older generations of townsman elites, moreover, did not simply fade away, but continued to persist in the form of the urban leisure class evoked by the terms *yoishū* (sometimes read as *yoishu*; good ranks, perhaps privileged ranks or well-born) and *rekireki* (pedigreed or long-established families), reproducing themselves through intermarriage with the higher ranks of the newly wealthy. The demographic transformation of urban society in the latter half of the seventeenth century is better understood as a diversification and stratification, given that the *chōnin* status group developed its own internal hierarchies based on new distributions of economic, social, and cultural capital. Along with that diversification and stratification was also a fundamental reconfiguration of the social and spatial basis of townsman identity as the influence of the *chō* receded in the face of the fluid circulation of wealth and property in the interregional marketplace: a shift from the stability of urban community and property toward the spontaneous flows of liquid capital across local and regional boundaries.

In a sense, the narrative of a generational shift from feudal privilege to market-driven entrepreneurship is a literary one in that it personifies large and complex historical processes into intelligible and engaging human drama. Indeed, this narrative is at least in part Saikaku's literary invention, given the many treatments of early modern social and economic history that have drawn on his stories as documents of such shifts. Throughout *Eternal Storehouse*, Saikaku depicts historical figures from throughout the seventeenth century, but portrays them almost universally as "sudden millionaires" (*niwaka bungen*) or "wealthy men of the moment" (*ima chōja*), placing them before his late seventeenth-century readers within a framework of recent success through entrepreneurial effort. And in depicting the rise of these new entrepreneurs, Saikaku effaces the complex negotiation between competing commercial regimes, along with the critical links between new money and old privilege. In place of this effaced historicity, he constructs the myth of the self-made townsman, the heroic entrepreneur who succeeds only by his individual wit and effort, without depending on feudal patronage or hereditary privilege. To understand the nature of this reimagining, we must reconstruct in some detail the historicity behind Saikaku's narratives of entrepreneurial success.

The shape of the narrative of the entrepreneurial townsman is seen most clearly in the exemplary case of the Mitsui Echigoya department store in Edo, fictionalized by Saikaku in "In the Past on Credit, Now Money Down" (*Mukashi wa kakezan ima wa tōzagin*, vol. 1–4).[20] The story is framed by a discussion of the increasing decadence of popular fashion, evoking the emergence of a consumer economy and rising standards of sumptuary display among both warriors and commoners in the latter half of the seventeenth century. Against this historical backdrop, Saikaku's narrator describes the rise and fall of the clothiers of the Edo Hon-chō district, who once had thrived as appointed clothiers to the Tokugawa house and to *daimyō* in alternate attendance on the shogun. The narration stresses that this business was conducted by the neighborhood as a whole: The clerks and shop hands of the Hon-chō clothiers, perpetually attending on the warrior households that were their clients, "worked in unison, cheering one another on" (*tomo-kasegi hagemiai*), suggesting less a competitive marketplace and more the collective practice of what was essentially a local clothing cartel. But Saikaku's narrator notes that, as *daimyō* finances became increasingly strained by the demands of conspicuous consumption, the privileged relationships that had originally underwritten the clothing business were jettisoned, and clothiers gradually were forced to compete with one another and bid for contracts, driving down profit margins. At the same time, the privileged relationships with shogunal and *daimyō* authorities became a liability because clothiers were compelled to take large orders with low margins simply for the prestige of association; because these orders were based on credit, with payments frequently withheld by struggling *daimyō* households, many shops declined.

It is in this context that Saikaku's narrator introduces an entrepreneurial fellow named Mitsui Kurōemon, who sets up a shop in the neighboring district of Suruga-chō. In Saikaku's rendition, Mitsui's key innovation is the model of storefront sales, as he operates "on a policy of selling everything for cash with no markups" (*gengin uri ni kakene nashi*). He also has a large staff of "forty resourceful clerks," with one responsible for each product line, and "dozens of tailors on hand," rationalizing his operations to scale for greater volume of business and to allow the tailoring of clothing to order on demand. In contrast to the Hon-chō clothiers, who had depended on large orders on account with significant markups supported by long-term, service-intensive relationships with elite warrior households, Mitsui's innovations allow him to offer his goods at a lower price; this also allows him to incorporate less elite customers like low-ranking warriors (as opposed to *daimyō* households) into his clientele, and to conduct a huge volume of business on small orders with low profit margins. To Saikaku's narrator, these innovations, framed as a move from the saturated field of elite clothiers to the opportunities of the emerging consumer clothing market, make his shop "one of the world's treasures" (*yo no chōhō*) and him "the model of a great merchant" (*ōakindo no tehon*).

In this concise episode, one that is uncharacteristically brief and lacking in ironic twists, Saikaku not only gives a vivid image of Mitsui's innovative business practice, but also situates that entrepreneurial innovation in the context of a plausible narrative of seventeenth-century cultural and social history, linking the rise in sumptuary standards and the emergence of a consumer economy to shifts in the finances of warrior households and the conditions of the clothing industry. Much of this narrative stands up to historical scrutiny, a testament to Saikaku's shrewd economic sensibility and to the astuteness of his grasp of his historical moment. But Saikaku also elides aspects of Mitsui's historic innovation, and these ellipses illuminate what was at stake in the literary image he produces of "the model of a great merchant" and thus in the (literary) narrative of a historical shift from privileged townsmen to entrepreneurial merchants.

Perhaps most obviously, Saikaku's rendition omits the historical privilege of the Mitsui house itself. In the early seventeenth century, the Mitsui house, based in Matsusaka (Ise Province) and headed by Mitsui Norihei, had been a moneylender and dealer of saké and soybean paste, a member of the local mercantile elite, and an archetypal example of the old guard of privileged townsmen who would, in the textbook narrative, supposedly be displaced by entrepreneurial merchants. As early as the 1620s, Norihei's heir, Toshitsugu, had established the first Echigoya dry goods store in the fourth block of the Hon-chō district before expanding to several other locations in Edo and Kyoto. Norihei's fourth and youngest son, Takatoshi, was apprenticed to Toshitsugu before returning to Matsusaka to become a minor lender to *daimyō*, but after his brother died, he began a meteoric rise to become one of Japan's greatest merchants. In 1673, Takatoshi directed the simultaneous opening of two clothiers: one in Kyoto (Muromachi Yakushi-chō), acting as supplier and managed by his eldest son, Takahira; and the other in Edo Hon-chō, acting as vendor to the Edo market and managed by his second son, Takatomi. Both were known by Takahira's shop name of Hachirōemon but were likely heavily directed by Takatoshi himself.[21] An interregional family conglomerate operating under the direction of a house patriarch, who was himself a privileged townsman of the old guard, with all the capital resources of a *daimyō* moneylender: This Saikaku writes into a story about the individual commercial wit of a singular heroic entrepreneur—Mitsui Kurōemon.

Takatoshi seems also to have been heavily influenced by his mother, Shuhō. According to Mitsui house documents, Takatoshi's father, Norihei, much like Saikaku's Matsuya, had been more concerned with living the rich and cultured lifestyle of the privileged townsman and amusing himself with linked verse than with managing the family trade, which he left to his wife; but the house nevertheless thrived due to her diligent efforts and shrewd business sense. Later generations would attribute even Takatoshi's historic success to his mother's wisdom and legacy, and consider her, rather than Norihei or Takatoshi, the house progenitor—in spirit, if not in letter. Takatoshi himself was also supported by a talented and diligent wife, Jusan.[22] The efforts of these accomplished women, perhaps unsurprisingly, are elided in Saikaku's narrative of the heroic male entrepreneur, as well as in most scholarly accounts of Mitsui's historic success.

More subtly, "In the Past on Credit, Now Money Down" also obscures the ways in which the success of the Mitsui house was predicated on the symbolic collapse, or rather defeat, of the *chō* as a local urban community. Yoshida Nobuyuki reconstructs this drama as follows.[23] Before the location in Suruga-chō described by Saikaku, Mitsui's first Edo clothier had been located in the Hon-chō district. Most of the Hon-chō clothiers were Edo branches of Kyoto firms, but, as a relative newcomer to the Edo clothiers' trade, the Mitsui Hon-chō shop was of a smaller scale and in many ways an outsider to the Edo community. Although it would expand to comprise two stores in neighboring blocks, both were rented spaces with relatively few clerks and initially lacked *daimyō* clients. In contrast to its illustrious neighbors, the Mitsui house eked out an existence by auctioning goods to street peddlers, who would sell the merchandise to individual (non-elite) consumers in Edo and the surrounding areas. The Echigoya's pivotal innovation, as Saikaku correctly observes, was the model of storefront sales: Abandoning the service-intensive practice of selling on credit to elite houses, Echigoya shifted to selling directly to individual consumers (whether elite or lower status), and, by keeping prices low, was able to attract enough business to make massive profits despite lower margins. But this innovation had in fact been appropriated by the Echigoya store from the street peddlers who were originally its sole wholesale clients: Such peddlers generally operated in largely public spaces such as riverbanks, bridges, and crossroads, but it was also not uncommon for them to set up temporary shops in front of the wholesalers from which they procured their wares. This was the template for Echigoya, which incorporated the paradigm of literal "storefront" (*tanasaki*) cash sales into its establishment, resulting in the archetypal department store. In other words, the Echigoya appropriated the sales model and likely livelihood of its main customer base, claiming the peddlers' business of consumer retail while enacting private enclosure of the storefront, which had been a semipublic space between the private space of the shop and the public space of the street itself.[24]

Meanwhile, the Echigoya's neighbors—the community of Hon-chō clothiers, who in spite of decreasing profit margins had remained bound by their commitment to collective commercial norms, and who had respected a symbiotic relationship with the professional associations of street peddlers—were naturally unenthusiastic about its success. When one of the dominant Edo clothiers lost a major *daimyō* contract to Echigoya, the Hon-chō clothiers conspired to expel the Mitsui house from the trade association and block its supply of goods from Kyoto. When these measures failed to slow Mitsui's success, they supposedly called on the cooperation of Echigoya's landlord (a *chō* member alongside Mitsui's competitors), who installed a toilet for the neighboring property to drain directly past Echigoya's kitchen in an effort to drive it out of the neighborhood. Whether

THE COMMUNITY OF THE MARKETPLACE

in response to these altercations or to damage incurred by a fire in 1682, the Mitsui house purchased a new property a few blocks away in the moneylending neighborhood of Suruga-chō, where it opened a shop in 1683 to establish the business described by Saikaku. Tensions with the surrounding neighborhood continued to afflict the Echigoya, however. Soon after the move, threats of arson were repeatedly posted on the *chō* gate, stating that if Suruga-chō were to allow Echigoya to move there, the store would be burned to the ground, putting the entire community at risk of fire. The source of these threats is unclear—the Mitsui house had made many enemies—but the Suruga-chō council, deliberating on the matter, concluded that "allowing a clothier into a neighborhood of moneychangers is like mixing oil and water," and that Echigoya should close. The new Echigoya simply responded by adding financial services to its operations, thus following the letter of the law if not the spirit.[25] In the following decades, the Mitsui house would buy out some of its former competitors in Hon-chō while purchasing extensive property in Suruga-chō, decisively demonstrating the subjugation of the *chō* as a self-governing local collective in the face of the commodification of urban property and the expansion of merchant capital across community boundaries. Yoshida compellingly summarizes these developments as the decisive defeat of "the logic of the *chō*" at the hands of "the logic of the merchant."[26]

The historic innovation of Mitsui's Echigoya—a storefront sales model, cannily promoted through the handy catch phrase "cash payment, no markups"—thus conceals an episode of economic intrigue that blends entrepreneurial transformation, latent class conflict, and local neighborhood politics, pitting the old Hon-chō and Suruga-chō neighborhoods against the upstart Mitsui house, likely managed by missives from Matsusaka by the nominally retired but still energetically active and brazenly cunning patriarch Takatoshi. To observe this element of local politics, which is lost in Saikaku's rendition, is not to downplay the significance or originality of the Echigoya's historic innovation, but to suggest that it was more than a matter of a generational shift, of new and independent entrepreneurs outwitting old and privileged families. Takatoshi was an established townsperson of the highest rank in Matsusaka, and Echigoya's success was a product of his ferocious ambition to extend the power of that capital across geographic boundaries to better exploit evolving urban markets. This success was possible only in defiance of local commercial norms that had been regulated at the level of the *chō*: The Mitsui house was an outsider (a mere renter) in Hon-chō, one that thus felt little compunction about violating the community's collective norms in what may be seen as a winner-takes-all resolution to the textbook problem of economic game theory. The framework of the *chō* never entirely disappeared (it remained present as an administrative unit and basic social community when Saikaku was writing, and would continue to exist into the modern era), but the rise of Mitsui's Echigoya reveals that, by the late seventeenth century—amid historic shifts in patterns of consumption, the increasing integration of transportation and communication networks, the movement of merchant capital across local boundaries, and the commodification of urban property—the local community of the *chō* was ceasing to define the social, spatial, and economic practices of its individual members. What emerged in the wake of its collapse—or, rather, the force that exploited and orchestrated that collapse from within—was the individual commoner household (*ie* 家), which would replace the *chō* as the atomic unit of urban society and the orienting nexus of urban commoner identity.

Seen from this perspective, the genesis of the Echigoya appears not as a generational shift, but instead as a reorientation of the socio-spatial structures around which *chōnin* identity and community were organized. If the logic of the *chō* was based in the concrete social relationships within that community and manifest in its unique, local spatiality, then the logic of the merchant structured a new form of urban spatiality, drawing a large and indeterminate audience of urban consumers into the orbit of the singular commercial storefront. Not every merchant to succeed in the new economy would operate at the same scale—even among the emerging stratum of large shops (*ōdana*) that oriented increasingly large cross-sections of the urban population, the Echigoya was a singular case—but those who prospered would have to think not in terms of local community and privileged relationships with authority, but in terms of the new set of networks, both interregional and intracity, that connected the individual merchant to a larger urban marketplace.

Regardless, my purpose in reconstructing the historical circumstances surrounding Mitsui's innovation is not to take Saikaku to task for misrepresenting or obscuring a historical truth that precedes the text. The question is what kind of narrative sense he makes of this tremendously complex set of historical contingencies and social shifts: what perspective he assumes, how he accounts for Mitsui's success, what the nature of his narrative reveals about his reimagining of the urban social imaginary, and what was at stake in that reimagining. In rewriting the circumstances around Mitsui's historic success, Saikaku pushes the intricacies of local community politics and the presence of interregional networks of hereditary capital into the background and renders them invisible. The ideologically charged narrative to resolve into focus in the foreground is that of the individual entrepreneurial merchant confronting, apprehending, and effectively exploiting the historical shifts of the marketplace and thus rising to wealth by his individual merits. The Echigoya is thus remade into an exemplary signifier of the emerging ideology of the newly imagined urban community: the supremacy of individual effort and entrepreneurial wit. Indeed, despite the truly singular status of the Mitsui house in the emerging economic landscape of the late seventeenth century, and despite the fascinating drama surrounding its historic success, Saikaku's Mitsui Kurōemon is almost totally generic, a blank cipher of individual entrepreneurial talent: "There was nothing to distinguish him from other men but his exceptional brilliance at his given trade" (*hoka no hito ni kawatta tokoro mo naku, kashoku ni kawatte kashikoshi*).[27] Here Mitsui has become more myth than man: an interregional and transgenerational commercial conglomerate personified as the individual entrepreneurial hero, nothing but a pure signifier of commercial wit.

This transformation was not necessarily a matter of authorial intent, but the product of the same networks of communication and media circulation that were transforming the urban community in Saikaku's time. Saikaku, who may or may not have traveled to Edo in his lifetime, was unlikely to have known about the intricacies of local intrigue surrounding the Echigoya, which historians have reconstructed largely from records kept by the Mitsui house. Documents from the Hon-chō and Suruga-chō wards might tell different stories (it is a testament to the richness of Mitsui's historical records, and to the sympathies of the historian, that the perspective of the local community comes through so vividly), but the subjectivity of the *chō* was only ever local. The narrative of the Hon-chō community—one that might foreground the ways in which the Mitsui house's business practice flouted the norms of the Edo clothiers' trade, and in doing so might reassert the boundaries of that particular community's local identity—would have no reason to circulate and would find no place in print. Although it is conceivable that some insider gossip might have reached Saikaku's ears, the author was ultimately an outside observer, a perspective that comes through clearly in his writing. Much of the information conveyed in Saikaku's rendition likely came from the Echigoya's advertising campaign, a promotional leaflet printed and distributed in large numbers throughout Edo following the move to Suruga-chō:

> Echigoya Hachirōemon of Suruga-chō announces the following. Henceforth, by way of my own innovation, I will be selling any and all garments for extraordinarily low prices. Please visit my shop for your purchases. Goods will not be delivered to any personage, regardless of status. Individual transactions are calculated and charged on the spot with not a single copper of markup and no discounts for haggling. All goods must, of course, be paid for upon purchase, so you won't pay a copper's worth of interest.
>
> Garments sold for cash, low prices with no markups!
> SURUGA-CHŌ 2-CHŌME ECHIGOYA HACHIRŌEMON[28]

The advertisement articulates the key points that a general consumer will need to know about the Echigoya: storefront sales, no delivery, payment in cash, no markups, no haggling, no payment on account or interest on late payments. More subtly but more importantly, it attributes these policies to the "personal innovation" (*watakushi kufū*) of the individual Hachirōemon—though this name merely represented the corporate agency of the Echigoya shop, and the innovation was likely of Takatoshi's conception. (The Echigoya's former customers, the street peddlers, would no doubt have read in this claim of personal innovation a particularly bitter irony.) Here is the critical stroke, the kernel of the Echigoya's promotional campaign that Saikaku elaborates into the myth of the individual entrepreneur: the heroic visionary whose mercurial wit apprehends the shifting contours of culture (rising sartorial standards) and the economy (increasing consumer spending) to find opportunity within the contingency and complexity of a historical moment. Saikaku's story, like the Echigoya's advertisement, would assume the perspective of, and be directed at, a broad and indeterminate audience (marketplace) of urban consumers.

MAPPING THE COMMUNITY OF THE MARKETPLACE

The cases of Mitsui, Matsuya, and Abumiya reveal two parallel tendencies in Saikaku's depictions of urban commerce. On the one hand, all three register a historical shift away from the socio-spatial structure of the *chō* and toward an endorsement of new forms of commerce based on the circulation of merchant capital across social and geographic boundaries. On the other, they also suggest a more fundamental reimagining of the nature of urban community and the underlying logic of economic practice. Despite the differences of status, occupation, and geographic position separating these characters, they are all ultimately measured against the same standard: an ethos centered on the interests of the individual household, on the effort and ability of the individual entrepreneur, and above all on the mercurial entrepreneurial cognition that aids the individual merchant in apprehending, navigating, and ultimately exploiting the dynamic energies of the consumer marketplace. This ethos is arguably based on the practice of the interregional merchant capitalist, but the more fundamental point is that it is a portable and universal set of values and practices imagined to apply regardless of social or geographic position: It allows the old townsman to live on, just as it enables the merchant capitalist to thrive—although the former is at a natural disadvantage to the latter.

In light of Saikaku's apparent celebration of the hollowing out of the *chō* and its displacement by the influence of the individual merchant house, one is tempted to conclude that what Saikaku depicts in *Eternal Storehouse* is not community at all, but precisely the dissolution of local urban communities in light of the commodification of urban property, the increasingly interconnected nature of the early modern city, and the growing force of merchant capital, like that of the Mitsui house, circulating across geographic boundaries—that what we have here is another instance in which, to borrow the Marxian cliché, all that is solid melts into air. Certainly, these historical processes were under way at the time, and Saikaku's writing attempts to make sense of them; the question is what kind of sense. If the late seventeenth century saw the decay of the *chō* and its displacement by new regimes of commercial practice, Saikaku produces out of those new regimes an image of a novel and different type of (imagined) urban community, an image of the interregional urban economy that is all the more ideologically powerful because it is imagined as a community.

David Harvey, drawing on Georg Simmel, uses the term "community of money" to refer to the new set of social relations enabled by and mediated through money exchange: the simulacrum that dissolves existing communities, only to become, in Marx's words, "the real community." But Harvey's description of the community of money is largely the community as theorized by the scholar (Simmel's broad sketches of urban alienation, individualism, and intellectual rationality) rather than as concretely imagined by the urban dweller.[29] Saikaku, while registering the impact of money on social relations, offers a detailed and diverse but ultimately normative vision of a field of social positions and economic roles, reflecting on where they stand in relation to one another. *Eternal Storehouse* maps the possibilities of mobility within the domestic money-based economy, presenting as exemplars those who, like the imagined figure of Mitsui Kurōemon, are able to exploit its opportunities. The inhabitants of this new economy constitute what I call the community of the marketplace. The community of the marketplace is, paradoxically, both diverse and normative, inclusive and stratified: It includes protagonists of diverse positions and offers them the equal promise of wealth and mobility, but in practice favors some and pushes others to the margins. It reorganizes the urban community according to the logic of the marketplace.

The old townsman, proxy of the *chō*, remains present throughout *Eternal Storehouse*, but, as we have seen, is rarely situated explicitly in a local context. Instead, he is regarded as a member of a generational milieu defined largely by the decadent comportment of its individual members: the recurring image of the broker millionaire. Although the story of Abumiya illuminates the links between this outward ostentation and the demands of the broker's trade, generally speaking the perceived self-indulgence of the old townsmen is presented as a matter of individual conduct, as with the deceased Matsuya. The decline of the established house is often blamed on a dissolute heir or simply on an incompetent one. "When a Paper Fortune Falls in Tatters" (*Kamiko shindai no yabure-doki*, vol. 3–5) traces the decline of a household in the elite Hon-chō clothiers' district of Suruga: Having been brought to wealth by the efforts of an inventive patriarch, the house collapses in thirty years at the hands of a feckless son.[30] But the failures of a dissolute heir may also present the opportunity for his entrepreneurial redemption, provided that he earns his living outside the framework of hereditary privilege. One of the most striking examples is "Daikoku, Who

Wore Wit as His Shelter" (*Saikaku o kasa ni kiru Daikoku*, vol. 2–3): A young degenerate named Shinroku is formally disowned by his father and thus is removed from the *chō* community, only to embark on an individual journey from rags to riches.[31] Along the way, he meets a number of beggars who are fallen townsmen. One is a man from Sakai who boasts of an exemplary pedigree of training in all the leisure arts (calligraphy, tea ceremony, Chinese verse, linked verse, *nō* dance and drumming, Confucian thought, kickball, *go*, shamisen and *shakuhachi* playing, *jōruri* chanting, and so on and so forth), but is left resenting the parents, who never taught him the practical skills to make a living. Another is the heir to a family that "from his parents' generation was homegrown Edo, with a grand estate in [Nihonbashi] Tōri-chō, and without fail would take in six hundred gold *ryō* every year in rent alone," but who lost his fortune due to simple lack of thrift. The story of Shinroku thus is premised on the renunciation of the *chō* and the framing of its proxies, the privileged townsmen, as insolvent decadents.

If the old townsmen are seen to decline due to their individual dissolution, then new types of entrepreneurial merchants are shown to rise to wealth by their individual wit. The paths to wealth are manifold, but one can observe within them a few general tendencies. One route to riches starts with street peddling (*furi-uri*), the most rudimentary form of commercial practice and the most accessible to those without capital resources, such as recent migrants from the countryside. In "The Ten Virtues of Tea, Gone in an Instant" (*Cha no jittoku mo ichido ni mina*, vol. 4–4), an enterprising tea dealer based in Tsuruga makes a fortune by selling tea by the cup to merchants at the morning wholesale markets.[32] The tea seller, Risuke, who is introduced as living "on the outskirts of the *chō*" (*chō-hazure ni*), is able to build some capital before long and establish himself among the local tea wholesalers. Eventually, he succumbs to an unbridled lust for wealth and begins buying up used tea dregs from around the province; as word leaks out of his unethical business practices, he goes mad and transforms into a demonic manifestation of merchant avarice. But his rise to wealth, from a peddler on the outskirts of *chōnin* society (and of the *chō* itself) to a wholesale merchant, remains a paradigmatic narrative of rags to riches. In another example, "Making a Living by Yodo Carp" (*Yowatari wa yodo-goi no hataraki*, vol. 5–2), the heir to a Yodo-based oil dealer wearies of his house trade, falls into poverty, and then finds a new calling as a peddler of fresh carp from the Yodo River.[33] At first, he catches the fish himself, but once he has made a name and a reputation for fresh fish, he begins simply buying his stock in markets at Ōmi and Tanba and selling it for a markup; as he continues to rise in the world, however, he abandons this trade entirely and shifts to a moneylending business. As these examples suggest, the entrepreneurial ethos that structures the community of the marketplace is, by and large, an amoral one. Saikaku has a particular interest in, and systematically notes, the places where opportunity is predicated both on minor transgression and on the concealment of such transgression. In rare cases, such as that of the tea dealer Risuke, characters are judged as having gone too far and face worldly consequences. But these are transgressions of degree, remaining within the entrepreneurial community of the marketplace as cautionary tales marking the limits of the moral liberties that can be taken in the pursuit of wealth; implicitly, then, the other transgressions marked in passing by Saikaku's narrators are authorized as legitimate. (The moral dimensions of commerce are taken up in greater detail in chapter 2.)

Many of Saikaku's protagonists (the successful ones) move nimbly between trades, ultimately graduating into the business of finance as the ultimate manifestation of the logic of the marketplace. As Harvey notes, the community of money is marked by "the rise of a variety of occupations (from the street vendor to the banker) which have no other content than making money."[34] Next to street peddlers, moneylenders of various stripes are central to Saikaku's vision. A few stories focus on what would now be called microfinance: Once the protagonist is able to pull together even a small fund of capital, he lends it at interest to other peddlers or new entrants to the urban economy. The question is only how to secure an initial fund—hard work, simple thrift, or some other more inventive scheme. Like the street peddlers, Saikaku's moneylenders are often of the renter class or otherwise on the margins of the local community. In "Scattering Coins Like Seeds of Good Fortune" (*Shiawase no tane o makisen*, vol. 4–3), we have a glimpse of an Edo moneylender of modest appearance and comportment, who worked his way to wealth in a rented shop with a mere nine-foot frontage, lending small sums to actors in the neighboring theater district.[35] A close cousin of the entrepreneurial moneylender is the pawnbroker. In "Plucking Out the Very Eye of the Boddhisattva Kannon" (*Yo wa nukidori no Kan'on no manako*, vol. 3–3), the Fushimi pawnbroker Kikuya no Zenzō, like the tea dealer Risuke, dwells "on the outskirts of the *chō*." As if to emphasize his marginal relationship to urban property, Kikuya no Zenzō is described as "not possessing even a storehouse, but rather a single wheeled chest" that he uses as both a personal closet and a safe for pawned goods. But he still supports a household of eight and amasses a small fortune through small-scale lending and shrewd bargaining.[36]

In contrast to the moneylender with his mobility, the figure of the working craftsman is pushed almost entirely to the margins of the community of the marketplace. In setting the scene for the pawnbroker Kikuya no Zenzō, Saikaku describes the dereliction of Fushimi: "Among the craftsmen making wicker baskets and bamboo blowguns, there are still some pedigreed families, but it's difficult to string together even a humble living selling rings for wood-tiled roofs, pins for folding fans, moxa tweezers, and packing ropes."[37] The difficulty of an artisanal trade is that its business fails to scale: One can make only so many moxa tweezers in a day. Similarly, in "Gentle Trade Winds for the Good Ship Jinzū" (*Namikaze shizuka ni Jinzūmaru*, vol. 1–3), Saikaku describes a diligent box-carver from Osaka: "Though he sold coin boxes to the wealthiest financiers, his hands were too busy making constant measurements to grasp any of the money that those boxes would hold, and when one of his apprentices came of age and set up his own shop, he too knew only how to make tinderboxes and lids to serving dishes."[38] The working craftsman, too immersed in the technical details and time-consuming manual processes of production, has little opportunity to exert the entrepreneurial wit necessary to truly profit from the historic opportunities of the new economy.

The few cases of craftsmen successfully working their way to wealth largely result from a pivot to the practice of the merchant. One vivid example is "A Votive Mat, a Sign of Prayers Answered" (*Inoru shirushi no kami no oshiki*, vol. 4–1), the story of a Kyoto couple by the name of Kikyōya whose trade is dyeing fabric.[39] The couple is introduced as diligent and honest. But despite their efforts, they have fallen to the brink of poverty and have taken to praying not to the god of wealth for succor but instead to the god of poverty, for whom they construct a votive altar and effigy. The god, pleased by their uncommon devotion, appears in an oracular dream, where he promises to "save their share of poverty for some decadent heir" and vouches that they will soon find prosperity. He leaves the dream chanting a cryptic declaration: "There are many ways to make a living; willows are green, and flowers are crimson." The husband, transfixed by the dream, interprets these words to refer to crimson dye, but notes that the Kyoto market is controlled by another dyer named Kobeniya and that "Kyoto is full of clever people, so it will be difficult to make a profit by ordinary methods."[40] Nevertheless, he takes to experimenting day and night, and soon comes up with a new and cheaper method of dyeing that is indistinguishable from ordinary crimson. He then begins dyeing in secret (*himitsu shite*), carrying his product himself to sell to wholesale dealers in Edo and picking up local textiles on the way back to sell in Kamigata, and within ten years succeeds in amassing a fortune of one thousand *kanme* of silver. Kikyōya's path to wealth turns on an artisanal innovation—a new method of dyeing—but his success is not merely a matter of craftsmanship: It depends on exploiting interregional trade networks to find a market for what is essentially a high-quality knock-off good, likely sold at a lower cost. (One might take the intervention of the god of poverty as a metaphor for a shift of attention from elite customers, the market of which is saturated, to a larger customer base that is willing to accept an attractive but inauthentic alternative.) As with many of the success stories in *Eternal Storehouse*, there is an element of moral ambiguity here, given that Kikyōya must dye fabric in secret and take his goods to Edo personally, both to circumvent the saturated trading networks of the Kyoto marketplace and possibly to lower the chances of his being discovered selling inauthentic goods. All of this, as much as the artisanal innovation itself, marks Kikyōya as much more than a technically innovative craftsman: He is now an interregional merchant.

Although the stories in *Eternal Storehouse* focus largely on urban spaces of various shapes and scales, Saikaku also makes select excursions to the countryside, revealing the ways in which agricultural production is being reshaped by the evolving interregional market. "Tengu by Name, with a Windflower Crest" (*Tengu wa iena no kazaguruma*, vol. 1–4) depicts the travails of a whaler-cum-fishing magnate from Kii Province by the name of Tengu Gennai.[41] Gennai is initially renowned for his exceptional bravery and skill as a whaler, and the story begins by narrating his heroic success in harpooning the largest whale the town has ever seen. But his true accomplishment comes after the fact as the villagers are processing the whale carcass. Once they have carved away the marbled slabs of meat and fat, Gennai makes off with the bones, regarded by his peers as waste, and boils them to extract the oil: "How foolish that no one had thought of this before." Building on this success, he then invents a fishing net suitable for whaling, deploying it in one bay after another: "Though he once lived in a shack on the beach, he now owns a large tenement of cypress, housing over two hundred fishermen with eighty boats."[42] No longer a fisherman and whaler himself, he has successfully consolidated a regional whaling concern with his former peers as his employees. In the last episode of the story, we learn how he also invents a technique for transporting live fish over long distances, situating his transformation from fisherman to merchant within the development of interregional trade networks. All the innovations in this story were historic shifts that transformed the fishing trade.[43] As in other stories, Saikaku reimagines them as the products of the entrepreneurial wit of a heroic individual.

"A Bathtub Tycoon for the Provinces" (*Kuni ni utsushite furogama no daijin*, vol. 3–2) is a simpler example.[44] A merchant's heir in the town of Funai (Bungo Province) secretly plants rapeseed over undeveloped land in the surrounding countryside, and then petitions for official authorization to develop the land, receives a grant for ten years without taxation, provides housing and equipment to local peasants, and begins shipping produce by boat to Kamigata—effectively incorporating the provincial town of Funai into national trade networks based in the urban centers of central Japan. His downfall comes when he likewise emulates the sumptuary habits of the capital, renovating his residence in urban fashion. Although this vision of the community of the marketplace seems almost so capacious as to blur the distinction between town and countryside, it does not negate difference between peasants and urban commoners. If Tengu Gennai is a townsman in spirit if not in name, then the fishermen who work for him remain peasants, as do those who cultivate the land on the outskirts of Funai: One transforms from peasant to merchant by organizing the ongoing labor of one's peasant neighbors.

What Saikaku narrates in these stories, along with the transformation of rural entrepreneurs into merchant capitalists, is the incorporation of the provincial countryside into what Henri Lefebvre calls the "urban fabric": not simply "the built world of cities but all manifestations of the dominance of the city over the country."[45] The urban phenomenon, and thus the imagined community of the marketplace, cannot be localized in cities, but permeates every place where life is transformed by urban networks and processes. Indeed, Saikaku's use of the term *chōnin* itself is remarkably loose, even in depictions of provincial settings; *chōnin* comes to be functionally indistinguishable from merchant. It is a matter of lifestyle rather than of formal status. The characters who are incorporated into the imagined townsman community are those who can perform the ethos of the entrepreneurial merchant. Peasants who remain bound to the agricultural economy and its demands of daily labor are excluded and largely rendered invisible or exploitable (see chapter 2).

Other exclusions are more conspicuous. The absence of women from the community of the marketplace is not altogether surprising. Although Saikaku had elsewhere explored with great nuance the economic agency of women both inside and outside the home—most famously in *The Life of an Amorous Woman* (*Kōshoku ichidai onna*, 1686)—he rarely conceived of it as a path to social mobility, nor even of permanent independence from the patriarchal frameworks of male property (whether that of the *chō* or that of the household). Saikaku's sense of women's economic activity was framed largely by an awareness of the floating world in its most pessimistic sense: various ways of getting by in the world, but very rarely any way of controlling one's fate or gaining wealth and status. In *Eternal Storehouse*, women appear most commonly as figures for the temptation of sumptuary indulgence, whether in the form of dalliance by an otherwise scrupulous male protagonist in the prostitution quarters, or in the form of wives and daughters who manifest the desire for conspicuous consumption of the latest fashion. (Conspicuous consumption was, of course, a male desire as well, but it tended to be projected onto women, and Saikaku was no different in this regard.)

Other women, however, invert (not to say subvert) this stereotype by supporting the male protagonist's efforts at thrift in the role of wife. In "Shippers and Packhorses in the Courtyard of Abumiya," Abumiya's wife is praised for having a modesty uncharacteristic of the wife of a broker, and in "Three *monme* and five *fun* at New Year" (*San-monme go-fun akebono no kane*, vol. 5–5), an uncommonly jealous wife saves the finances of the household by browbeating her husband out of any attempt to consort with ladies of the night.[46] Such representations are in keeping with the values of their time concerning women's labor. As historians have long observed, women played many important functions in the townsman household, but those functions were generally oriented by the dual roles of wife and mother and contained within the domestic space of the house. The distinction between the outward-facing economic agency of the husband and the domestic duties of the wife was of course more flexible in the lower rungs of urban society, where women had to take on all kinds of work to survive; but in the propertied and upwardly mobile strata, the agency of women was, with a few notable exceptions, generally consigned to a supporting role within the home.[47] At the same time, such roles were likely more flexible in the newer generations of entrepreneurial merchant households than they had been within the community of the *chō*, which tended to extend and reinforce the patriarchal structures of shogunal rule; over the course of the Tokugawa period, women would play increasing roles in the marketplace at various social strata.[48] But these developments remained inchoate in the late seventeenth century, and Saikaku's stories register at best an ambivalence regarding women's economic agency outside domestic roles. Several stories, like that of Kikyōya the Kyoto dyer, open with a focus on a hardworking couple, only to shift seamlessly to focus on the entrepreneurial creativity of the male partner.

The more telling examples are those that foreground the question of women's economic agency and thereby chart precisely the gendered margins of the community of the marketplace. One, as we have seen, is Matsuya's widow in "A Lucky Bid from the World of Greed." The widow, who like all the female protagonists in *Eternal Storehouse* is left nameless, is praised both for her feminine modesty—a model widow in refusing to remarry—and for her entrepreneurial wit, but is still unable to maintain a household herself. Her wit succeeds only in exchanging her property (and status) for liquid wealth, but we have no trajectory from there toward a new commercial endeavor. The most striking example is "Gentle Trade Winds for the Good Ship *Jinzū*."[49] Here Saikaku depicts an impoverished woman, a widow and single mother, who makes a living by sweeping up spilled rice at the Kitahama rice market in Osaka, a marginal trade that places the woman in the ranks of nonhereditary outcasts and beggars. One year, the market is overflowing with rice, which she "sweeps up along with piles of dust"; even after subtracting her daily meals, she is able to amass a small surplus. Realizing the opportunity before her, she scrimps for a year and ends up with a store of seven and a half bales, which she sells in secret (waste rice could of course not be sold legally). Within twenty years, she has collected a modest capital fund of more than twelve *kanme* of silver. But despite her many years of thrift, hard work, and morally ambiguous entrepreneurial insight, real mobility is only possible for her son. As the narrative continues, the woman's son from a young age builds a business by selling woven threads for stringing together copper currency; when he matures, he establishes a moneylending shop that makes short-term loans to travelers and recent migrants; within ten years, he has become one of Osaka's premier financiers. Eventually, he is adopted as the heir to a pedigreed house, but retains his mother's old dust broom as a house treasure and an object of private veneration. That the son's mobility is predicated on his mother's entrepreneurial vision only underscores the ways in which women's economic agency, even in the open-ended community of the marketplace, is ultimately envisioned as subordinate to male entrepreneurship. It remains compartmentalized, as in the case of the historical Mitsui house, as a matter of the household's private legacy rather than its public face.

What unifies all of these participants in the evolving market economy—what unifies the community of the marketplace—is not a shared social position, trade, or geographic location, but a shared sense of mercantile values, practices, and lifestyles: an entrepreneurial ethos. We will see in chapter 3 that this ethos itself was shot through with tensions and contradictions, but in the broadest sense it was composed of the familiar merchant values of thrift and hard work, balanced with a dynamic entrepreneurial cognition able to imagine inventive solutions to common problems and to perceive opportunity where others may not. The idea of a shared ethos was symbolically powerful because it articulated a form of community and narrativized forms of social mobility in ways that anyone could aspire to regardless of any particularities of their position or the historical contingencies they might face. As Saikaku describes the great (imagined) merchant Mitsui Kurōemon, "There was nothing to distinguish him from other men but his exceptional brilliance at his given trade." The community of the marketplace is oriented by this ethos: The characters who succeed are those who are best able (whether by ambition, disposition, or circumstance) to embody it.

What is perhaps most striking about this vision of urban community, and the ethos on which it is based, is how it seems totally void of conflict, even of concrete and reciprocal relationships among its members. For his remarkably precise apprehension of shifts in the nature of the Japanese economy, Saikaku only occasionally hints at an understanding of the community of the marketplace as a space of competition; when he does,

THE COMMUNITY OF THE MARKETPLACE

victory is achieved not through direct conflict, but by circumventing one's peers by addressing new and different markets. When the fictionalized Mitsui Kurōemon invents a new system of storefront sales for cash, he does not do so by defying the community-based business practices of the Honchō clothiers or by appropriating the sales practices of his primary customers: His innovation appears as a new solution to a collective problem, one that makes him not a pariah but a model for his peers. In the few cases when characters meet with karmic justice for their avarice, it is not in response to any specific injury inflicted on customer or competitor, but a matter of individual excess, their performance of the entrepreneurial ideal having been taken too far. Taking Saikaku's marketplace as a community of money, it is one in which money does not connect individuals or set them into intelligible relations with one another, but instead is simply a metric that places them on the same playing field and enables their comparison, singling out some as "models" and "mirrors" and rendering others invisible or negligible. The marketplace is a community of atomized individuals, and their membership and standing within that community is a remarkably pure function of whether and how they manifest its values.

Throughout his townsman pieces, Saikaku repeatedly quotes the aphorism "a thousand households can make a living together" (*sen-gen areba tomosugi*), indicating an awareness that, once an urban community reaches a certain size, it can sustain itself in reciprocal relations of supply and demand. We hardly see this economic reciprocity in Saikaku's stories, however. As if to reflect this altered consciousness of the nature of urban community, Saikaku twists the proverb further, replacing the character *tomo* 共 (among companions or together) with the homophonous character 友 (friends).[50] Similarly, the text's table of contents imagines Saikaku's protagonists as neighbors—and yet we have no sense of connection or meaningful relationship between them: just a series of disparate voices in a crowded marketplace, each calling out its sales cry to an indeterminate audience of potential customers that parallels Saikaku's indeterminate audience of readers. We have an image of an urban marketplace imagined as a neighborly community, a shared commercial endeavor more collective than competitive. It is collective not in the sense of all being in it together, as it were, but simply of all being in it—subject to the same challenges and presented with the same tactics to navigate and strategies to master them.

TOWARD THE TOWNSMAN AS TEXT

In *Eternal Storehouse,* Saikaku articulates a new urban imaginary and new sense of urban identity based on a shared set of values, lifestyles, and practices, one that unifies a broad, diverse, and unbounded urban population in the face of significant differences in social position, life prospects, and economic interest. It is a sense of urban community paradoxically predicated on the rejection of local community, especially of the *chō* and the forms of social and economic practice that it structured, and centered instead on the figure of the entrepreneurial merchant and his relationship to a large and indeterminate audience of potential customers. The *chō* has not vanished from this new urban imaginary, but its influence is waning, and the entrepreneurial merchant does well to operate outside it and across its boundaries. The human proxies of the *chō*, townsmen of the old guard, are viewed as decadent and degenerate, or otherwise as the managers of massive and cost-burdened operations that lack the agility to fully profit from the new economy, in which all that matters is the wit, diligence, and entrepreneurial talent of the individual merchant in finding ways to profit from the shifting whims of the urban market. The newly imagined urban community is porous. It extends into the countryside, to agricultural communities and fishing villages, along with the networks of transportation, communication, and trade that connect such sites with urban centers of consumption and distribution. It dictates the terms of participation in the larger interregional urban marketplace and promises rewards for doing so, modeling entrepreneurial participation in the evolving domestic economy. It makes little distinction between peasant and townsperson, but only as long as the former refashions his agricultural endeavors after the commercial practices of the latter. Any well-to-do peasant may begin cultivating for the interregional economy, and even an impoverished and propertyless villager may abscond to the city to take up a new trade as a street peddler and work his way up the urban socioeconomic hierarchy. The community of the marketplace pushes to its margins forms of productive labor, most notably that of the craftsman, favoring the mobility (both geographic and social) of merchant capital, its profits limited by only the vision of the heroic entrepreneur. Although imagined as a community, it is not bound by any concrete sense of social collectivity and reciprocal obligation, whether that of the *chō*, the village, the city, or the trade association. It takes as its basic unit the individual merchant household (*ie*), where it compartmentalizes women's participation in social and economic life.

I wish to stress that this was a fundamentally new way of understanding urban identity and community: a shift in the social, spatial, and economic logics by which the individual understood his relationship to and place in a larger social imaginary. To the extent that this is understood in narrative terms as a generational shift—from old, privileged townspeople to new, entrepreneurial merchants—it is fundamentally a literary narrative, one that personifies historic socioeconomic shifts in the form of individual exemplars and thereby makes human sense out of the abstract and often incomprehensible forces of economic change. Saikaku made intelligible the diverse, stratifying, and contradictory world of the seventeenth-century city by transforming it into a set of stories, constituting a newly capacious understanding of urban community and urban-commoner identity through the narrative logic of entrepreneurial effort and reward.

Another way to understand this reimagining of urban community is in terms of a shift from the particular and local to the universal and general—from the idiosyncratic, historically and geographically situated, irreducible particularity of the local community to a generic, rational, portable set of values that anyone can aspire to or attempt to emulate. Each member of this newly imagined urban community has their own particularities of position, trade, geographic location, and historical moment, but the ineffable and dynamic entrepreneurial virtue of wit allows them (so we are to believe) to apprehend those circumstances as opportunities rather than as constraints. The diverse economic developments of the seventeenth century are thereby included within this model, transformed into didactic (or cautionary) exemplars existing in the timeless, ahistorical space of the "Eternal Storehouse." If the imagined community of the nation, in Anderson's formulation, is built on a temporal framework of simultaneity and collective progress through linear history, then the imagined urban community of the late seventeenth-century *chōnin* is built on the looser contemporaneity of an eternal present: Customs may change in constant flux and situations differ from year to year, town to town, and province to province, but the fundamental problem of how to make a living, and the strategies one might deploy to do so, will never change so radically that the sufficiently enterprising individual cannot find a way to carve out a space for himself and his household. The arrangement of the pieces may differ, but the rules of the game—the ethos that enables mobility and membership in the urban community—remain the same.

Incidentally, among Saikaku's protagonists, a few truly transcend place and position and exist as pure ethos—pure signifiers of entrepreneurial exemplarity. In closing, consider "Greatest Among the World's Renters" (*Sekai no kashiya-daishō*, vol. 2–1), Saikaku's revisionist rendition of the legendary miser Fujiya Ichibei, affectionately known to posterity by the portmanteau Fuji-ichi.[51] Saikaku's title refers to the fact that Fuji-ichi was renowned for having accumulated a great fortune while remaining in humble rented lodgings: The narration describes his frontage as a mere six feet, the smallest possible for a commercial renter. Like many of Saikaku's protagonists, he eschews the obligations associated with *chō* membership to enjoy the freedom of life on its margins. As if to reinforce the irony, Fuji-ichi comes into possession of property when one of his debtors defaults on a mortgage, and he "laments that he had for the first time become a householder" (*hajimete iemochi to nari, kore o kuyaminu*). His is a trajectory, then, from the freedom, mobility, and economy of renter status into the propertied townsman class, but a reluctant one, in keeping with the values of Saikaku's urban imaginary. As the episode progresses, it becomes clear that Fuji-ichi's rejection of community is due to the costs and obligations associated with formal townsman status and *chō* membership: mandatory participation in community rituals such as funerals and New Year celebrations "along with the rest of the *chō*" (*chō-nami ni*).

According to later accounts, the historical Fuji-ichi seems to have begun his career as a clerk in an established business in Kyoto and built a fortune through shrewd international trade in Nagasaki, ultimately succeeding to the position of household head.[52] But in Saikaku's rendition, Fuji-ichi's trade is all but effaced: The subtitle, which for most of the stories in *Eternal Storehouse* serves to index the protagonist's trade, identifies him only as "an inventive individual, renowned throughout the capital" (*kyō ni kakurenaki kufūmono*). His wealth results not from any apparent trade but from his individual comportment: "This Fuji-ichi, due to his cleverness [*rihatsu ni shite*], was in a single lifetime able to achieve such worldly wealth."[53] Saikaku's Fuji-ichi is marked neither by membership in a particular local community nor by participation in a particular trade: the perfect model for the new entrepreneurial merchant, free of any particularities that might constrain the accumulation of wealth for its own sake. To the degree that

THE COMMUNITY OF THE MARKETPLACE

Fuji-ichi's status and trade are rendered illegible, Saikaku offers a vividly articulate description of his personal conduct, modeling not only thrift but also the full repertoire of materialist virtues and commercial practices that constitute the text's entrepreneurial ethos. Blessed with a firm constitution, Fuji-ichi spends every day within the confines of his shop, brush in hand, turning the pages of a ledger assembled from odd scraps of paper. When not calculating transactions (what kind is left obscure) and keeping accounts, he is plying his customers and passersby for information—developments in the international trade in Nagasaki, prices of various commodities in Edo, fluctuations of currency exchange rates—to take down diligently in his ledger. A proper merchant rationalist, he knows the value of information and dedicates himself to its collection, inscription, and constant correction, and in doing so becomes a reliable scribe for the city: "a treasure of the capital" (*rakuchū no chōhō*). Every day, he wears the same outfit, a single undergarment and a sole padded kimono, tying the sleeves at the wrist to avoid undue wear and tear; when forced to leave his shop, he wears durable leather-soled sandals, taking care never to run and risk damaging them. His few formal garments are of the most modest sort, with generic printed designs rather than a custom family crest.

And so on and so forth, the largely plotless narrative continues through increasingly elaborate and eccentric manifestations of a highly rationalist, utilitarian ethos centered on personal household economy. But what is most striking about Saikaku's portrait of Fuji-ichi is how it reflects on the entrepreneurial ethos as both performance and signification: not just self-fashioning but self-representation. "It is not that this man was born a miser, but that he wished that in all things his conduct might become a mirror for others" (*kono otoko mumare tsukete shiwaki ni arazu, banji no torimawashi, hito no kagami ni mo narinu beki negai*).[54] Fuji-ichi's eccentric behavior is not simply focused on thrift and the accumulation of wealth, though it is that. More importantly, it is intended to instruct, to model, to communicate, to signify, to represent proper conduct to others. Indeed, in contrast to Fuji-ichi's conspicuous illegibility in social registers—unmarked by trade, status, community—his conduct is lucidly legible as a signifier of the merchant virtues of thrift, diligence, rationalism, pragmatism, sound health, and invention. "Greatest Among the World's Renters" likewise lacks an overarching plot and consists instead of a series of short episodes, each of which reflects the protagonist's disposition in different ways. Just as Fuji-ichi wishes to become a "mirror" for his peers, Saikaku renders his conduct into a text that the reader may probe for lessons. Fuji-ichi is, in a word, the townsman as text: an abstract figure, lacking in any social position or content, whose individual conduct acts as a didactic representation of portable, universal merchant values.

One might push further here and observe that entrepreneurship itself is predicated on acts of self-representation, manifesting an ethos (in the rhetorical sense) that invites trust as the basis for commercial transaction, and that many of Saikaku's protagonists are not precisely who or what they represent themselves to be. This topic is taken up in chapter 2; here I simply use the example of Fuji-ichi to suggest that Saikaku's vision of urban community operates according to a literary logic of signification. The entrepreneurial townsman, transcending the particularities of occupation or geography, becomes a pure signifier of an entrepreneurial ethos that his peers (and Saikaku's readers) are left to interpret from his conduct and from the stories that Saikaku's narrator spins around him. This reimagining of urban community from the particular to the universal was inextricably related to its inscription in writing and, in particular, to its circulation in print, a reflection of the increasing integration of disparate communities into an interconnected and loosely unified (though stratified) urban public: The community of the urban marketplace was, in this sense, a reflection of the community of readers. Saikaku reimagined urban community for the age of print, and his most striking characters, those who best represent the entrepreneurial ethos at the heart of the new urban commoner identity, are figured precisely as texts. As Saikaku's narrator describes Mitsui Kurōemon, "He was the model of a great merchant"—a model or, more literally, a primer (*tehon*), a text to be read as a template for emulation.

Chapter Two

THE POETICS AND POLITICS OF TOWNSMAN PROPERTY

> Without the aid of an inheritance, one sets to work by way of wit; he who gathers five hundred *kanme* of silver is called a man of means, and above a thousand becomes known as a millionaire.
>
> —IHARA SAIKAKU, *JAPAN'S ETERNAL STOREHOUSE*

> Strategies pin their hopes on the resistance that the *establishment of a place* offers to the erosion of time; tactics on a clever *utilization of time*, of the opportunities it presents and also of the play that it introduces into the foundations of power.
>
> —MICHEL DE CERTEAU, *THE PRACTICE OF EVERYDAY LIFE*

The late seventeenth century saw the emergence of a new sense of urban identity, one based not on the collective practices of local communities (*chō* 町) but instead on a sense of shared entrepreneurial values guiding participation in an interregional urban marketplace. To be a townsman was to claim one's place in the community of the marketplace, and, through personal ingenuity and effort, begin a trade, build a fortune, and establish a name. Hereditary privilege and warrior patronage, though advantageous, were no longer deemed necessary, and the hierarchies of status that they represented were liquidated in the face of emerging hierarchies of raw wealth. As Saikaku's narrator declares in *Eternal Storehouse*, "Regardless of name or lineage, riches alone will become the townsman's pedigree" (*zokushō sujime ni mo kamawazu tada kingin ga chōnin no uji keizu ni naru zokashi*).[1] The community of the marketplace turned on the possibility of social mobility. The tantalizing promise of worldly success through individual effort underwrote an image of entrepreneurial self-fashioning that set the poor street peddler next to the privileged townsman and the interregional merchant as fellow players on a supposedly level field, measured only by the depth of their coffers. It was one thing to suggest that anyone could internalize the values of the marketplace, but yet another to suggest that those values, in some sense, worked: that they not only brought the individual into a loose and abstract community oriented by certain shared values, but could allow the anonymous individual to establish the material property that would supposedly become his pedigree. Saikaku brings in various principles to explain how an individual can accumulate wealth—thrift, hard work, physical well-being, patience, resourcefulness—but in *Eternal Storehouse*, the poiesis of townsman property turns on the mercurial principle of "wit" (*saikaku*), a homophone so fortuitous that one is tempted to imagine it as an authorial signature. In a word, wit was the flash of nearly magical insight that allowed the anonymous individual to seize opportunity from the unpredictable flux of the urban marketplace and to alchemically extract stable and secure property from the liminal flows of the floating world. The nature of this entrepreneurial wit is the topic of this chapter.

The idea of an unpropertied and anonymous entrepreneur building a fortune from nothing was potentially problematic, for the Tokugawa polity was conceived as a social order in which each individual knew their place. In the early decades of the seventeenth century, when the memory of the social upheavals of the previous century remained fresh, warrior authorities were keenly aware that an individual's ambition to escape his given station could take the subversive form of "the low overcoming the high" (*gekokujō*). Shogunal administrators enacted various measures to constrain the possibility of both social and spatial mobility, rendering existing social distinctions and hierarchies into objective and permanent realities. The administrative framework of mandatory registration at Buddhist temples, originally intended as a way to enforce the ban on Christianity, gradually evolved into a general system of residential registration that provided the framework for a universal policy of status administration, intended to fix residents in geographic and social place.[2] In theory, each individual had a given place in the realm, and the harmonious coexistence of communities of disparate wealth and privilege, a reflection of the virtuous rule of the governing authorities, was seen as a static order that would carry on in perpetuity. This is not to say that Tokugawa society offered no room for mobility. In spite of the shogunate's attempts to establish a hereditary social order through its systems of status administration, geographic movement would become increasingly common over the centuries, whether in the form of tourism under the guise of religious pilgrimage, or in the form of impoverished peasants absconding from their villages to find work in cities, or in the form of the everyday movements of merchants between regional markets. Regardless of the nominal status distinction between peasant and townsman, migration between the countryside and cities was in fact quite fluid (if usually one-directional) and became more so as the centuries progressed; it was this mobility that drove the explosive growth of cities throughout the seventeenth century and the formation of an unpropertied urban stratum who hoped, like Saikaku's protagonists, to make their way up in the world. Indeed, vertical movement up the economic ranks of commoner society was possible, at least in theory, as long as the boundary separating commoners from warriors was respected.

Saikaku's vision of entrepreneurial self-fashioning unfolds within the spaces of mobility provisionally tolerated within Tokugawa society. I mean space here both figuratively and literally: In *Eternal Storehouse*, social mobility is predicated on spatial mobility, and wit is none other than a set of spatial tactics for navigating the complex, multidimensional, and steadily evolving networks of the interregional urban marketplace. In the readings that follow, I am concerned both with the practical mechanics of this spatial wit and with its politics. Entrepreneurship operates in the interstices of a fixed moral and social order, in the spaces of lateral movement that were tolerated by the authorities; it decisively did not upset the hierarchy separating commoners from warriors. But this is not to say that it was without political import. To the commoner entrepreneur, the acquisition of name and property was intertwined with the renegotiation (and reproduction) of status hierarchies within commoner society itself, with the canny navigation of the boundaries separating the propertied townsman from the peasantry and the urban laboring strata, and ultimately with the drawing of strategic distinctions between proper townsman society and the marginalized populations of beggars and outcasts. It is this commoner politics that was at stake in Saikaku's vision of a townsman community unified by the possibility of entrepreneurial self-fashioning. In examining the operation of Saikaku's wit, I aim to illuminate both the poetics and the politics of townsman property.

In describing Saikaku's wit as a set of spatial tactics, I draw on the tactic as theorized by Michel de Certeau: the contingent, situational moves made on the fly by those who lack the security of a stable position and who thus must perceive and act on moments of opportunity to get by. Certeau's tactics are figures for the practices by which the dominated classes navigate, appropriate, and make use of the spaces and systems created and administered by hegemonic power, systems that the dominated agent lacks the power to shape but simply must exist within. Certeau contrasts the "tactics" of the dominated classes with the "strategies" of authority: The latter refers to the use of power to structure space and society in a fashion that will ensure the integrity and reproduction of the hegemonic subject. The notion of the "proper" (inflected variously in cognates of property and proper name) is central to this schema, where it describes the capacity of the hegemonic subject to define itself and assert its boundaries, intertwined with its ability to reproduce itself and its structures of power in perpetuity; tactics are the modes of everyday operation of those who lack a proper place.[3] My interest in Certeau's schema is for the nuance with which it articulates how nonhegemonic agents (in his terms, the "common man" or "everyday people") operate within social and spatial systems they lack the ability to shape: It offers a useful framework for understanding the agency of the early modern townsman as a subject position that was explicitly alienated from the realm of political power, and especially for understanding the position of the unpropertied and nameless entrepreneurial agents who operated outside the (proper) spatial locus of the *chō*. Moreover, the analogies that Certeau constructs between spatial and textual practice—Certeau's prototypical tactics are walking on the one hand and reading on the other—illuminate the ways in which Saikaku's wit, and the vision of townsman community that it enables, was coeval both with new spatial practices emerging from the early modern city and with new textual practices mediated by commercial print.

But in regard to the political implications of wit, my apprehension of Certeau is more ambivalent. Certeau's schema is rooted in a stark and immutable opposition between those with and those without power, from which perspective the common man so easily becomes an agent of heroic resistance, heroic precisely to the degree that he never properly possesses hegemonic authority in his own right. There is a certain seduction in the inclination to see the tactical as essentially subversive.[4] The same seduction is always present in scholarly treatments of the emerging subjectivity of the early modern townsman, so often the hero in narratives of the cultural rise of a politically disenfranchised class and its implicit challenge to warrior hegemony. Indeed, Saikaku's work seduces the reader in a similar fashion: to see his characters as trickster heroes even and especially as they operate within spaces of moral ambiguity accessible only by stepping outside the realm of the proper. But to celebrate Saikaku's entrepreneurial wit as "an art of the weak" would be to disregard the capacity of the townsman class to generate its own forms of property and social power.[5] This is not the place to interrogate the historical conditions that informed the stark binarism of Certeau's schema (in a word, those of capitalist modernity), only to observe that the situation looks significantly different in an early modern status society characterized by different, competing, and asymmetric forms of social power, and in which a unitary vision of "the common man" conceals a conflictual space of competing status communities with varying forms of both resistance to and complicity with the strategic frameworks of warrior hegemony. Within such a conflictual space, forms of everyday practice that appeared from the top-down vision of shogunal authority as mere tactics (operating within the affordances of the status system but never challenging the hegemony of the warrior class) could also operate as strategies: marking off boundaries and structuring spaces for the local assertion of social power, albeit in dimensions orthogonal to the power exerted by warrior authority.

The space of the *chō* is a case in point. Having emerged as a tactical response by the commoner residents of the Heian capital to the collapse of the administrative structures of the *ritsuryō* state, it had by the late medieval period transformed into a strategic locus of commoner property in its own right and, with the dawn of the Pax Tokugawa, proceeded to reproduce itself through systematic relationships with shogunal authority. As we saw in chapter 1, the institution of the *chō* was by the late seventeenth century hollowing out, its strategic power giving way to the tactical operations of the individual merchant household. The merchant household was likewise not fated to remain in the ephemeral and improper realm of the tactic, but would itself come to embrace the strategic assertions of power in the name of expanding merchant capital. In other words, the tactic also contains the possibility to transform into, or to be repurposed as, a form of strategy, and thus suggests a politics more multifaceted than a simple schema of top-down authority and bottom-up resistance or subversion. By simultaneously applying and problematizing the distinction between tactics and strategies, I wish to understand the political implications of the entrepreneurial genesis of property other than as the heroic resistance of the common people to shogunal control. Using a sustained dialogue between Certeau and Saikaku, this chapter articulates a new vision of the politics of the entrepreneurial townsman subject, one in which the tactical creativity of the entrepreneur both conceals and legitimates a process of strategic accumulation that is both symbiotic with existing structures of warrior authority and predicated on the creation of new social and economic hierarchies within the townsman status group.

One of the challenges in apprehending this wit, a form of tactical operation that by its very nature must resist apprehension, is that it is irreducibly contingent: It is embedded in ephemeral specificities of time and place. Accordingly, it is expressed not through explicit principle (didactic narration) but instead through narrative, through stories of characters moving through space and time to claim opportunity from the liminalities separating here from there. It is inextricable from the narrative poetics of Saikaku's stories and, in particular, depends on his ellipses. Saikaku's stories often signify precisely through the details and contexts and conclusions that they omit, that are revealed as significant only through the reader's active reflection, and the principle of wit is likewise centered on the apprehension of opportunity and value that might otherwise remain unnoticed. In other words, wit is, like Certeau's tactics, a form of reading—a kind of close reading of one's environment, scrutinizing one's surroundings for opportunities to grasp something of value that others have missed—and Saikaku's stories are about careful and inventive readers, those who learn to appropriate (cite) selectively from the affordances of the urban text in order to compose their own narrative trajectories of social mobility. In keeping with this spirit of wit, an ethos of close and appropriative reading that evolves into a narrative poetics, this chapter presents detailed readings of three stories from *Eternal Storehouse*. I pay particular attention to their loaded silences, to the narrative gaps and ellipses from which Saikaku and his heroes extract the generative kernel of value, and to the seamless transitions from tactics of opportunistic appropriation to strategies of systematic accumulation.

THE TACTICS OF LIVELIHOOD

In *Eternal Storehouse*, the dialectic between the tactical and the strategic plays out through competing constructions of economic activity. Warrior authorities generally understood the activities of the commoner classes through a discourse of socially productive "occupation" (*shokubun*):

Economic activity was meaningful and morally legitimate to the degree that it contributed in recognized ways to the collective functioning of the realm.⁶ This discourse of occupation was often expressed through the trope of the "four estates" (*shimin*) of "warriors, peasants, artisans, and merchants" (*shinōkōshō*). Contrary to many modern interpretations, these four estates did not represent a moral hierarchy of labor as much as a figure for the moral necessity of each occupation: executive leadership of both the administrative and moral variety (warrior-bureaucrats), agricultural production (peasants), creation of craft goods (artisans), and transportation and distribution of resources (merchants). But the discourse of occupation was still in essence strategic, linked to the institutional frameworks through which the shogunate structured and administered the Tokugawa polity: Status communities (such as individual *chō*) were granted a stable place within the Tokugawa polity only when they could claim to serve a legitimate occupation, expressed in the form of material "duties" (*yaku*) owed to the state. Private accumulation of wealth for its own sake and entrepreneurial mobility across space and social hierarchy fell outside this rubric.

The discourse of occupation generally reflected the perspective of the ruling authorities, but over time came to be embraced by commoner ideologues as a way of legitimating their place in a shogunal social imaginary. For example, the Nagasaki merchant-intellectual Nishikawa Joken elaborated the idea of commerce as a form of resource distribution through an analogy with primitive exchange, arguing that the merchant merely responds to resource differentials and redistributes goods to satisfy social needs:

> In ancient times, no one used money, but simply exchanged one thing for another. This was known as "trade" [*kōeki*]. The true merchant is the one who judges the quality and quantity of goods, and, calculating costs and benefits without claiming excessive profits, exchanges that which he possesses for that which he lacks; he takes the things of his province and exchanges them for those of other lands, and by circulating the realm's precious goods, fulfills the needs of the state.⁷

Joken did not deny the townsman's right to profit from the services that he provided in distributing goods, a form of labor he believed to be morally legitimate to the degree that it fulfilled the public needs of the realm. But he maintained that the desire for private profit for its own sake was morally unjustifiable. In parallel with this, he advocated an ethos of knowing and embracing one's proper "station" (*bunzai*): accepting a given position and living by standards that are appropriate to that position. He also had no place for the imperative to accumulate wealth in perpetuity. He saw wealth as a public good that served a moral purpose only to the degree that it circulated, and considered private accumulation, if not explicitly immoral, then at least as essentially impermanent, an epiphenomenon of the flux of the marketplace and the ebbs and flows of the floating world.[8] He chided his fellow merchants for clinging too closely to their fortunes, observing that "when one's own fortune declines, that of another increases; and when one's own increases, the other's declines."[9] (One suspects that his readers would nevertheless have been greatly disturbed by the former scenario and proportionally delighted by the latter.) Although Joken had a merchant background and was writing as an apologist for the townsman's lifeways, the substance of his thought, which was heavily indebted to the conceptual vocabulary of the Song Confucian tradition, often cleaved closely to shogunal orthodoxy.

However, the late seventeenth century saw the rise of an alternative discursive construction of economic activity, one that reflected the realities and values of the entrepreneurial townsman. This was the idea of "livelihood" (*nariwai*). The word *nariwai*, often rendered with the characters 生 (living) and 業 (craft) and literally translated as "the craft by which one lives"—along with cognates such as *sugiwai* (craft by which one gets by) and *misugi* (making a way for oneself)—referred to the labor by which a person makes a living, conceived not in terms of official social function or moral merit but in terms of individual necessity. Any economic activity that allowed the individual (or household) to survive was, from the commoner perspective, deemed legitimate, regardless of whether it carried broader social value. Through synonyms such as *tosei* 渡世 ("making a way through the world"), the idea of livelihood was also semantically linked to the notion of the "floating world" (*ukiyo* 浮世) in its more pessimistic valence. If those of commoner status regarded worldly existence as a universal condition of existential insecurity and flux, in which one could not truly control one's fate even in the best of circumstances, but merely flow along with the world's shifting currents, then one had to simply do what one could to make one's way through the world. In a word, the idea of livelihood was tactical.

David Howell underlines this tactical quality of livelihood when he juxtaposes it to occupation, which had clear and explicit political significance, linked to the place of status communities in the Tokugawa polity. In Howell's interpretation, the concept of livelihood acted as a gloss for the complex and diverse forms of economic activity that fell outside of the political framework of occupation and that thus existed only at the level of practice: "Livelihood had no meaning as an economic activity divorced from status."[10] But this was merely the (strategic) perspective of warrior authority, which was naturally unable to grasp the tactical logics of the townsman's everyday practice. In contrast, Hiraishi Naoaki suggests that the concept of livelihood did not refer to a set of practices as much as to an emergent discursive construction, a way of conceptualizing the purpose of economic activity and its place in a larger social imaginary, albeit not that of the four estates. In other words, the forms of (officially) invisible economic practice carried out by commoners outside the institutional frameworks of occupation would over time giving rise to the explicit (if still inchoate) articulation of a distinct commoner worldview. Indeed, Yokota Fuyuhiko has argued that this idea of livelihood was at the center of a commoner social imaginary, first articulated in the late seventeenth century and disseminated through popular print.[11] In contrast to the mandates of moral and social utility dictated by official discourses of occupation, the commoner ideology of livelihood was oriented by the sole imperative for the individual household to survive and perhaps accrue wealth. Saikaku's fiction was part of this process by which this worldview was articulated in language and given textual form.

It is within the amoral and tactical space of livelihood, apprehended through an ethos of entrepreneurial wit, that Saikaku finds the possibility of social mobility and the genesis of townsman property. Though *Eternal Storehouse* lacks an authorial preface, its first story, "Fortune Comes Riding on the First Horse Day of Spring" (*Hatsumuma wa notte kuru shiawase*, vol. 1–1), begins with a cryptic and rhetorically dense passage that has long been observed to frame the larger themes of the work.[12] Through a *haikai*-esque oscillation between the high (the divine, the moral, the transcendent) and the low (the material, the mundane, the everyday), Saikaku teases out space for the amoral and purely economic activity of livelihood: a tactical negotiation par excellence, one that finds space within orthodox moral discourses without upsetting their order and authority.

> The Way of Heaven speaks not, but the realm and its land are rich in blessings. Man has his truth but is also full of falsehood; his heart is originally empty but changes to reflect that which it encounters, leaving no trace of what it had previously been. To dwell in the space between good and evil and make one's way boldly through the upright reign of the present day: this is the mark of a true man, though most men fall short. The most important matter in a man's life is the means by which he makes his way in this world. Not only the four estates of warriors, peasants, craftsmen, and merchants, but equally the bonzes, clerics, and others: each must entrust himself to the oracles of the Great God of Thrift and store up wealth, for it grants life as if a third parent. Taking a long view, human life fades like the morning dew, and in the short view, one never knows at dawn what even dusk may bring; heaven and earth are like a traveler's inn, the days and months its lodgers. The floating world is said to be no more than a dream, turned in an instant into clouds of smoke. When we die, what good is wealth—gold and silver are no better than rocks and debris, and wealth will serve us no use in the world beyond. Nevertheless, it will remain to benefit our descendants. Thinking to myself, it occurs to me that, of all the things in the world you might wish for, those that cannot be granted by money surely are counted at five in all of creation, no more than that. Even the most fantastical of imagined treasures could not offer more. A cloak and cap of invisibility, worn by a devil on some far-off island, even such magical garments would do you no good in a sudden storm, so abandon your distant ambitions for that which is closer at hand, and dedicate yourself to your house trade. Fortune is found in a firm body, so never slack from dawn to dusk; root yourself in benevolence and rightness, and respect the gods and Buddhas. This is the custom of our realm.[13]

The passage is structured by an oscillation between the spheres of the divine and the human, a vertical symbolic motion modeled after the interplay of *ga* (elegant or classical) and *zoku* (vulgar or contemporary) in linked-verse poetics. Saikaku's narrator opens by evoking the absent presence of the divine—"The Way of Heaven speaks not" (*tendō mono iwazu shite*)—and

THE POETICS AND POLITICS OF TOWNSMAN PROPERTY

here we must keep in mind the persistent metaphor linking heaven to the Tokugawa hegemony, a connection reiterated a few lines later in the reference to "the upright reign of the present day" (*sugu-naru ima no on-yo*). But the elevated and implicitly moral perspective of the divine immediately gives way to the morally ambivalent figure of man, who "has his truth" (*jitsu atte*) but is also "full of falsehood" (*itsuwari ōshi*); man is an essentially amoral being, "dwelling in the space between good and evil" (*zen'aku no naka ni tatte*). As the narration shifts from the moral dimension of the divine to the amoral dimension of human endeavor, it pivots to the topic of money. Although Saikaku cites the trope of the four estates, it is not to affirm the social or moral value of each occupation, but to reduce all of them, including the divine occupations of the Shinto and Buddhist priests, to mere livelihood: merely "the skill by which he makes his way in the world" (*mi o suguru no waza*). And yet, as soon as we arrive at the universal, amoral, and mundane imperative to "store up gold and silver" (*kingin o tamu beshi*), we return to the divine: here a Buddhist discourse of impermanence that reduces wealth to "no better than rocks and debris" (*gaseki ni wa otoreri*). The divine perspective is then inverted again and brought back down to the mundane imperatives of the social world, as the narrator notes that, although wealth is worthless in the afterlife, "it will remain to benefit our descendants" (*nokoshite shison no tame to wa narinu*) by its worldly and material value. The vertical oscillation between the divine and the human accelerates through the end of the passage, juxtaposing the need to "respect the gods and Buddhas" with the materialist imperative to dedicate oneself to the accumulation of worldly wealth.

In a thought-provoking Marxian interpretation, Hirosue Tamotsu reads this passage as Saikaku's symbolic effort to establish money as an independent measure of value, one that exists in a relativistic space of competing value systems.[14] In Hirosue's reading, Saikaku accomplishes this with his progressive and repeated denial of "the absolute, the metaphysical, and the superior." These registers of moral value cannot be separated from the symbolism of the Tokugawa hegemony, linked to the authority of heaven, and Hirosue's reading is indeed oriented toward finding traces of symbolic resistance to warrior hegemony. That resistance takes the form of an acknowledgment of the leveling force of money, which reduces all human relations to relative terms (relative quantities): All occupations are merely methods of livelihood. Hirosue is also careful to note that here money does not come to supersede or displace orthodox systems of moral value, but instead continues to exist in tension with them, and it is this unresolvable tension between competing value systems that drives the spontaneous and unpredictable proliferation of Saikaku's prose, spewing forth through constant twists and inversions that resist any sense of finality or ideological closure. In short, Saikaku seems, through a kind of dialectical rhetoric rooted in linked-verse poetics, to be teasing apart the moral and the economic as measures of value. However, within the bounds of this opening passage, this distinction still remains only implicit, and indeed it is easy to read this preface as ultimately affirming that money and morality can coexist as part of a harmonious social totality: Work hard, stay healthy, stay rooted in benevolence, trust the gods and Buddhas—as is the custom of our realm. The story that Saikaku spins out of this preface—and, indeed, the entire text—elaborates this gesture: finding space within existing frameworks of moral value and political authority for the individual accumulation of worldly wealth while still affirming the legitimacy and authority of heaven.

Following the preface, we are introduced to the Mizuma Temple, in the rural hinterland to the south of Osaka, where men and women of all ranks come to worship. The pilgrims come to pray for "wealth in keeping with their station" (*sono bunzai hodo ni tomeru o negaeri*), and the bodhisattva responds austerely: "You have been granted your station as peasants. The husband tills the field, and the wife works the loom, both working morning 'til night. Thus it is for all people" (*domin wa nanji ni sonawaru. otto wa tauchite, fu wa hata orite, chōbo sono itonami su beshi. issai no hito, kono gotoku*). Although the bodhisattva's reply reiterates the logic of occupation and the social station of the peasant, the narrator sardonically comments that these words fail to reach the ears of the pilgrims, who have come "not out of faith, but as fellow travelers on the road of desire" (*mina shinjin ni wa arazu, yoku no michizure*). The temple is known to lend small amounts from its donations as an expression of the bodhisattva's mercy. Interest is high—loans are customarily returned in double in a year's time—but the narrator notes that, because this is the bodhisattva's money, none dare default on the loan, and regardless the sums lent are in the order of a few coppers each.

Having thus set the scene, the remainder of the story focuses on one enterprising individual who exploits this system to rise to wealth and fame.

The anonymous entrepreneur is distinguished by his indistinguishability, and Saikaku introduces him with a virtuosic rendition of genericity. A man of twenty-three or twenty-four, sturdy of frame, outdated in hairstyle and dress, his sleeves and hems slightly too short, his garments and undergarments both of the same rough pongee—Saikaku is often descriptive by way of listing, and here that technique is used to evoke a character whose appearance signifies precisely nothing and nobody-ness. This anonymous man, of humble stature but not identifiably peasant nor townsman, approaches the alms table without ceremony, as if it were a mere afterthought following his pilgrimage, and asks for a loan of a thousand coppers. The temple typically would receive requests for a mere copper or two, and the priest on duty, at a loss when faced with the gall of such an outlandish demand, simply acquiesces without even asking the man's name or address—he is a figure for the anonymous, after all—and he disappears without a trace. The monks later review the matter and decide that this was an unprecedented exploitation, that they never expect to see the money returned, and that in any case they should refrain from lending such a sum again. The anonymous borrower, meanwhile, is revealed to be a resident of Edo, where he operates a small shipping concern. Using the funds borrowed from the Mizuma Temple, he begins lending to local fishermen under the shop name of Amiya, explaining the divine provenance of his funds and promising his borrowers the benefits of the bodhisattva's compassion, and his fortune grows year by year. Thirteen years later, he calculates the interest owed to the Mizuma Temple and, in spectacular fashion, sends a team of packhorses down the Tōkaidō laden with the precise sum of 8,192,000 coppers to repay his debt. The monks of the temple celebrate this as a tale for future generations (and, no doubt, as a handy bit of advertising for their own lending concern) and raise a pagoda in his honor. The narrator concludes that the true millionaire is one who, without the aid of hereditary wealth, "makes his way by his own wit" (*sono mi saikaku ni shite kasegi idashi*). But what is it exactly in this snappy anecdote that constitutes wit? What, ultimately, is the source of Amiya's fortune?

One is tempted to take this as a felicitous story about the divine provenance of wealth, for in some sense the fortune that Amiya produces is intertwined with the spiritual authority of the Mizuma Temple. Lending by temples, though not particularly common in Saikaku's time, had a long history as a form of proto-finance throughout the medieval period.

According to a loosely standardized set of lending practices, major temples and shrines, which received tributary donations of crops grown on their lands, would lend rice to peasants, to be returned following the year's harvest with a high rate of interest. Fabio Rambelli has observed that temple-based lending was rooted in Buddhist conceptions of the divine origins of worldly wealth: Wealth was bestowed by the gods and Buddhas, through the mediating grace of religious institutions, and made materially manifest through the steady accumulation of agricultural products that were returned to the gods in a donation that functioned effectively as interest. Even as economic practice shifted away from agricultural production and toward the marketplace, the spaces in which commodities moved, changed hands, and produced a surplus of wealth were seen as standing apart from the hierarchies of the secular world and suffused with the quality of the divine.[15] Saikaku's story likewise concerns the appearance of wealth out of such liminal interstices, and still depends in some sense on the authority of the divine as the origin of wealth, as suggested both by the opening passage and by the constitutive role played by the Mizuma Temple. However, it would distort the spirit of Saikaku's text to suggest that the story is ultimately about the divine provenance of wealth, for its focus is on how the enterprising Amiya is able to wield divine authority opportunistically to grasp some portion of that wealth as the basis for his own name and fortune. My point is not to suggest that Saikaku found the origins of worldly wealth within the quasi-divine liminal spaces of the road, but to ask how such spaces became sites of tactical operation and ultimately strategic accumulation—how the ethos of wit cannily exploited such liminalities to produce its own hierarchies and forms of property. The question is how Amiya is able to use the authority of the temple to appropriate wealth, name, and property for himself.

Amiya's wit is spatial. His success turns in large part on the distance between the rural outskirts of Osaka, where he receives the historic windfall of an unduly large loan, and the city of Edo, where he lends dubiously acquired funds. The accumulation of wealth becomes possible in the interstices and flows between cities and in those separating city from countryside. It depends both on distance—Amiya's ploy could never work if he borrowed from a temple closer at hand, because he must both escape and extend the temple's authority—and on the possibility of unexpected itineraries of movement across that distance. The spatiality of wit is lateral,

THE POETICS AND POLITICS OF TOWNSMAN PROPERTY

one of movement across geographic space and through the emerging networks of trade, transportation, and communication that were progressively, though still imperfectly, connecting disparate locales; it is this movement that allows for the appropriation of value without disturbing or subverting local forms of power and authority. The lateral spatiality of wit is categorically distinct from the vertical orientation of the opening passage, which juxtaposed human action with the authority of heaven: It eschews that morally charged verticality to open an amoral dimension of lateral space in which entrepreneurial appropriation is possible. The ultimate representation that Amiya makes of his entrepreneurial virtue, depicted dramatically in the illustration for the story, is a splendid signifier of the poetics of the trade network: the mass of packhorses, laden with specie, sent down the Tōkaidō (figure 2.1).

As an ethos emerging from the liminal spaces of the road and the marketplace, wit is extemporaneous. It is defined by the exploitation of a specific opportunity occurring at a certain time and place and by the

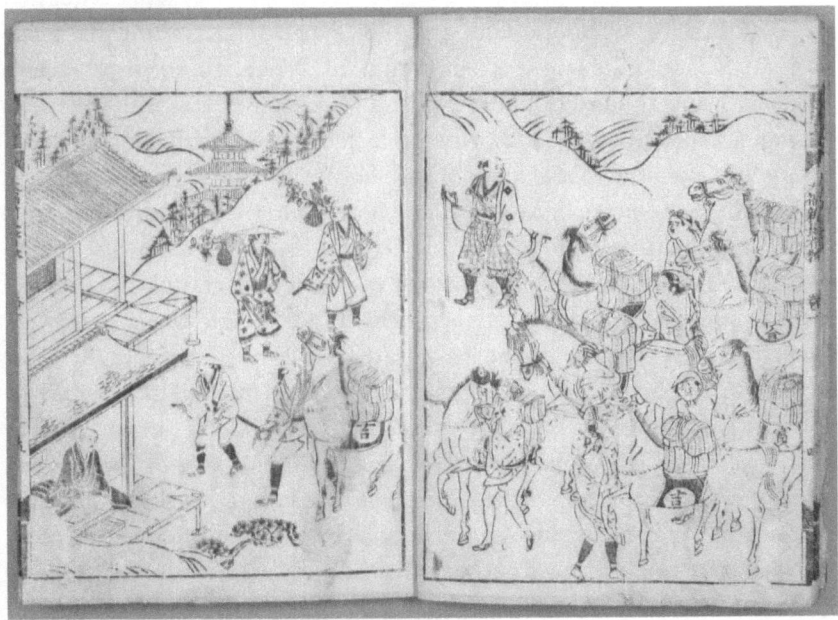

FIGURE 2.1 *Nippon eitaigura*, Morita edition. Illustration to "Fortune Comes Riding on the First Horse Day of Spring" (vol.1, 4u–5o). Courtesy of Waseda University Library.

affordances within existing systems of power and authority. To borrow from Certeau, "it must vigilantly make use of the cracks that particular conjunctions open in the surveillance of the proprietary powers."[16] The anonymous entrepreneur who would later establish himself as Amiya snatches the opportunity that he perceives at the Mizuma Temple with such an exemplary performance of spontaneity—casually, dressed as a nobody, as if merely stopping by on his return trip—that the clerk tending the lending booth is caught totally off guard, at a loss of what to do other than assent. (A formal audience and business proposal clearly would not do; whether truly spontaneous or not, surprise is of the essence.) Amiya's entrepreneurial appropriation also proves to be a singular opportunity: After his brazen ploy succeeds, the temple priests convene to declare that no such sum shall ever be lent again. Wit perceives the opportunity in a door left open a crack and soon to be closed; it is not concerned with whether the door remains open for others. It is precisely the virtue of seizing momentary opportunities out of the interstices of existing systems of money and power: Resources appropriated from the proprietary powers become property conjured out of nothing. Yet, despite this tactical quality, wit is ultimately symbiotic with authority. Having carved out his place within the amoral, lateral space of livelihood, the entrepreneur takes care not to disrupt or subvert the hierarchical, vertical relationship between human action and divine authority. Protected by the lateral distance separating him from the spatial locus of such authority, Amiya enthusiastically admits the provenance of his funds and his debt to the Mizuma Temple. It is not only the temple's funds but also its very name and authority that he borrows. Claiming unofficial status as its agent—"narrating the details" (*shisai o katarite*) of the provenance of his funds, he offers his borrowers by proxy the promises of the bodhisattva's blessing—he goes to great lengths to reaffirm the authority and property of the lending temple in spectacular fashion. In different terms, and contra Certeau, Amiya does not subvert the logic of the proper—the authority invested in and exerted by property and proper name—but instead appropriates it for his own use, ultimately constituting his name and property and fortune through the tactical use of borrowed authority.

As with many of Saikaku's stories, the dazzling flash of entrepreneurial wit conceals a colorful legal and moral underside. Religious institutions such as the Mizuma Temple were authorized to lend small sums at rates that were forbidden to private moneylenders. Because the enterprising Amiya repays his debt (with interest) in full, calculated to the last copper, also covering the cost of shipping the funds by packhorse—eschewing gold or even a bill of exchange in favor of repayment in heavy loads of copper, a feat that has been calculated to require 197 horses—one must naturally conclude that he has made far, far more off the investment, namely, by lending at shorter terms and higher rates of interest. The practice of borrowing at high rates to lend in small sums for even higher interest was known as "copper wheel" (*kuruma-sen*) or "wheel lending" (*kuruma-gashi*); this commonly took the form of lending small amounts of money with daily interest, known as "dailies" (*hinashi*), sometimes at rates as high as 10 percent per day. These practices were illegal, though the frequency of shogunal edicts aimed at their suppression indicates that they were nonetheless widely practiced.

Based on such associations, Saikaku scholar Yano Kimio takes Amiya's spectacular return of the loan as a paranoid demonstration meant to conceal or otherwise deflect potential criticism of the illicit practices on which his fortune was built. He thus finds in this opening episode a veiled critique of entrepreneurial merchant practice: Saikaku's ironic exposé of the underhanded tactics underlying many of the economic successes of his contemporaries.[17] But I am reluctant to take this story (or *Eternal Storehouse* as a whole) as a veiled social critique, for Saikaku's narrative offers no hint of judgment about Amiya's appropriative commercial trajectory. Instead, it celebrates the poetics of livelihood, expressed through spatial tactics of entrepreneurial wit freed situationally from moral and legal constraint. In true tactical fashion, Amiya's rise to wealth and property is predicated on moral ambiguities that are briefly glimpsed in the flow of money, goods, and people, but once those ambiguities close, the adept entrepreneur takes care to realign himself on the side of moral and political authority. The anonymous entrepreneur is successful in carving out a momentary space for entrepreneurial movement, appropriation, and exploitation that is fertile precisely to the degree that it is amoral and successful to the degree that it persistently reaffirms vertical symbols of authority and thus solicits both their toleration and their symbolic support. When the no-longer-anonymous entrepreneur returns the interest on his loan to the priests of the Mizuma Temple, it is not a paranoid concealing of vice but a spectacular performance of virtue, one that renders the appropriation virtuous and is, indeed, celebrated by the priests themselves as an act of exemplary karmic merit. Amiya's gesture does not conceal moral transgression as much as produce, in the true sense of a performative act, a symbiotic relationship between the material pursuit of wealth and the authority of heaven. This symbiosis is already implicit in the opening passage: "Root yourself in benevolence and rightness, and respect the gods and Buddhas. This is the custom of our realm."

Saikaku's central concern is with exploring the possibility of real social mobility at a historical moment of dramatic economic expansion that nevertheless remained within the political bounds of a society marked by rigid social and ideological constraints on status and place. He does so by radicalizing the potential for tactical appropriation within the amoral discourse of livelihood. But though the author's exploration of the spatially dynamic and temporally contingent quality of entrepreneurial wit invites understanding as a kind of tactic, something in the final legitimating gesture troubles Certeau's notion of the tactical. To Certeau, the tactic is only ever contingent, seizing opportunities within the gaps of existing frameworks of social and political power, but always on the run and never claiming a secure and proper place of its own: "What it wins it cannot keep."[18] Amiya, to the contrary, has through the tactical operation of wit claimed a name for himself, entering into the realm of the proper while affirming the prior authority of the temple and respecting "the gods and Buddhas." Wit is not merely a matter of seizing fortune on the fly, but also of transforming ephemeral fortune into permanent property. Once it has succeeded in creating space in a fixed system of moral value, it must enable its agent to transform tactical space into proper place. It moves subtly from the contingent realm of tactical appropriation to stable forms of strategic accumulation—from tactics to strategies.

TACTICS OF READING, STRATEGIES OF WRITING

Many of Saikaku's stories of entrepreneurial success are spatial stories, but where Amiya finds the flash of opportunity in the liminal interstices of interregional financial networks, others find their fortunes amid the hustle and bustle of the city streets. Here again I am drawn to Certeau, for whom urban walking is the tactical operation par excellence, forming emergent patterns of practice within an urban environment structured and planned to serve the interests of governing authority. Certeau observes that the act of "walking in the city" has an enunciative quality akin to that of reading a text. This is an active, creative, and appropriative (tactical) kind of reading: the borrowing of passages and the selective, opportunistic use of structures and inscriptions intended for perhaps other purposes but turned to serve the reader-walker's needs and inclinations.[19] Saikaku depicts similar appropriative acts of spatial reading, as with Amiya, who creatively cites the divine authority and economic clout of the Mizuma Temple extemporaneously on the way back from a pilgrimage, and who cannily exploits the affordances of the interregional transportation network—its capacity to both connect and separate—in order to claim his own unofficial status as the bodhisattva's economic proxy. Saikaku's stories of urban entrepreneurship are stories of reading: of literal acts of reading, of the reading of people and the social positions and values that their conduct signifies, and of the reading of the city itself as a text, the examination of which promises to divulge the contingent flash of fortune. Wit means carefully combing the urban text for opportunities for intervention and invention, for opportunistic turns of foot and turns of phrase, and for hidden meanings that carry undiscovered and unexploited registers of value.

"Medicine Prepared in Abnormal Fashion" (*Senjiyō tsune to wa kawaru toigusuri*, vol. 3–1) begins with a splendid example of appropriative reading. A nameless lad, proxy for the reader, solicits a wealthy man for his wisdom: This was the framing device of many seventeenth-century entrepreneurial guidebooks, which would go on to dispense didactic principles of thrift and hard work in the voice of the millionaire.[20] (These texts, and the principles within them, are discussed in detail in chapter 3.) In Saikaku's story, the protagonist is an anonymous, middle-aged resident of Edo who approaches a local tycoon with a query: "The pains of poverty sickness! Is there no way to cure these ills, a method that relies upon neither wisdom nor wit?" The wealthy man responds by rehearsing the platitudes of seventeenth-century entrepreneurial literature in the form of a figurative medicinal prescription: five parts early rising, twenty parts house trade (*kashoku* or *kagyō*), eight parts midnight oil, ten parts economy, and seven parts good health, followed by a long series of routine prohibitions on sumptuary excess, leisure diversion, costly religious devotion, risky speculation, unnecessary quarrels, and so on. The millionaire holds forth in monologic fashion, and the anonymous protagonist's apprehension of the advice resembles an act of passive reading: principles to be applied in rote fashion (the metaphor of the medicinal elixir suggests ingestion), requiring "neither wisdom nor wit" (*chie saikaku ni mo yorazu*). One might indeed imagine the protagonist not as one who has spoken with a millionaire himself, but simply one who has just finished enthusiastically paging through a didactic work, assured that its insights will bring him wealth in short order. Our anonymous protagonist is an anonymous reader.

Venturing forth, the aspiring entrepreneur resolves to follow this precious prescription, but in the bustling capital city of Edo, things are not so simple. The millionaire's advice had centered on house trade, but the anonymous protagonist has neither house nor trade. Moreover, the labor market is saturated and any trade he adopts is likely to find competition, so he recognizes that simple hard work will not be enough. He needs an original business idea. Mulling his predicament, he goes to the southern end of Nihonbashi to watch the crowds, and the earnest enthusiasm with which he had embraced the wealthy man's insights is replaced by an opportunistic gaze that is equal parts lazy and cunning. Palpably reluctant to engage in any kind of material labor, is he looking for inspiration or simply hoping to snatch a few coppers from the crowd?

> However, no one dropped anything of value, and no matter how intently he looked, he couldn't find a single coin. Reflecting on this, money is something that truly must not be spent lightly. "I must try my hand at a trade," he thought, and in spirit at least he was toiling away, but these days the only way to make money with empty hands is as a grappling instructor or a midwife. Without planting a few seeds, you can't grow a single cent, let alone a gold coin. Then it occurred to him: "If only there were a way to make something from nothing!"[21]

In one of the author's characteristic tonal pivots, the high-handed didacticism of the wealthy man's lecture gives way to a comical glimpse into the opportunistic mentality of our hero. Although he initially resolves to leave his fate up to the advice he has received, "working tirelessly from dawn to dusk" (*chōbo yudan naku*), he instead spends the day (indeed, from morning to night) watching the crowds at Nihonbashi, hoping for a way to "make something from nothing" (*nani to zo tada toru koto o*). Comic though it may be, our hero's wry opportunism is underwritten by the observation that

THE POETICS AND POLITICS OF TOWNSMAN PROPERTY

making money without capital or an established trade is no small feat; the millionaire's advice offers little by way of practical starting point for someone who lacks the privilege of an established house, trade, and name. The narrative that follows, centered on the problem of how to grow a fortune from scratch, is less one of diligent effort than one of intellectual invention, and our protagonist exemplifies this as someone who is outwardly lazy but who, the narrator notes with tongue partly in cheek, "is toiling away in spirit" (*kokoro wa hatarakinagara*). His posture combines outward inertia with energetic mental activity and sharp observation: From the passive reading of the didactic handbook, we shift subtly to a mode of actively reading the complex, dynamic, and ephemeral urban text. The illustration strikingly juxtaposes the flow of people across the bridge with the flow of water beneath it (figure 2.2).

The apprehension of the city as a space of flux and ephemerality was itself somewhat novel, a reflection of a distinctly commoner worldview. The city as designed by its planners and administrators was conceived as a static

FIGURE 2.2 *Nippon eitaigura*, Morita edition. Illustration to "Medicine Prepared in Abnormal Fashion" (vol. 3, 3u–4o). Courtesy of Waseda University Library.

order, the spatial projection and material reification of the hierarchies of status. The nigh-universal template that structured the built environment of urban Japan in the seventeenth century was the castle town (*jōkamachi*), divided into discrete districts of townsman communities (*chōnin-chi*), warrior residences (*buke-chi*), and religious institutions (*jisha-chi*)—all placed in felicitous orbit of the central castle, a striking vertical symbol of ruling authority.[22] An urban topology that rendered social distinctions as spatial and visual signifiers, the castle town was also an expression of the ideology of occupation, arranging status communities in a distribution that served the ruling authorities' needs for different forms of labor and material production. The households of high-ranking warrior vassals, placed in close proximity to the central castle, provided administrative labor and military defense, and townsman communities were often summoned by the ruling household to manage marketplaces, distribute essential commodities, and direct the artisanal production of military materiel, luxury clothing and housewares, and craft goods for everyday use. The shogunal seat of Edo had been meticulously planned in this fashion in the early years of the Pax Tokugawa, and by the late seventeenth century had grown into a sprawling microcosm of the Tokugawa polity; its topology of properly differentiated districts was materially palpable in the urban maps that were produced in increasing numbers toward the end of the century.[23]

Within this highly ordered visual topography, the great public bridge of Nihonbashi was significant for its ambivalent position between warrior authority and commoner culture. On the one hand, the bridge had an elevated status linked to the public authority of the shogunate: the center of shogunal Edo and of the realm, the point from which all distances were measured. On the other, it was already, in the late seventeenth century, shifting toward a place in the popular imaginary as a cultural site associated less with political authority than with commoner culture: the center of townsman Edo.[24] Nihonbashi was the point at which the visual strategies of warrior hegemony met the tactile and tactical negotiations of the commoner crowd, and where the built environment structured by shogunal will interfaced with the contingent and liminal flows of the floating world. It was the site of flows both figurative and literal: Commoner Edo, later to be known as the "low city" (*shitamachi*) for its sea-level elevation, was in its early years a network of canals and waterways, a ubiquitous flow of water that structured also the flow of people and things. Jinnai Hidenobu has elucidated the spatial logic of this "city of water," both its systems of social organization and its visual iconography. As Jinnai observes, Edo's major temples and sacred sites were generally located at the margins where the city intersected with nature—especially, for commoner Edo, with the flows of water, whether on the Sumida River or against the sea. Such sacred sites, and the imagery of water, were also closely linked to spaces of urban leisure—most notably, the theater and prostitution districts—which thereby took on a quality of the divine or otherworldly, becoming semi-sacred spaces in which everyday status hierarchies were suspended.[25] However, although this sense of liminality informs Saikaku's depiction of Nihonbashi as a site of urban flows to a degree, this is not a story that finds subversive energy in such flows, or that aligns the subjectivity of the townsman with the carnivalesque sites of urban leisure. Instead, it unfolds by building a productive itinerary that links the liminality of the public bridge, the stability of warrior authority, and the formation of stable townsman property.

Regarding the depiction of urban space in Saikaku's works, Matsuda Osamu has written that the author always approaches the city from a street-level view. This is particularly conspicuous in scenes where he presents sweeping vistas of the urban setting. Elsewhere in *Eternal Storehouse*, Saikaku offers a view of the endless waves of roof tiles and glimmering white walls of the plaster storehouses of Osaka, but, as Matsuda observes, the view is from an ever so slightly elevated perch on Naniwa Bridge, Osaka's premier public bridge, passing over the Yodo River with a splendid view of the city's commercial districts. "Hegemony and authority are manifest through a vertical will: the donjon of the castle, the five-storied pagoda. The horizontal Osaka of Saikaku's works is the Osaka of the townsmen."[26] In "Medicine Prepared in Abnormal Fashion," likewise, the view from Nihonbashi is squarely on street level, focused on the human spectacle of waves of people of all ranks and social stripes passing over the shogun's bridge. Even as the protagonist attempts to scrutinize the flows of the crowd in his effort to "make something from nothing," he is himself a part of the crowd that he aims to observe, and his vision of it is thus incomplete. To Certeau, the sense of vision is of the order of strategy, and the visual experience of the city is that of the planner and administrator, who produce and deploy the top-down vision of the urban map, with its clear social and spatial topologies. Those who inhabit the world below learn to tactically navigate the city streets in an almost tactile fashion: Their "bodies follow the thicks and thins of an urban 'text' they write without being able to read it."²⁷ Certainly in comparison with the view of shogunal authority—Matsuda's "vertical will" of hegemony, the donjon of the castle—Saikaku's perspective on the city is embedded and enmeshed, narrative rather than visual. But though lacking the bird's-eye view of the administrator or mapmaker, our anonymous urban entrepreneur is not without a certain vision and a certain remove from his object. Through an apprenticeship of careful observation, he is slowly learning to set himself off from the crowd to observe and make sense of its dynamics—not just to follow the urban text (or to be carried along with the flows of the floating world), but also to read it carefully, probe it for the meanings and opportunities that may be hidden within it, and to discern a chance to turn them to his advantage. Although lacking the totalizing vision of the view from above, the anonymous entrepreneur builds an image and indeed a reading of the city out of the shifting views from its streets and waterways.

As the anonymous hero watches the crowds at Nihonbashi, he encounters a group of tradesmen coming back from a day of construction on the *daimyō* estates just to the east of the shogun's castle. This is just one group amid the myriad flows passing through Nihonbashi, but Saikaku's treatment of this group of laborers, focalized through the eyes of his hero, is far from the indistinct and heterogeneous mass of the urban crowd evoked a few lines before. The development of the narrative, and of the anonymous hero's entrepreneurial ability, turns on the cultivation of a capacity for perspicacious vision, one that simultaneously sets the viewer apart from the crowd and scrutinizes it for social distinctions: "Chattering loudly with their hair in comical disarray, dirt around their collars, waistbands tied around their coats, and sleeves fraying at the cuffs, some leaned on their measures as walking sticks and others held their hands in their pockets, bent at the back from the day's work. They may as well have had a signboard labeling them as craftsmen."²⁸ The hero's discerning gaze notes in detail the outward manifestations of manual labor as seen in the figure of the working craftsman, and the narrative voice, which like the gaze merges with the position of the hero, discriminates almost instinctively against the material signs of physical labor—after all, the aim is to get something for nothing. It is this probing and opportunistic gaze, which precisely repeats his posture in viewing the crowd at Nihonbashi, that finally leads him to discover the opportunity that becomes his path to wealth: collecting and

THE POETICS AND POLITICS OF TOWNSMAN PROPERTY

reselling the wood scraps that the teams of craftsmen leave in their wake. On discovering this windfall, the budding entrepreneur exclaims that "Only in the very seat of the sovereign could one find such generosity!" (*korera made ōyō naru koto, tenka no go-jōka nareba koso*). He then retraces the carpenters' path along the bustling commercial boulevard (sometimes called Tōri-chō) from the intersection of Suruga-chō, just north of Nihonbashi, to the Sujikaibashi Bridge over the Kanda River, at which point he has gathered more wood than he can carry.

Here the spatial logic of the story shifts from one that is embedded in the flux of the floating world to one of keen apprehension of the opportunities afforded by the topology of the castle town. Whereas the commoner districts surrounding Nihonbashi were largely commercial—focused on wholesale trade, luxury goods, and moneylending—the Kanda district historically consisted of communities of craftsmen, many of which had been organized by shogunal fiat in the early years of the seventeenth century. It was also one of the points at which such neighborhoods of laboring craftsmen abutted and overlapped with warrior Edo, the *daimyō* estates just to the southwest of Sujikaibashi and the bannerman residences beyond them. Whereas the working craftsman navigated this spatial nexus according to the logic of occupation dictated from the seat of authority—crossing into warrior spaces to provide productive labor—Saikaku's protagonist is cagier in his movements, tracking such itineraries in order to poach resources left as waste amid the productive labor of construction. His movements become steadily more complex but always systematic as he pivots from collecting wood scraps to establishing a business of selling chopsticks and toothpicks to nearby neighborhoods of greengrocers, an inventive citation of the urban text of the castle town to produce new spatial itineraries of collecting and selling. By the end of the story, he has returned to the elite center of commoner Edo near Nihonbashi, where he has now established himself with both name and property as one of the leading figures of the Zaimoku-chō lumberyards. By now, he has given up his entrepreneurial perambulations of the city in favor of directing the flow of capital through new and larger spatial networks that link the city of Edo to the forested mountains from which were extracted the resources driving urban expansion. This progression is rendered in a rapid and accelerating series of elliptical narrative pivots as the protagonist transforms from scrappy entrepreneur into wealthy lumber magnate:

Lamenting how long he had gone without realizing the opportunities that had been falling at his very feet, every day from then on he eagerly awaited the dusk, watching for when the carpenters would return, whereupon he would gather up all he could from the roadside, and there was never a day when his haul was less than five loads. On rainy days, he would carve the scraps into chopsticks and sell them wholesale to the grocers of Suda-chō and Setomono-chō, and before long he had accumulated great wealth, renowned throughout the Kamakura riverbank as Hashiya [Chopstick] Jinbei. Soon these wood scraps grew into great trees, and he purchased a great mansion in Zaimoku-chō, where he kept more than thirty clerks. The forests he bought up were no less impressive than those of Kawamura, Kashiwagi, or Fushimiya, and his spirit was as broad as the sea: once he had made a sturdy fortune, he bought up materials for ships' masts, and his profits were all he could have wished. Before long, forty years had passed, and his coffers held a hundred-thousand *ryō*. All this was truly a testament to the millionaire pills he had taken in his younger days.[29]

Hashiya Jinbei's wit is inextricable from a set of spatial practices rooted in a novel apprehension of the evolving urban text of the late seventeenth century. Jinbei's Edo is not the city as imagined by shogunal administrators, in which labor is performed as a socially sanctioned occupation in service of the ruling warrior household, nor is it the Edo of the privileged community of the *chō*, organized as a local collectivity in which labor is carried out in service of the community and its shared property and trade. Here the city is defined by a more fluid and mobile form of walking that emerges and evolves as a reflection of the liminal flows of people, materials, and money between spaces and communities. Although shaped by and taking form within all these frameworks, Jinbei's Edo emerges as an extemporaneous itinerary through and across status communities, a singular case of a livelihood made by "making one's way" through an urban world in flux.

But this walking is not precisely Certeau's, for it flows seamlessly into the strategic consolidation of wealth. Jinbei does not merely poach the waste disposed of by others in a perpetual survivor's hustle, but also steadily and systematically transitions from modes of appropriation to those of accumulation—claiming a proper name, purchasing an estate, and ultimately subjecting the land itself to the force of his personal property as he buys up forests to feed his growing lumber concern. Jinbei's assertion of the authority of townsman property, siphoned off the labor of the working craftsman, is symbiotic with the structures of warrior hegemony. It was in large part the need for construction and renovation of warrior estates (as suggested by the movements of the craftsmen themselves) that drove the profitability of the lumber trade. The lumber merchants of Zaimoku-chō provided the raw material by which the top-down vision of the castle town was inscribed on the earth to give shape to the early modern city. Indeed, the character of Hashiya Jinbei is likely based on the historical personage of Kamakuraya Jinbei, a Zaimoku-chō lumber merchant who had established himself by at least the 1640s and subsequently served as an appointed lumber provisioner for the shogunate—an implied context that situates Jinbei's historic success against the visionary rebuilding of Edo in the wake of the Great Meireki Fire (1657).[30] Entrepreneurial merchant capital flourishes in the embrace of shogunal authority and participates in the shogunal strategies of spatial inscription: "Only in the very seat of the sovereign!"

As with Amiya, Saikaku's narrator takes care to retroactively legitimate the entrepreneur's appropriative excursions. In this story, the stakes are lower—accumulating wood scraps would have fewer legal implications than borrowing money illicitly to fund usurious lending—but the glimpse that Saikaku offers of the mercurial genesis of merchant capital, parasitically extracted from the socially productive but relatively unprofitable labor of the craftsman, is hardly a savory one. The final narrative declamation that Jinbei's success was "a testament to the millionaire pills he had taken in his younger days" (*wakai toki nomikomi shi chōjagan no shirushi*), which, like the focalization throughout the narrative, seems to reflect Jinbei's voice as much as an objective narrator's, is precisely parallel to Amiya's legitimating gesture in repaying the interest on his borrowed funds to the Mizuma Temple. It says, "All of this was virtuously done. I have followed the rules we all recognize, my success being both a sign of my virtuous efforts and a just reward for them." The irony of this legitimating gesture is that few, if any, of the virtues of the millionaire pills are in evidence. In place of the tycoon's didactic platitudes—which focus on a standard ethos of thrift, hard work, and individual austerity—Jinbei succeeds through wit. The irony is not simply that, after enthusiastically taking in the millionaire pill recipe as precious advice, he sets out for Nihonbashi to wait for a windfall of "something for nothing," but moreover that he succeeds in this hope; it is by this hope that he succeeds. As if to reflect the shift from steady accumulation of merit through hard work toward the generative intellectual flash of wit, the narrative time of "Medicine Prepared in Abnormal Fashion" is weighted heavily toward the cognitive processes of the protagonist as he learns to read the urban landscape, following in minute detail his inner monologue and focalized observations as he slowly realizes the opportunities that are hiding in plain sight. The long years of diligent effort after the moment of entrepreneurial insight are glossed over in a few lines. Seen from this perspective, the closing citation of the millionaire pills is precisely that: a citation, the last of a series of tactical borrowings through which Hashiya Jinbei alchemically extracts name and property from the flows of the floating world and the interlinear space of the urban text.

But once the entrepreneurial protagonist is given the authority to narrate the moral legitimacy of his own economic success, we are already far beyond the space of tactics. Narrative itself has become the legitimating strategy of entrepreneurial townsman property. Certeau contends that narrative is essentially tactical. The written text is a mere trace artifact of the spontaneous act of its composition, a reification and objectification of the fickle path that the hand takes over the space of the page, just as a graphic trail of a spatial itinerary, as one might inscribe on a map—a walk from Suruga-chō to Sujikaibashi, or a chopstick peddler's rounds through the greengrocers' districts—is merely the spectral projection of a series of fugitive enunciative acts.[31] But, to the contrary, it is through such an act of writing, punctuated by the felicitous citation of established didactic truths, that the improvised itinerary of entrepreneurial walking is transformed retroactively into a mythic narrative of commercial success through diligent effort, and the place of the townsman is rendered stable and permanent and legitimate. However much Saikaku's writing grappled with the flux of the marketplace, the contingent ephemerality of urban life, and the existential insecurity of the floating world, his writing of prose fiction could not be tactical in the fashion of, say, the extemporaneous appropriations of linked verse. The author's townsman pieces ultimately channel the contingent opportunism of the tactic, and the everyday appropriations that transpire under the rubric of livelihood, into strategies for the accumulation and legitimation of merchant capital: from acts of tactical reading into modes of strategic writing. Saikaku's writing was, as his narrator states in the conclusion to *Eternal Storehouse*, meant to be a lasting resource, a form of capital preserved in Japan's eternal storehouse as a sign of a realm at peace.

THE POLITICS OF WIT

By now, we have a clear enough vision of the narrative logic of entrepreneurial wit. The anonymous or otherwise disenfranchised protagonist, casting about amid the uncertain flows of the floating world, happens to perceive the flash of opportunity. In many cases, the act of seizing opportunity from the jaws of fortune is morally ambiguous; in others, it is legally suspect. The forms of moral transgression, though, are to a degree justified or at least glossed over by the need of the vulnerable to somehow get by. Even as the amoral tactics of the unpropertied transform into the strategies of upwardly mobile merchant capital, the moral lapses witnessed along the way and perhaps smuggled into new forms of strategic accumulation are transmuted into the heroic spectacle of entrepreneurial success. Moreover, that success is usually accompanied, as with Amiya and Hashiya Jinbei, by performative acts of self-narrating moral legitimation that reaffirm a symbiotic relationship with established authority. Neither of these merchant paragons subverts or even relativizes the political powers and moral discourses that define the socio-spatial structures in which they operate and out of which they seize opportunity: The goal of entrepreneurial endeavor is to claim property as part of the system rather than in the face of it.

But there is another and yet more subtle side to the tactics of livelihood and to the politics of entrepreneurial wit, one that is all the more ideologically forceful to the degree that it is barely perceivable in the ellipses of Saikaku's stories, in the social and moral limits that they depend on but leave unstated, and in the socio-spatial boundaries they limn but painstakingly refrain from crossing. As the moment of tactical appropriation transmogrifies into the strategic articulation and accumulation of townsman property, the navigation of social space becomes a reassertion of social boundaries, in particular, those that separate commoner society from the urban margins. For in each of these stories are marginal populations that the narrative simultaneously excludes and depends on as the target of tactical appropriation: the fishermen to whom Amiya lends the bodhisattva's wealth and mercy through unauthorized acts of usurious microfinance; the disheveled craftsmen who Hashiya Jinbei observes with contempt while collecting the scraps that fall at their feet, and who no doubt will continue their daily exertions long after he has purchased his mansion in Zaimoku-chō. As noted in chapter 1, the boundaries of the community of the marketplace, though porous, tended to exclude manual labor: Craftsman and cultivator might join the community to the degree that they abandon productive but repetitive work in favor of the mobile flash of wit, but otherwise their trades were to be at best pitied, at worst scorned, and in any case avoided. At the same time, the adoption of wit was not equally accessible to all, and indeed was predicated precisely on the presence of such marginal and wit-less figures from whom to appropriate. Although symbiotic with authority, wit was parasitic on the marginalized. Saikaku's spatial stories, a form of writing that translated the tactical operations of wit into the strategic narratives of townsman property, act in subtle but powerful (powerful because subtle) ways to mark those boundaries, setting the townsman proper apart from the denizens of the urban margins. It is in this constitutive assertion of social boundaries that we may see the contours of an alternative politics of urban entrepreneurship and of the literary voice of the townsman.

Saikaku's most exemplary story of wit is also his most systematic study of the moral ambiguities opened up by the tactical space of livelihood and of the politically charged boundaries of the townsman community. "Daikoku, Who Wore Wit as His Shelter" (*Saikaku o kasa ni kiru Daikoku*, vol. 2–3) follows the fate of a certain Shinroku, the prodigal heir to a wealthy Kyoto merchant house, in his transformation into a paragon of entrepreneurial success.[32] Although born into significant wealth, Shinroku falls into dissipation and indiscriminate spending; when stern reprimands by the father and his clerks fail to correct his ways, he is disowned. This scenario was not uncommon, whether in fiction or in life, but Saikaku takes care to mark that Shinroku's is a case of legal disownment (*kyūri o kitte*). This formal process not only nullified the bond between parent and child, but also removed the child from the family name register and thus from the community of the *chō*, which would no longer bear responsibility for any fate, legal or otherwise, that might befall him. Shinroku thus transforms quite literally into a man without a place: a lumpen townsman, barred from both hereditary wealth and community support. Exiled from the security of proper place, he must rise into wealth by navigating the tactical space of livelihood.

I have suggested that the idea of livelihood was largely amoral, but in fact it was a bit more than that, for the contingent necessity of making a living was seen as authorizing forms of conduct that, in certain ways and

THE POETICS AND POLITICS OF TOWNSMAN PROPERTY

to certain degrees, were considered morally transgressive. The occupational encyclopedia *Illustrated Encyclopedia of Humanity* (*Jinrin kinmōzui*, 1692) avers that "Truly it is the way of the human world that one must, in the course of making a living, accrue some amount of moral demerits."[33] This remark is made in relation to the figure of the hunter, whose profession demands transgressing Buddhist injunctions against the taking of life; this kind of moral leeway, though, was but one reflection of a wider view that the need to make a livelihood in an uncertain world would occasionally necessitate and even justify behaviors that otherwise were marked as morally wrong. For example, Nishikawa Joken, who otherwise embraced a moral understanding of occupation and cautioned against the excessive desire for individual profit, acknowledged an element of truth in the aphorism that "Merchant houses are like folding screens: They need to be a little crooked or else they'll collapse."[34] This provisional toleration of the morally problematic is key to Saikaku's tale, for from the beginning, Shinroku is sketched as a person whose conduct frequently and even systematically transgresses social and moral norms.

As the narrator notes, for a father to formally disown his son is surely due to the son's "uncommon wickedness" (*ōkata naranu akushin*), and it is the evolution of this seed of wickedness that drives forward a narrative of appropriative wit. As if mere disownment were not enough, when his father discovers him in a bathhouse on the outskirts of Kyoto, he is sent packing with barely the clothes on his back. The season is late in the twelfth month, just before the New Year. Without even a sedge hat to stop the snow from falling into his collar, he stops to rest at a teahouse but has not a single copper to warm himself with a cup of tea. Instead, he skulks near the entrance, watching carefully as customers come and go. Shinroku's posture here is that of the still-anonymous Hashiya Jinbei, perched perspicaciously on the edge of the crowds of Nihonbashi, waiting for someone to drop something of value. But, in comparison with Jinbei, here the (im-)moral valence of opportunistic appropriation is clear: "Under cover of the hustle and bustle of the crowds" (*ōzei no dosakusa magire ni*), he steals sips of tea to wet his throat and snatches up a straw raincoat that one of the customers has just thrown off. "Feeling for the first time the urge to steal" (*hajimete nusumigokoro ni natte yuku ni*), he makes his way to the village of Ono, and his "uncommon wickedness," which has expressed itself as the "urge to steal," continues to shape the tactics that he uses to proceed steadily on a path eastward. At the same time, the narrator also remarks on Shinroku's desperate straits, being sent on the road with neither cash nor travel garments and hardly even his own loincloth: "If only there were a way to endure this cold!" The urge to steal that drives his movement forward is balanced by an empathetic framing of the material depravation he faces outside the security of townsman society.

In the village of Ono, he finds a group of children mourning the death of a large dog, the carcass of which he handily appropriates, wrapping it in the straw raincoat he had taken from the teahouse. He has plans for the carcass as well. When he encounters some peasants digging in the fields, he calls them over: "This dog is a miracle cure for colic! For three years, I've been feeding him all kinds of medicines, and now I'm going to burn him black!"[35] The charred remains of a dog, especially a large one, were believed to be an effective cure for *kan*, a form of childhood colic, but Shinroku, the budding entrepreneur, inflates the value of his wares with claims that he has been feeding the animal medicine, the benefits of which are presumed to enhance the curative properties of the ash. The peasants lend him a tinderbox to help him burn the animal, after which he gifts the villagers "sparingly" (*wazuka ni*) with a small share of the resulting ash, claiming the rest for himself. As his itinerary moves eastward, his snake-oil hustle becomes more elaborate: He disguises his voice in the local dialect so as to appear as a local peddler and passes off the charred dog as charred wolf, believed to be a cure for abdominal pain—this being an attested form of fraud at the time.[36] Saikaku's narrator is frank in labeling Shinroku's business as one of "foisting" (*tsukitsuke akinai*) his wares on unwitting customers, who are "swindled" (*katararete*), and his marks even include savvy travelers and fellow itinerant peddlers. Shinroku's social trajectory follows the logic of livelihood as a largely amoral practice of doing what one must to survive, and his itinerary becomes very precisely a spatial process of "making a way" from Kyoto eastward toward Edo. The flash of wit is reiterated in each of Shinroku's opportunistic appropriations and exchanges: the stolen straw raincoat, the acquisitioned carcass, the tinderbox borrowed in exchange for a parsimonious dispensation of the resulting ash, the dog powder passed off as wolf powder.

This series of exchanges recalls the folkloric mode of the "rice stalk millionaire" (*warashibe chōja*) a genre of folktale in which the protagonist initially acquires a single stalk of rice and comes to wealth through a series of fortuitous and unexpected trades. This narrative trope was popularized in the Edo period in the form of the late Muromachi tale "Daikokumai" ("The Dance of the God Daikokuten"), in which an exceptionally filial son, on pilgrimage to the Kiyomizu Temple, is blessed by the gods in response to his virtue: Given a single stalk of rice along with an oracular message, he exchanges one thing for another until he achieves great wealth.[37] Not unlike "Fortune Comes Riding on the First Horse Day of Spring," this story thus seems to situate the origin of wealth within the semi-sacred liminal space of the road. But rather than presenting wealth (and wit) as divine per se, Saikaku ironically repurposes this narrative trope, transforming the exceptionally filial son of "Daikokumai" into the disowned, amoral scoundrel Shinroku. Through this cynical parody of the folkloric trope of the rice stalk millionaire, Saikaku also presents a wry commentary on the nature of interregional commerce when seen through the lens of livelihood. Recall that Nishikawa Joken, discussing commerce in terms of the moral mandates of occupation, asserted that "the true merchant is the one who judges the quality and quantity of goods, and, calculating costs and benefits without claiming excessive profits, exchanges that which he possesses for that which he lacks," and in doing so serves the needs of the realm.[38] Shinroku likewise carries out a series of exchanges as he moves from Kyoto to Edo, but rather than redistributing resources, he relies on the distance from town to town and on the anonymity of the itinerant merchant to obfuscate the provenance of his fraudulent goods, foisting counterfeit medicine on unsuspecting locals. From this perspective, Shinroku's itinerary is a parody of commerce as occupation in the form of commerce as livelihood: exchange of resources, but purely for personal benefit and at the expense of the trading partner. It is also, like the story of Amiya, a kind of entrepreneurial opportunism that can happen only in the spatial interstices of interurban trade and travel, a flash of opportunity that emerges in the liminal moment of transit, a reflection of the poetics of the transportation network.

If, on the one hand, Shinroku's wit depends on the liminal possibilities of the road, then on the other, and despite that liminal quality, it retains and reaffirms a certain set of social and spatial distinctions. Indeed, Shinroku's wit is fundamentally predicated on social difference. Through Shinroku's eastward migration, the countryside is defined as a space to be passed through in transit between urban marketplaces, a field of opportunistic appropriation where one might find and extract resources and exploit locals, who always appear as objects rather than subjects of wit: They are there to be "taken in" and "foisted upon." In this regard, the provincial locals who Shinroku cheerily exploits as he makes his way to Edo recall the fishermen who are pushed to the margins of Amiya's narrative, but on whose borrowing his success is built, and the craftsmen in Hashiya Jinbei's story, whose manual labor he dismisses but whose wood scraps he cannily claims for himself. But, more important, and all the more significant to the degree that it is unspoken and virtually invisible, is the boundary between commoner and outcast status. The geographic territoriality of outcast communities overlapped in complex ways with the socio-spatial structures of commoner society, and it was widely recognized that outcast communities retained exclusive rights to the disposal of animal carcasses within their territory; this was both an obligatory occupation through which such communities gained a secure (albeit marginal) place within the Tokugawa polity and a livelihood through which they supported themselves.[39] Shinroku, of course, give little thought to these recognized privileges as he passes through the countryside on his way to Edo. Although the appropriation of the dog carcass conjures unspoken associations with outcast status, Saikaku is careful not to identify Shinroku's activities too closely with that of the outcast: The identification of his business as foisting (*tsukitsuke akinai*) remains within the space of "trade" (*akinai*), though at its amoral margins, rather than within the space of outcast practice, which was tangential to religious practice (disposal of corpses) and craft labor (preparation of animal hides). Shinroku carefully navigates the boundary between moral liminalities that can be resolved into the amoral space of everyday economic livelihood and those that are inexorably excluded from commoner society.

The story's concern with outcast status deepens as Shinroku arrives in Edo. Reaching Shinagawa with a small reserve of cash, he disposes of the remains of the dog and spends the night in the company of a group of three beggars. Like Shinroku, all are former townsmen who have fallen through the cracks of proper commoner society, and all are associated to one degree or another with the old class of privileged townsmen. One is described as a born-and-bred Edo local (*Edo no jibae*) whose income had come from rent, marking him as a fallen member of the highest ranks of townsman society. Due to his spendthrift ways, however, he has fallen into ruin, and Saikaku's narrator describes him as "a beggar, and not even one of Kuruma

Zenshichi's guild"—referring to one of the heads of the Edo beggar community. Remaining outside the jurisdiction of official beggar administration, these characters belong to a category distinct from that of official and hereditary outcast status: lumpen townsmen who, like Shinroku, have been removed from their family name registers and thus expelled from the community of the *chō* but not yet incorporated into the status order of outcasts, which had its own limited protections.[40] Nor does Saikaku's narrator allude to the amorphous ranks of lumpen-townsman street performers who would later be roughly systematized under the label of *gōmune*.[41] Indeed, the various forms of occasional begging and performing that were occasionally practiced by commoners who had fallen on hard times are virtually absent from Saikaku's townsman pieces, which are systematic in their rejection of established but modest methods of economic survival in favor of novel and inventive (though precarious and contingent) modes of mobility. Shinroku acts as a figure for the possibility of braving the profoundly insecure and protean liminalities of the urban margins without the security of membership in a status community, whether commoner or outcast.

After explaining his situation, Shinroku solicits his companions for advice. Their first response is to suggest that he might find a way to mend bridges and return to his birth family: "Isn't there any way you could apologize?" "Don't you have an aunt or someone [to intercede on your behalf]?" "Better if you hadn't come to Edo in the first place!" All these beggars, in keeping with their characterization as failed merchants who have fallen into ruin due to their incompetence at business, are only able to imagine their financial recovery through a return to earlier frameworks of privilege. Shinroku, in contrast, seems (claims) to reject the logic of hereditary privilege, recognizing that "one cannot return to times past, but must plot instead for what's to come" (*ato e kaeranu mukashi, ima kara saki no shian nari*), and continues to press his three companions for novel ideas for business opportunities that require little capital. They reply with three suggestions: collecting discarded shells to burn into lime ash, peddling shredded seaweed and shaved strips of dried bonito, and buying cotton scraps to be cut up and sold as hand towels. Shinroku takes inspiration from this advice, giving the three beggars three hundred coppers for their trouble—the last in a series of exchanges, here taking the form of payment for information on local market conditions. Although he does not share his inspiration with the beggars, it turns out that he has settled on the third option; in typical elliptical form, Saikaku does not explain why, inviting the reader to speculate on Shinroku's reasoning. Taken in historical context, the first two options serve known social needs: Lime ash was used in housing plaster, which, following the Great Meireki Fire, was mandated in 1660 to be applied to all roofs in Edo as a fire retardant; and shredded seaweed and dried bonito were key components in easily prepared dishes that found a ready market in Edo's predominantly unwed, male, laboring population. However, as Saikaku notes elsewhere in *Eternal Storehouse*, productive labor does not easily scale, and its opportunities for profit are finite; Shinroku, whose consciousness has taken the form of entrepreneurial wit, chooses the third option of selling hand towels.[42] Shinroku has taken another, more subtle piece of advice from his companions as well. Despite his recognition that one cannot return to the past, he nevertheless makes use of the intangible networks of existing social capital furnished by prior privilege: He tracks down an old family relation among the cotton wholesalers of Tenmachō, explains his situation, and receives the support of the master, who offers a stock of cloth to cut into hand towels.

One can imagine an alternative version in which Shinroku refrains from giving all his leftover profits from the dog powder to his fellow beggars, uses some to purchase scraps of cloth, and makes a fortune from literal rags to riches. This is not the story that Saikaku is telling. It is critical that Shinroku offer payment for the advice to the beggars, who praise him for his generosity and bless his enterprising endeavors—entrepreneurship becomes virtue. And despite the pretense of a narrative of rags to riches, Saikaku takes care to explicitly mark where entrepreneurial endeavor depends on prior connections, strategically deployed. Strategically, rather than tactically, for this is the point where this narrative, like the others, pivots seamlessly from the ephemeral space of tactical operation to that of strategic accumulation, systematically deploying stable and reproducible forms of social power to carve out a place for individual property. Shinroku's ultimate entrepreneurial gambit is to wait for a festival day at the Tenjin Shrine in Shitaya, attached to the great shogunal temple of Kan'eiji, and set up shop next to the ritual washbasin, selling hand towels to pilgrims as a talisman of good fortune. Here the narrative precisely parallels that of Amiya as Shinroku establishes a symbiotic relationship with local religious authority (and, through the connection with Kan'eiji, implicitly with the symbolic authority of the shogunal auspices), while securing through that felicitous connection a place for his own property: Within a dozen or so years, Shinroku has come into fantastic wealth, himself bandied about as a Daikoku-esque deity of good fortune by Edo locals.

As with the story of Amiya, one is tempted to take "Daikoku, Who Wore Wit as His Shelter" as a work of veiled social critique, one that suggestively, if indirectly, exposes the ways in which the everyday economic practices of the entrepreneurial townsman class may conceal forms of fraud and exploitation. Certainly, Saikaku's work does reveal this, but it would be wrong to frame this revelation as a critical one. To the contrary, Saikaku authorizes such morally ambiguous practices in service of narratives of entrepreneurial success. The moral ambiguities of livelihood become legitimate to the degree that they operate as tactics by those who are understood to exist outside the frameworks of power and hereditary privilege. But for entrepreneurial wit to be truly successful as such, it must move out of the space of flux and ephemerality to merge with or transform into stable strategies that allow for the accumulation of wealth and power under the proper name of the townsman household. One of Saikaku's key insights was to observe that the generally amoral and occasionally immoral space opened up by the ideology of livelihood need not be allowed simply as a way for the disenfranchised to get by—an unsavory tactical necessity allowed provisionally to those lacking proper place—but that it contained the possibility of positive accumulation. The chance opportunities and fortuitous turns of fate that characterized the space of livelihood need not be experienced merely as the uncertain ebbs and flows of the fortunes of men in the floating world: One could conceivably chart a course through them and engineer out of those contingencies a stable platform on which to build a name, trade, and fortune. Even as the tactics of the weak gave way to the strategies of townsman property, the possibility of moral transgression would always include the promise of further mobility as long as it could be plausibly justified as still falling under the necessarily tactical repertoire of an entrepreneurial underdog such as Shinroku.

The ultimate political import of Saikaku's vision of wit, however, was a matter less of the moral lapses it authorized and the amoral appropriations it legitimated than of the social positions it excluded and the social boundaries it reaffirmed. In tandem with the emergence of a capacious and upwardly mobile (urban) commoner society based on shared entrepreneurial values, the late seventeenth century and the turn to the eighteenth also saw the dramatic reassertion, on both legal and ideological grounds, of the boundaries that separated commoner society from the marginalized classes of beggars and outcasts.[43] The years following the publication of *Eternal Storehouse* saw a flurry of shogunal edicts that stigmatized begging as a form of illicit extortion, framing beggars as a latent criminal element and calling for the increased consolidation and control of the begging classes. At the same time, and despite the moral flexibility embraced by the discourse of livelihood, commoner-oriented texts such as the *Illustrated Encyclopedia of Humanity* came increasingly to describe beggars as lazy, incompetent, morally degenerate, and—mirroring the shogunal decrees—latently criminal and thus requiring social control. Similar dynamics played out around the class of hereditary outcasts (*eta*). Tokugawa Tsunayoshi's controversial "edicts of compassion for living beings" (*shōrui awaremi rei*), part of a program of moral leadership intended to reframe those in the warrior class as moral figureheads and the Tokugawa house as a benevolent hegemon, were used to justify the ongoing marginalization of the *eta*, whose occupations came to be seen not only as immoral in themselves but also as reflective of an intergenerational karmic taint, a hereditary moral debt that could never be escaped. In sum, as the seventeenth century gave way to the eighteenth and as warrior rule was increasingly framed as a function of benevolent moral leadership, the emerging townsman community was also learning how to legitimate its own moral standing in the realm, a move accomplished in part by conspiring with the warrior authorities in the systematic marginalization of the underclasses, who were excluded both from the benefits of benevolent rule and from the implicit moral freedoms of commoner livelihood. Seen in this context, Shinroku's entrepreneurial journey in "Daikoku, Who Wore Wit as His Shelter" becomes a striking allegory of the formation of the commoner subject, one who exists by defining himself against the outcast, whose proprietary rights to animal carcasses may be disregarded in acts of tactical appropriation; against the rural cultivator, who becomes an easy mark for a trade of foisting specious goods; and against the declassed beggar, who can lend experiential expertise at navigating the economic opportunities afforded by the urban margins, but who lacks the wit to convert that expertise into effective strategies of accumulation and is therefore deemed to be deserving of his miserable lot.

TOWARD "THE WAY OF THE TOWNSMAN"

When reading an author like Saikaku, the townsman entrepreneur is the heroic underdog. We read this way in part because of the narratives that we have been given about the townsman as a dominated class, and in part because Saikaku himself frames his narratives as stories about those without property or secure position; to a certain degree, the narratives we have been given are Saikaku's invention, extrapolated by generations of scholars into a narrative of cultural history. Certeau's theory of the tactic does much to illuminate the logic of such narratives, casting into clear relief the logic of how the unpropertied entrepreneur navigates and apprehends the affordances of the city and the interregional marketplace. But the distinction between tactics and strategies is not absolute, and it is precisely the valorization of the tactic as the agency of the weak that allows for the emergent strategies of local hegemony to operate invisibly under the guise of mere tactics. Saikaku's wit begins, certainly, as a tactical cognition and mode of reading the urban text: It surveys the diversity of the urban world for lessons on how to make a living, pivoting to opportunities for material appropriation—viewing beggars as potential sources of lessons and lifestyle models, watching tradespeople to perceive the value that they produce and that they are unable to exploit, observing local lending practices and imagining how they could be creatively redirected toward new enterprises. But Saikaku's townsman entrepreneurs are never purely tactical, focused as they are on constructing and legitimating their own forms of property. The ethos of wit culminates in a shift from tactical reading to strategic writing, ultimately becoming narrative itself. Entrepreneurship in its purest form, the magic of producing something from nothing, is none other than the magic of self-representation. Saikaku's star entrepreneurs, like the author himself, are master storytellers, their narratives authorized and legitimated by the inscriptions of Saikaku's brush.

Saikaku finds the possibility of social mobility and the genesis of townsman property within the space of livelihood, which allowed for movement outside of the moral strictures and socio-spatial structures that defined the official vision of the Tokugawa polity. However, livelihood was not just a matter of practice, a lived reality that operated outside the ideological and discursive structures of shogunal authority. In the late seventeenth century, livelihood was turning into an ideology in its own right: a discursive figure, rendered in language and disseminated in didactic texts, that oriented a commoner worldview and a sense of townsman identity. And once we have stepped out of the realm of lived practice and into language—into writing and into print—and moved from a condition of existential uncertainty to an ethos of building property, we have moved beyond the realm of the tactical. Saikaku's fiction was part of the historical process by which the townsman's lifeworlds were put into writing and developed into new forms of narrative art. Through such new modes of inscription, the tactical operations of the commoner everyday were transformed into new strategies of townsman power.

Later writers would work to render the moral value of the merchant legible and his social power visible and thus legitimate them in a more public sense. Building on the premises of moral commerce explored by merchant intellectuals such as Nishikawa Joken, later thinkers such as the ideologues of the Kaitokudō merchant academy and, most influentially, Ishida Baigan's heart learning movement would develop an ethos of ethical commerce that aimed to integrate the townsman's practical understanding of commercial exchange with the morally normative social imaginary of the four estates and the shogunal ideology of occupation—what some scholars identify as "the way of the townsman" (*chōnin no michi*).[44] The irony of the putatively moral way of the townsman was that, despite legitimating the practice of commerce under the rubric of socially sanctioned occupation, it also largely served to orient all the obligations of the individual merchant through the institution of the household and its imperative toward self-preservation and reproduction. It was not the case that the morally upright merchant worked to serve a social purpose. Instead, he would naturally be serving a social purpose as long as he worked diligently for the economic benefit of his own household. In other words, such discourses simply built on the emerging commoner ideology of livelihood, suggesting that the perpetual existence and incremental increase of townsman property was not merely a matter of private interest or practical necessity, that it was morally legitimate and indeed morally imperative in its own right. The way of the townsman was none other than the logic of livelihood disguised in the rhetoric of occupation.[45]

The way of the townsman of course had other sides. In addition to morally legitimating the private accumulation of wealth in the name of the townsman household, ideologues such as Baigan worked to impose (or at least to propose) limits on the townsman's private self-interest and moral strictures on his conduct in both private and public. Seen from the perspective of Saikaku's morally unconstrained entrepreneurs, one can see why.[46] But just as the "way of the warrior" was a variable ideological construct that oriented but never fully prescribed the actions of individual warriors, it would be naive and nostalgic to assume that an idealized vision of moral commerce such as a putative way of the townsman ever truly circumscribed (or even accurately described) the practices of the entrepreneurial townsmen of early modern Japan. There is theory and then there is practice; what makes Saikaku unique among townsman writers and thinkers was his ability to depict all the messy complexities of the latter but to do so without ultimately unsettling the moral confidence of the former. In contrast to later merchant ideologues, Saikaku's writing grappled ambivalently with the complex and amoral spatial practices through which social mobility was possible and out of which townsman property might congeal. To use an orthogonal spatial metaphor, Saikaku's way of the townsman was a meandering pathway of livelihood that charted a course from the poor and unpropertied into the privileges of property and power. Its logic was to appropriate resources through spatial movement and social subterfuge, to assert the legitimacy of commerce while systematically marginalizing the peasantry, working poor, beggars, and outcasts (who were needed as objects of exploitation), to establish that legitimacy through strategic alliances with sites of orthodox social power, and in the end to assert that all of this had been accomplished honestly and auspiciously. The irony of Saikaku's writing is that, precisely to the degree that it renders such trajectories visible, it also renders them legitimate, as stories of heroic entrepreneurial underdogs. Just as tactics transform seamlessly into strategies, Saikaku's narratives of entrepreneurial practice integrate seamlessly with the theoretical legitimation of the townsman subject.

Chapter Three

FROM TOWNSMAN CULTURE TO TOWNSMAN NARRATIVE

The writings of Ihara Saikaku have long been a fixture of cultural histories of Genroku townsman culture: the late seventeenth-century efflorescence of urban cultural production, named for the Genroku era (1688–1704) and taken to mark the emerging cultural voice of the townsman.[1] The cultural products of this moment are diverse—the materialist metaphysics of Itō Jinsai and his followers, Matsuo Bashō's efforts to elevate linked verse—but cultural and even social historians have fixated on Saikaku's works, especially *Eternal Storehouse* and the townsman pieces that followed it, as documents of an urban zeitgeist that expressed the emerging voice of the townsman status group. The interpretations produced through this attention range in focus but share certain premises. Positing the Genroku townsman as a coherent and self-consistent category of historical subjectivity and Saikaku as an exemplary spokesman for the same, they attempt to extract from the author's fiction a consensus of values, generally centered on the possibility of accumulating wealth through individual effort and built on a belief in the primacy of lived experience and rational calculation. In such a reading, Saikaku's fiction is essentially didactic, representing the author's beliefs (and by extension those of the Genroku townsmen) more or less transparently through the pronouncements of his narrators:

Each must entrust himself to the oracles of the Great God of Thrift and store up wealth, for it grants life as if a third parent. (vol. 1-1)
    shimatsu daimyōjin no go-takusen ni makase, kingin o tamu beshi. kore, futaoya no hoka ni inochi no oya nari.

Verily one becomes even a millionaire by virtue of one's own mettle. (vol. 1-3)
    onore ga shōne ni yotte, chōja ni mo naru koto zo kashi.

Slack not for even a moment, and wealth come 'round in good time; set your will upon it, and it can hardly fail to accumulate. (vol. 4-1)
    zanji mo yudan suru koto nakare. kingin wa mawarimochi, nenriki ni makase, tamaru majiki mono ni wa arazu.[2]

From statements like these, memorable perhaps more for their epigrammatic nature than for their originality of conception, we may take an image of an approximate constellation of keywords—thrift (*shimatsu*), diligence (*kinben*), physical and mental well-being (*kengo*), dedication to house trade (*kagyō*)—with particular emphasis on those qualities that rely on the activity of the mind or will over that of the body—cleverness (*rihatsu*), judgment (*funbetsu*), mettle (*shōne*), will or intention (*nenriki*), and, as seen in chapter 2, wit (*saikaku*). Taken together, these keywords seem to comprise a materialist ethos of upward mobility that might be called a Genroku dream: a belief, supported by the rapid development of domestic consumer markets during the 1660s and 1670s, that adherence to certain principles will allow the enterprising individual to rise from obscurity to great wealth in a single generation.

As I have argued, Saikaku was writing at a moment when such values came to constitute the basis for a newly portable and capacious sense of townsman identity, defined not by locality, occupation, status, or class, but instead by a shared sense of values, practices, and lifestyles: an entrepreneurial ethos. What oriented the unifying ethos of the emerging urban community was the premise that entrepreneurship was possible through rational will, and that one could become a townsman—that one could come into name and trade and property—simply by choosing to live as one. That the marketplace and the economic logics that govern it could be understood and could be mastered meant that, by embodying the values and practices and self-representations of the entrepreneurial merchant, those on the city's social and spatial margins could achieve real social mobility into the urban community. But I have also suggested that this new sense of townsman identity, built on the promise of social mobility, functioned to gloss over—not to say resolve—the distance and at times tension between what were in practice very different strata of urban society and different regimes of economic practice. The danger of an approach of cultural history that would use Saikaku's fiction to reconstruct townsman identity, an approach that might be called ethnographic in its assumption of the assumed coherence of an underlying consensus of values, is that it risks mistaking the symbolic and ideological coherence of this constructed ethos for the social coherence of the urban community of the late seventeenth century. In my view, the key question is not what values the townsmen shared but rather how a particular set of values, and the texts used to disseminate those values, could account for the disparities and tensions that persisted within that (only) nominally unified urban community.

Indeed, Saikaku's fiction is significant for how keenly it registers the contradictions within the townsman's entrepreneurial ethos and the moments where that ethos seems to fail in the face of the increasing stratification of urban society.

> In this world, only money makes money. (vol. 2–3)
> *tada kane ga kane o tameru yo no naka*

> It is difficult to become wealthy unless wit is aided by fortune! There are fools among the rich, while some quite clever men remain poor. (vol. 3–4)
> *bungen wa, saikaku ni shiawase tetsudawade wa narigatashi. zuibun kashikoki hito no hin naru ni, oroka naru hito no fūki*

> But even wisdom and wit are no good if they can't make you a living. (vol. 5–2)
> *tada chie saikaku to iu mo, yo watari no hoka wa nashi*[3]

There is no reason that an industrious person cannot make a fortune, but nevertheless money tends to reproduce itself. One can make a fortune by one's wits, but wits are no good if they can't make one a living. The central contradiction at the heart of *Eternal Storehouse* is that a sense of townsman identity built on the premise of economic rationality and success through individual effort would always be incomplete, and would eventually fail when confronted with the raw historical contingency of the distribution of wealth. The question is how Saikaku's text registers these contradictions and what sense it makes out of them.

In light of the palpable tension between an optimistic belief in success through individual effort and a cynical recognition of the contingency of worldly wealth, *Eternal Storehouse* is recognized as a contradictory work, and many of its most illuminating interpretations come from scholars attempting to make sense of its contradictions. In one paradigm-defining reading, Teruoka Yasutaka proposed that Saikaku's fearless engagement with and astute apprehension of social reality drove him to produce a blunt depiction of the world as it is. Teruoka argued that *Eternal Storehouse* was conceived as a didactic work, intended to express the author's optimistic belief, as an exemplary spokesman for the townsman community, in a radically egalitarian vision of social mobility through individual effort. However, Teruoka also took Saikaku to be a committed realist, one whose writing evolved in tandem with a deepening grasp of social reality. In Teruoka's reading, the contradictions of *Eternal Storehouse* were products of the confrontation between the author's ideals and his increasingly pessimistic apprehension of the difficulty of making a living, let alone a fortune, in the stratified economy of the late seventeenth century. In other words, Teruoka took *Eternal Storehouse* as a work of failed didacticism and a point of transition toward the socially conscious realism of the author's late works.[4] In contrast, I contend that Saikaku's accomplishment in *Eternal Storehouse* was the development of a narrative form that could depict contradiction without necessitating its resolution, and that could thus contain the failures of a sense of townsman identity built on the premise of economic rationality and success through individual effort. He did so by using a highly sophisticated structuring of the interplay between didactic voice and narrative content.

Much of Saikaku's fiction is distinguished by a unique narrative form, in which the didactic pronouncements of an opinionated narrator seem, on occasion, to be contradicted or subverted by the details of the story being told. Scholarly interpretations of this form are various, but many have focused on the question of whether and how such a form functions to subvert hegemonic ideologies, implicitly those of the ruling warrior class. For example, Jeffrey Johnson has read Saikaku's dynamic narrative style through Mikhail Bakhtin's theory of the carnivalesque to argue that the author's ironic use of the didactic voice acts as a mode of "festive critique" that serves a function of "overturning all hierarchies."[5] Johnson suggests that Saikaku's fiction is ideologically relativistic rather than explicitly subversive, but his analysis (like that of Bakhtin) still centers on the capacity of such a literary form to decenter dominant worldviews, a concern shared by much Saikaku scholarship (as of Tokugawa popular fiction writ large). In a convincing revision to such approaches, David Gundry has suggested that "the reigning sensibility [of Saikaku's work] is not iconoclastic or egalitarian but rather that of the ambitious and assertive bourgeois who is concerned with social self-advancement rather than with leveling social distinctions."[6] Based on this premise, Gundry poses an alternative interpretation of the author's narrative style, wherein the ironic deployment of a moralizing voice aligned with political authority serves to draw attention to, and ultimately affirm, the alternative hierarchies of wealth and distinction embraced by the wealthier strata of townsman society.[7] In line with this interpretation, Gundry suggests that the seeming failures and contradictions of the didactic voice give form to a floating world aesthetic of metaphysical impermanence and epistemological indeterminacy, rooted in the popularization of Buddhist belief, that lends aesthetic value to commoner experiences previously considered to not merit literary representation.[8] My analysis extends this line of thinking, but the forms taken by the didactic voice in Saikaku's late works, including *Eternal Storehouse*, differ from those in the early works analyzed by Gundry and Johnson. Here the principles given expression through the didactic voice are for the most part not moral but economic, and the voice that is seemingly undermined is the incipient rationalism of the entrepreneurial townsman himself. Moreover, the didactic voice, I argue, is not parodied or deconstructed, though it seems at times to be relativized or thrown into question. Paradoxically, this provisional questioning renders the didactic voice more robust by allowing it to accommodate degrees of exception.

This chapter explores the nature and functions of this unique textual form. Rather than treating *Eternal Storehouse* as a document of townsman culture, transmitted more or less directly through the voice of its narrators, I consider it a symbolically powerful work of townsman narrative, one in which the formal structures of narrative function to contain the contradictions within the townsman's sense of self and the tensions within the urban community. In other words, the ideological import of this work is to be found not in its content as much as its form. Like Teruoka, I take this form to be essentially didactic; but where Teruoka saw it as a failed didacticism (and prized it for its failures), I see it as a form of didacticism that is ideologically powerful precisely for the degree that it can represent and account for such failure without ultimately throwing its didactic premises into question. This is a complex and ambivalent form of didactic literature, made possible by the author's highly sophisticated deployment and manipulation of narrative voice. My aim in this chapter is to illuminate the textual genres and genealogies that informed Saikaku's writing and how he used them in developing new forms of narrative. In particular, I focus on the connections between Saikaku's fiction and the long historical tradition of anecdotal narrative (*setsuwa*), and on the seventeenth-century genre of entrepreneurial guidebooks, both of which had their own strategies for containing the failures of didactic principle. After tracing those traditions and their intersection with Saikaku's writing, I present a series of readings that show how *Eternal Storehouse* represents a new didactic mode: one that approaches didactic principle empirically, through situational observations that may be modified by future evidence, and that ultimately sublimates the failures of didactic principle into moments of heightened affective experience. It is through this aesthetic sublimation that Saikaku acknowledges and thus contains the failures of economic rationality, the contradictions of the early modern marketplace, and the tensions and fault lines within the emerging townsman community.

SETSUWA-ESQUE DIDACTICISM

In most narratives of Saikaku's writing career, *Eternal Storehouse* marks the second of two turning points in theme and social topos. The first pivot, represented by *Saikaku's Stories from the Provinces* (*Saikaku shokoku-banashi*, 1685) was a turn from the eroticism of the author's early "amorous" (*kōshoku*) works to a more eclectic set of themes and a more socially and geographically diverse collection of settings, resulting in a highly heterogeneous corpus of works sometimes referred to as his "miscellaneous pieces" (*zatsuwa-mono*), a category that sometimes includes his pieces focusing on warriors and those focusing on male-male sexuality. In *Eternal Storehouse*, Saikaku turned his attention to the everyday and usually economic realities of the urban townspeople with his townsman pieces.[9] Like most narratives of literary history, this piece of biographical shorthand is at best heuristic and risks glossing over significant continuities between the various periods, but it becomes more illuminating when considered in terms not of themes and social settings but of genres and textual forms. As Nakamura Yukihiko has argued, the author's early works were driven by an iconoclastic grappling with the classical canon, expressed formally through frameworks of parody and the *haikai*-esque inversion of the high and low, but in his middle period, his inspiration shifted from the classical canon (and from *haikai* poetry) toward the various genres of contemporary popular prose. Along with this shift in intertextual influence, his "compositional consciousness" (*sōsaku ishiki*) shifted away from parodic iconoclasm toward a more serious and affirmative (if always still ambivalent) exploration of the didactic mode.[10] One of the forms that this exploration took was an interest in the body of anecdotal narrative known to modern scholars as *setsuwa*.

The term *setsuwa* most commonly refers to a corpus of written collections of oral stories, centering on medieval collections such as the *Collected Tales of Times Now Past* (*Konjaku monogatari shū*, ca. 1120), *Collection of Things Written and Heard in the Past and Present* (*Kokon chomonjū*, ca. 1254), or *Collection of Tales from Uji* (*Uji shūi monogatari*, ca. early thirteenth century). Beginning with the *Record of Miraculous Events in Japan* (*Nihon ryōiki*, ca. 787–824), which reported strange and miraculous occurrences to illustrate the imminent reality of the workings of karma in this life, many such collections throughout the medieval period were set in writing by Buddhist monks and scribes and centered on themes of Buddhist karmic causality and retribution. Not all collections were Buddhist in orientation, however. Some, such as the *Compilation of Ten Precepts* (*Jikkinshō*, ca. 1252), were centered on more general didactic principles colored by Confucianism; many others lacked any didactic premise and simply compiled engaging stories of human drama, supernatural occurrences, or other objects of narrative interest. Any given collection might manifest a tension between didactic meaning or frame and plot content, in that some stories may satisfy the orienting frame better than others; the same tension runs even through individual stories, which may reveal a narrative complexity that cannot be reduced to a single driving principle. This is even and especially true within the more morally inclined Buddhist collections, in which many stories demonstrate a palpable tension between lively plotting and the moral principles that the compilers attempted to find in the episode: a tension between the voice of the narrator and the content of the plot, which complement but never precisely complete one another.[11] Reflecting the dynamic nature of a form of narrative built on the interplay between textual and oral transmission, the same story might also be transformed and adapted to different didactic ends in different texts.[12] To approach the ambivalently didactic functions of such anecdotal narrative, I follow Charlotte Eubanks' gloss of *setsuwa* as "explanatory tales," with the caveat that the explanatory quality can assume various valences. On the one hand, the anecdote may explain (illustrate or exemplify) didactic principle; on the other, the principle may be brought in to explain, justify, or rationalize an otherwise incredible occurrence.[13]

The canonical *setsuwa* collections were produced in the medieval period, but the genre lived on into the Tokugawa period.[14] But the implications of the term in this context grow more ambiguous, because the genre splintered further as it interacted with various emergent literary forms. On the one hand, medieval texts such as the *Collection of Tales from Uji* found a wide readership in new woodblock-print editions, becoming, like other texts of the emerging popular canon, objects of respectful emulation as well as parodic citation.[15] But more broadly and as a living genre, the paratextual form of the *setsuwa* collection—a loosely unified but eclectic and potentially contradictory collection of short narratives—was incorporated into the heterogeneous corpus of variously didactic, informational, and entertaining prose literature known as *kana-zōshi*. As Laura Moretti has shown, this body of texts exhibited a robust symbiosis of the didactic and the entertaining, as instructional frameworks, whether moral or practical, fused seamlessly with a plurality of content; that plurality sometimes spilled beyond the bounds of didacticism but did so without decisively unsettling the works' instructional aims.[16] But the role didactic frameworks played in seventeenth-century prose was neither uniform nor stable. As a broad tendency, in tandem with the general drift toward a more secular society, the didactic elements within the *kana-zōshi* either followed the rising influence of Song Confucianism as a model for popular morality, shifted to focus on matters of more practical instruction, or else faded into the background as writers and readers were drawn more to stories with pragmatic informational content or raw entertainment value.[17] At the extreme end of this trajectory was the genre of tales from the provinces (*shokoku-banashi*), which generally dispensed with any coherent moral frame in favor of a focus on the pure entertainment value of the singular anecdote. This genre was quite productive during Saikaku's active years. The author's *Saikaku's Stories from the Provinces* was published almost contemporaneously with Nishimura Ichiroemon's *Sōgi's Tales from the Provinces* (*Sōgi shokoku monogatari*, 1685), and the choice to include Saikaku's name on the cover title, singular among Saikaku's prose works, was likely driven by the demands of competition.[18] The booming popularity of such anecdotal compilations of amusing episodes from the provinces is a testament to the curiosity of urban readers for knowledge about other parts of the country—a curiosity no doubt driven by the increasingly active and robust trade and communication networks connecting the major cities to the countryside. As a product of what might be called the poetics of transportation networks, *Saikaku's Stories from the Provinces* anticipates *Eternal Storehouse*, which itself could be considered a *shokoku-banashi* style compilation of stories from all throughout the country, albeit one organized around commercial themes. But despite the general shift away from didactic principle, even into the eighteenth century, much prose narrative continued to be framed in relation to some kind of central didactic principle or message.

The question is what role didactic frameworks play in Saikaku's fiction, what his formally innovative and ideologically ambivalent style of narrative does to and with the didactic principles that its narrators often seem to profess. Nakamura Yukihiko articulates this question in terms of what he calls the *setsuwa*-esque character (*setsuwa-sei*) of Saikaku's writing. In Nakamura's interpretation, medieval Buddhist *setsuwa* treat their human characters as mere manifestations of universal principles, in relation to which humans lack any sense of individual agency. To the *setsuwa* writer, human drama is a perfect reflection of a transcendental moral order. But in Saikaku's fiction, humans become agents, and though Saikaku retains certain didactic frames, they are reoriented around the challenges of making sense of complex and contradictory human actions, as concretely manifest in vividly sketched narratives of the social world.[19] For the most part, I follow Nakamura's account, but where Nakamura stresses the distinction between Saikaku's fiction and the didacticism of the *setsuwa* tradition, my reading emphasizes their continuity. The medieval *setsuwa* had always contained a certain tension between, on the one hand, an objective and documentary attention to the fascinating and occasionally inscrutable idiosyncrasies of the human world and, on the other, a moralistic desire for narrative mastery, a desire to render the singularity of the anecdote intelligible, to domesticate the anomaly by parsing it in terms of universal and accepted moral principles. It is precisely this dialectical tension, which generally plays out in the dissonance between the didactic frame (narrative voice) and the details of the plot (narrative content), that I see as the *setsuwa*-esque element in Saikaku's writing.

In *Eternal Storehouse*, the principles in question are economic rather than moral—practical maxims concerning how to live one's life and run one's business in the pursuit of wealth—and the *setsuwa*-esque didactic form has been adapted to make sense of economic rather than karmic causality. Rather than positing economic principle as an iron law that structures narrative on a fundamental level, Saikaku's stories are structured by the *setsuwa*-esque interplay between abstract principles and observed realities, unfolding through the tension between narrating voice and narrated content. Principles are posed and set up against particular cases, tested for their validity, and new models prescribed. Most critically, this dialectical process is always incomplete because the logic of the distribution of wealth ultimately eludes final prescription or even perfect description. It is this epistemological aporia that drives the ongoing proliferation, elaboration, and movement of narrative. But just as the explanatory incompleteness of didactic principle is a feature rather than a flaw of his writing, this endlessly replenishing narrative motion still depends on the supposition of didactic principle to drive it forward. If *setsuwa*-esque narrative always involved a certain tension between didactic principle and the singular narrative episode, then Saikaku was unique in his perception and celebration of this constitutive tension.

In *Eternal Storehouse*, the *setsuwa*-esque tension gives rise to a narrative structure defined by three tendencies. First is what some Saikaku scholars have referred to as an "omnibus" narrative form: a tendency to compile a series of thematically or topically related anecdotes into a single, loosely woven narrative that lacks a clear central plot. Second is a tendency to subject these disparate threads to a didactic narratorial consciousness that probes them, often through explicit juxtaposition, to abstract and interpret how they reflect on the central thematic concern—here, the economic logic behind the distribution of wealth and the practical ethos necessary to harness it for individual gain. Third, through that juxtaposition, is a tendency to recursively foreground, at the diegetic level, parallel acts of didactic narration and interpretation: lectures by aged millionaires, exchanges of stories by merchants in the marketplace, shop hands comparing notes, all of whom make different claims concerning the economic logic that separates the rich from the poor and good business from bad. Relativized by the nested interplay of narrating voices, interpretation is never final and often contradictory, but the imperative to interpret is never extinguished.

For example, consider "Gentle Trade Winds for the Good Ship Jinzū" (*Namikaze shizuka ni Jinzū-maru*, vol. 1–3).[20] The story centers on the bustling Kitahama rice market in Osaka and claims to illuminate the reasons why the rich are rich, why the poor are poor, and how the latter might manage to assume the place of the former. It does so by using a series of loosely linked subnarratives, framed by the narrator's didactic musings. The story begins with an auspicious anecdote of a certain Karakaneya who builds a massive ship (the titular Good Ship Jinzū) to become a wealthy shipping magnate; the narrator then surveys the lifestyles and personal backgrounds of the wealthy brokers of the rice market, then enters into a discourse on the fates of clerks and apprentices to merchant houses, and concludes with an anecdote of how the son of an impoverished sweeper woman is able, through some combination of thrift, wit, and fortune, to rise to the heights of Osaka merchant society. What unifies these disparate threads is the narrator's concern with economic causality, the question of what determines an individual's economic fortunes. The story is structured and driven by an unfolding tension between a didactic voice based on the assertion of rational principle and narrative content that resists totalizing explanation.

The story opens with a rhetorical question that frames the economic fates of men as a matter of karma: "The many *daimyō*—what karmic seeds must they have sown in their previous lives?" (*sho daimyō ni wa, ika naru tane o, zenjō ni makitamaeru koto ni zo arikeru*). But the narrator's concern is not with the *daimyō* so much as with the elite strata of the merchant class, and not with moral karma in a Buddhist sense but with economic principles of effort and reward. After discussing Karakaneya's ship, the narrator concludes that "verily his house came over time to flourish because he was fastidious in all his dealings" (*shidai ni ie sakaekeru wa, shoji ni tsukite, sono mi chōgi no yoki yue zokashi*)—that the success of an individual household is the product of individual comportment. As the narrator's attention shifts to the elite brokers of Kitahama, it remains focused on revealing the logic and history behind the accumulation of wealth: that many of the current elite were born as peasants, adopted as clerks and apprentices, and eventually made their way into great wealth. But this is not to say that all apprentices meet with such success, because some are too irresponsible, are dismissed or disowned, and end up peddling goods on the street: "Verily one becomes even a millionaire by virtue of one's own mettle!" (*onore ga shōne ni yotte, chōja ni mo naru koto zokashi*). But not just mettle. The narrator goes on to reflect on how much one's fortune depends on one's master. An apprentice to a humble craftsman will rarely exceed his master in wealth, but might become a great merchant if apprenticed elsewhere.

As if to sidestep this contingency, the final anecdote is of an entrepreneur who forgoes apprenticeship altogether, pulling himself up by his proverbial bootstraps through a series of opportunistic pivots from one opportunity to the next, mobilizing resources dynamically and on the fly to realize ever greater profits. The trajectory from rags to riches begins with an impoverished widow and single mother who makes a living sweeping up spilled rice at the rice market. One year, amid an economic boom prompted both by shogunal policy and good harvests, the market is overflowing with rice, which she "sweeps up along with piles of dust," and, even after subtracting her daily meals, is able to amass a small surplus. Realizing the opportunity before her, she scrimps for a year and ends up with a store of seven and a half bales, which she sells in secret (waste rice could not be sold legally), and within twenty years has collected a modest capital fund. The woman's son inherits the widow's bent for moneymaking. When he comes of age, he establishes a moneylending shop making short-term loans to travelers and recent migrants from the countryside and within ten years has become one of Osaka's premier financiers. After the man's meteoric ascent to the upper rungs of the Osaka financial world, the narrator remarks that some among his peers might occasionally investigate his background (wondering, like the narrator the beginning of the story, what karmic seeds and past lives gave rise to his fortune) and scoff to learn that he is the son of an outcast. But the same people, in a pinch, will swallow their pride and come to beg him for a loan. At this point, the question of economic causality is moot, as what matters is simply who has the money: "Such, verily, is the authority of wealth!" (*kingin no isei zokashi*). Meanwhile, the entrepreneurial son venerates his late mother's rice-broom as a house treasure and a private document of the provenance of his wealth. The story thus shifts from a discourse on economic causality to a reflexive study of whether, when, and how such causality may be narrated—to the question of who has authority over its narration.

Throughout the story, Saikaku's narrator applies, supposes, and extracts a series of didactic principles in an attempt to explain why the rich of Kitahama are as rich as they are. But these principles are posed hypothetically, or else in retrospect—individual cases are accounted for, but exceptions proliferate, and a totalizing answer is not forthcoming. Not that this incompleteness poses a problem for Saikaku or his narrator. Saikaku was a writer who delighted in the unpredictable development of narrative in new and, indeed, contradictory directions. But just as the explanatory incompleteness of didactic principle is a feature rather than a flaw of his writing, this endlessly replenishing narrative motion still depends on the constant supposition of didactic principle to drive it forward. The story is thus structured by a productive tension between didactic (economic) principle and the singularity of the anecdote, which simultaneously demands and resists rational explanation.

One of the most compelling attempts to account for this idiosyncratic narrative form is Hirosue Tamotsu's "space of the collection" ("shū" no kūkan). Hirosue's term alludes to the paratextual form of the collection of short narratives, nominally unified by theme but in practice comprising a diversity of narrative content that resists reduction to a single frame or worldview, that originated in the medieval *setsuwa* collection and was inherited by the *kana-zōshi*. In Hirosue's reading, Saikaku's fiction realizes the symbolic potential within the paratextual form of the collection and manifests it at the level of narrative form on a story-by-story basis: in the form of diffuse narratives with more lateral than forward motion, shaped by often random or unexpected encounters that occasion radical shifts in perspective and even voice. Saikaku's stories thus resist both narrative and ideological closure, as each perspective is relativized, in turn, by the possibility (even if left unrealized) of further twists and inversions.[21] But as I suggest in the introduction to this book, Hirosue perhaps overemphasizes the anarchic nature of Saikaku's narrative practice. Despite using the paratextual collection as a figure for an ideologically and narratively open-ended textual space, Hirosue ultimately traces Saikaku's ideological ambivalence not to the existing tradition of prose fiction, but to the ever-shifting vision of linked-verse poetics: His interest is in *haikai*-esque linkages as a kind of centrifugal force that perpetually rebels against thematic unity. Although this is certainly a tendency in Saikaku's work, I suggest that the *setsuwa*-esque quality of a text like *Eternal Storehouse* constitutes an equally assertive centripetal force that persistently demands and seeks a minimum of coherence and unity in the face of this perspectival fragmentation and ideological diffusion.

The balance of these forces suggests an understanding of the space of the collection that is both more concrete and more ambivalent than Hirosue's formulation. In my reading, this is a *setsuwa*-esque space: Its didactic claims are not residual traces of an official ideology that Saikaku cites ironically in order to decenter it but instead constitutive elements that give the text narrative direction through the always incomplete imperative to interpret. As in "Gentle Trade Winds for the Good Ship *Jinzū*," Saikaku's shifting vision tends to spill out of or otherwise reconfigure the posited didactic principles, but this is counterbalanced by a narrative voice that continues to attempt to make economic sense of a complex, fragmented, unstable, and even contradictory series of events and perspectives. The *setsuwa*-esque space of the collection functions to contain such complexities and contradictions, transforming them into complications, exceptions, nuances, and details that enrich and exemplify and explore but never fully dislodge the orienting frame. Despite the complications, the narrative posits an underlying logic, albeit one that always remains at least partially obscure.

APHORISTIC RATIONALISM

In representing the underlying logics of economic causality that supposedly underwrote the distribution of worldly wealth, *Eternal Storehouse* borrowed its didactic language from a small but robust tradition of get-rich guides: instructional tracts focused on the accumulation of material wealth. Such works had been a minor but perennially popular genre since the dawn of the Tokugawa period. The archetype was *The Millionaires' Teachings* (*Chōjakyō*): a short treatise consisting of a short dialog on the importance of thrift and personal discipline, followed by various aphorisms and mnemonics on the same themes. *The Millionaires' Teachings* seems to have circulated in manuscript form as early as the turn of the seventeenth century, and, following the rise of commercial woodblock printing around the 1630s, saw multiple reprintings throughout the century.²² The theme of monetary accumulation would be taken up occasionally in other eclectic works such as *Foolish Tales* (*Iguchi monogatari*, 1662), *Mirror for Posterity* (*Shison kagami*, 1673), and *Tales of Recent Millionaires* (*Ima chōja monogatari*, 1675). Saikaku was not subtle in announcing his debts to this didactic tradition. *Eternal Storehouse* carried the subtitle of *Daifuku shin chōjakyō*, an overwrought portmanteau combining *daifuku chōja* (wealthy man of great fortune) and *shin chōjakyō* (new millionaires' teachings), and thus positioned itself as a modern update to what was by Saikaku's time a popular classic. Moreover, Saikaku's publisher, the Osaka bookseller Morita Shōtarō, had in the previous year released his own get-rich guide, a text called *The Elixir of Wealth* (*Kingin mannōgan*), and clearly envisioned *Eternal Storehouse* as the next volley in an expanding line of didactic texts that would appeal to the commercial ambitions of new generations of urban entrepreneurs.²³

Such texts generally preach a simple gospel of steady, incremental material accumulation through hard work, thrift, other platitudes of personal austerity, and the power of compound interest through careful lending. Their didactic thrust, which ultimately boils down to a two-note ethos of thrift (*shimatsu*) and diligence at one's house trade (*kashoku* or *kagyō*), likely had little practical value for the aspiring entrepreneur with neither trade nor capital: They have plenty of advice concerning how not to waste money but very little to say about how to make it. As cultural historian Fujiwara Noboru has observed, the model of thrift and incremental effort as the basis for material accumulation seems to reflect the roots of the genre in the agricultural economy of the late medieval period.²⁴ The guides do little to illuminate the workings of the marketplace, nor do they meaningfully distinguish between the livelihood of the merchant and other forms of (agricultural or craft) labor. Entrepreneurship as such falls outside their purview: They have little advice on how to choose or build a trade or how to find a new market. Laura Moretti has made the provocative observation that these texts did little to empower readers for commercial success but much to explain the difficulty of mobility and thus ultimately to rationalize the unequal distribution of wealth: "Their efficacy was in declaring the sway of money, portraying the complexities of moneymaking, and eventually justifying the status quo in which rich and poor coexist."²⁵ Many of these texts begin by appealing to the reader with the optimistic suggestion that material wealth is not only achievable in this life but indeed imminent with effort, but they ultimately revert to encouraging the reader to accept their position in life as a matter of fate and commit to working hard to make an honest and morally upright living.

Eternal Storehouse is indebted to this didactic tradition but also innovates on it. For one, Saikaku's text shifts emphasis away from familiar principles of hard work and thrift and toward intellectual virtues of cleverness (*rihatsu*), judgment (*funbetsu*), wisdom (*chie*), and of course wit (*saikaku*). It is through the astute application of the intellect in perceiving opportunity that the poor but clever individual is able to extract value where it did not exist (or was not perceived) before. This shift—from an ethos of thrift and incremental effort to one of entrepreneurial creativity—was in part a reflection of the rise of new generations of merchants operating outside frameworks of hereditary privilege and shogunal patronage, but more broadly a reflection of the steady integration of the agricultural economy and its modes of accumulation with an emerging market economy based on interregional trade, high-interest lending, speculative investing, and the development of new consumer markets.[26] However, this is not to say that entrepreneurial virtues such as wit displace the principles of thrift and hard work proposed in the existing tradition of entrepreneurial literature. Instead, wit becomes one central element within a loosely defined collection of lifestyle principles proposed to enable the accumulation of worldly wealth. Saikaku took more from the tradition of entrepreneurial literature than its conceptual content, however. He also borrowed a certain rhetorical form, manifest in textual structures and styles of language. What is striking on reading the works of this genre is less their explanatory failures than the remarkable degree to which, much like *Eternal Storehouse*, they are able to sustain the pretense and, indeed, the appearance of explanatory efficacy—how they are able to contain the incompleteness of their didactic claims.

For example, consider *The Millionaires' Teachings*. This short treatise is eminently prosaic in content, endorsing a simple ethos of thrift and steady effort. It begins as an anonymous but "intelligent lad" visits three famed millionaires to ask for their instruction on the path to wealth. The three millionaires then hold forth on the principles of capital accumulation, most of which (perhaps unsurprisingly) boil down to thrift and hard work, combined with shrewd lending, but are evoked through memorable metaphors and mnemonics. "One begets two, and two begets three; dust piles up and becomes a mountain.... When climbing a ladder, you take one step at a time; if you aim to go more quickly and take two at once, you will fall."[27] The comments of the three millionaires give way to a series of lists, evolving from a simple enumeration of virtues to more substantive aphorisms:

> Principles to practice at all times:
>
> 1. To use judgment.
> 2. To be upright.
> 3. To be patient.
> 4. To regard every man as a thief and every fire as a conflagration.
> 5. To restrain one's emotions and follow advice.
> 6. That regret is without benefit.
> 7. That conceit is to be despised.
> 8. That small talk is useless.
> 9. That restraint is only half a virtue.
> 10. That one need not be intimate with all men. However, one should make close acquaintance with the great and the virtuous alike. The skilled socialite knows to act like a chicken—not too distant nor too close.[28]

The remainder of the text consists of several series of didactic verses in *tanka* form on topics such as "things to study," "reliable people," "useless things," and "cautionary verses"; a list of the names of "the ten sons of the god of fortune" and the "ten sons of the god of poverty" (all mnemonic devices evoking various virtues and vices); and so on. The treatise closes with an unsuccessful interjection by the god of poverty, who makes a spirited case for living a humble but happy life, but whose advice is soundly mocked by the three millionaires as sour grapes.

Even at a mere eighteen short leaves, *The Millionaires' Teachings* strikes the reader as plodding and repetitive, and indeed the path to wealth that it prescribes is one of plodding and repetition. But despite this prosaic content, this text retains traces of an ideological complexity and dynamism that transcends its seemingly one-dimensional ethos—a complexity that manifests not in didactic content but in form, in a style of language. Here the language of material accumulation takes the form of the aphorism: the handy, quotable, eminently memorable turn of phrase that encapsulates an unquestioned truth akin to folk wisdom. Citation of the aphorism brings not the flash of new insight, but the confirmation of an already known truth; its virtue is not to be original but to be pithy. The aphorism communicates by its rhetorical force, not without a hint of mystery (there must be some deeper truth behind this), rather than by the content of its claims. The effective aphorism is memorable and thus overlaps with the mnemonic; the doggerel *tanka* verses that appear throughout the entrepreneurial manuals are a testament to this.

In a recent study of the aphorism as a rhetorical form, Andrew Hui explores the historical tension between philosophy and the aphorism, juxtaposing the systematicity of the former with the fragmentary quality of the latter. But, he stresses, the aphorism itself is not a rejection of systematic thought, as it always exists in relation to a larger project of understanding; instead, it oscillates between fragment and system, pointing toward the incompleteness of the system and the need for semiotic supplementation to complete or transcend it. "Though an aphorism is by definition succinct, it almost always proliferates into an innumerable series of iterations," including those that precisely oppose it.[29] The aphorism is thus also a paradoxical form, seeming to affirm and delimit a basic and finite truth while also containing, by virtue of its fragmentary nature, the possibility of an infinite plurality of further possibilities and interpretations. The idiosyncrasy of this rhetorical form, and its functioning in *Chōjakyō* and beyond, is illuminated by contrast with another short genre, what Gary Saul Morson refers to as the "dictum": the equally pithy, memorable turn of phrase that means what it says, no more and no less. His example, from Marx and Engels, is: "The history of all hitherto existing society is the history of class struggles." To Morson, the dictum is a figure of totality, certainty, and clarity, one that accommodates neither objection nor exception.[30] Some of this resonates with a text such as *The Millionaires' Teachings*, which after all is making simple, universal, and quite lucid (if unconvincing) claims about how to achieve wealth. But what is most distinctive about this text's rhetorical style is its never-quite-completeness. It is here that I am drawn to Hui's treatment of the aphorism, which seems self-contained but still, by its fragmentary form, holds an endless potential for supplementation and inversion.

The aphoristic quality of seventeenth-century entrepreneurial discourse becomes clear when we consider its medieval prehistory. Noma Kōshin places *The Millionaires' Teachings* in a textual genealogy, focusing on didactic instruction on the path to wealth but equally shaped by medieval Buddhist thought, that dates back at least as far as Yoshida no Kenkō's *Essays in Idleness* (*Tsurezuregusa*, ca. 1330).[31] Although that work's historical context and ideological content differ greatly from those of *The Millionaires' Teachings* and *Eternal Storehouse*, Kenkō's famously aphoristic collection sheds useful light on the stylistic and ideological issues at play in these later texts. In the 217th *dan*, a wealthy man holds forth on the path to wealth, followed by Kenkō's sardonic commentary.

> A certain wealthy man of great fortune once said, "A man should set all else aside and devote himself single-mindedly to acquiring a fortune. Life is not worth living when one is poor, and only the rich man may truly be called a man. If you would like to make a fortune, the first thing you must do is to cultivate the proper frame of mind, which is precisely this: the abiding conviction that human life is eternal. You must never, even for a moment, reflect on its impermanence. This is the first caution. Next, you must refrain from satisfying all of your needs. In this world there are innumerable desires, arising from both within and without. If you should aspire to satisfy those desires, even one with a million coppers will soon find himself penniless. Desire is unending but fortune finite; it is impossible to follow unlimited desires with limited means. If desires should sprout in your heart, you must fear them as evil thoughts come to destroy you, and restrain them firmly. Do not gratify even small wants. Next, if you treat your money as a servant, you will never escape poverty for long. You must fear it and bow before it as if it were a master or even a god, and never once use it for your own ends. Next, you must never become angry or resentful, even when faced with humiliation. Next, you must be upright and honor your promises. Any man who abides by these principles as he seeks after profit will find that riches come to him like a fire spreading through dried brush or water flowing downstream. Once he has gathered an inexhaustible store of wealth, he will find that, though he gives no thought to carousing or carnal pleasure, and though his dwelling remains humble, and though his desires remain unfulfilled, his spirit is eternally at peace and full of delight." Thus spoke the wealthy man.
>
> But one seeks wealth to fulfill one's desires, and money is precious precisely as a means to obtain what one wants. If a man has desires but does

not satisfy them, has money but does not put it to use, he is no different from a poor man. What pleasure could he possibly take from this? The millionaire's prescriptions seem to suggest that man should abandon worldly desire and not lament poverty. But it is better not to have money at all than to take pleasure simply in gratifying a lust for wealth. One suffering from boils, rather than taking pleasure in washing them, would be better off being cured of the affliction. At this point, there is no difference between poverty and wealth: transcendence is the same as delusion, and the man with great desires resembles one absent of all desire.[32]

In Kenkō's reflection, the wealthy man's thesis of materialist accumulation and radical austerity is ultimately denied in favor of an antithesis of enlightened poverty. This is at least in part a consequence of Kenkō's embrace of a Buddhist ideal of impermanence, which throughout *Essays in Idleness* is aestheticized as a topos of sublime beauty. Kenkō's idiosyncratic work, in which a posture of Buddhist detachment blends and intersects with a humanistic appreciation for the diversity of the contemporary urban world, met with an enthusiastic reception in the seventeenth century, when it saw multiple printings and garnered many commentaries, becoming one of the most popular of the classical Heian texts.[33] Saikaku, whose grasp of the classical canon was so notoriously spotty that he was occasionally derided as illiterate, drew especially strong influences from Kenkō, who likely shaped his humanistic embrace of ideological flexibility and his sensibility of erotic refinement and urbane detachment. Perhaps unexpectedly, one of the works to show the most frequent and concrete references to Kenkō's text is *Eternal Storehouse*.[34] My point, however, is not to stress the direct impact of Kenkō's work on Saikaku's writing; instead, I wish to draw attention to the ways in which Kenkō's ideological multivalence was also retained in *Chōjakyō* and, indeed, woven into the very rhetoric of material accumulation.

In *The Millionaires' Teachings*, Kenkō's rebuttal to the wealthy man is echoed by the god of poverty, who interrupts the three millionaires to interject that even among the rich are those who are so miserly that they live as if in poverty, and that even among the poor are those who enjoy life as if they were rich. He concludes his case with a concise set of three aphorisms explaining why being poor is easier than being rich: "Those without treasures need not fear thieves, those without houses need not fear fires, and those without riches need not care for the rising and falling of prices."[35] The god of poverty concludes his tirade with a smug look on his face, but his words are disregarded as "a crone passing as a sage or a beggar who says he's fasting" (*akujo no kenjaburi, mata wa kotsujiki no danjiki*)—an aphoristic expression as good as any other—and the text concludes with a reiteration of the supreme value of money. This is not to say that the god of poverty has been proven wrong, only that his objections have been contained: acknowledged, set aside, and thus diffused. In contrast to the wealthy man in *Essays in Idleness*, the materialist millionaires in *The Millionaires' Teachings* have the last laugh, and the language has shifted far in the direction of a prosaic kind of rationalism. But this rationalism has absorbed the form and the rhetorical force of aphoristic language. The narrator concludes by imploring the reader to "reflect carefully on the precious sayings of these three men"—their "precious sayings" (*kingen*), or perhaps their aphorisms; we are thus invited to believe that, despite the work's prosaic content, it contains nuggets of hidden wisdom to be revealed by deep reflection.

To describe this style of thought, the worldview given form by the aphoristic and always incomplete enumeration of didactic principles, I propose the term *aphoristic rationalism*. Rationalism in that, like Morson's dictum, it seeks to explain a particular situation (the distribution of wealth) as a case of a finite set of stable, predictable, and rational principles: work hard, wake up early, avoid legal entanglements and unnecessary social obligations, reject luxury and limit personal consumption, be fastidious about details of household management, cultivate physical well-being, and so on. But aphoristic in that each principle—indeed, any finite set of such principles—is never quite enough to explain, once and for all and without exception, the secret to achieving material wealth. Each principle seems true enough in itself—each evokes the feeling of a deeper truth hiding behind its pithy expression—and yet also lacking, not quite enough to account for the situation it attempts to explain. Charged with both a surplus and a deficit of meaning, it gives way to rearticulation, permutation, even inversion. In this regard, *The Millionaires' Teachings* is truly an exemplary text: not one millionaire but three, each picking up on the discourse of the previous one to expound from a new direction; followed by a series of lists of principles, maxims, and mnemonics that all seem simultaneously repetitive and incomplete; and leading up to symbolic inversion in the voice of the god of poverty—the exception that (so goes the old saw) proves the rule.

CONTAINING CONTINGENCY

In *Eternal Storehouse*, the language of aphoristic rationalism blends with the framework of *setsuwa*-esque didacticism to create a narrative form capable of accounting for and making sense of the complexities and contradictions of the urban economy. The basic structure is as follows. A story of commercial success or failure is framed by certain didactic principles. In *setsuwa*-esque fashion, the story that unfolds often seems to have a complexity that resists reduction to those principles, and when that surplus of complexity grows too great, the narrator (or a character) interjects an aphoristic response, bringing in new principles to account for it; but this accounting is never complete, and the story moves forward in new directions that require new forms of accounting. Generally speaking, this open-ended play of didactic signifiers moves toward a grappling with moments of raw economic contingency, what Saikaku sometimes glosses as "fortune" (*shiawase*)—literally, circumstances transpiring (*shi-*) into one another (*awase*) or "coming together" fortuitously. But despite the presence of traces of raw contingency that resist didactic reckoning (which after all may only be apparent to the careful reader), the story concludes with an affirmation of the efficacy of didactic principle. Despite its complexity and contradictory nature, *Eternal Storehouse* invites reading—has been understood historically by generations of readers and scholars—as ultimately a didactic text. Rather than suggesting that such a reading is incorrect or lacking in nuance, I contend that Saikaku's accomplishment was precisely in creating a form of didactic narrative that is all the more powerful and robust because it can acknowledge and accommodate its limitations and contradictions without requiring their resolution.

Throughout *Eternal Storehouse*, Saikaku's narrators remark frequently on the contingencies of fortune. As Saikaku writes in "A Burial Mound for Debts on Mount Kōya" (*Kōya-san shakusen-zuka no seshu*, vol. 3–4), "It is difficult to become wealthy unless wit is aided by fortune! Some very clever men are poor, and fools rich. . . . one may writhe like a centipede but nevertheless remain insolvent, nothing to be done about it."[36] Both intelligence and effort are subordinate to fortune. The surest path to wealth and safest shortcut past the whims of fate, Saikaku frequently reminds his readers, is to already have money. "A Clockmaker's Hands Move Slowly" (*Mawari-dōki wa tokei-zaikaku*, vol. 5–1) concludes with a scene of three clerks—one from

Edo, one from Osaka, one from Kyoto—gathered in Nagasaki, trading stories of their respective houses to while away the time on a rainy day, but "not a single one of them had grown to be a millionaire from nothing" (*sono tane nakute chōja ni nareru wa, hitori mo nakariki*). After each relates the provenance of his master's fortune, the narrator concludes that "the starting point for great wealth is usually out of reach" (*daibungen no hajime, tsune nite wa oyobi-gatashi*) and that "the circumstances of each were terribly different from the last" (*mina hito shisai zutsu, kakubetsu no kawari ari*).[37] In other words, not only is the path to wealth out of reach for those without capital to begin with, but the question of how to acquire capital in the first place is a matter of such contingency that it can hardly be reduced to rational principle. By the same token, money tends to accumulate in the hands of those who already have it: "These days money makes money, so one can hardly get by slacking off" (*ima wa kane ga kane o mōkuru jisetsu nareba, nakanaka yudan shite tosei wa narigatashi*).[38] But now we are back to square one. Despite the supremacy of wit over effort, of good fortune over wit, and of prior wealth over good fortune, one still has no choice but to work hard to try to grasp some tiny fund that might grow into something larger, with some combination of all of these.

Such apparent contradictions have led some scholars to speculate that Saikaku's grasp of the market economy shifted as he composed the work, resulting in a subtle transformation in his deployment of the didactic form. Teruoka Yasutaka observed that the last two volumes of the work tend to be simultaneously more fatalistic, reckoning pessimistically with the decisive influence of fortune over the economic fates of men, as well as more blunt in their didacticism. In Teruoka's reading, this shift was a product of the author's dawning awareness of the deepening stratification of townsman society and his increasing pessimism over the possibility of entrepreneurial success through individual effort; the didactic voice rings hollow, endlessly reiterated as if to compensate for its failures.[39] Teruoka's reading was ultimately a speculative one, rooted in his imaginative reconstruction of Saikaku's authorial consciousness and the evolution thereof, but it was supported by evidence of a range of paratextual and orthographic discrepancies between the first four volumes and the last two, suggesting the possibility of multiple manuscripts representing different stages of composition, and by some documentary evidence that a manuscript of the text may have been circulating in some form in the years before its commercial publication.[40] To this day, much scholarship on this text has focused on the question of the order of textual composition (*seiritsu*), but the interpretations offered vary widely; in the absence of any empirical evidence concerning supposed manuscripts, the debate remains inconclusive, speculative, and to a large degree interpretive, reflecting how individual scholars choose to navigate the text's apparent contradictions.[41] Despite the evidence of a subtle shift in didactic voice between the first four volumes and the last two, both fragments remain well within the parameters of the space of the collection and its capacity to integrate seemingly contradictory threads into a heterogeneous whole. What is most significant about the text is that the tension between the didactic voice and the recognition of fate runs, in different forms, through all of its stories—to the degree that the nature and significance of any possible shift in compositional consciousness remain open to debate. In my view, the unanswerable question of authorial consciousness is less illuminating than that of textual structure: What strategies do Saikaku's narratives use to make sense of the *setsuwa*-esque tension at the heart of the text?

For example, let us briefly revisit "Medicine Prepared in Abnormal Fashion," the story of Hashiya Jinbei, treated in detail in chapter 2. The story begins with a precise citation of the narrative scene of *The Millionaires' Teachings*: an anonymous, aspiring entrepreneur asking a wealthy man for advice. The millionaire responds with an exhaustive exposition of didactic principles, dressed up memorably in the mnemonic form of a medicinal recipe:

* Early rising: five parts * House trade: twenty parts * Midnight oil: eight parts * Economy: ten parts * Good health: seven parts

Grind these components to a fine dust, and follow the instructions precisely with great care not to err in calculation of quantities. If you ingest this morning and night, you will become rich without fail. However, it is of great importance that you abstain from the following poisons!

* Rich foods, sexual dissipation, and silken garments worn casually * Private palanquins for wives, *koto* and poem-card lessons for daughters * Percussion lessons for sons * Kickball, archery, incense, and linked verse * Parlor renovations and fondness for tea * Flower-viewing, boating excursions, and daytime bathing * Nighttime outings, gambling, and board games * Martial arts among townsmen * Religious pilgrimage and thoughts of the next life * Mediating in others' troubles * Lawsuits over reclaimed fields,

speculation in mines * Drink with meals, tobacco, and unwarranted trips to the capital * Backing and organizing sumo matches for charity * Schemes outside one's house trade and fancy sword accessories * Socializing with actors and spending time in brothels * Borrowing at a monthly rate of more than eight to the thousand.[42]

The protagonist seems to accept this advice, but throughout the tale remains skeptical, observing the urban world to draw his own conclusions. His appropriative vision overlaps with the *setsuwa*-esque imperative to interpret the obscure logics of economic causality, which he perceives to be operating just below the surface of the urban text. As he watches the ebb and flow of traffic over Nihonbashi, frustrated that nobody would drop even a single copper, the narrator concludes, "Reflecting upon this, [money] is not something that should be spent lightly" (*kore o omou ni, ada ni tsukau beki mono ni wa arazu*). But a few lines later, almost as if proposing an antithesis to the imperative of thrift, we are given the aphoristic aside that "without planting a few seeds, you can't grow a single cent, let alone a gold coin" (*tane makazu shite, koban mo ichibu mo haeru tameshi nashi*); in other words, thrift and diligence may well be meaningless if one lacks a fund of capital to begin with. After Jinbei has made his fortune—first collecting and selling waste scraps of wood, and eventually becoming a lumber merchant—the *setsuwa*-esque climax to the story occurs as Jinbei narrates his success, asserting (despite all evidence to the contrary) that "All this was truly a testament to the millionaire pills he had taken in his younger days."

As I argue in chapter 2, this story exemplifies the tactical logic of opportunistic appropriation through wit, which here seems to displace the moralistic ethos of thrift and hard work conveyed in the millionaire's citation of *The Millionaires' Teachings*. In light of the flexibility of the form of economic rhetoric I have called aphoristic rationalism, perhaps it is more accurate to say that Saikaku integrates this vision of wit with the existing matrix of entrepreneurial lifestyle principles and practices: The retrospective narrating gesture suggests that, without fussing about the details, one can basically get rich by following some of these principles. But more important, Saikaku acknowledges that even the ephemeral cognition of wit ultimately still depends on the whims of fortune to present opportunities for it to apprehend—and the historicity of such opportunities is easy to glimpse in the ellipses and allusions of Saikaku's stories. As noted in chapter 2, the historical inspiration for Saikaku's character was likely the lumber magnate Kamakuraya Jinbei, of Zaimoku-chō, who had served as an appointed lumber supplier for the shogunate in the mid-seventeenth century; Hashiya Jinbei's entrepreneurial success in collecting wood scraps makes sense against a background of extensive construction, as of Edo in the first half of the seventeenth century and in the wake of the Great Meireki Fire (1657). This is precisely the historical contingency glossed as fortune. Through such contingencies, Saikaku's stories set didactic principle in relation to economic history, or rather economic historicity: the raw happenstance, just beyond the optimistic but only approximate premises of didactic principle, that underlies the distribution of wealth. The unfolding tension between the form of didactic narration and the content of economic contingency reveals the ways in which aphoristic rationalism acts as a compensatory mechanism, never totally capable of accounting for what it attempts to explain and thus always driven to further attempts. Despite this, "Medicine Prepared in Abnormal Fashion" has for the most part been read as among Saikaku's most frankly didactic stories, one that most directly manifests the imperatives of earlier get-rich guides. The question is not whether this assertion is right or wrong, but how Saikaku (or his protagonist) is able to contain such a complex and contingent story within a set of straightforward didactic principles without collapsing into self-evident contradiction—how a complex story built on the historical contingency of opportunity is transformed into a signifier of didactic principle.

How should we make sense of this tension between the complex contingencies of historical fact and the didactic principles that such contingencies are adapted and restructured to serve? To understand the necessary but subordinate role played by history in this text, I take inspiration from Roland Barthes's theorization of myth. In *Mythologies*, Barthes identifies myth as a particular type of sign and a particular type of image: the sign that not only charges the image with ideological meaning, but, more important, renders that meaning natural and self-evident—as though the image could never signify anything else. To be effective as myth—to not appear simply as an ideological caricature—the mythic image must possess a certain richness and complexity. Myth depends on history to furnish such richness but likewise impoverishes that history, for only by obscuring the complexity and contingency underlying the image and its production—by obscuring its historicity—can the mythic image become an exemplary token, a signifier of values that thereby have been naturalized and rendered unquestionable. The operation of myth is to tame the complexity of the image, evacuating it of its history in order to fill it with meaning that thus appears self-evident.[43] By such a formulation, the story of Hashiya Jinbei, functioning as myth, depends parasitically on the example of Kamakuraya Jinbei and the complex network of historical conditions that enabled his economic rise, to furnish it with a richness and specificity that, paradoxically, makes the ultimate meaning of the story—the efficacy of hard work, thrift, and some amount of wit—all the more convincing. The function of the narrative is not so much to observe from history that diligent effort is rewarded as it is to forcefully subject the contingencies of history to the demands of didactic (mythic) meaning. The historic success of Kamakuraya Jinbei, despite and through its complexity, becomes (like that of the Mitsui house, discussed in chapter 1) an exemplary myth of merchant entrepreneurialism. As Barthes notes, "Myths tend toward proverbs," for the proverb is the genre par excellence of self-affirming common sense.

In some stories, however, the contingency of fortune proves more difficult to contain. At some moments, the failures of economic rationality and entrepreneurial principle become undeniable; didacticism palpably collapses and raw contingency comes into view. The most striking example is "A Winter Thunderbolt Brings Injury" (*Kega no fuyu-gaminari*, vol. 2–2), which tells the story of a poor soy-sauce dealer in Ōtsu named Kiheiji.[44] Kiheiji is introduced as a thoughtful but unsuccessful street peddler who has learned to accept his station in life, working diligently and living happily day by day. Despite laboring tirelessly on his daily rounds, despite having an intelligent and industrious wife, and despite not envying (and thus attempting to emulate) those of richer station, he is still never able to pass the new year with more than a pittance in savings. Still, as someone who has accepted his lot happily, he celebrates his fortune in at least passing each year without falling into debt—until one year, when on the twenty-ninth day of the last month, lightning strikes his abode, shattering the family cooking pot into tiny pieces. Because this is one of the few material possessions that even the poorest family cannot do without for even a day, he is at last forced into debt to fund a replacement.

Kiheiji's story seems to contradict the didactic premises of *Eternal Storehouse* by showing a character for whom hard work and diligence have failed to lead to material success. But more than a reflection on the possibilities or

FROM TOWNSMAN CULTURE TO TOWNSMAN NARRATIVE

limitations of a particular set of values, Kiheiji's story is a strikingly subtle study of the capacity of Saikaku's narrative form to contain the failures of didactic principle. The episode opens, "Even if it were to sink amid the gentle waves of Lake Ōmi, a one-*masu* pot is what it is" (*sazanami ya Ōmi no mizuumi ni shizumete mo, hito-masu iru tsubo wa sono tōri nari*), a poetic variation on the standard aphorism "A one-*masu* pot is one-*masu*" (*hito-masu tsubo wa hito-masu*). In other words, everyone has their proper station; some things never change no matter how you might try. The pot, of course, is Kiheiji. Surrounded by the bustling commerce and material opulence of what was emerging as a thriving trading post, the humble but reflective Kiheiji stops amid his itinerant rounds, sets down his goods, and reflects on his lot:

> "Nothing in the world shows such heights and depths as the fortunes of men," he thought, setting his load down and reflecting on the sad nature of existence. "As I make my rounds, I see joy and sadness, wealth and poverty, but none of it is as one would expect. The wise often wear paper rags, and fools adorn themselves in fine silks. I suppose that there's more to good fortune than good judgment. But if you don't put yourself to work, money won't just fall from heaven or bubble up out of the ground—not even a single copper. Then again, just doing an honest job won't get you anywhere, but you still have to find a business suited to your station and not slack at it." Thinking this, he lived happily day by day.[45]

Kiheiji's soliloquy is a striking attempt to understand economic causality using the language of aphoristic rationalism. Trying to explain and to infer based on his lived observation of the social world, he cycles through one maxim after another—"The wise often wear paper rags, and fools adorn themselves in fine silks," "If you don't put yourself to work, money won't just fall from heaven," "You still have to find a business suited to your station"—in a kind of semiotic supplementation, each aphorism appended to compensate for the explanatory deficiency of the last. The ultimate logic of economic causality and the distribution of wealth—why "nothing in the world shows such heights and depths as the fortunes of men" (*shindai hodo kōge no aru mono wa nashi*)—eludes him, as it does the reader. Of course it does: This is the horizon beyond which the aphoristic-rationalist consciousness will never reach, the irreducible surplus of historical contingency that drives its attempts to explain but always eludes explanation. Nevertheless, and even though his "reflecting on the sad nature of existence" (*mujō o kanjikeru*) evokes a pessimistic and Buddhistic reckoning with impermanence, Kiheiji is able to satisfy himself and "live happily day by day" (*ichinichi-gurashi o tanoshimikeru*).

Following this moment of inconclusive reflection, the story proceeds as a series of short anecdotes, framed as the observations of Kiheiji as he makes his rounds. Here the omnibus structure of the space of the collection, reproduced in microcosm through Kiheiji's perspective, overlaps with the diverse and stratified urban community. Each resident of Ōtsu becomes the protagonist of a short narrative, part of a collection centered on *setsuwa*-esque inquiry into the logic of economic causality in this particular setting. Throughout his perambulations, the narrator's focalization through Kiheiji manifests a *setsuwa*-esque desire for didactic interpretation—creating meaning out of his observations—that lacks complete knowledge or authority. As in his opening monologue, his reflections on the economic lifestyles and fortunes of his Ōtsu neighbors are expressed through aphoristic language. First, we have the impoverished doctor Moriyama Genkō, who, though acknowledged as an accomplished physician, is unable to cure the seasonal colds that afflict the residents of Ōtsu. Lacking patients, he lives a life on the margin between idle boredom and desperation: In place of income from a medical practice, he rents his space as a parlor for *go* matches, selling tea for three coppers a cup. The narrator concludes, "There are those who consider it a great fortune merely to stave off death each day." Next, we meet Sakamotoya Jinbei, a once-great merchant who has fallen on hard times. Having lost his fortune, sold his property, and failed at one new venture after another, he finally has lost the confidence of his relatives and is sustained by only the magnanimity of his mother, who lends her retirement savings to support him with the interest, a sum of eighty *monme* of silver per month. The description of Jinbei focuses on the difficulty of supporting a family on a meager income. Jinbei heads a household of five: husband and wife, one child, a chronically ill younger brother, and a crippled former wet nurse the family has taken in—many dependents, but none who can contribute to the household's finances. Living a life of severe austerity, the family manages to barely stretch its allowance to cover expenses each month. But, the narrator concludes, "there are those who, versed in the path of commerce, can comfortably support a household of seven or eight with

FROM TOWNSMAN CULTURE TO TOWNSMAN NARRATIVE

less than one hundred *monme*." How, we are not told: Aphoristic consciousness rushes to note the exception, not to explain but to contain it.

Finally, we read a pair of short descriptions of households getting by on the opposite ends of urban society. On the one hand, a widow disguises her daughter as a pilgrim begging for alms on the way to Ise, or, as the narrator puts it, "a woman who has made a living on the same lie for the last twelve or thirteen years." On the other, a needle maker, despite his apparently humble profession, prepares to furnish his daughter with a fantastic dowry. At this point, the *setsuwa*-esque drive to interpret, mirrored by Kiheiji's speculative inquiry into economic causality, seems to break down, confronted with the insurmountable tension between appearances and realities. If some households survive on lies and swindles and others possess incredible and inexplicable stores of wealth, on what grounds can an outsider attempt to divine a logic behind their respective fates? But the narrative desire for didactic meaning does not completely collapse. Instead, it is transformed into an aestheticized wonder at the unfathomable complexity of the urban economy, one that echoes and elaborates Kiheiji's earlier Kenkō-esque meditation on "impermanence" (*mujō*): "The logic of people's finances is truly mysterious, for even here in Ōtsu, it takes all kinds!" (*hito no naishō wa shirenu mono, kono Ōtsu no uchi ni mo samazama ari*).

It is precisely this sublime surplus of contingency that is ultimately allegorized in the winter thunderbolt, striking on the eve of the New Year to send the happy but poor man into debt (figure 3.1). In the thunderbolt, we have the mirror image of fortune: the unpredictable catastrophe, to which the poor are always more vulnerable than the rich, that belies the myth of happiness within humble means. At first glance, this looks very much like parody. Kiheiji uses didactic language to try to understand his place in the world and how to achieve material success; the didactic logic fails, and he is defeated by the fickle finger of fate. In such a reading, Saikaku reveals that, in reality, honest work and penny-pinching often amount to nothing. To the contrary, "A Winter Thunderbolt Brings Injury" is not about the failure of didactic principles, but about the proper functioning of the language of aphoristic rationalism. Like "Medicine Prepared in Abnormal Fashion," it is about the power of a form of language that is able to account for, however incompletely, and ultimately to contain contradiction, tension, and uncertainty, and to subject the contingency of history to the demands of didactic meaning. The tension between the narrating voice and the

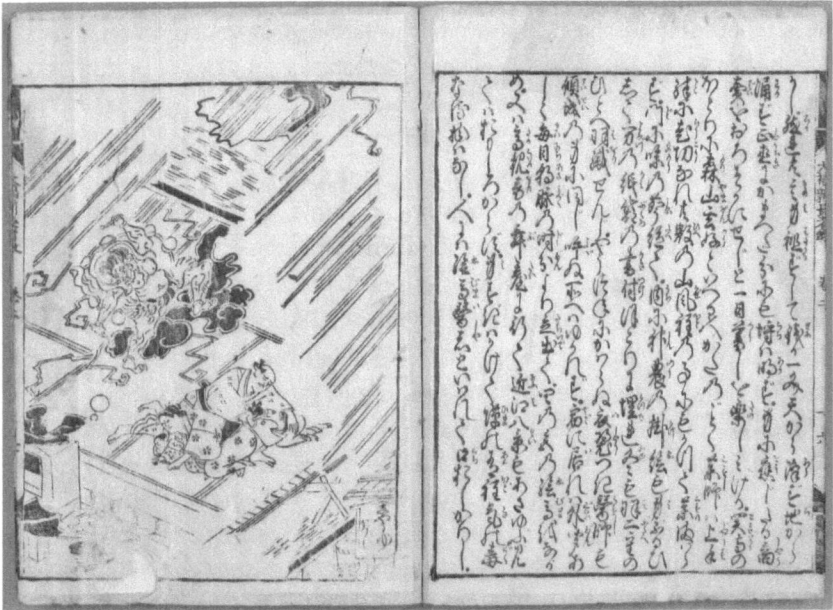

FIGURE 3.1 *Nippon eitaigura*, Morita edition. Illustration to "A Winter Thunderbolt Brings Injury" (vol.2, 6u–7o). Courtesy of Waseda University Library.

complex and contradictory narrative content does not invalidate that language, but attests to the capacity of language to accommodate contradiction. When Kiheiji himself comments, "In life, nothing ever goes the way you expect" (*atedo no kanarazu chigau mono wa yo no naka*)—perhaps, the best-laid plans of mice and men—he is correct: Truer words were never spoken. His situation has been accounted for, simply chalked up to fate, but a fate that has been apprehended and made tolerable by the eternal truths of folk wisdom.

Made tolerable, but also made aesthetic. When Saikaku confronts his reader with raw contingency—the inscrutability of fate, the seemingly arbitrary nature of the distribution of wealth, the irreducible historicity of men's fortunes—he sublimates that confrontation into aesthetic response, here laughter: The thunderbolt is a darkly comic punch line, to which Kiheiji responds with a kind of bemused vexation but the reader responds with laughter. Teruoka Yasutaka has observed several types of laughter running through Saikaku's work: on the one hand, an elevated and intellectual form of humor deriving from the juxtaposition of high and low in *haikai* poetics and typically taking the form of wordplay, and, on the other, a lower and more plebeian form deriving from oral joke telling (*hanashi*) and typically taking the form of the punch line (*ochi*). Kiheiji's fate is clearly of the second type, revealing the author's debt to the oral tradition and its set of techniques for sublimating incongruity and tension as objects of laughter. But this story also points to what Teruoka identifies as a third, more nuanced kind of darkly tragicomic humor that took shape in Saikaku's late works, in part a reflection of his deepening attention to the absurdity of everyday human life and to the incongruous balance of pathos and egoism in the human heart—in a word, a form of laughter that reflects Saikaku's evolving humanism.[46] In *Eternal Storehouse*, this laughter emerges as a response to the inscrutability of fortune—fate so fickle that one can only laugh at it.

Indeed, it is in this register of wonder that Saikaku both begins and ends *Eternal Storehouse*, and the auspicious conclusion to the work is particularly revealing of the nature of the tension between the text's didactic claims and its recognition of the contingency of fate. The short concluding story, "A Measure of Wisdom from a Rice Ladle at Eighty-Eight" (*Chie o hakaru hachijū-hachi no masukaki*, vol. 6–5), is less a story than an awed panegyric to wealth—both to its fantastic power and to the inscrutable mysteries of whom it favors.[47] The narration is a rapid-fire tour de force of aphoristic rhetoric:

> Now one cannot but be struck by how wide the world is. For half a century, men far and wide have complained of lack of prospects in trade. But even when times are tough, there are those who seize opportunity with their bare hands and rise to the ranks of the pedigreed! And even when rice can be bought for pocket change, there are still beggars. When one examines the private accounts of men's houses, one sees how each furnishes its own necessities, to live on the whole at a higher standard than generations past, and for every house that has fallen into ruin many more have been made.
>
> Surely nothing shows such variety as men's household accounts, and the ways of making a way in the world are diverse. There are couples who barely eke out a living together and huge households supported by the labor of one man; for those who meet with unusual success as mere townsmen, it is by virtue of their personal invention. All people have eyes and noses, and are

born with arms and legs, including the highborn and the masters of the arts, but a townsman makes a name in the world by virtue of his wealth! One must toil in youth—what a waste to not leave a name in keeping with one's merits! For regardless of bloodline or clan, a townsman's wealth is his only pedigree. Even if one is descended from a noble family of old, as long as one lives in a townsman's house, to be poor is to be no better than a monkey trainer or a beggar! Pray for fortune, for becoming wealthy is a goal above all others! And keep a big heart, for a millionaire's fortune is built by able clerks.

A fellow from Osaka began brewing saké for the Edo market and raised even his relatives to prosperity! There are those who speculate on mining concerns and come into wealth overnight! Yoshino lacquer tycoons with hidden fortunes, ferrymen who become shipping magnates; some become rich by lending for mortgages, while others build a steady fortune as iron brokers! These are the new merchants of recent years, products of just the last thirty years.[48]

Written to be rattled off in a breathless stream, the narration sees prescriptive language give way to mystified wonder, and didactic non sequiturs ("a millionaire's fortune is built by able clerks") set alongside broad moral pronouncements. Above all, the reader is left in stunned marvel at the sheer fact of wealth in its multifarious manifestations; generic description yields to a listing of random cases, without rhyme or reason. At the climax of this ecstatic ode to the unfathomable wonders of money, the book closes with a paradox: "As money gathers where it lies, so do its stories, passed on and inscribed here in the Great Ledger of Japan, so that for all time, those who read them might profit thereby, resting securely in the Eternal Storehouse of a realm at peace."[49] On the one hand, we have the aphoristic recognition of the contingency of fortune—"money gathers where it lies" (*kingin aru tokoro ni wa aru*); it is where it is, and those who have it, have it—and on the other, nevertheless, we have the stubborn insistence that these are didactic stories, that "those who read them might profit thereby" (*kore o miru hito no tame ni mo narinu beshi*).

THE BIRTH OF TOWNSMAN PROSE

Eternal Storehouse shows tremendous nuance and ideological ambivalence in its treatment of the contradictions of the market economy. Nevertheless, if one dispenses with some of the details and acknowledges that the economy is no simple matter and that individual fortunes are shaped by multiple, complex, and competing factors, then one can, despite these contradictions, observe a loose, approximate, and conditional ethos emerge from these statements and narratives. It generally advocates for diligent effort and honesty, thrift and personal discipline, entrepreneurial wit and broad-ranging intelligence, as well as some measure of happy circumstance. Indeed, what makes *Eternal Storehouse* remarkable is its ability to contain these contradictions without necessitating their resolution. What is most striking about the innovations in narrative form that Saikaku accomplished with this work is how its distinctive narrative textuality operates to make sense of those complexities: It sets them in service of rational principle and didactic imperative, acknowledging the existence of the historical contingencies and social forces that stood between the aspirational townsman and the full mastery of his destiny while containing the fundamental threat they represented to the constitutive myth of the Genroku dream. Despite the nearly universal recognition of *Eternal Storehouse* as a contradictory text, it is one in which contradictions appear as nuances that render the image more complex and thus, paradoxically, more plausible. Saikaku created a form of narrative to embody an aspirational image of an entrepreneurial ethos that was experienced as compelling, inclusive, and powerfully normative despite its self-evident contradictions.

It accomplishes this through Saikaku's adaptation of *setsuwa*-esque didacticism, which constructs links between narrative content and didactic frame and suggests that didactic principles may be expressed in complex, indirect, incomplete, and contradictory ways; through the deployment of aphoristic rationalism as a narrative voice that never claims total finality and that thus accommodates contradiction while remaining centered on a set of ideologically charged principles; and through the sublimation of failures of didactic rationality into heightened moments of aesthetic experience. Using these techniques, Saikaku created a vision of the townsman as master of his own fate. In slightly different terms, *Eternal Storehouse* reveals that, in the face of the inexorable contingency of fortune and the complexities of the social world, the townsman's will toward mastery played out at the level of literary form, as a narrative structure and a register of language that could acknowledge the limits of townsman agency, sublimating them as aesthetic experience, whether laughter or wonder. Textual form thus perfected the project of the townsman's self-fashioning in a way that reality rarely could. Despite the apparent contradictions within Saikaku's townsman pieces—between an optimistic ethos of upward mobility and a pessimistic recognition of the arbitrary distribution of wealth and of the practical difficulties of navigating its hierarchies—*Eternal Storehouse* is ultimately a powerfully normative text, for it gives the ethos that defined the townsman a coherence that could only exist as text: the contradictions and tensions of economic reality given symbolic resolution in the dynamic forms of townsman prose narrative.

Indeed, *Eternal Storehouse* has, since its initial publication, been read overwhelmingly as a didactic work. Hōjō Dansui, Saikaku's premier disciple and the de facto executor of his literary estate, would later write in an editor's preface to *Saikaku's Loose Threads Tied Off* (*Saikaku oridome*, 1694) that *Eternal Storehouse* was the first of a planned trilogy, to be followed by works titled *Mirror of Townsmen of Our Realm* (*Honchō chōnin kagami*) and *The Hearts of People in the World* (*Yo no hito-gokoro*), that "when examined by the merchant and artisanal classes would become paragons to aid in making a way through the world" (*shōshokunin no kemi suru ni, hiyō yo o wataru tatsuki ni kokoro o ubeki kikan taru beki mono*).[50] Although we have no guarantee that Dansui's reading was paradigmatic, it is the voice of a careful reader, indeed one close to Saikaku, describing and thus mandating a didactic style of reading for Saikaku's work. Modern scholarship, likewise, has with relatively few exceptions read the work as a didactic one, notable more for its value as a historical document than as a work of literary merit or aesthetic nuance. My point is not to suggest that such readings are incorrect, but rather to show how, despite the palpable contradictions that militate against such a reading, the text itself induces us to read it didactically, and surely did the same for its historical readers.

The genre of *setsuwa*-esque narratives of rags to riches would prove a productive form of prose fiction in the decades that followed, beginning with Yuirakuken's *The Merchant's Ledger of Worldly Success* (*Risshin daifukuchō*, 1703).[51] Dansui himself would go on write a spiritual sequel to *Eternal Storehouse* in the form of *The New Eternal Storehouse of Japan* (*Nippon shin eitaigura*, 1713). Perhaps unsurprisingly, Dansui's work was much less nuanced than Saikaku's, favoring instead a form of bluntly didactic narrative—more dictum than aphorism—that excised both the social complexities and aesthetic sublimity of Saikaku's apprehension of

FROM TOWNSMAN CULTURE TO TOWNSMAN NARRATIVE

the urban economy in favor of a simplistic image of virtue and its earthly reward, or equally vice and its immanent punishment. Dansui's moralizing (and deeply un-Saikaku-esque) tone is apparent from his preface, as brief as it is dire.

> A day's negligence becomes a year's sloth, and a lifetime is wasted, never to return. Townsmen of the recent past have forgotten their house trades in the pursuit of leisure and lost the precious treasures of gold and silver. One night, the god of fortune knocked upon my gate and requested that I write something admonishing such folly, and so here I have gathered anew in six volumes the names of such millionaires, safely stored in a New Eternal Storehouse.[52]

Meanwhile, other works in the genre, such as Getsujindō's *Pillar of Progeny* (*Shison daikoku-bashira*, 1709), took precisely the opposite approach of setting aside didactic pretense to simply offer entertaining and unusual stories drawn from the world of commerce.[53] The later evolution of the genre thus split into two distinct genealogies reflecting the two elements of the *setsuwa*-esque narrative—the centrifugal pull of a didactic frame and the unpredictable energy of diverse narrative episodes—that Saikaku had brought into a symbolically powerful balance. However, although the direct progeny of *Eternal Storehouse* would prove unable to sustain the dialectical tension that gave Saikaku's text such ideological weight, the forms of townsman prose narrative would be taken in new directions by Ejima Kiseki—Saikaku's most enthusiastic epigone, who would use new permutations of the space of the collection to explore the contradictions within the townsman household and indeed the townsman self.

PART II
Copying Characters

Chapter Four

THE MISFORTUNE OF BEING SAVED BY ONE'S ARTS

> To objectify romantic, fictional illusion, and above all, the relationship with the so-called real world on which it hinges, is to be reminded that the reality against which we measure all our imaginings is merely the recognized referent for an (almost) universally recognized illusion.
>
> —PIERRE BOURDIEU, "IS THE STRUCTURE OF *SENTIMENTAL EDUCATION* AN INSTANCE OF SOCIAL SELF-ANALYSIS?"

> The realm is divided into the four estates of warriors, peasants, craftsmen, and merchants. Each works at his allotted occupation, and as his descendants inherit his craft, his household is sustained. Among these, the commercial dealings of the townsmen are various, but all are merely a matter of making money on interest.
>
> —MITSUI TAKAFUSA, *A RECORD OF OBSERVATIONS ON TOWNSMEN*

THE HOUSEHOLD AND ITS DISCONTENTS

In the 1720s, amid the energetic shogun Tokugawa Yoshimune's Kyōhō Reforms, Mitsui Takafusa, the third-generation head of the Mitsui Echigoya clothier in Edo, set out to document the recollections of his father, Takahira. The result was *A Record of Observations on Townsmen* (*Chōnin kōken roku*), a lengthy manuscript consisting of anecdotal histories of major merchant houses of the seventeenth century. The text narrates in vivid detail and severe tone the rises and falls—mostly the falls—of the old milieu of "privileged townsmen" whom the great patriarch Mitsui Takatoshi had outfoxed and outlived to establish what had by Takafusa's time become the premier merchant house in all of Japan.[1] Although largely lacking in literary ambition or aesthetic elaboration, the collection is in many ways a counterpart to Ihara Saikaku's *Eternal Storehouse*, attempting to account for the laws of karmic-cum-economic causality that had led so many of Mitsui's peers to fail where Takatoshi had succeeded. The work is shot through with an austere pessimism: a unifying anxiety, bordering on religious terror, that the slightest slip into imprudent business dealings or, even worse, decadent personal comportment would inevitably lead the household into imminent ruination, whether in one's own generation or in the next. Like so many didactic works, the collection is much more invested in depictions of failure than prescriptions for success. Once the house fortune had been established through the heroic efforts of its founding patriarch, the obligation of each future heir was to act as merely a custodian of the household's estate, preserving it from generation to generation and increasing it incrementally through consistent and conservative business practices rather than growing it in new directions through new entrepreneurial endeavors. Indeed, and in contrast to the *Eternal Storehouse*, the text shows remarkably little concern for any positive and substantive understanding of what the business of commerce entails as a creative act in itself. As Takafusa remarks at the opening of his preface, regardless of the differences among the various trades, all are in the end "merely a matter of making money on interest" (*mazu wa kingin no risoku ni kakaru yori hoka nashi*).[2]

Takafusa's preface is a particularly artless admission, by one of the very paragons of the early modern townsmen, of one of the unstated truths of merchant capital—or, perhaps more precisely, of its unstated fictionality. Throughout the didactic literature of the seventeenth and eighteenth centuries are scattered frequent endorsements of house trade (*kagyō* or *kashoku*)—as in the preface to *Eternal Storehouse*: "Never slack at your house trade from dawn 'til dusk!"—and house codes like that of the Mitsui Echigoya likewise placed house trade at the very core of the townsman's identity. But in practice, the category of house trade was remarkably flexible. Most of Saikaku's protagonists, the successful ones, move up from simple artisanal practice or street peddling into larger enterprises, and ultimately graduate into the trade of moneylending, banking, and other financial services. As both Saikaku and Mitsui keenly understood, the townsman's house trade was itself a fiction of a sort, a fluid and semantically vacuous term that often merely signified the accumulation of wealth on behalf of the household. All the better when that labor was not really any labor at all, when it was marked by neither concrete specificity nor any identifiable social function by way of "occupation"—when it was "merely a matter of making money on interest."

The late seventeenth century saw the establishment of the household (*ie* 家), sometimes translated as "stem family," as a nearly universal model of social organization throughout all ranks of Tokugawa society.[3] The institution of the household had of course existed in earlier eras: In slightly different forms, it was the orienting unit of medieval warrior society, and had been adopted by the more elite ranks of urban commoners between the late medieval period and the early Tokugawa era. Not until the explosive economic expansion and social dynamism of the seventeenth century began to settle down, however, did the household become truly universal, the basic unit through which the Tokugawa social order was reproduced from generation to generation.[4] One driving force in the dissemination and normalization of the household and its values around the turn of the eighteenth century was the influence of popular print: The body of informational and didactic literature that flourished from the Genroku era into the eighteenth century was increasingly focused on the interests and norms of the propertied household. In the case of the townsman, the household was seen as owing its existence to the efforts of a founding patriarch who through heroic entrepreneurial efforts wrought from nothing the three components that defined the household: name, trade, and estate.[5] This definition may seem peculiar for placing the objective externalities of the household above its human members. Of course, the household could not exist without human proxies and was centered on the atomic collective of husband, wife, and children (though it could also include the older generation as semimembers in a state of retirement or dependence, as well as apprentices, clerks, and servants). But it was the very nature of the household that it transcended, contained, and to a certain degree dictated the individual will of any of its members, whose interests were subordinated to the sustained existence of the household and whose energies were thoroughly instrumentalized in service of its reproduction from one generation to the next.[6] This was true of even the household head, who—despite his significant privilege as the male patriarch who held near total authority over his wife, children, and other dependents—was himself ultimately only serving in a temporary and custodial role. He was subordinate to the authority of the household as a corporate entity driven by imperatives that transcended any individual head and that were often enforced by older relatives. To enjoy the security of the household was also to be subject to its stringent demands. And many of the literary heroes of the moment were precisely those who were unable to bear the pressures and obligations wrought by the household and its custodians.

A vague but pervasive sense of alienation runs through the literature and theater of the eighteenth-century townsman, as if he were always wishing, striving, or simply pretending to be someone else. Saikaku's protagonists had, in their own ways, been part of this striving. They had refashioned (or simply re-presented) themselves, with no small amount of literal dissembling, from peasants, impoverished craftsmen, and unnamed vagrants into heroic entrepreneurs. In doing so, however, they had discovered the possibility, however fleeting, of mastery over their destinies amid the morally ambiguous ebbs and flows of the urban marketplace. In contrast, the protagonists of eighteenth-century fiction are almost invariably children of established houses, whether those of the newly wealthy or of old and pedigreed families: those who have not made their names and fortunes themselves but inherited them, those for whom the primary imperative is to reproduce the norms modeled for them by their parents, those who find themselves in a secure and stable positions but utterly stultified by them. These depictions register a condition of alienation that was at the very heart of the townsman household, which sought to thoroughly instrumentalize the energies of all its members in service of its reproduction across successive generations. Chikamatsu Monzaemon's romantic heroes, like Kamiya Jihei of *Love Suicides at Amijima* (*Shinjū ten no Amijima*, 1721), are those who, despite having achieved (or inherited or married into) a respectable name and estate, and despite enjoying the love of family and regard in the world, choose to catastrophically throw it all away in the tragic pursuit of true feeling not constrained or prescribed by familial obligation and social role—of authentic action, in defiance of the cynical truth that the lot of the townsman was "merely a matter of making money on interest."

But the most incisive critic of the townsman household was Ejima Kiseki (1666–1735).[7] Kiseki was a veritable exemplar of the degenerate heir that the patriarchs of the Mitsui house so feared and reviled. Born Murase Gonnojō, Kiseki was the scion of a successful Kyoto rice-cake business—the "Great Buddha rice-cake" (*daibutsu mochi*) shop—that dated to the dawn of the Tokugawa era. The Murase house was of the elite milieu of old families that the Mitsui document decried as undisciplined and decadent; indeed, many of Kiseki's relatives appear in *A Record of Observations on Townsmen* as individuals who led their households to ruin through high living and risky lending.[8] Kiseki assumed the position of household head and the hereditary shop name of Shōzaemon in 1695, but just as he was assuming the responsibilities of a fully fledged townsman patriarch, he was also beginning to pursue leisure pastimes that would ultimately come to displace his house trade. A habitué of the theater and a self-styled connoisseur of Kabuki acting, Kiseki began a side career as a writer by penning a series of puppet plays for the chanter Matsumoto Jidayū that were released by the Kyoto publisher Hachimonjiya Hachizaemon (Jishō), who would become his ongoing patron.[9] Kiseki's first great success came with *The Actor's Vocal Shamisen* (*Yakusha kuchi jamisen*, 1699), an innovative and massively influential book of actor reviews, lavishly illustrated by the woodblock artist Nishikawa Sukenobu, and the trio of Hachimonjiya, Kiseki, and Sukenobu soon branched into popular fiction with *The Courtesan's Amorous Shamisen* (*Keisei iro jamisen*, 1701).[10] Over the decade or so that followed, Kiseki dedicated increasing amounts of his time and energy to his dalliances in the lesser literary arts of actor reviews and popular fiction before making the fateful decision, in 1714, to abandon his hereditary trade and name, establishing a publishing business under the name of Ejimaya and branding his works with the pen name by which he is still known. The Ejimaya would fold in less than a decade, but it represents Kiseki's romantic attempt to trade the alienations of the townsman household—"the constraint on entrepreneurship that follows from the submission of person to lineage and hereditary calling"—for some combination of the autonomy of the artist and the agency of the entrepreneur.[11]

The iconic work of Kiseki's quixotic career as a townsman dropout was *Characters of Worldly Young Men* (*Seken musuko katagi*), published as a flagship release for the Ejimaya imprint in 1715. A collection of fifteen stories in five volumes, *Worldly Young Men* is a comic exploration of the petty vices of contemporary young men that cause their households to fold. In its basic didactic conception, it was far from original: Saikaku's *Twenty Unfilial Exemplars of Japan* (*Honchō nijū fukō*, 1686), from which Kiseki borrowed liberally in both spirit and letter, had presented a series of explorations of contemporary vice, situated within the framework of the household (mostly, though not exclusively, that of the townsman) and its norms. But Saikaku's interest was less in the household per se and more in the fate of the strong-willed individuals whose conduct it failed to constrain; in spite of the title of the work, he was not concerned narrowly with the norms of filial piety but more broadly with good, evil, and moral causality writ large. In contrast, Kiseki's character pieces are squarely focused on the household and on the alienated consciousness that it structured: They act as a house of mirrors, taking the idealized, normalized image of the proper townsman and refracting, inverting, and twisting it to comic effect. Despite presenting his works in a seemingly didactic frame—holding up his characters as cautionary tales of the fates awaiting children gone wrong—the target of his satirical pen was not the screw-ups and dropouts of townsman society: It was the household itself.

In its deconstruction of the townsman household, *Worldly Young Men* foregrounds the disruptive potentialities of leisure—the seductive appeal of play, which the ideology of the household persistently, though always incompletely, sought to excise in favor of work. In this regard, Kiseki's stories shared thematic concerns with Saikaku's early erotic pieces and with Chikamatsu's domestic dramas. Such works tended to focus on the temptations of the brothel districts, which were perceived to have an addictive quality that could ensnare otherwise upright townsmen and lead them into dissolution. But to an equal and even greater degree, townsman culture of the late seventeenth and early eighteenth centuries was defined by another form of leisure: the "leisure arts" (*yūgei*), sometimes simply the "various arts" (*shogei*), consisting of amateur training in various cultural accomplishments. More than even the brothel districts, the leisure arts were objects of intense anxiety, subject to complex and contradictory discourses that aimed to dictate what type and degree of involvement were appropriate for the proper townsman, and what place they had in the respectable townsman household. They brought the transgressive, liminal, boundary-blurring quality of the "bad places" (*akusho*) of urban leisure into the private, inner spaces of the townsman household itself; both a part of townsman culture and a mode of transgression against that very culture, they reflected a fissure in emerging norms of townsman selfhood. *Worldly Young Men* was among the first literary works to explore the central place of the arts in the townsman household and their role in the formation, and de-formation, of the townsman self.

Kiseki's seminal work would spawn a series of sequels—*Characters of Worldly Young Women* (*Seken musume katagi*, 1717), *Characters of Old Men of the Floating World* (*Ukiyo oyaji katagi*, 1720), and *Characters of Worldly Clerks* (*Seken tedai katagi*, 1730)—and would ultimately become the template for a genre. The character piece (*katagi-mono*), as modern scholars know it, consists of compilations of comic sketches on a range of social types taken from across urban society, and its works vary widely in theme; even Kiseki's later *katagi-mono* would explore different sides of the household, and to different ends. These works are taken up in detail in the following chapter, where I explore the nature of the term *katagi* and the genre that it came to name, but the readings in this chapter touch on them selectively where they extend the concerns with townsman leisure framed by *Worldly Young Men*. Before the *katagi-mono* became a genre, this text was a singular broadside against the ideology of the household, played out through romantics like Kiseki himself: Absorbed in impractical fancies and alternative selves fashioned through artistic cultivation, Kiseki's young men reveal through their very folly the hollowness of a life defined only by work with no space for play.

FOR THE HONOR OF THE HOUSEHOLD AND ITS REPUTE IN THE WORLD

Just as Mitsui attempted to account for the rises and falls of the households of his fellow townsmen, Kiseki opens *Worldly Young Men* with his own trenchant diagnosis of the degenerate conduct and insolvent finances of his peers. In the opening story, "Selling Scouring Rushes to Scrub the Heart Clean: The Character of an Honest Peasant" (*Tokusa-uri wa kokoro o migaku shōjikina hyakushō katagi*, vol. 1–1), Kiseki begins by citing a time-worn aphorism: "The father strives, the son indulges, and the grandson begs." The remainder of the story asks why: Why do heirs tend so often toward prodigality, and why do they ruin the households that their fathers have built up with such care and effort? In answering these questions, Kiseki presents a tongue-in-cheek but provocative and original critique of the townsman household and its values.[12]

The story introduces an anonymous old man, a peasant peddler of scouring rushes from Oku Tanba (to the northwest of Kyoto) and the husband of an aging couple that has neither children nor property and is resigned "to be a couple of but one generation"—that is, not to beget a household. As the old man heads into the city to sell his wares, he encounters a strange child of eleven or twelve, resembling a Buddhist acolyte, who reveals himself to be a supernatural emissary of the local deity, sent to the city to chastise parents for being too lenient with their children: parents who, like so many of Saikaku's protagonists, have moved away from their rural hometowns into the city, become townsmen, and raised their children amid urban culture. According to the acolyte, contemporary young men tend toward wickedness because their parents lack discipline and spoil them, and thus the parents who disown their sons are in fact the ones to blame. The old peddler objects, citing the orthodoxy of townsman common sense to say that parents love their children above all else, and for a son to warrant disownment he must be truly wicked. The acolyte counters by asserting that doting and permissive parents lead their children to selfishness and vice, cutting through the platitudes of filial piety that place the blame for poorly behaved children solely on the moral failings of the younger generation. By Kiseki's time, such critiques were themselves commonplace. Similar comments were made by no less of a moralist than Kaibara Ekiken (1630–1714), whose discussion of commoner education in *Vernacular Precepts for Children* (*Wazoku dōjikun*, 1711) was likely Kiseki's template for this passage.[13] However, the distinguishing point in Kiseki's diagnosis of this common social ill is the attention that he gives, in the words of the acolyte, to the influence of the polite arts, which contain the seed of the household's downfall:

> Parents these days, even more than those in earlier times, have become decadent and put on airs beyond their stations. They indulge their children in the leisure arts while taking it upon themselves to carry out the house trade. Year in and year out, they prod the young ones to practice the *nō* drum, and on the occasion of *chō* gatherings delight in being told, "I had the pleasure of hearing the young master's drumming the other day during practice at Higashiyama. He made quite the impression—some were even saying that a paid performer-in-residence could hardly compare!" The father comes to be rather puffed up about it, and before long is using his connections to get the child placed in the *nō* retinue of some lord or another, thinking, "For the honor of the household and its repute in the world!"[14]

As the young aesthete associates more and more with the urban elite, he "knows not the toil of the floating world" and, in place of his house trade, immerses himself in the pursuit of refined forms of urban leisure until his spending gets out of hand and he faces disownment. Even then, the acolyte narrates with sadistic glee, the prodigal son is unlikely to reform, only to resent his parents all the more. Abandoned by his family, he falls in with unsavory companions, taking on the ruffian demeanor of a street tough and pursuing various schemes of fraud and extortion; as he falls into the morally corrupt depths of urban society, there is not the slightest chance for his reform.

A certain malice is clear in the acolyte's tirade, a sneering tone that delights in revealing the unsavory truths of townsman society and the vanity, dysfunction, and intergenerational resentment concealed by the image of the household as a harmonious and stable domestic unit. Unlike Saikaku's perspective in *Honchō nijū fukō*, Kiseki's vision is not of honest, hardworking parents and ungrateful, wicked children: It is of successive generations of prideful, petty opportunists who resemble and indeed deserve one another. To Kiseki, the fall of the household was inevitable, not a consequence of any individual failing, but born out of the contradictions of the institution itself. The acolyte's ultimate argument, directed at the "couple of one generation" with neither property nor heir, is that, in fact, one is better off doing without children in the first place—nothing less than a wholesale renunciation of the townsman household and its existential imperative to reproduce itself from one generation to the next.

At the core of Kiseki's broadside against the household was an acute sensitivity to the role of the arts in townsman society and to their fraught place in the household. It is through training in the arts (here, the *nō* drum) that the vain father wishes to enjoy the fawning admiration of his peers and neighbors within the *chō*, to hobnob with warrior elites, and generally to increase "the honor of the household and its repute in the world" (*ie no menboku yo no gaibun*); and it is through the very same arts that the son falls into moral degradation and social obscurity. If the house trade of the townsman was a symbol of his entrepreneurial will-to-power, then, to Kiseki, the arts contained the seed of his fatal hubris.

The leisure arts were a set of aesthetic practices—such as the tea ceremony, flower arrangement, and *nō* chanting and drumming—that had originated as leisure pastimes among elite warriors and court aristocrats but had spread widely through commoner populations. By Kiseki's time, the arts included diverse leisure practices and forms of cultural training, ranging from Sinitic scholarship, medicine, classical poetry in Chinese and Japanese, calligraphy, and formal etiquette; to elite arts such as *kemari* (kickball) and incense appreciation; to popular forms like shamisen performance, *jōruri* chanting, and *kouta* popular melodies; to board games such as *go* and *shōgi*. In contrast to earlier eras, when formal artistic training was, like literacy, the exclusive purview of elites (*daimyō* and elite samurai, the old Kyoto aristocracy, the privileged townsmen, and high-ranking clergy) or else a marginal trade practiced by itinerant performers, the seventeenth century saw the popularity of all manner of literary, visual, and performing arts spread widely among commoners, especially among urban commoners of all ranks. As commoner populations gained a modicum of surplus income and leisure time, and with the support of a flourishing print culture, the various arts became objects of intense fascination by large circles of aspiring amateurs who used them as opportunities for cultural finishing, self-expression, and socialization across otherwise strict social hierarchies. This explosion in the popularity of amateur artistic training was one reflection of the emergence of a commercial marketplace for culture as established systems of aesthetic practice, which had historically been the exclusive property of families with their own artistic genealogies and systems of direct transmission from teacher to student, became objects of instruction to wide audiences of aspiring amateurs in exchange for tutelage fees.

Cultural historian Moriya Takeshi has observed that the leisure arts served important social functions as a metric of "repute" (*gaibun*), marking the relative standing of the individual household within the diversified townsman community of the late seventeenth and early eighteenth century.[15] A modicum of cultural sophistication by way of the arts was the mark of the successful household and the model townsman. Refinement of taste in culture and the arts was most strongly associated with the old families of privileged townsmen, who were increasingly thought to be commercially ineffectual and borderline degenerate, but who were nevertheless the paragons of urban success and sophistication with whom new generations of entrepreneurial merchants (perhaps despite themselves) sought to associate—indeed, who they wished to emulate, in cultural if not financial terms. Saikaku, before his explorations of the entrepreneurial ethos in his late townsman pieces, had incisively commented on the stratification of townsman society and the cultural anxieties that it entailed. In *The Great Mirror of Myriad Elegance* (*Shoen ōkagami*, 1684), the writer comments on the "pocket directories" (*sode kagami*) of the capital: lists of the premier merchant households, intended both as a reference for commercial purposes and as a social who's who of upper-class urban society.

The pocket directories of the capital make three distinctions: the well born, the wealthy, and the newly rich. According to popular custom, the well born are those who have not practiced a trade for generations and simply pass on exquisite antiques from one generation to the next, enjoying tea with the snow and poetry with the flowers, sparing no thought from morning 'til night of worldly affairs. The wealthy are those recognized by local society, who do not cease business but leave the matters of the house up to their clerks and do not involve themselves in the details. The rich are those of recent good fortune, who have profited from the rising price of rice, met with success in speculation, or made money through lending, and still check even the ledgers themselves. But the mere possession of ten thousand *kanme* of silver hardly means that one can enter the company of the pedigreed families.[16]

The category of "well born" (here *yoishu*, usually read as *yoishū*) was particularly fraught. The paradigmatic figure for this stratum was the *shimotaya*, sometimes *shimōtaya* (literally, "closed-up shop"): the long-established, elite townsman family that had ceased business, retired from trade, and continued to exist through the strategic lending of its profitable reserves of hereditary capital and through the purchase and rental of urban property. The *shimotaya* households of old Kamigata, especially in the historic neighborhoods of Kyoto and Sakai, were also known for their aesthetic sophistication because the heads of many had abandoned their house trades to dedicate themselves to poetry, kickball, the tea ceremony, antique appreciation, and all the finer arts of the old urban elite.[17] As noted, such figures are lambasted throughout *A Record of Observations on Townsmen* as decadent degenerates. The text reserves particularly stern criticism for the patriarch Takatoshi's elder brother Mitsui Toshitsugu. In a striking parallel to the opening story of *Worldly Young Men*, Toshitsugu, having developed an interest in *nō* theater, built a stage and encouraged his son to perform; in the end, the son had "nothing of the spirit of the merchant" (*akindo kokoro wa kore naku*) and is described as an aesthete who immersed himself in *nō*, the tea ceremony, and board games and who "mastered all manner of other leisure arts" (*sono hoka yūgei ni yoku tasshite*) to become "a model of the extremes of townsman decadence" (*shigoku no chōnin no eyō-mono nari*).[18] In this regard, the apple fell close to the tree: Takatoshi's father, Norihei, was a paragon of the old guard of privileged townsmen, having left the business in the hands of his more-than-capable wife as he amused himself with linked verse. However, despite these anxieties, Saikaku's quote reveals a rarely spoken but widely understood truth running through late seventeenth- and early eighteenth-century townsman society: that wealth alone was not the mark of the man. The stigma that an entrepreneurial paragon such as Mitsui sought to impose on the *shimotaya* was merely the neurotic mirror image of this nearly universal aspiration toward the cultural refinement and leisurely existence of the well born. Within the stratified upper reaches of urban society, training in a range of leisure arts took on the value of a formally optional but practically obligatory form of cultural finishing, a critical signifier of the public persona of the proper townsman household.

To a degree, the role of the arts as a signifier in service of "the honor of the household and its repute in the world" was a symbolic one, the kind of pecuniary performance of surplus that Veblen identified with the leisure class: the conspicuous demonstration of unproductive activity that performs the privileged status of its agent. But the entrepreneurial townsman's concern for repute also had more pragmatic dimensions, for as the arts increasingly became the basis of polite socialization in the late seventeenth and early eighteenth centuries, basic fluency in a wide range of popular arts became a key professional qualification in the fields of urban commerce.[19] Repute was a key attribute that placed the merchant among his peers in the community of commerce; the arts became a concrete tool for navigating social networks that were also economic networks, connecting and establishing rapport with potential business partners. If the pursuit of cultural finishing through the leisure arts was in part a reflection of the social posturing of the newly wealthy, it was also colored by the deep pragmatism of a class that had not yet secured a stable position among the urban elite in either economic or cultural terms. The value of the arts as a signifier of status was a manifestation of the symbolic economies of a society in which the hierarchies of money intersected in increasingly complex ways with those of culture, and in which the entrepreneurial merchant was endlessly striving and competing within both fields at once—a context in which, ironically, the arts hardly had the quality of leisure at all.

This is not to say that the only reason for the townsman's participation in the arts was out of a mercenary lust for cultural capital that could be readily converted to the social and ultimately to the economic. Eiko Ikegami has argued that the leisure arts drove the formation of "aesthetic publics": spaces in which the categories and hierarchies of the hereditary status system could be provisionally suspended or transgressed, and in which individual practitioners of diverse backgrounds felt "their aesthetic enclave identities to be more profoundly rooted to their true selves than were their feudal categorical identities."[20] Similarly, Nishiyama Matsunosuke argues that the leisure arts were a fundamentally autonomous space of aesthetic play that was independent of any social determination or constraint. By pursuing training in a given art, and ultimately donning an alternative artistic sobriquet (*geimei*), the amateur practitioner participated in a utopian "fiction" (*kyozō*) of freedom and equality that temporarily upended the feudal strictures that were the unequal "truths" (*jitsuzō*) of everyday life.[21] To a degree, certainly, the arts held the potential to transgress or suspend even the most fundamental status distinctions on which the Tokugawa polity was built. Thus, in Kiseki's story, the father sponsors his son's training in *nō* drumming, which had been among the arts most prized by elite warriors before being adopted as an object of emulation and aspiration among urban commoners; he does so in the interest of placing the child (and himself) among the prestigious company of elite commoners, even to rub elbows with *daimyō* and their retinues. Yet Kiseki, who was keenly attuned to the petty vanity of his townsman peers, makes clear that the company of warriors and even lords is ultimately incidental to a far more mundane kind of status display: that which takes place among the father's immediate community of townsmen, "on the occasion of *chō* gatherings" (*chō sankai ni*). Is the goal of such ostentatious display of distinction to transcend the status position of the townsman or to strategically reaffirm it?

If the arts enabled forms of socialization across boundaries of status and underwrote emerging forms of identity and community built on aesthetic experience, then we must nevertheless keep in mind that, as Pierre Bourdieu reminds us, aesthetic distinction and sensibility are never entirely free from social determinations, whether those of status, class, or gender: Taste "functions as a sort of social orientation, a 'sense of one's place,' guiding the occupants of a given place in social space towards the social positions adjusted to their properties, and towards the practices or goods which befit the occupants of that position."[22] One is inclined toward the aesthetic forms and practices that are appropriate or proximal to one's station and that therefore have come to symbolize legitimate membership in, and exemplary status within, one's class. Aesthetic taste and cultural expression thus come to both reflect and reify the structures of the social field, legitimating everyday social hierarchies both by rendering them culturally legible and by positing them, through a symbolic sleight of hand, as innate and natural distinctions of personal substance. In other words, aesthetic practice does not transcend the everyday categories of social identity. It is instead through the aesthetic expressions of taste that distinctions of class and status come to be recognizable and taken for granted. Bourdieu perhaps overstates the determination and unconscious quality of such processes, which also allow for individual performances to innovate on or subvert social norms even while citing and reproducing them.[23] This indeterminacy, which is particularly pronounced in the interstices of the social system, gives rise to the possibility of appropriation, adaptation, and misrecognition—in short, all the messy negotiations of identity precipitated by movement between stable social positions and fixed identities. To the degree that taste is determined unconsciously by habitus, it may also be shaped aspirationally and deployed strategically in self-aware processes of performative self-formation, though always at the risk of charges of inauthenticity: pretense, affectation, or putting on airs. It is this tendency to strategic self-cultivation and performance, oriented toward the concrete and mundane goal of upward mobility and status prestige, that we see running through the culture of the leisure arts in Kiseki's time as new generations of upwardly mobile merchants attempted to join the polite ranks of urban society and old families clung to claims of cultural distinction as their economic clout waned in the face of the onslaught of new money.

To the degree that the leisure arts may have allowed a space for free socialization and self-expression unencumbered by status of birth, they were also, like the salaryman's game of golf or the middle-class daughter's classical-music training, a tactic for incremental position-taking within the steadily ossifying strata of townsman society. If the arts could suspend social hierarchies, they could also be used strategically to navigate those hierarchies and in doing so reinscribe them in the space of culture. When the wealthy townsman father boasts to his peers of his son's accomplishments in *nō* drumming, it is hardly out of the belief that such an art is closer to his true self (his son is doing the drumming, after all) than his role as a respected and wealthy townsman is. Instead, it is through the exemplary performance of proper taste that the status of townsman is affirmed and reproduced, and by dutifully reproducing such taste, the father seeks to claim for himself repute within the community of fellow townsmen. As Kiseki frankly acknowledges, the subject of this repute is neither father nor son but instead the corporate household, on the behalf of which the father has compelled the son to perform. This is not to deny that the arts provided access to certain forms and degrees of boundary trespass, or that such transgressions could be experienced as liberating. Many of Kiseki's hapless townsman antiheroes are precisely those who find their leisure personae to be more true than their hereditary status and familial role. But it must be kept in mind that townsman society as a whole was at best ambivalent and usually intensely anxious about the threat that such boundary crossings represented to the everyday status quo. Moreover, the status quo that was threatened by such experiences of ludic liberation was, at least for the wealthy townsman, not that of the hereditary status system writ large, but of the townsman household itself, which sought to instrumentalize the energies and efforts of its members toward the single imperative to sustain and reproduce the estate established by the founding ancestor.

Indeed, townsman ideologues were intensely anxious about the influence of the arts if not carefully channeled in service of repute. Warnings against the deleterious influences of the leisure arts can be seen in the earliest piecemeal articulations of urban-commoner values in the merchant house codes of the seventeenth century. The Hakata merchant Shimai Sōshitsu, whose seventeen-article testament to his heir, written in 1610, has perennially been mined for insights into merchant values, strictly forbade all forms of leisure practice, including board games, *nō* chanting and dancing, and the tea ceremony, along with sightseeing, pilgrimage, religious practice, and any kind of spending on ostentatious clothing and household goods.[24] The frequent didactic admonitions made against the arts, which were widely seen as unproductive activities with addictive potential, were but one manifestation of the tensions surrounding consumption that were at the heart of townsman culture: the opportunity to profit from the domestic consumer economy, much of it driven by luxury spending on urban leisure, paired with the imperative to resist active participation in the same and thus avoid temptations and expenditures that might lead one to financial insolvency. But even among the various temptations of urban leisure consumption—clothing, home renovations, lavish entertainment in the theater districts or (for men) the brothel quarters—the leisure arts were the object of a particularly intense and contradictory set of strictures. The direst warnings were reserved for the prodigal son or degenerate household head who became so lost in his leisure pastimes that they displaced his house trade as the focus of his energies. Saikaku's townsman pieces are replete with such figures. For example, in "Daikoku, Who Wore Wit as His Shelter" (see chapter 2), the protagonist Shinroku encounters a beggar, who he learns is the fallen scion of an old merchant house of Sakai and who enumerates at exhaustive length his impressive pedigree in a range of polite arts, only to "lament that, instead of the various arts, his parents had never taught him how to make a living" (*shogei no kawari ni, mi o suguru tane o oshie-okarenu oyatachi o uramikeru*).[25] Even in the rare case of a talented artist who knowingly opted out of his house trade in an attempt to make a career as a cultural professional, the individual in question would in all but the most exceptional cases be viewed by his relatives and peers as little more than a failed townsman.[26] Henri Lefebvre's diagnosis of the place of leisure in early modern Europe applies here: "In so far as the man of those times was *genuinely* separated from social practice and devoted to leisure alone—to laziness—he was doomed both in a personal sense and from the point of view of class."[27] Thus goes the aphorism, "the misfortune of being saved by one's arts" (*gei ga mi o tasukeru hodo no fushiawase*).

Yet the townsman could not do without the arts entirely because they were bound up in his mode of social being and his processes of self-formation. The instructional almanac *A Record of Great Treasures for Men* (*Nan chōhōki*, 1693), which may be considered an introductory textbook of the basic cultural literacies expected of the proper townsman male, dedicates a full two of its five volumes to laying out the basics of a range of widely popular and respectable leisure arts: volume 2 to calligraphy, Sinitic poetry, *waka*, linked verse, and *nō* chanting, and volume 3 to the tea ceremony, flower arrangement, and board games.[28] Saikaku had already understood how the identity of the townsman was inextricable from the culture of the arts that formed his taste and thus distinguished him from other classes. Elsewhere in *Eternal Storehouse*, Saikaku wrote about the elite moneylenders of the Kitahama rice market in Osaka: "By and large, the wealthy of Osaka have not been thus for many generations. For the most part, they are those who were once laborers and servants but worked their way up into wealth with some amount of good luck. Without even meaning to, they became versed in the ways of poetry, kickball, archery, the *koto*, the flute, the drum, incense, and tea, and thus came also into good company, and before long their countrified accents have vanished."[29] If the old families like those of Kyoto could use their long pedigrees of cultural refinement to distinguish themselves from new money, then for the newly wealthy, the arts served a dual function. On the one hand, pursuing training in the arts, whether for themselves or for their children, was a way of coming into "good company" (*yokihito-zukiai*), with all the benefits both tangible and intangible that such brought. On the other, though, it was the way the entrepreneurial townsman distinguished himself from his roots in the peasantry or in the urban laboring classes. As much as the mobility of money, it was the mobility of culture that made the townsman who he was, that defined the townsman self by distinguishing him from his others. As we saw in chapter 2, the entrepreneurial townsman was constituted by drawing a clear boundary between the townsman proper and the laboring and outcast classes, and through the cultural finishing of the arts such distinctions were made to appear as natural substances. The constraints and imperatives that the ideology of the townsman household placed onto the arts were reflections of its many class anxieties—both those directed at the classes it wanted to emulate and those directed at the lesser selves that the upwardly mobile townsman hoped to leave behind. These alternative selves, the townsman's others, would become spectral images haunting the deviant conduct of Kiseki's comic antiheroes.

THE TOWNSMAN'S OTHERS

To a humorist such as Kiseki, the townsman's conflicted fixation on the arts offered a gold mine of rules to be comically broken and anxieties to be antagonized in the course of a relentless lampoon of the household and its values. Kiseki's comic antiheroes are, by and large, those who resist the mandate to engage in leisure cultivation "for the honor of the household and its repute in the world." Indeed, they are the deviant sons who risk bringing shame or at least disrepute on their households through their often willfully bizarre leisure pastimes. Kiseki is concerned with the amusing situations that stem from this eccentric conduct, but he also attends to its social consequences, tracking the fates of his deviants as they are pushed out of their households to drift toward the margins of townsman society.

In "Wounded by His Own Strength: The Character of a Sumo Wrestler Who Tossed His Own Fortune" (*Dairiki wa mi no kizu shindai nageta sumō-tori katagi*, vol. 2–3), Kiseki narrates a father's frustration as he reflects on the unbecoming conduct of his three sons.[30] The father, a fabulously wealthy Kyoto merchant and a leader among the trade association of moneylenders, retires and leaves the household in the hands of his eldest son, Magotarō, who promptly begins spending the family fortune on the courtesans of the Shimabara brothel district. Magotarō is disowned and the position of household head is passed to the second son, Magojirō. But Magojirō is of a somewhat more eccentric disposition: Unlike his suave and refined elder brother, "he was tall and swarthy, his arms and legs strapped with sinews, and had from a young age boasted of his strength." In keeping with his impressive physique and rowdy comportment, he becomes infatuated with sumo wrestling, spending his hours tossing the servants about in a homemade ring, inventing new throws, and competing in charity matches and nearby village festivals. The father soon disowns Magojirō as well and passes the household's duties to his third son, Magosaburō. But this son, too, has his quirks: He has become obsessed with *jōruri* puppetry, has transformed his room into a miniature stage, and invites the servants of nearby houses over to watch his amateur performances. In the end, the father gives up on all three sons and adopts an heir (figure 4.1).

The humor of the story centers on norms of townsman leisure, norms that aimed to regulate not only the degree to which the heir might indulge in leisure activities, but also the kinds of pastimes that were deemed acceptable or advantageous to the interests of the house. The central joke, to which Kiseki returns repeatedly throughout *Worldly Young Men*, is that in the end one could do much worse than spend time in the brothel districts, which, by the early eighteenth century, were deemed a perfectly acceptable form of leisure for the wealthy townsman if indulged in moderation. In contrast to the run-of-the-mill profligacy of the first son, the hobbies of the second and third sons seem willfully eccentric, as if designed to violate the elite townsman's sense of propriety. Witnessing Magojirō's intransigent attachment to sumo wrestling, the father reprimands him: "Now, a man might amuse himself with the *koto*, chess, calligraphy, and painting, or even tea, kickball, archery, and *nō* chanting. But stripping down naked and putting your body in harm's way for sport! Is this the conduct of the son of a pedigreed townsman, one who makes loans even to *daimyō*? From now on,

FIGURE 4.1 *Seken musuko katagi*. Illustration to "Wounded by His Own Strength: The Character of a Sumo Wrestler Who Tossed His Own Fortune" (vol. 2, 12u–13o). Courtesy of Waseda University Library.

put a stop to this and find a more appropriate form of recreation."[31] A similar class anxiety extends to Magosaburō, who is absorbed not in *jōruri* chanting or shamisen playing, both of which were low and marginal arts but not without popular followings among townsmen and even warriors, but with puppetry, a highly specialized art strongly associated with the outcast status of its practitioners. Despite the persistent stigmatization of the leisure arts in didactic discourses of the townsman household, the father's issue is not with the pursuit of leisure itself, which he acknowledges to be acceptable and even laudable for the upper-class townsman son, but with forms of leisure that are out of keeping with that position.

In selecting such eccentric arts, Kiseki pokes fun at a set of anxieties about the role of leisure practice as a fundamental piece of the townsman's processes of self-formation: in particular, a fear that unconventional leisure practices could produce dysfunctional townsman selves—indeed, that they could lead away from a proper townsman self and toward the townsman's others. As the story approaches its conclusion, Kiseki's tableau of eccentric leisure practices transmutes into a study of modes of social existence at the margins of townsman society. The narrator briefly summarizes the fates of all three sons: The eldest becomes the proprietor of a low-grade illicit brothel in the unlicensed prostitution district of Miyagawa-machi; the second becomes a cart driver in Shimo-Toba; and the youngest becomes the door-crier for a sideshow. Kiseki refracts the arts of erotic play (*iro-asobi*, the codified mores of the licensed prostitution quarters and etiquette of interacting with high-ranking courtesans, taught as a leisure art in its own right), sumo wrestling, and *jōruri* puppetry into marginal occupations, tracing a trajectory out of upper townsman society and toward the social periphery. Through these trajectories, Kiseki prods a pervasive anxiety toward the townsman's others, the modes of social being that the upwardly mobile townsman had rejected and defined himself in opposition to: the laboring underclass, out of which many now-respectable townsmen had pulled themselves up by their proverbial bootstraps, and the demimonde, which offered the male townsman an idealized experience of refined and unfettered play, but which always carried the eerie aura of misery and ruination. And yet, along with that apprehension, one detects in Kiseki's humor a parallel fascination with the exotic allure of the alternate forms of social existence that might exist beyond the boundaries of polite society—a desire to see eccentric dispositions cultivated through deviant arts and realized as alternative livelihoods, even if marginal ones. Rather than moral satire, Kiseki's work expresses an unsettling empathy with the household's deviants and dropouts.

As they shift from anxieties about the boundaries of townsman identity toward a phantasmal fascination with the townsman's others, Kiseki's stories offer hints of an alternative narrative of opting out of proper townsman society. By and large, Kiseki accomplishes this by inverting the hierarchy of work and play, reconfiguring livelihood as an extension of leisure practice, or transforming leisure into anything other than a hollow signifier of repute. A telling if somewhat facile example may be found in one of Kiseki's later works, *Characters of Worldly Clerks*. In "Chanting His Way into His Clients' Pockets, *Jōruri* Became Business Capital" (*Tokuigata o kataritsukeru jōruri wa akinai no motode*, vol. 2–3), two brothers are adopted as clerks for different businesses, the elder to a seller of Buddhist robes and the younger to a dealer in sundries.[32] Both are diligent enough, but become absorbed in their preferred leisure arts, the elder in *jōruri* chanting and the younger in Buddhist scholarship. These pastimes cause problems for their respective businesses when the elder brother regales his customers (members of the Buddhist clergy) with *jōruri* gossip, and the younger, selling cosmetics and accessories to the maids of his customers, attempts to lecture them on Buddhist morality. The problems are resolved when the two trade positions, each ending up in a job whose customers share his leisure tastes. When the elder brother subsequently has a falling out with his new master, he sets up his own business in sundries, relying on the popularity furnished by his amateur *jōruri* ability to steal his master's clients. *Worldly Clerks* is a much less cynical work than *Worldly Young Men*, using ingenious narrative twists to move toward conclusions that maintain the integrity of the household, albeit through the diligent and clever labors of its clerks rather than the efforts of its head. *Worldly Young Men*, in contrast, is deeply skeptical of any handy resolution of the dialectical tension between work and play, especially one that would serve and reproduce the interests of the household. Leisure arts reshaped and redirected in accordance with house trade, play in the service of work—to the contrary, the deviant protagonists of *Worldly Young Men* are unsatisfied until play has displaced work altogether as the very core of the townsman's self.

It goes without saying that this trajectory mirrored the career of Kiseki himself. Whether Kiseki believed his fate to be one of misfortune, this was very likely the feeling of his relatives and peers when he established his Ejimaya imprint in 1710, and all the more so when, in 1714, he bequeathed his long-established rice-cake business to a relative, effectively ending his family line. The precise reasons for Kiseki's decision to start this enterprise at the late age of forty-four are open to some degree of conjecture. Later anecdotal accounts would attribute the fall of the house of Murase to Kiseki's individual dissolution, framing Kiseki as the typical degenerate townsman scion who frittered away his inherited fortune in the brothel quarters; although such accounts would form the basis for modern authorial portraits, they should be taken as more hearsay and literary conceit than fact.[33] Rather than prostitution, Kiseki's main pastime as a youth had been the Kabuki theater, a cultural literacy that he ultimately converted into an amateur career as a writer of actor reviews and, in time, into a fraught career as a quasi-professional author of popular fiction—whether out of necessity or ambition one can only speculate. Fiction, though, was far from an established leisure art at the time. Saikaku had come to be celebrated as a popular writer, but his authorial persona had built off his reputation as a celebrated linked-verse poet. Kiseki's grandfather, better known by his retired Buddhist name of Sōkyū, had been a student of classical linked verse, once scolded by the by the poet Satomura Shōtaku for being too critical of his peers (Shōtaku is said to have remarked, "Let the mochi shop stick to making mochi"), and Kiseki's father likewise was a *haikai* poet who dabbled in other polite arts.[34] In comparison with such arts, which were recognized (if sometimes contested) as the proper pedigree for the wealthy townsman, the writing of fiction likely appeared to Kiseki's relatives as a nonsensical indulgence, something akin to sumo wrestling or puppeteering.

GENDER AND THE ARTS

The townsman culture of the leisure arts was, in Kiseki's time, overwhelmingly male. Nineteenth-century Edo would see the widespread involvement of women in the leisure arts and participation in aesthetic publics at both the amateur and professional levels, but such was not common until at least the middle decades of the eighteenth century.[35] Nevertheless, cultivation in a small range of polite and largely aristocratic arts was allowed and even encouraged for women within the home. The almanac *A Record of Great Treasures for Women* (Onna chōhōki, 1692) dedicates many of its pages to the marriage ceremony, pregnancy, and childbirth, but also devotes a volume to a range of arts—reading and calligraphy, classical poetry, *koto*, poem-matching games, and incense appreciation—as well as the more practical skills of home remedies and stain removal.[36] As was true of the arts the elite townsman son pursued, the daughter's participation in the arts was primarily a vehicle for status ambitions, a form of conspicuous leisure that signified the stature of the household within the townsman community, often as a necessary qualification for marriage into elite social ranks. But as with the male culture of the arts, this was not just a matter of conspicuous leisure. For the married woman, artistic practice overlapped with the critical forms of social and emotional labor that she was depended on to carry out in the household's interest: They would aid her in hosting and entertaining, and thus maintaining the interpersonal and professional relationships that secured the household's place in its social and commercial networks.[37] To the townsman husband, the shop front (*mise*) was a space of work, whereas the inner room (*oku no ma*) and parlor (*zashiki*) of the house were spaces of rest and recreation; but to the wife, whose labor was theoretically contained within the home, these were spaces of work, and the leisure arts that took place in them became a semi-obligatory form of labor.

Just as *Worldly Young Men* sees men's arts overflow the bounds of proper leisure to disturb the household's equilibrium of work and play, *Worldly Young Women* occasionally probes the norms surrounding women's arts to reveal a distinct set of anxieties about gendered forms of labor and leisure. Kiseki is less keen in his observations about daughters than he is about sons, and the stories contained in this work are equally if not more about the male patriarchs, often emasculated by the unbecoming conduct of their wives and daughters, as they are about the female household members in question. For example, in "A Poem-Loving Daughter Who Couldn't Count a Hundred Coins" (*Hyaku no zeni yomi-kaneru uta-zuki no musume*, vol. 1–3), a long-established but unintelligent and middling mirror dealer marries a highly pedigreed woman who spent time in the service of a lady-in-waiting of the Kyoto court.[38] Through her time in service, in addition to adopting many of the refined mores and manners of speech of the court aristocracy, the wife was able to attain significant accomplishments in classical poetry. The husband, despite a nagging sense of inferiority at his own uncouth simplicity, spends his days delighting in refined pastimes with his wife and lets his business decline. As the couple's fortunes falter, the wife is forced to abandon her aristocratic demeanor and exquisite fashions but retains her artistic refinement, expressed above all through her literacy. When the husband confesses that he lacks the competence to revitalize the household, it falls on his intelligent and educated wife to come up with a plan to support them. In narrating her efforts to rebuild the household through her wits and the skill of her pen, Kiseki traces a subtle navigation and renegotiation of the boundary that conventionally kept women out of the public-facing space of work.

Although the story initially frames the wife as accomplished in classical poetry, Kiseki's true concern is with the social and narrative possibilities within literacy itself, especially the act of writing. The wife's first enterprise is to open a classroom offering instruction in basic literacy to young women. Female instructors of neighborhood schools were far from unheard of, and many taught not only what was called the "woman's pen" (*nyohitsu*)—the vernacular *hiragana* script and its proper calligraphic expression—but the full curriculum of basic education to students of both genders.[39] Kiseki's heroine, however, finds that enrollments are slow to increase and, to make ends meet in the short term, begins offering her services as a surrogate scribe for the illiterate, lower-ranked prostitutes working in local teahouses and brothels. Thanks to the exceptional elegance of her calligraphy, credited to her experience in court service, she comes to be employed even by elite courtesans, and the household is able to survive comfortably on her earnings. Trouble arises when the husband's stern relatives, having discovered voluminous reams of love letters written to various local youths in his wife's distinctive hand, reprimand him that this could easily breed gossip of adultery and that he must put a stop to her scribal work. With this opportunity closed off, the wife pivots to preparing documents for legal disputes and lawsuits, a form of consulting that was believed to open the gateway to legal fraud and extortion schemes. Here the story seems to closely mirror that of the three eccentric sons, who see their leisure pursuits transformed into variously unsavory livelihoods on the margins of urban society, but Kiseki had different outcomes in mind for his literate heroine. Just as her business opportunities are closing off, the household's financial troubles are resolved by a deus ex machina as one of the *chō* elders passes away and the husband is invited to replace him—a sinecure with modest compensation that allows the couple to live comfortably. The husband's troubles are not over, however, because his public position requires him to mediate disputes among *chō* residents, a task that he is too dull to accomplish alone. The final narrative arc details an episode in which the hapless husband repeatedly is forced to consult his wife surreptitiously over matters of *chō* deliberation, a comical state of affairs that continues until the other elders decide that both husband and wife should be present for all future meetings, effectively acknowledging the literate wife as a member of the council of *chō* elders. As the narrator remarks in closing, she would accompany him even for summons by the samurai authorities, "and he ended up a laughingstock" (*waraigusa to natte hatekeri*).

As in many of Kiseki's stories, several of these narrative turns are inspired by moments from Saikaku's fiction. The most conspicuous textual poaching is from *Kōshoku ichidai onna* (*The Life of an Amorous Woman*, 1686), from the well-known story "Etiquette and Calligraphy for Women" (*Shorei onna yūhitsu*, vol. 2–4).[40] Saikaku's amorous woman is the daughter of a fallen court noble father and a commoner mother, but has spent her youthful years as a lady-in-waiting and owes her literacy and aesthetic refinement later in life in part to time spent immersed in the culture of the Kyoto aristocracy. In keeping with the spirit of Saikaku's early erotic works, the author is quick to link this refinement, infused with the rarified erotic ambiance of court culture, with the sexual marketplace. Many chapters trace a subtle pivot from aesthetic refinement, often in the form of one art or another, into a marketplace for gendered labor and from there to various forms of prostitution. In this episode, the amorous woman draws on her sophisticated literary accomplishments to open a school of penmanship for girls, but ends up instead writing love letters for a local young man; before long, through channeling her erotic energy into these letters, she develops feelings for the man and seduces him. As Yokota Fuyuhiko has observed, the late seventeenth century saw an intensification of anxieties concerning the figure of the woman working outside the household: Women's labor in the marketplace tended to be sexualized and placed on a spectrum with prostitution, and independent working women tended to be regarded as sexually available.[41] Saikaku cannily links these erotic associations to women's literacy. The act of writing carried an erotic charge that moved ambiguously across class distinctions, linking literate commoner women both to court aristocrats and to courtesans, and the story plays with the erotically charged desires and anxieties surrounding those class boundaries. To Kiseki, by contrast, the central anxiety bound up in women's literacy is not that of class but that of gender. Teaching penmanship, and even writing letters for courtesans, does not inspire erotic desire in Kiseki's heroine nor draw her into some form of prostitution, but it does decenter her husband's authority: both by displacing him as the breadwinner for the household and by implicating him in the gossip (not the reality of adultery, but the gossip concerning its possibility) that represents "a shame upon the family" (*ichimon no tsura-yogoshi*). When the incompetent husband is forced to beg his wife to close her classroom and find another business, he bluntly inverts the hierarchy of gendered labor on which the household was built: "From now on, stop all this writing love letters for courtesans, and think of some other novel way to make money. If you can [make enough to] provide for me, I'll cook all your meals and take care of the laundry, and even make the beds!"

Scholars of women's history have long observed that the critical roles played by women's labor within the early modern household represented a significant form of social agency, but it was nevertheless the case that, at least within the context of the wealthy townsman household, the labor of social (and biological) reproduction was seen largely as subordinate to the public-facing labor of the household head's house trade.[42] In "A Poem-Loving Daughter Who Couldn't Count a Hundred Coins," the husband's offer to do the housework is intended to make him out not as a generous and anachronistically progressive husband but as an impotent fool. Similarly, though it was not entirely unheard of for a wife to assume the public-facing role of household head and even to represent her household or community in transactions with authority, such instances were truly exceptional, most often in the case of widows without adult sons. Like the conclusions to many of Kiseki's stories, the transformation of the highly literate wife into a de facto *chō* elder is pure fancy, only reinforcing the emasculation of her husband as an illiterate laughingstock. Even worse than the misfortune of being saved by one's arts, it seems, is the misfortune of being saved by one's wife. Yet despite the significant censure and mockery that the story directs at the incompetent husband, the wife herself comes off, more so than Kiseki's haplessly idealistic townsman dilettantes, as sympathetic, accomplished, loyal, and attractive.

THE PROBLEM OF LITERACY

Kiseki maintained an ambivalent sympathy with the fools whose deviant dispositions led them out of polite townsman society, but his most wicked humor and most nuanced social commentary were reserved for the exemplary townsman, the well-heeled heir who effortlessly manifests the ideals and norms of the household. Kiseki delighted in finding twists and potholes that would send the earnest scion precipitously into straits that were just as unenviable as those of the most unrepentant of degenerates. It was through such exemplary figures that he was able to deconstruct the household on its own terms, showing that its norms were riddled with contradictions and that its ideals were thinly concealed pathologies. Kiseki's prodigal children were not mere deviants. They were, in the proper sense, enfants terribles, embodying the ways in which the household, and the townsman's idealized self-image within it, contained the seeds of its own ruination.

As we have seen, one of the core contradictions at the heart of townsman society was the place of the arts in the household. It was through the

THE MISFORTUNE OF BEING SAVED BY ONE'S ARTS

arts that the townsman performed his status as an exemplar among his peers, but the same arts carried the ever-present threat of status transgression and material ruination. One provisional resolution to this tension—one discursive move made to contain it—was to prioritize a small and relatively practical set of key cultural literacies, centered above all on literacy as such: on the skills of reading and writing, along with basic arithmetic. Kaibara Ekiken wrote in *Vernacular Precepts for Children* that commoner children "should be taught only arithmetic and writing, and should focus on their house trades," and that they should, under no circumstances, be exposed to the "harmful, useless, miscellaneous arts" (*itazura, muyō naru zatsugei*).[43] But Kiseki, whose highly deviant leisure art of choice was the very act of writing, was aware of the subversive potentialities concealed even within literacy itself: how the basic skills of reading and writing were inextricably linked to higher level literacies that verged into more transgressive forms of leisure and contained the troubling possibility of fashioning alternative selves.

The problem of literacy and its ambivalent status within the townsman household is the topic of "Unheeded Advice Makes for Ineffective Medicine: The Character of a Doctor Who Wouldn't Mend His Own Ways" (*Iken wa kikanu kusuri kokoro o naosanu isha katagi*, vol. 2–1).[44] Like many of the stories in *Worldly Young Men*, this one is framed by didactic admonitions against the baleful influence of the arts, but here these warnings are directed specifically against the pursuit of the polite arts in the service of townsman vanity and repute. Kiseki's narrator, echoing the good sense of Ekiken, suggests that the responsible townsman son should instead focus on the skills of writing and "after training in penmanship, take up scholarship." We are then introduced to just such a diligent son, who, on hearing such sound advice, "promptly ceased the myriad arts that he had begun learning" setting instead on a course of Confucian study; as if to underline the juxtaposition with the misbehaving *nō* drummer in the opening story, the illustration shows him having his drumming equipment destroyed (figure 4.2). But the young man quickly comes to focus on scholarship at the expense of his responsibilities to his house trade, taking on the moralizing postures of a Confucian scholar. The young man's scholarly affectation stands in the way of business when, in response to routine compliments from customers, he criticizes them for flattery by quoting from the *Analects*, in literary Sinitic: "It is said that 'Benevolence is seldom found

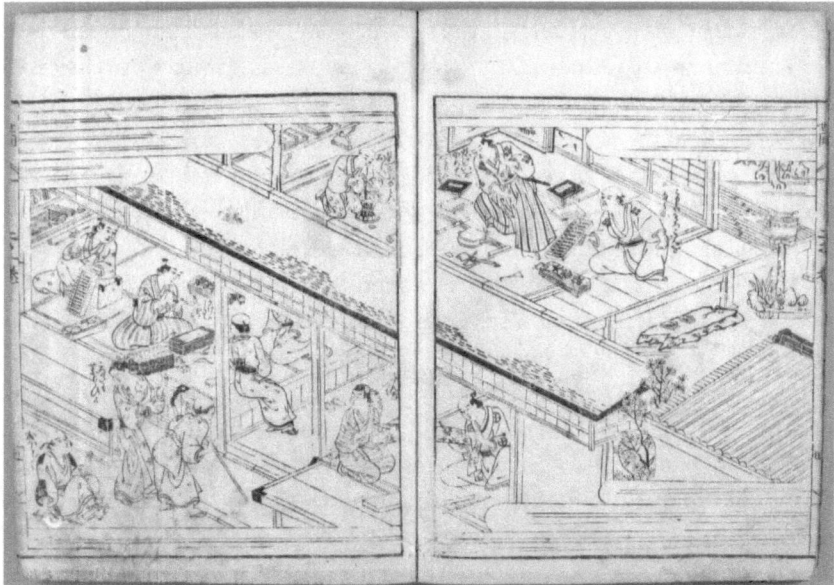

FIGURE 4.2 *Seken musuko katagi*. Illustration to "Unheeded Advice Makes for Ineffective Medicine: The Character of a Doctor Who Wouldn't Mend His Own Ways" (vol. 2, 4u–5o). Courtesy of Waseda University Library.

alongside skilled words and an ingratiating countenance.' People like you, who live only by insincerity, miss my true virtue." As long-time customers are put off by the son's pedantic rebuffs, the house clerks intervene, complaining to the father that "the young master's learning [*gakumon*] will be the end of this household.... If he would only spend a bit of time learning the abacus instead, it would do the house a great service!" But the son remains intransigent and begins, as an extension of his new persona as would-be Confucian scholar, to study and practice medicine, to catastrophic results: offering unsolicited and untested medicines to servants, neighbors, and tenants. When the situation gets out of hand, the father recognizes that his son's behavior has crossed a line and finally disowns him.

Although the story opens by criticizing the townsman culture of leisure arts as superficial and positing Confucian scholarship as a more wholesome pastime, scholarship is ultimately just as harmful as the "useless, miscellaneous arts." The amusing crux of the story is in witnessing how a path of modest and responsible learning goes immediately awry. But behind this flip comic inversion is Kiseki's close attention to the ideologically problematic gray area between, on the one hand, a modest program of pragmatic study that serves the households interests and, on the other, indulgence in scholarship as a leisure art in its own right, one that contains the possibility of displacing house trade to catastrophic effect.

The boundary between the basic study of literacy and arithmetic and the higher forms of scholarship was, after all, poorly defined. Laura Moretti has observed that popular conceptions of literacy in the seventeenth century were based on a distinction between *tenarai* and *gakumon*: the former essentially reading and writing and the latter referring to "the study of books written in literary Chinese and designed in such a way as to teach correct behavior—in other words, ethical knowledge."[45] Despite the appearance of a dichotomy between the two that seems to parallel the dichotomy between vernacular Japanese and literary Sinitic, Moretti contends that the two were merely ends of a continuous spectrum. Basic vernacular literacy offered many gateways into higher forms of learning through the intersection of multiple literacies, and, even through self-study mediated by printed texts, "the modulations between the two poles of *wabun* [Japanese writing] literacy and *kanbun* [Chinese writing] literacy ensured that some bridging between *tenarai* and *gakumon* was possible."[46] This continuity and ambiguity, between limited and pragmatically oriented training in basic literacy and the open-ended, potentially limitless horizons of *gakumon*, caused no small amount of anxiety in the educational philosophy of a pedant such as Kaibara Ekiken. Was training in advanced literacy and intellectual discourse to be embraced as a natural, desirable, or even obligatory extension of basic education, or should it be dismissed as an impractical and potentially distracting form of recreation akin to "the harmful, useless, miscellaneous arts?" The problem that Ekiken's didactic works were unable to solve was just this: If any orthodox program of education charted a continuous trajectory from *tenarai* into *gakumon*, and if the mandate of *gakumon* was an unending program of intellectual and moral cultivation through textual study, then did not literacy itself contain the latent potential to subvert, relativize, and transcend the ideological frameworks of the townsman household? This is the threat satirized by Kiseki's deviant townsman scholar.

A further irony of this character is that his investment in the scholarly arts is at once both too deep and too shallow: too deep, in that his obsessive interest in learning distracts from and comes to displace his house trade, but too shallow, in that his learning is lacking in substance and is a mere dilettantish affectation. The opening narration, which borrows at some length from Saikaku's *New Laughable Record* (*Shin kashōki*, 1688), decries the efforts of townsman amateurs in the tea ceremony, medicine, flower arrangement, and other polite arts as undercooked manifestations of bourgeois vanity, a reflection less of dedication to aesthetic refinement than to mercenary pursuit of reputation and standing among one's peers.[47] To Saikaku, who was a highly accomplished cultural professional (poet) in his own right, this was an incidental failure of his fellow townsmen, who could be proper artists if they were to pursue the arts in the proper spirit. But Kiseki's key insight, the deeper truth he found within Saikaku's sardonic commentary and developed into his own original critique, was that this failure was hardly incidental. It was no accident that townsman practitioners tended to be superficial in their knowledge of the arts because, to the townsman, the arts were merely a vehicle of "the honor of the household and its repute in the world," a medium of social intercourse and shared cultural literacy rather than a means of spiritual cultivation or self-expression. In other words, the arts to the townsmen were valued above all as signifiers.

The accepted standard was one of being conversant rather than being a specialist: One only needed to be as competent as one could expect one's peers to be, and by the same token, functional competence in a modest range of arts was more desirable than a very high level of specialization in one. Ekiken gives this anxiety a Confucian color: "Even for the useful arts, if you give excessive affection to only one . . . then your spirit will become biased toward it rather than commuting with all things."[48] The standard of broad but shallow cultural literacy is nowhere better exemplified than in a textbook like the *Record of Great Treasures for Men*, which gives only the most rudimentary introduction to terminology and entry-level "gist" (*omomuki*) of the arts discussed—just enough to keep up with a conversation on the topic, perhaps, but hardly enough to satisfy a demand for independent self-instruction. Although "Unheeded Advice Makes for Ineffective Medicine" begins with a critique of townsman dilettantism, such dilettantism was precisely the point, for the alternative path of serious scholarship was, from the perspective of the household, likely to cause as much harm as good. Once the seemingly diligent son has "mostly gotten through the enunciation of the Four Books," he grandly declares himself to be a scholar, but his failure is neither that of choosing the wrong art nor of having not studied it deeply enough, but of not recognizing that his learning was always supposed to be superficial: a practical tool set in service of commerce, or else a signifier of a refined self and an instrument of the repute of the household, but nothing more.

SIGNIFIERS OF REPUTE AND SIGNIFIERS OF DEVIANCE

Concealed within Kiseki's seemingly satirical stories of the ignominious failures of townsman screw-ups and eccentrics is a nuanced commentary on the values and norms of the household. Takahashi Akihiko identifies Kiseki's *katagi-mono* as inaugurating a genre of "fool's tales" (*gujintan*): narratives of comic failure by those who diverge from society's norms. Although the fool's tale appears at first glance as satire, with the reader and author residing safely on the side of common sense to ridicule and thus police the kinds of conduct that defy it, Takahashi sees the satirical form as a pattern that can be inverted and deployed to different ends. In Takahashi's reading, the *katagi-mono* is an ironic genre that "harbors as its orienting axis a skepticism toward all values"; it twists the satirical form to throw into question the norms themselves, which exist only to be frustrated and turned on their heads for comic effect. But while questioning the legitimacy of any orthodox or mainstream values, the fool's tale also demonstrates the impossibility of imagining a legitimate alternative: The doxa is itself a fiction, but anyone who should attempt to escape it through antiheroic transgression is doomed to be a fool and a failure.[49] Indeed, Kiseki's insight was a step deeper than this, for he knew that the norms of the household and the modes of their transgression were merely two sides of the same coin, the ideologies of the household pathologies in disguise, both rooted in a superficial grasp of culture as a mere set of signifiers lacking in substance. The amateur townsman enthusiast, who has internalized this very logic, is, even in his most deeply felt and passionately pursued leisure arts, unable to escape this alienation: If the normative arts of the townsman house were mere signifiers of repute, then *the unbecoming arts of the townsman eccentric were to Kiseki mere signifiers of alternative selves*. In attempting to opt out of the household to cultivate a persona as a cultural professional, he is doomed to be inauthentic, for inauthenticity is all he knows.

Even and especially in his most grotesque caricatures, Kiseki finds an unsettling pathos in this condition. In "Strung Along by Those Better Versed in the Ways of the World: The Character of a Poet" (*Seken no hito ni hanage o yomaruru kajin katagi*, vol. 3–1), Suketarō, the bright and diligent adopted heir of an Edo merchant, eschews the usual youthful vices of the pleasure quarters, taking his leisure instead in the study of classical poetry.[50] Like the would-be doctor's initial pursuit of Confucian learning, this is presented as a sign of his good sense, propriety, and modest sophistication, and as an exemplary signifier in service of the repute of his household. One evening while on a boating outing with his father-in-law, he is moved by the beauty of the Musashino moon over the water and composes a verse, whereupon he is overheard by one of his fellow revelers, a certain Dōtetsu, who senses an opportunity to insinuate himself into wealthy company. Complimenting the young man on the quality of his verse, Dōtetsu goes on to remark that his wife maintains correspondence with an aristocratic household in Kyoto in which she had once served, and that he might include the verse in his wife's next letter; if all goes well, the master might offer his evaluation or even include the poem in a future anthology. Suketarō, floored by the possibility, insists that Dōtetsu go himself and offers to pay for his trip and all its attendant expenses. When Dōtetsu reappears several weeks later, he reports the aristocrat's supposed response:

> After taking some time reciting it, the nobleman responded, saying, "The idea is interesting, but the poetry of a mere commoner after all can hardly be sublime, possessing as it does a natural vulgarity. Townsmen always have their hearts set on how to make a living and are caught up in their own lust for profit; thinking intently on such things day and night, their poetry is profoundly vulgar. Fun'ya no Yasuhide's poetry may have been like a merchant wearing silk, but this is like someone in cotton garb trying to judge incense. It's regrettable however you look at it."[51]

The reference is to the *kana* preface to the *Collection of Ancient and Modern Poems* (*Kokin wakashū*, ca. 905), in which Ki no Tsurayuki writes of the poet Fun'ya no Yasuhide that his words are skilled but not fitted to the content, "like a merchant wearing fine silks." The simile of "someone in cotton garb trying to judge incense" comically transposes this sentiment to the Edo period, when merchants were expected to wear cotton and judging incense was seen as an aristocratic pastime, while more subtly invoking the concern with authenticity that was part and parcel of the class-specific nature of aesthetic distinction. Dōtetsu has in fact fabricated the story and simply pocketed the money, but the invented response of the aristocrat is revealing, for it shows a stereotypically aristocratic attitude toward the capacity for cultural production: The commoner can compose only vulgar poetry because the social being of the commoner is fundamentally vulgar. Although Dōtetsu intends these remarks to come off as callous and cutting, the oblivious Suketarō receives the response gratefully as earnest advice, interpreting it to mean that he will write better poetry if he distances himself from commerce, and begins dressing and conducting himself like an aristocrat. His sartorial performance of aristocratic mores immediately collapses into travesty, for, in terms of the status distinction between townsman and aristocrat, clothes alone hardly make the man. The grim and terribly precise irony of Kiseki's conclusion is that Suketarō, having been chastised for writing poetry that is merely elegant signifiers lacking in elegant substance, can only respond with a proliferation of more signifiers, his appearance collapsing into a grotesque cosplay of the poetic tradition:

> He abruptly changed his trade, setting up shop as a seller of "incense oil" and buying up a dealer in face powder to boot. Whenever he wrote a poem, he would sign it with great delight, writing in black ink: "Cheap Verse" Fujiwara, Deputy of Musashi. He was afflicted with the illness known as *waka*, and as soon as his father passed away, his estate fell rapidly into ruin, and he came to live in a pitifully small tenement in Kanasugi. His "mighty paper jacket" in tatters, he became a "vagabond from a distant land," and, spiraling into debt, he wanted for even a "single demon's mouthful" to eat, but even if he furrowed his brow like [poetic immortal] Sarumaru Dayū, he couldn't find a way to get by. In the end, he broke the "ore-red earth" and, carrying a load of thirty scallions on his shoulders, made a living selling his deep-rooted poetic spirit.[52]

As the story concludes, it devolves into nonsense as Kiseki closes with a series of progressively more far-fetched plays on words. Like most puns, the wordplay is virtually untranslatable. Suketarō switches his business to selling hair oil, known colloquially as "incense oil" (*kyara no abura* or *kyara-abura*), simply because the term *kyara* (incense) carries aristocratic connotations. His pen name, "Cheap Verse" Fujiwara (Fujiwara no Yasubun 安文), alludes to the name of Fun'ya no Yasuhide while suggesting the literal meaning of cheap writing. The nonsensical "mighty paper jacket" (*chihayafuru kamiko*) and "vagabond from a distant land" (*hisakata no tenjiku rōnin*) are plays on conventional epithets: "mighty" (*chihayafuru*) on *kami* (god), which here becomes *kamiko* (paper jacket), and distant (*hisakata no*) on *tenjiku* (India) but here in the compound *tenjiku rōnin* (vagabond). The reference to a "demon's mouthful" (*oni hitokuchi*) alludes to the Akutagawa episode of *The Tales of Ise* (*Ise monogatari*), and so on and so forth. The coup de grâce is "thirty scallions": a pun on *misojihitomoji* (thirty-one syllables), an elegant term for *waka* that Kiseki breaks into *misoji* (thirty) and *hitomoji*, a feminine word for Japanese scallions (*negi*); deeply rooted (*nebukaki*) suggests *nebuka*, another synonym for scallions. The passage is not intended to make narrative sense or present a coherent vision of this character and his social prospects: It is simply a pastiche of vocabulary variously linked to the traditions of classical verse. Narrative collapses into nonsense.

Or perhaps not nonsense, for this language is ordered by a different sort of sense: that of poetic association, punning, and other forms of associative linkage that constitute a culture of poetic verbal play with roots in the tradition of classical verse. But neither is this a terribly authentic evocation of that tradition, for Kiseki, who lacked Saikaku's training in linked-verse poetics and the grasp of the vernacular canon mediated through that, invokes only the most common of pillow words, allusions, and classical references. Kiseki's verbal play is a broad aping of the poetic tradition, a clever play of signifiers but one that inevitably comes across, indeed, as lacking in substance. Kiseki was in many ways a pastiche artist who cobbled together textual mosaics through citations drawn widely from the world of popular print, and this ingenious travesty of poetic language, which obliquely and loosely evokes associations of the Kyoto aristocracy, was a showpiece of his writing craft. But along with this technical showpiece and buried just beneath the cartoonish caricature of the traditions of classical verse, we are also given the chilling portrait of the fractured consciousness of the lumpen townsman dilettante. Like many of Kiseki's protagonists, Suketarō is unable either to recognize or to accept the proper limits of townsman leisure, but equally unable to recognize the limitations of his own poetic ability and the utter impossibility of his cultural ambitions. He is unable to see that his own language is a travesty, that he is doomed to be both a failed merchant and an inauthentic living parody of an aristocratic poet. In his elaborately costumed pantomime of aristocratic mores, we see the dilettante who has been so consumed by fantasy that he has lost his grasp on reality. In the very language with which Kiseki closes the episode, we have the linguistic trace of a consciousness that, in the absence of both a deep understanding of poetry and a substantive connection to aristocratic culture, has collapsed into a fetishistic attachment to the signifiers that stand in for them.

The reader, of course, retains the distance to laugh at what is, to most appearances, a preposterous and absurd fate, and takes the closing sequence as merely a round of amusing wordplay. But lest this be mistaken for a purely didactic laughter, one that functions to police the boundaries of acceptable conduct by singling out Suketarō as the object of scorn and derision, Kiseki makes it clear that Suketarō, as he delights in his preposterous aristocratic cosplay, is laughing along with the reader. To the degree that Kiseki uses laughter to mark the boundaries of acceptable townsman conduct, there are also eerie echoes of laughter from the other side of that boundary, from the space of social oblivion that awaits the townsman who abandons his status of birth.

This is not to say that, in reality, it was impossible or unthinkable for a townsman to become a poet, scholar, or any other type of cultural professional. As Nishikawa Joken remarked in the opening to *The Townsman's Satchel* (*Chōnin bukuro*, 1719), "Thanks to the peaceful reign of the past hundred years, it has come to pass that many of our scholars, doctors, poets, tea masters, and practitioners of the various refined arts come from the ranks of townsmen."[53] Joken himself was, despite his merchant birth, a scholar of some renown and a successful writer of both scholarly tomes and popular instruction; Saikaku had abandoned his hereditary trade to pursue a career as a professional poet and, ultimately, writer of fiction; and other townsman masters of the arts were not uncommon. Kiseki's failure to imagine the transformation of the wealthy townsman into an independent cultural professional did not represent a clear reflection of the realities of the cultural professional but instead his keen sensitivity to the ideologies of the townsman household. His works refracted what the ideologues of the household imagined the townsman could or should be, a vision that was almost claustrophobic in its reluctance to imagine the possibility of positive outcomes for the townsman who was forced or who opted to live by his arts—such could be seen only as misfortune.

THE (IM)POSSIBILITY OF TOWNSMAN AUTHORSHIP

The townsman household offered the promise of security amid the existential uncertainty of the early modern economy and the unpredictable ebbs and flows of the floating world. To the generation of entrepreneurs who had worked their way into wealth and property during the rapid economic growth of the mid-seventeenth century, it was a mark of success, of having earned a place among the rarified upper strata of urban society; many likely wanted to spare their progeny such efforts. But to the younger generation that was born or married into such a position, the household's significant privileges also came with a share of alienations. The alienation of inheriting a name rather than making one, of being explicitly forbidden from entrepreneurial creativity in favor of an ideal of passive stewardship of a name and estate made by one's father or grandfather. The alienation of living in a time of stasis and consolidation, when movement outside one's position of birth was increasingly unlikely—as well as a time of intense normalization, when the wealthy ranks of urban society were unified around shared ideals of polite sophistication, and when the obligation of the proper townsman heir was above all to be splendidly normal, just like his peers but hopefully just a little better at it. The alienation of having all of one's energies subordinated to the household and its potential to sustain and incrementally increase its estate in perpetuity—and to have even one's leisure pastimes relegated to mere signifiers of repute in a game of keeping up appearances. To be born as a propertied merchant in this moment was to be born into a role that preceded you and that you were simply born to fill, as if a character copied from a primer. Kiseki's *Worldly Young Men* was an iconic reflection of this moment, and a rebellion against it.

It was also a reflection of Kiseki's career. Scholars have long gestured toward the possibility of an autobiographical reading of *Worldly Young Men* and its sequels, whether as an expression of the intransigence of a rebellious heir or the circumspection of an erstwhile prodigal son when faced with the responsibilities of a father.[54] I would suggest that Kiseki's genre-defining work was also a bitterly ironic piece of self-parody of his career as a writer. In parallel with the middling and darkly comic careers of his characters, Kiseki's biography traces an attempt to grapple with the ideologies of the townsman household, to chart a new course through its fraught dialectics of work and play, and to imagine the (im)possibility of townsman authorship. To Kiseki, who renounced the stability of the household to carve out a path as a cultural professional, this was indeed a desperate attempt, the fruits of which were none other than *Worldly Young Men* and the genre that it spawned.

Regarding the figure of the modern author, Pierre Bourdieu writes that to understand "any writer, major or minor, is first of all to understand what the status of writer consists of at the moment considered; that is, more precisely, the social conditions of the possibility of this social function, of this social personage."[55] To Bourdieu, the condition of possibility for the modern author is the existence of a literary field that was largely autonomous from the commercial and political concerns of bourgeois society. The leisure arts of Kiseki's time did not represent the formation of a fully autonomous artistic culture, but instead one in which practices of play and leisure identities existed only in symbiotic relation to everyday social roles and hierarchies. This was especially true in the context of the townsman class, where the ideologies of the household operated to place ludic practice in a subordinate position to the centrality of labor by reducing the polite arts to a mere signifier of status and constitutive element of the townsman's processes of self-formation. In such a context, fiction writing was neither recognizable as labor nor as leisure. Kiseki's career thus makes him a figure not for the author as "a sovereign position which proclaims itself free of any determination," but for the contradictions within the social institutions of eighteenth-century townsman society that constrained the possibility of autonomous authorship.[56]

Kiseki's early works published by Hachimonjiya were all written anonymously, a fact that modern scholars have often attributed to the relatively low status afforded to fiction at the time: Kiseki, as the master of an elite townsman house, would not wish to be known to be moonlighting as an author of actor reviews and amorous stories.[57] We have little concrete evidence, though, that authorship was explicitly stigmatized. It was simply culturally illegible: At the turn of the eighteenth century, there was no coherent notion of authorship for popular fiction. The most common form of authorship in Kiseki's time was the writer-publisher (perhaps more precisely, the publisher-writer): booksellers who produced their own works or had them composed in an ad hoc fashion by close acquaintances, likely viewing textual composition as a relatively minor part of what was primarily a commercial trade. The paragon of the publisher-writer was Saikaku's erstwhile imitator and competitor Nishimura Ichirōemon, and many others would follow this mode: Nishizawa Ippū (Kyūzaemon); Yama no Yatsu (Yamamoto Hachizaemon); and, indeed, Hachimonjiya, who for all intents and purposes was understood to be the author of the works penned by Kiseki, and would continue to be so into the modern era. Certainly, there were exceptions to this pattern, including writers such as Miyako no Nishiki, who claimed to have made a living by their brushes, but such cases were rare. The greatest exception was Saikaku himself, but Saikaku's renown as a writer of fiction had been built on his spectacular efforts in the field of linked verse—his leisure art of choice—and, though little is known with certainty about his milieu, it is likely that he was well enough off to retire early, leave his trade to his clerks, and live a comfortable if eccentric life of writing and travel. It would be nearly a century before the subjectivity of the professional author would crystallize in the form of the *gesakusha*, and even then it remained far removed from the modern figure of the autonomous author as artist.

Authorship of popular fiction at the turn of the eighteenth century was in the gray area between intellectual labor and cultural play: an ambiguous surplus, both quasi-ludic and quasi-ergic, growing off of more established leisure identities (linked-verse poet, scholar) or commercial trades (bookseller). The ill-defined status of the writer worked to the advantage of an enterprising publisher such as Hachimonjiya Jishō, who could turn the spontaneous pastimes of an amateur theater aficionado like Kiseki into great profit. Inchoate forms of copyright had been developing since the 1680s in response to piracy and the emergence of derivative works, but such rights were essentially a matter of a publisher's rights to profits and held no guarantees for the author in the absence of any coherent concept of intellectual property.[58] Even so, Jishō was not unaware of the value that the name of a proven author could have as a form of advertisement for new texts. According to a later account by Kiseki in the preface to *Travel Baskets of Lads and Ladies* (*Yakei tabi tsuzura*, 1712), Jishō once requested that he be allowed to use Kiseki's name in connection with his works, but Kiseki demurred: "In the first place, they were not works that I had composed myself, but rather made by borrowing phrases from Saikaku, so it would seem truly impudent to put on airs and declare my own name [as the author]."[59] Kiseki, who was nothing if not open about the degree to which his work—indeed, his entire practice of writing—was built on copies of other writers, seems to have had reservations about making claims about the work as his own legacy and property. Instead, he agreed that the works could be released under Jishō's name; Jishō, the exemplary townsman entrepreneur, shared none of his friend's qualms concerning opportunistic appropriation of value generated by the labor of others.

Matters changed in 1710, when Kiseki opened the publisher Ejimaya Ichirōzaemon under the name of his son, entering a period of rivalry with Hachimonjiya that would last until their reconciliation in 1718.[60] Kiseki's motivations in establishing his own bookselling business were likely multifaceted. To one degree or another, by starting his own imprint, Kiseki sought to lay claim to more of the profits from his writing as a form of creative labor. Although the details of the prior financial relationship between Kiseki and Jishō regarding possible manuscript fees are open to speculation, it is probable that any arrangements took the form of an ad hoc agreement between publisher and writer, perhaps in the form of a one-time gratuity but likely not accompanied by any formal conception approximating royalties from sales. Perhaps out of respect for their long-standing friendship and professional relationship, Kiseki initially pursued an arrangement of joint publishing with his friend and mentor, which would amount to a specified stake (*kabu*) in the venture—that is, a percentage of profits.[61] (Jishō naturally balked at Kiseki's proposal of joint publication, which deviated from a precedent that had long worked greatly to his advantage.) At the same time, we cannot discount the possibility that Kiseki was also driven to a degree by the desire to dedicate himself undistracted to his leisure art of choice, to which he had already likely been devoting a great deal of his time and effort, perhaps at the expense of his inherited house trade. Despite his humility regarding his borrowings from Saikaku, he took a measure of pride in the dramatic success of several of his early works, and when Hachimonjiya, amid their increasing hostilities, found a replacement ghost writer in the otherwise obscure Miren (dates unknown), Kiseki would use his authorial prefaces to repeatedly blast this replacement as a mere amateur, expressing a growing sense of confidence and ambition as a seasoned professional.[62] Indeed, whether due to creative inspiration, interpersonal rivalry, economic necessity, or some combination of the three, this period of rivalry saw a flurry of productive output and formal innovation from Kiseki, who penned five new works in 1712 and five more in 1713.[63] The culmination of these years of rivalry came in 1714, when Kiseki passed his inherited rice-cake business to a relative and formally renounced any ties to what had been his house trade.[64]

Significantly, it was at precisely the same juncture that he began to use the name by which he is now known: Ejima Kiseki. The authorial subjectivity represented by the pen name Ejima Kiseki was predicated on a renunciation of the hereditary house trade in favor of the identity as writer that the erstwhile Murase Shōzaemon had cultivated as a leisure art—albeit one that was quite eccentric for a townsman of his stature. But the dark irony of this shift was that Kiseki could not exist in the world as an autonomous author, but had to channel his leisure art into, indeed, a new house trade: professional bookseller. Along with bearing the misfortune of being saved by one's arts, Kiseki was destined to face the truism that a hobby changes when it becomes a job, and that the real prospects of the working cultural professional diverge from the idle fancies of the townsman dilettante—a dynamic that he projected onto his various townsman screw-up sons, who become immersed in their eccentric arts only to find that, once they have fallen or opted out of their hereditary trades, they lack the ability to make it as cultural professionals.

Much like the fates of his protagonists, Kiseki's new house trade proved far from secure. With the exception of his wildly successful character pieces, most of the works he released through his imprint saw middling sales; even after severing ties with his old family business, the address of the Ejimaya shop moved almost every year, likely indicating uneasy finances, and Kiseki's output was slow and inconsistent. Although he continued to wage an increasingly bitter (or perhaps simply petty) war of public opinion with Hachimonjiya in the prefaces to his works, the two would reconcile in 1718; the reasons for this reconciliation remain unclear, as do its terms, but likely resulted in a compromise in which Kiseki's authorship was recognized but Jishō retained the controlling share of profits—in other words, not far from the pair's original arrangement, but with nominal credit for authorship given to Kiseki.[65] Although this recognition of Kiseki's authorial agency might be seen a victory and validation of his creative labor throughout his career, it equally marked the end of his ambitions toward independence as an author-publisher. The Ejimaya imprint released no more works and formally folded in 1722 or 1723. Kiseki, who thus had presided over the collapse of two houses—that of his inheritance and that of his entrepreneurial invention—spent his remaining years churning out works for Hachimonjiya and other Kyoto publishers, the majority in the mode of theatrically inspired period pieces, along with the occasional character piece, jest book, illustrated erotica, and works in other minor genres. In his late years, he seems to have largely been in the care of various relatives, bouncing from one residence to another along with his youngest son, Genkichi, who would become an occasional author in his own right before being adopted as an heir in the household of a more financially stable relative.[66]

Kiseki's world was one without an autonomous literary or cultural field, one in which the practice of the author could not sustain itself through a wholesale rejection or inversion of the economic logics that constituted the townsman doxa. Nevertheless, Bourdieu's observation, made of Flaubert as a figure for the modern author, rings true: that authorship "is rooted in the sterile dilettantism of the bourgeois adolescent, temporarily freed from social determinations."[67] Indeed, Kiseki's case feels all the more sterile and dilettantish than that of Bourdieu's Flaubert, for Kiseki's dilettantism could not be refracted into an idealized image of the author as artist, and it remains difficult to read a work like *Worldly Young Men* without feeling that palpable sterility. But precisely for that reason, the understated desperation, which in the figure of the townsman poet spirals into nonsense, attests to Kiseki's ambition, his effort both to imagine and to personally manifest a form of social and aesthetic agency that could barely be glimpsed in the interstices of the status system; it attests also to his keen understanding of that very predicament. Townsman authorship was impossible, barely imaginable, predicated on failure and on ridicule, even on recognition of the superficial, derivative, myopic, antisocial, and inauthentic nature of the alternative self that was constituted through leisure practice. Kiseki, though he confronted this fact in both his writing and his life, was hardly a didactic pedant and refused to condemn it. To the contrary, his understanding of this condition allowed him to perceive and to reveal the contradictions and alienations on which the townsman household was built—indeed, to reveal the fictionality of the household itself.

As we saw in part 1, the townsman household was a fiction of sorts, built on modes of appropriation, exclusion, and exploitation that were coeval with new textual practices and modes of narration. The successful townsman was none other than the townsman who mastered the signifiers of entrepreneurship and thus represented himself as a success, and the deployment of the leisure arts as signifiers of repute in the urban community was no more than an extension of that strategic dissembling. Kiseki was uniquely astute in observing just how precarious the fictions sustaining the household were; how any of the household's virtues could become vices; how any of its members could, through minor eccentricity, upset its tenuous balance and send it spiraling into ruin; and how, even in the best of times, the imperative toward house trade at the heart of townsman identity was, as Mitsui Takafusa was happy to acknowledge, "merely a matter of making money on interest." But despite his awareness of the tenuous fictions on which the everyday reality of the townsman was built, Ejima Kiseki knew too well that there was no escape, for outside the fiction of the household was the sobering truth of obscurity and ostracization, balanced only by the private pleasures of the socially deviant.

Chapter Five

REPRESENTING NORMALITY

In modern Japanese, the word *katagi*, conventionally written with the Sinitic compound *kishitsu* 気質 and often translated as "character," refers to the distinctive disposition or personality associated with a particular social type or occupation. In what is perhaps its most common usage, *shokunin katagi* (character of the craftsman) evokes the quality of exacting, distempered perfectionism associated in the modern era with the figure of the artisan and the ethos of artisanal craft. But there is a curious tension within *katagi*, apparent from even the phrase "character of the craftsman." What is taken as typical is simultaneously marked as the unique quirk of a particular type, as if to say that craftsmen are an odd bunch but generally odd in the same way. From the perspective of a normatively middle-class society centered on white-collar office work, the "character of the craftsman" is deemed eccentric, but even when the term *katagi* is applied to the office worker—*sararīman katagi*—it comes with an implicit othering, a focus on the idiosyncratic that deviates implicitly from some imagined, more universal norm. To mark something as a *katagi* is to relativize it, to mark it as a deviation, and to acknowledge that what is normal or characteristic for one type might be peculiar for someone in another role. Yet, at the same time, it is to assume the context of a society in which such eccentricities are accepted, perhaps taken up as objects of mirth but rarely outright mockery or derision, accepted as charming and familiar quirks, even recognized as norms in their own right. This is not to say that a *katagi*-esque social imaginary is truly diverse: *Katagi* embodies an affectionate embrace of alterity only in familiar and domesticated forms, pluralism within a limited and stable horizon. Built on a dialectical tension between normativity and eccentricity, it suggests a vision of society in which everyone is a bit eccentric but certain forms and degrees of eccentricity are normal.

This use of the term was the invention of Ejima Kiseki, and the social imaginary that it reflected was that of the early eighteenth-century townsman. It was first given expression in his *Characters of Worldly Young Men* (*Seken musuko katagi*, 1715) and progressively articulated in the sequels *Characters of Worldly Young Women* (*Seken musume katagi*, 1717), *Characters of Old Men of the Floating World* (*Ukiyo oyaji katagi*, 1720), and *Characters of Worldly Clerks* (*Seken tedai katagi*, 1730). Kiseki's works established a textual paradigm that would become the dominant form of *ukiyo-zōshi* until the decline of Kamigata popular fiction in the late eighteenth century: the *katagi-mono*, or character piece, so named for the mellifluous use of the term *katagi* to brand collections of comic tales surrounding common social types. Later writers would produce similar collections centered on a vast range of social types, including mothers, mistresses, millionaires, maidservants, mothers-in-law, household heads, matchmakers, doctors, Buddhist priests and preachers, *haikai* poets, shogunal bannermen, theater enthusiasts, tea practitioners, cultural professionals of various stripes; and the titular trope of *katagi* would be repurposed to different ends by later Edo *gesaku* writers, as in Shikitei Sanba's *Characters of Drunkards* (*Namaei katagi*, 1813).[1] But despite the range of social types that the genre eventually came to comprise, the *katagi-mono* in its original form was situated squarely within the middle to upper strata of townsman society, framed by the social unit of the household, and focused on characters who transgress the norms of the household in various ways.[2] As we saw in chapter 4, this persistent fixation on eccentricity and transgression was rooted in Kiseki's keenly felt alienation at a sense of townsman identity that had been thoroughly instrumentalized by and subordinated to the interests of the household, and that consisted largely of acts of self-representation without authentic substance. But transgressions lose their bite as they are repeated, and forms of behavior that once seemed scandalous can, through repeated acts of representation, come to appear as familiar and even charming peccadilloes. This concluding chapter explores how Kiseki's satirical vision transformed as the *katagi-mono* evolved from a singular deconstruction of the townsman household into a stable genre in its own right, one that could organize a normative vision of a diverse urban society.

The *katagi-mono* is a paradoxical genre. On the one hand, it is based in a conception of self in terms of social role, expressed materially through dress, manner, and speech. In light of this tendency, the genre might be seen as an iconic literary reflection of the social logic of status group (*mibun*): a form of narrative in which selfhood is imagined in relation to social roles rather than in terms of (to give the modern foil) the unique individual, and in which such selfhood is represented through the externalities of material form and conduct rather than through the suggestion of interior depth. On the other hand, the *katagi-mono* rarely depicts characters who typify their roles: The works of Kiseki and his followers fixate on eccentricity and deviance, on characters whose conduct defies their given places in status society. Of course, stories in which characters transgress norms can be a highly effective way of communicating and reinforcing those norms; Kiseki claimed as much in the prefaces to many of his works. A common comparison is with the genre of Theophrastan characters—didactic sketches of commonly perceived moral vices or character flaws—that saw a brief flourishing in early modern England.[3] But whereas that genre was defined by its tendency to abstract common vices into generic types—the boor, the bumpkin, the sycophant—the *katagi-mono* tends, conversely, to defy the typical, even the typical vice, in an ever-escalating pursuit of unexpected eccentricity. Kiseki's characters are not wicked or deficient so much as odd. Indeed, the *katagi-mono* have often been criticized for seeming to say very little about their types, about what it means to be a townsman son or a daughter or a father, even by negation.[4] Each of Kiseki's works exhibits a chaotic heterogeneity of content that resists easy description. In this regard, the *katagi-mono* may be seen as the ultimate evolution of the "space of the collection": a symbolic form that represents diverse content by placing it within the centripetal pull of unifying norms.

This tension between normativity and eccentricity also defines the *katagi-mono* at the level of textual form. Kiseki is notorious for his liberal borrowings from Ihara Saikaku—to some degree from other contemporaries like Miyako no Nishiki and Yashoku Jibun, but above all from

Saikaku, whose work he seems to have taken as an object of self-conscious study and emulation, a corpus to be endlessly cited, remixed, and rewritten. Since the advent of modern textual scholarship, Kiseki has often been dismissed as at best a hack and at worst a plagiarist; more recent scholars have defended him on grounds that certain forms and degrees of borrowing and citation were expected and even celebrated in a textual culture without systematic notions of intellectual property, but it remains true that Kiseki was unrivaled in the frequency and systematicity of his liberal intertextual practice, and even his apologists consider him a competent popularizer who distilled Saikaku's eclectic works into a familiar set of conventions for textual reproduction.[5] However, it is hardly the case that Kiseki's writing was merely a direct reproduction, a straightforward emulation of his literary role model or a curated catalog of stock types and greatest hits. The *katagi-mono* is endlessly inventive in how it deploys its appropriations: It twists its citations and borrowed images in new directions, appropriating fragments of prose or narrative situations and repurposing them to new ends, and pursuing novelty even to the point of nonsense and narrative collapse. Yet, despite its chaotic heterogeneity, it would become the most stable genre within the *ukiyo-zōshi* corpus, the label of *katagi* an iconic signifier of genericity itself. The question is what kind of sense the *katagi-mono* made out of this formal tension between normative reproduction—of textual forms, of social norms—and eccentric innovation.

I argue that the *katagi-mono* reflected a new understanding of townsman identity, oriented around relatively narrow norms of conduct but flexible enough to accommodate certain forms and degrees of deviation. I refer to this as a regime of normality. By normality, I mean a kind of social consciousness structured primarily by the question of whether the conduct of any individual is in keeping with the expectations of a given role or class, a sense of social appropriateness in which the primary imperative assumed for any given social role is to conform to the role—for the conduct of the townsman to signify townsman-ness—and in which a great deal of attention, both positive and negative, is given to forms of behavior that defy such norms. It is a consciousness of the social self as viewed by others, but this social self-consciousness goes beyond the local level: It transcends the concerns of fitting into one's household (*ie* 家) or community (*chō* 町) and interfaces instead with abstract norms of class and status, expectations that would be placed on a generic someone of a given social standing.

Normality rejects and to a degree displaces any norms beyond those of social role, such as those of universal morality—the imperative is not to do good and reject evil, but simply to behave appropriately to one's status, to keep up appearances—and is certainly not concerned with the possibility of questioning or transcending or reconfiguring the political order that defines the social roles themselves. It is of the order of the everyday, of living in relation to a system of roles and routines that are taken for granted. Indeed, the crux and central paradox of the regime of normality is that its transgressions remain of the order of the everyday: Normality domesticates the imagination of social alterity into mere eccentricity while progressively reifying eccentricity itself into recognizable, familiar, and indeed normative forms. This is the nature of the *katagi-mono*: to digest the diversity of urban society into a robust sense of everyday normality that could accommodate certain modes and degrees of deviation as merely amusing eccentricity. It is a form in which norms are rendered more flexible through limited, situational transgressions and, conversely, in which norms may be transgressed endlessly but never undone—for the pleasure is in the transgression.

The emergence of this sense of normality is closely related to the formation of class-specific social norms. As discussed in chapter 4, the early eighteenth century was a time of intense interest in the question of how a proper townsman should or should not behave. The very notion that the norms of townsman society were distinct from those of other status groups—and that such a distinction should be given outward expression in material form—was in Kiseki's time a relatively new understanding of the social self. Throughout the seventeenth century, it was far from taken for granted that individuals of different status groups should dress and talk and behave differently. The categories of status were understood as structures of community and frameworks for administration but not as distinctions between materially differentiated selves. Over time, however, differences of status came to be seen as the basis of distinct social norms. The turn to the eighteenth century saw the emerging belief that people of different status were fundamentally different and should act accordingly. This is the moment of the clear articulation of what Pierre Bourdieu refers to as the habitus, wherein underlying social distinctions—the structures of the social field—are given material expression as distinct lifestyles: patterns of conduct, speech, taste, social cognition, a sense of one's place.[6] Of course, it was hardly the case that the early eighteenth century saw the diversity of urban society immediately resolve to reflect a unitary set of norms. In practice, it remained deeply stratified and differentiated by geography, occupation, and so on, and much ambiguity remained concerning what degrees and forms of divergence from the norm would be seen as amusingly eccentric and what would be problematically transgressive. The *katagi-mono* emerged as an iconic literary expression of the moment at which status was transfigured into habitus, and the tension between norm and deviation that structured the genre was a way of making sense of processes of social normalization that would always remain incomplete. The irony of the *katagi-mono* is that Kiseki's bristling work of townsman self-satire ultimately gave birth to a powerfully normative genre, a narrative form that could contain the transgressive energy and social diversity of a steadily normalizing urban society.

Incidentally, the paradoxical tension between normativity and eccentricity is built into the idiosyncratic spelling of *katagi* itself. Historically, the vernacular *katagi* most often referred to external patterns of conduct—not character or disposition, but something closer to the observable manners or mores of a given social type. In contrast, the Sinitic *kishitsu* 気質, rooted in the metaphysics of Song Confucianism, referred to the particularity of specific social classes or individuals, conceived as a morally problematic deviation from universal moral norms. Kiseki combined these terms as a bit of wordplay in the title of *Worldly Young Men*, glossing the Sinitic *kishitsu* with the vernacular *katagi*, and though his later works would use other characters, the paradoxical sense of conduct that is normative yet eccentric and typical yet transgressive would come to define the genre of *katagi-mono*. The playful usage in *Worldly Young Men* would quickly become standard: the idiosyncratic gloss that became a norm in its own right. To illuminate the significance of Kiseki's innovation, we must begin by excavating the earlier constructions of the status-based self contained within these seemingly opposing terms.

THE FORM-ATION OF THE TOWNSMAN SELF

It has often been observed that early modern Japan was a society of forms. Throughout Tokugawa society, externalities of form—manner, dress, conduct, speech—acted as signifiers of social role, marking the distinctions between warrior and commoner, townsman and peasant, and commoner and outcast, as well as illustrating the manifold hierarchies and social differentiations, occupations, and positions that multiplied within each group. If the categorical distinctions of status were fundamentally rooted in the structure of local communities and administered through the systems of residential and religious registration, then it was through the exteriorities of material form that those distinctions were made socially perceptible, that they came to appear not as ad hoc legalistic distinctions but as a priori social substances—the appropriate forms for appropriately differentiated selves. In David Atherton's memorable formulation, "Status was the grammar in which society spoke itself. And this grammar was made outwardly apprehensible—as a language is written in script—through visual and behavioral forms: styles of hair, types of dress, features of speech, modes of comportment."[7] Such observations are useful in capturing the unique social logics of the Tokugawa status system, as well as the nature of Tokugawa literature. As Atherton suggests, an attention to form allows us to track the interplay between highly conventionalized literary representations and formalistic sociopolitical realities. Such forms, however, did not materialize out of nowhere with Tokugawa Ieyasu's victory at Sekigahara. The development of a set of robust social norms and forms was a historical process. Only by being reproduced generation after generation, amplified and perpetually reconfigured through the influence of a didactic print culture, were nominal distinctions of status made palpable and self-evident in the differentiations of outward form. The historical process by which the objective structures of the social field, rooted in the bottom-up organization and top-down administrative interpellation of local communities, were progressively incorporated as subjective forms of identity (in other words, the formation of the habitus) was coming to fruition around the turn of the eighteenth century. The concept of *katagi* and the genre of *katagi-mono* was both product and agent of this moment of social form-ation.

The didactic print culture that emerged in the mid-seventeenth century in the urban hubs of Kyoto, Osaka, and Edo was centered on the description and dissemination of social norms, but this normalizing function of early print culture was rarely targeted at particular status groups. The heterogeneous body of popular print known to posterity as "vernacular booklets" (*kana-zōshi*) tends toward the universal in its moral outlook. Although the works within this corpus are diverse in both form and content to a degree that resists easy summary, one of the conceptual baselines underlying their didactic premises is an assumption of human universality across class and status: "The underlying concern that emerges from these texts is in a desire to help forge human beings worthy of this appellation."[8] The *kana-zōshi* may distinguish between inferior and superior individuals—the latter are the more literate, who used their literacy to cultivate themselves in the direction of universal human norms—but only rarely make clear distinctions of status or social class. Readers are readers. This is not to say that, within this vast body of printed prose, no works advocate for certain forms and degrees of social distinction. The Zen monk and shogunal ideologue Suzuki Shōsan (1579–1655) composed a series of short essays titled *Right Action for All* (*Banmin tokuyō*, 1661), in which he asserted that members of each of the commoner estates—peasants, artisans, merchants—should find merit in pursuing their social lot and dedicating themselves to productive labor rather than aspiring to higher social status (namely, that of the warrior). But Shōsan's endorsement of status as a fundamental framework of social distinction was a polemical outlier: The work merited publication precisely because it remained far from self-evident that different populations should have their own values, lifestyles, and measures of moral merit. Social distinctions were a lived reality, but when it came to discussions of how members of any given class should act or appear, the general assumption was that all classes should aspire to universal moral norms—though it was acknowledged that some social positions (warrior) were closer to the norm, whereas others might be congenitally deficient. Shōsan's essays were a reckoning with (and ideological justification for) the fact that de facto social distinctions may, in practice, conflict with universal moral norms shared across classes.

One expression of the belief in universal moral norms was the Sinitic term *kishitsu* 気質 (C. *qizhi*). This word derives from the thought of Song Confucian scholar Cheng Yi (1033–1107), whose notions of ethics and metaphysics were systematized in the work of Zhu Xi (1130–1200) and enjoyed wide circulation in seventeenth-century Japan through the commentaries of the Hayashi school. To be clear, in citing the thought of Zhu Xi, my aim is not to reiterate the outdated premise that Tokugawa society was structured according to an official ideology rooted in Song Confucianism, or to suggest that Zhu Xi's philosophy was the underlying worldview that defined and shaped the Tokugawa embrace of social form: Zhu Xi's metaphysics merely furnished one set of conceptual categories that thinkers applied to describe, interpret, and (to a certain degree) attempt to regulate the social world.⁹ However, although the discourses of Song Confucian metaphysics were never able to fully grasp or prescribe social form, they saw wide circulation at both elite and popular levels and provided a conceptual vocabulary that was used to understand and debate the nature of the self and its relationship to moral and social norms. Peter Flueckiger concisely summarizes the place of *kishitsu* in the thought of the Zhu Xi school:

> Zhu Xi equated the Confucian Way with a universal "principle" (*li* 理, J. *ri*) that inheres in all things in the cosmos, uniting them in a single moral order. Principle itself is purely abstract, but is always accompanied by "material force" (*qi* 気, J. *ki*), which allows things to exist as physical realities. While principle is entirely virtuous, material force can be morally either good or bad, depending on whether it facilitates or obstructs the manifestation of principle. In the case of humans, principle is represented by a purely good "original nature" (*benran zhi xing* 本然之性, J. *honzen no sei*), while material force, or the "material nature" (*qizhi zhi xing* 気質之性, J. *kishitsu no sei*), is represented by the emotions (*qing* 情, J. *jō*). The cultivation of humans as moral and social beings then involves correcting the emotions so as to recover the original nature that all people innately possess, but that can become obscured by immoral emotions.¹⁰

According to Zhu Xi, the "material nature" (alternatively, "particular essence") of the individual is morally compromised by the contingencies of material reality and tends to manifest as evil and selfish desire. The metaphysical category of *qizhi/kishitsu* represents the particularity of phenomenal reality amid a heavily normalized ethical system that was centered on universal moral ideals. At the level of theory, the Confucian orthodoxy maintained that this material nature was morally indeterminate rather than simply immoral, and that emotion (*qing/jō*) could give expression to moral norms as well as deviant particularities. In practice, however, adaptations of this thought in Tokugawa Japan tended to treat both material nature and emotion as deeply problematic and threatening to the moral integrity of both the individual and society. The material individuality of the self was seen as a form of deviant particularity that had to be studiously (though always imperfectly) disciplined by the vigilant individual in pursuit of moral perfection by asymptotic approximation to a true self that accords with universal principle.¹¹

By Kiseki's time, these premises had been variously contested. As Nakamura Yukihiko has argued, Saikaku's fiction was part of a late seventeenth-century zeitgeist centered on a humanistic curiosity concerning the diverse, material forms of contemporary society.¹² For example, Saikaku's later works came to focus on the ineffable contradictions of the "hearts of people in the world" (*yo no hito-gokoro*): an egalitarian sense that all people, despite and across the distinctions of status and class that divided Tokugawa society, share a certain basic and universal humanity, juxtaposed with an awareness that an individual's conduct, disposition, and moral scruples could easily change based on their circumstances. Saikaku's writing shared with the Confucian tradition a belief in the underlying universality of the human heart, but the author was more open-minded regarding the diversity of contemporary social forms, which he saw not as morally compromised epiphenomena but as objects of curiosity and empirical attention. As he wrote in the preface to *Tales of Samurai Honor* (*Buke giri monogatari*, 1688), "All people share the same heart, no different through all the multitudes. The man who carries a long sword is a warrior, the one who dons a court cap is a shrine official, and the one who wears black robes is a monk; he who grips a hoe becomes a peasant, he who handles a chisel is a craftsman, and the abacus is the mark of the merchant."¹³ Although this pithy observation suggests, on the one hand, a universal humanity that persists despite the social distinctions expressed at the level of form, it affirms, on the other, the salience of those social forms and their constitutive role in defining social selves. Indeed, as the title suggests, the work was focused on exploring the norms and structures that, in his view, defined samurai identity. In this regard, the work parallels his studies of townsman identity in *Japan's Eternal Storehouse*.

In depicting the diverse and sometimes radically nonnormative social forms that he saw proliferating in late seventeenth-century urban society, Saikaku occasionally deployed the vernacular term *katagi*. Most often written with compounds suggesting external forms or norms (形気・容気), this word at the time referred to external patterns of appearance and conduct, suggesting perhaps a translation as "manner."¹⁴ In the Japanese-Portuguese dictionary produced in 1603 by the Jesuits in Nagasaki, *katagi* (Port. *catagui*) is translated as "custom" (Port. *costume*); the term may have been related to older Sinitic compounds such as *gyōgi* 形儀 and *yōgi* 容儀, which referred to external comportment. Appended to a social class or social type, *katagi* evoked the observable manners of the given social category in a sense that was typical and occasionally normative. Whereas, in the metaphysics of the Song Confucian tradition, particularities of external form represented a morally compromised (if, in a sense, inevitable) divergence from universal norms, the vernacular *katagi* treated form itself as norm, with little suggestion of moral substance lying behind or above it. In fact, the earliest sense of the term *katagi*, occasionally rendered with the characters for "form" (*kata* 形) and "wood" (*ki* 木), was that of a carved wooden board or block, as used to impress patterns on cloth or, as in the case of a Buddhist sutra, characters on paper—in other words, a woodblock for printing.[15] The word thus contains a figure for normative conduct—the woodblock as a metaphor for externalized forms of behavior that become patterns for emulation and reproduction—and though this sense was rarely operative in the early modern era, the metaphor remains apt in the context of an emerging townsman culture in which norms of identity were created through processes of textual (re)production. Kiseki was keenly attuned to the ways in which the norms or "characters" of the townsman were being reshaped and reproduced by the mediation of the woodblock print.

Saikaku occasionally refers to *katagi* at points where his work verges into an almost ethnographic reportage and commentary on the newly emergent mores of late seventeenth-century urban society. In *Eternal Storehouse*, he uses the term in the story "Shippers and Packhorses in the Courtyard of Abumiya" (*Funabito umakata Abumiya no niwa*, vol. 2–5), about the "great broker" Abumiya of Sakata, whose brokerage hosts traveling merchants from throughout the realm. The narrator observes the manners of the various merchants, clerks, and shop hands who have come to carry out their business through his brokerage: "Examining the various manners of the merchants who came to this broker over the years" (*kono toiya ni sūnen amata akindo katagi o mioyobikeru ni*).[16] What follows is a series of micronarratives in the omnibus form: brief descriptions and commentaries on the forms of conduct that distinguish the successful merchant from the unsuccessful. The reference to the "manners of the merchants" (*akindo katagi*) acts as an indexing device that frames the juxtaposition and evaluation of a range of similar figures within a given role. The concept of *katagi* encompasses the diversity of conduct contained within the social category of merchant—the specific and idiosyncratic cases that necessarily complicate but ultimately make up the category—with the implicit function of comparison and evaluation, measuring which cases are more suited to and characteristic of that category. The aim in this story, as for *Eternal Storehouse* as a whole, is to extract and produce a primer of aspirational norms of townsman conduct: as Saikaku remarks elsewhere in the work, "the model of a great merchant" (*ōakindo no tehon*). In this way, Saikaku's deployment of the vernacular *katagi* was part of his reconfiguration of the "space of the collection," which in *Eternal Storehouse* is reoriented around the emergent norms of entrepreneurial commercial practice that in the late seventeenth century were coming to define a newly mobile sense of townsman identity. And, as we saw in part 1, the model of a great merchant is revealed by Saikaku to be none other than the merchant who represents himself as such: The ultimate form of entrepreneurial self-fashioning is the reduction of entrepreneurship to acts of self-representation, to the spectacular performance of the emerging norms that define the successful merchant.

Saikaku's work was part of a larger rearticulation of the terms in which status-based identity was conceptualized, as administrative distinctions and community structures were becoming incorporated as lived forms of embodied practice and sartorial performance. It was at this moment that Nishikawa Joken wrote that "Truly the townsman should reek of townsmanness" (*chōnin wa chōnin kusaki koso yoku haberu mono o*).[17] This subtle but fundamental shift was not limited to the townsman, but affected various status groups in different ways. For example, the late seventeenth century saw a radical change in administrative policies surrounding *rōnin* (declassed samurai). The *rōnin*, who had lost membership in their military households, often resided in commoner wards but were always required to be registered with government authorities, who feared that unregistered *rōnin* might be responsible for criminal schemes or outright rebellion. Such registration had originally been carried out by the propertied townsmen of the *rōnin*'s ward of residence, who would confirm his identity with his relatives or with the warrior household he had formerly served. In the late seventeenth century, however, registration policies and official edicts shifted to simply address "men carrying swords" (*taitōjin*): The mere act of carrying the samurai's long sword was enough, in the eyes of both commoner communities and warrior authorities, to mark the individual as a *rōnin*.[18]

REPRESENTING NORMALITY

Saikaku's pithy observation that the "man who wields a long sword is a warrior" thus approximated an emerging legal truth. It was also during this moment that shogunal sumptuary regulations were directed more frequently and forcefully (though never systematically) at the commoner classes of townsmen and peasants.[19] Although many scholars have taken such regulations as iconic representations of the logic of the status system as a method of social control, they are better understood as a historical response to the breaking down of the policies of community-based social administration and spatial segregation and the failure of such policies to constrain the fluidity of the contemporary world: If the *chōnin* was no longer defined by membership in his *chō*, then he would be defined instead by his appearance. These changing policies of status administration reflected a shift from *mibun* as a highly local and particularistic sense of community membership to *mibun* as a set of lifestyles, carrying distinct values and systematically marked by external distinctions in material form and conduct. The status system thus saw a shift toward a conception of *mibun* as a kind of *katagi*.

Early eighteenth-century print culture registered this shift, reorienting didactic frameworks from universal moral principles to status-based norms of conduct. The iconic genre representing this shift was the *chōhōki*, but the same transformation can be seen more subtly in the didactic tracts of Kaibara Ekiken. Ekiken was a humanist in the Confucian tradition, one whose works were radically new in parsing Neo-Confucian thought in simple, vernacular language for a wide, popular audience, and one of the principles he introduced in such a fashion was the Sinitic *kishitsu*. In many ways, Ekiken's adaptation of this principle cleaves remarkably closely to the stern moral rigorism of Zhu Xi: "Each person possesses a nature that is originally good, but each person is also hindered by their disposition [*kishitsu*] and desires, and that goodness is lost. Disposition is that with which one is born."[20] Following Song Confucian orthodoxy, Ekiken maintained that this particularity had to be diligently normalized through spiritual discipline and textual study until it resolved into a morally normative form. However, Ekiken was also careful to mark where the norms of conduct, learning, and education that he prescribed for commoner readers differed from those of the warrior class. As we saw in chapter 4, warriors were encouraged to pursue cultural training in a wide array of leisure arts as part of their class-based pedigree; in his popular didactic works, Ekiken would affirm that pedigree for warriors while insisting that commoner children "should be taught only arithmetic and writing, and should focus on their house trades," and, under no circumstance, be exposed to the "harmful, useless, miscellaneous arts."[21] Despite his embrace of a strain of moral universalism rooted in the Song Confucian tradition, Ekiken was a man of his moment in his recognition that the norms of the townsman differed from those of the warrior. Although he did not use the term *katagi* in his writings, his use of *kishitsu* had already been implicitly reshaped by a *katagi*-esque grasp of differing norms and forms for different status-based identities.

FROM MORALITY TO NORMALITY

Kiseki came to the Sinitic term *kishitsu* through the mediation of Ekiken's popular writings. This is not to say that Kiseki was deeply invested in Neo-Confucian metaphysics or that his writing manifested the moral seriousness endorsed by Ekiken; in spirit, he was closer to Saikaku's enthusiastic enumeration of the diversity of contemporary *katagi*. Kiseki's engagement with Ekiken's thought was largely opportunistic. Amid the increasingly conservative climate of moral didacticism that would culminate in the Kyōhō Reforms of the 1720s, Ekiken's work represented a burgeoning new sector of the publishing field. Kiseki, who was embattled in a bitter and protracted trade war with his former publisher Hachimonjiya Jishō, was drawn to the new style of didactic writing represented by Ekiken's work as a viable new product category. Put ungenerously, he likely sought to cash in on the historic popularity of Ekiken's didactic efforts by offering works that readers might take in a similar vein.[22] The result of this encounter was *Worldly Young Men*, the pioneering work of the *katagi-mono* genre and the first work to render the vernacular *katagi* with the characters of the Sinitic *kishitsu*. But Kiseki took Ekiken's concepts in a novel direction, from an idea of moral transgression to one of social eccentricity rooted in an acute apprehension of the townsman's proper habitus.

The nature of this shift is illuminated when we consider Kiseki's source material and the changes he effected in adapting it to his moment. Much of Kiseki's writing drew liberally from Saikaku's late townsman pieces, but in *Worldly Young Men* he took particular inspiration from *Twenty Unfilial Exemplars of Japan* (*Honchō nijū fukō*, 1686). In the opening preface, he alludes to this debt with the closing line "and carved it in catalpa wood, to spread throughout the world as an aid in the promotion of filial piety" (*azusa ni chiribame, kō ni susumuru ichijo naran kashi*), which was borrowed verbatim from Saikaku's preface.[23] But *Twenty Unfilial Exemplars* is a very different work from *Worldly Young Men*, concerned with universal norms of filiality and, ultimately, good and evil. Although Saikaku projected these issues into the economic affairs of the contemporary townsperson and explored that world with characteristic nuance and ambivalence, his ultimate concern in this work remained with moral universals more than social particulars. *Twenty Unfilial Exemplars* is not without its share of dark humor, but most of its stories ultimately resolve into stark morality tales surrounding the nature of evil and its grim consequences.[24] It is this severe sense of moral universals that Kiseki transmogrified into a humorous exploration of the townsman's social norms. The interest of the narrative is not in how universal moral dramas play out within the townsman's economic affairs, but in how the conduct of any given individual may reflect or defy the proper forms of townsman society.

Consider the story in *Worldly Young Men* about the amateur townsman sumo wrestler: "Wounded by His Own Strength: The Character of a Sumo Wrestler Who Tossed His Own Estate" (*Dairiki wa mi no kizu shindai nageta sumō-tori katagi*, vol. 2–3), discussed in detail in chapter 4.[25] Much of this story was, in fact, borrowed from a story in *Twenty Unfilial Exemplars*: "A Useless Show of Strength" (*Muyō no chikara-jiman*, vol. 5–3).[26] Saikaku's story concerns the scion of a wealthy merchant family who inexplicably dedicates himself to sumo wrestling, ignoring his father's reprimands and neglecting his family business. In the end, he becomes overconfident in his strength, is physically crippled due to an injury received in a match, and lives out his days berating his poor parents. This is one of the shorter and lighter stories in this collection, but within it are hints of the morally charged metaphysics of Zhu Xi. Indeed, of all of Saikaku's works, *Twenty Unfilial Exemplars* is the closest to a Song Confucian view of the corruptibility of moral essence. The story deals in part with the Confucian taboo of subjecting the body (a gift from one's parents) to harm, but Saikaku also associates the son's morally deviant character with his bodily physicality: "His limbs became ever more robust, until at the mere age of nineteen he looked to be in his thirties; his form changed to something truly extraordinary." Though Saikaku does not use the term "material disposition" (*kishitsu*), we have here a sense that the son's innate disposition, expressed in both bodily form and personal conduct, contains an inherent deviance that, if left uncorrected, carries the potential for moral and social ruination. In contrast, Kiseki's rendition concludes with the hapless failed wrestler being disowned and finding employment as a cart driver—a humble occupation to be sure, but a far cry from the dire punishment inflicted on Saikaku's unfilial son. Indeed, the consequences faced by these two characters clearly reflect the nature of their transgressions: The material disposition of Saikaku's protagonist defies the universal moral norms of filiality and his body is left crippled; Kiseki's deviant youth defies the townsman's ideas of propriety and so is pushed to the margins of townsman society.

The shift from stories of moral transgression to those of social impropriety is accompanied in Kiseki's *katagi-mono* with a lowering of narrative stakes. Transgressions are minor, amusing improprieties that are met with annoyance, scolding, and laughter; bad behavior often goes unpunished, and indeed it is the eccentrics who are doing the laughing.[27] Kiseki's worldview has no place for stark moral dramas of good and evil, of murder and theft; nor does he give us glimpses, as does Saikaku in *Eternal Storehouse* and his other late works, of the desperate grappling with opportunity and deprivation that takes place outside the security of townsman property. In Saikaku's work, disinheritance is a trigger for dramatic narratives of social mobility, but to Kiseki it marks the boundary of narrative itself, often in a very precise sense. In the story "Unheeded Advice Makes for Ineffective Medicine: The Character of a Doctor Who Wouldn't Mend His Own Ways" (*Iken wa kikanu kusuri kokoro o naosanu isha katagi*, vol. 2–1), about the eccentric would-be Confucian scholar who becomes a quack doctor, the narrative ends with the voice of his father: "Disowned, disowned!" (*kandō kandō*).[28] Where we do get glimpses of life outside the wealthy townsman household, it is overwhelmingly and improbably rosy. Kiseki's protagonists tend to land on their feet and delight in their fates; every eccentric has a place, albeit on the social margins. The author's narrative purview was situated squarely within the realm of the everyday lives of the urban townspeople.

One driving factor in this shift was no doubt Kiseki's efforts to address a widening reading public, one that had come to embrace reading itself as a form of casual leisure. Kiseki's erstwhile publisher, Hachimonjiya, had made wide-ranging and systematic efforts to expand the readership of commercial-print fiction—for example, by attracting the theatergoing audience with new forms of illustrated librettos and actor reviews, and by standardizing and simplifying book formats to drive down production costs and book prices.[29] Kiseki was similarly sensitive to the needs and tastes of his widening readership and focused on producing accessible works with broad entertainment value. In developing new forms of popular comic narrative that would appeal to an audience with a taste for accessible and easily digested amusement, he drew significant inspiration from the practice of oral joke-telling (*hanashi* or *shōwa*) and the booming genre of "jest books" (*hanashi-bon*).[30] Although this influence is most obvious in the formal qualities of his writing—the use of gags and minor twists or punch lines, often in the form of wordplay—it also comes through in the tone of his stories, which, to the degree that they jettison serious moral messaging, present an ultimately optimistic and provisionally inclusive (though still normative) worldview. Those who deviate from the norm are mocked but suffer no severe consequences, no transgressions are so grave as to upset the collective well-being of the community, and every eccentric has a place as long as he is willing to endure the fate of light-hearted ridicule. This is the world of the sitcom, sometimes ridiculous and occasionally subtly subversive but always comfortable and familiar.

Kiseki's work also normalized a range of minor transgressions that in the previous generation were generally framed as morally irredeemable. One motif running through *Worldly Young Men* is the suggestion that the merchant's son who indulges here and there in the brothel districts is, taking the larger view, not all that bad—certainly less troubling than the other eccentrics and deviants whose foibles Kiseki takes such delight in enumerating. What in the previous generation had been seen as a grievous and potentially catastrophic transgression against the norms of the household here becomes a mere youthful indiscretion. In "Weary of Leisure: The Character of a Retiree Laid Up to Recover" (*Yūkyō ni kutabirete yōjō ni hikikomu inja katagi*, vol. 5–2), an otherwise responsible son begins wiling away his time and fortune in the company of courtesans, but his magnanimous father decides to treat this is a mere phase, granting him a generous allowance with the advice to have his fun in moderation. The story concludes with a narratorial aside: "The appeal of these places is really in the challenge of keeping one's doings secret, and to play around so openly takes most of the fun out of it. The young man soon found the pleasure quarters quite distasteful and lost all interest, lamenting that he'd rather visit a temple."[31] The young man's lament (*nagekarekeru*) over the loss of the transgressive pleasure of leisure stands in sharp contrast to the palpable delight expressed by Kiseki's other deviant sons in the face of their disownment and social marginalization. As the dialectical tension between normativity and transgression pushed Kiseki progressively further in the pursuit of novel forms of eccentricity, old tropes like dallying in the company of courtesans emerged as norms in their own right. This articulation of social norms went hand in hand with the progressive (re-)production of textual norms: This story in its entirety was taken virtually verbatim from "Taking Inventory" (*Tana-oroshi*, vol. 4-1) in Yashoku Jibun's *Cure for Love's Ills* (*Kōshoku haidokusan*, 1703).[32] Although this appropriation was likely driven by a degree of pure opportunism, it also reflected Kiseki's astute perception that Yashoku Jibun's comic story fit precisely into the themes of *Worldly Young Men* as one of the poles of its exploration of the new normality of townsman society.

Shinohara Susumu has observed elements in *Worldly Young Men* of "an urban sense of indifference" (*tokai-teki bōkan shugi*) that is interested in and amused by the diversity of contemporary habitus, but also detached from and undisturbed by it.[33] We might paraphrase this, by way of Georg Simmel, as a blasé quality.[34] Saikaku, despite his reputation as a worldly sage in the fashion of Kenkō, retained a sense of wonder and occasional horror at the diversity and dynamism of the contemporary world; as he famously wrote in the preface to *Saikaku's Stories from the Provinces* (*Saikaku shokoku banashi*, 1685), "people transform in a flash like shape-shifters, and the world contains anything you might imagine" (*hito wa bakemono, yo ni nai mono wa nashi*).[35] This was the perspective of someone who had come of age during the rapid economic expansions of the late seventeenth century, when newly formed communication networks regularly exposed individuals to new sights, sounds, and communities, and when the explosive growth of the market economy was transforming the urban world at a dizzying pace. In contrast, in Kiseki's time, the sights had been seen, and the riveting dynamism of the floating world had been lessened by years of economic stagnation. This is not to say that urban society in the early eighteenth century was in any real sense less diverse than it had been in Saikaku's time. To Kiseki, though, this diversity was not an object of wonder or threat; nor did it represent a universe of unrealized social possibility. It was merely a source of amusement and passing distraction. Regardless of whether his protagonists are ludicrous eccentrics whose outlandish conduct pushes them outside society's upper ranks, or whether they are by and large responsible heirs going through the throes of adolescent rebellion, they are all ultimately harmless.

Above all, in the background of Kiseki's interest in eccentricity was an increasingly predictable sense of a normative townsman society. For all of Kiseki's interest in deviance, eccentricity, and alternative life paths, the ground on which his works were built was an image of a generic townsman normality that was, in all senses, unmarked. This generic quality is nowhere more clear than in the spatial setting of his stories, which are set nearly without exception in the three urban hubs of Kyoto, Osaka, and Edo. Saikaku, in contrast, had a wide-ranging geographic consciousness, setting his stories in locales ranging from the urban to the rural and across all the provinces of Japan. He was exquisitely attuned to how the historical contingency of economic opportunity was bound to time and place: His stories center on modes of entrepreneurial cognition that are born of and evolve in relation to the particular conditions of the port city, the fishing village, the market town, the working-class slum, and so on. Kiseki has none of this sense of spatial specificity. The narratives of the *katagi-mono* could happen anywhere with the basic infrastructure of urban entertainment: commercial districts, teahouses, theaters, brothels. His settings are occasionally marked with proper names, but these are almost always elite commercial districts such as Kyoto Muromachi—markers of a general milieu rather than a precise sense of place—and have little bearing on the stories that unfold within them. On the rare occasions that Kiseki provides a concrete description of a setting, it is usually in prose borrowed from Saikaku and often from a different city entirely, transmuting the local specificity of Saikaku's grounded descriptions into a generic downtown urban imaginary of bustling thoroughfares and imposing warehouses. In terms of social class, likewise, Kiseki's protagonists are only rarely marked by particular trades, and only the most generic ones—moneylenders and clothiers—within the mid- to upper strata of the townsman class, just high enough to be both relatable and aspirational to his readers.[36] To the degree that Kiseki's relentless pursuit of narrative novelty and social eccentricity expressed a deep sense of alienation from the normativity of such a setting, it also endlessly reproduced and progressively distilled a generic sense of ordinary, unmarked townsman existence.

THE POETICS OF NORMALITY

The tension between normative settings and eccentric characters is pushed further in *Worldly Young Women*. This work is less coherent in theme than its predecessor: It lacks the systematicity of method and clarity of vision with which *Worldly Young Men* dissected the contradictions of the townsman household. *Worldly Young Women* has more of a formalist character, developing the narrative poetics by which Kiseki created his characters and crafted stories around them. These formal poetics operate on two levels, following the dialectical structure of the *katagi-mono*. On the one hand, Kiseki produces exquisitely generic frames, placed as descriptive openings at the beginning of his stories and painstakingly crafted through a refined practice of appropriative pastiche. On the other, he uses such generic frames as the ground for increasingly extreme caricatures and outlandish twists, pushing past eccentricity into nonsense.[37] Through the combination of these elements—the production of generic frames and the depiction of extreme caricatures—*Worldly Young Women* acts as a symbolic form to reflect on the nature and boundaries of the new normality of townsman society. Through the creation of a generic social ground, Kiseki casts into clear relief the kind of conduct that had once been deviant and now was regarded as normal; further, paradoxically, through the escalation of deviance ad absurdum, he defines and reaffirms the absolute limits of normality while carving out space for a domesticated vision of minor, harmless eccentricity.

At the heart of *Worldly Young Women* is a set of norms of townsman femininity that had long circulated in print and that were being rearticulated and reconfigured in the didactic literature of Kiseki's time. In the preface, Kiseki declares, "In the end, the path of the woman is not to be found in possessing ability or wisdom greater than others; it is to devote her heart to chastity and rid it of obscenity, to dedicate herself to managing her household and serving her husband."[38] This was a transparent and certainly facetious citation of the short treatise "The Greater Learning for Women" (*Onna daigaku*), long mistakenly attributed to Ekiken, that had been published the previous year in *A Treasure Chest of Greater Learning for Women* (*Onna daigaku takarabako*, 1716). One of the publishers of this text was Ogawa Hikokurō, the Edo distributor of Kiseki's imprint Ejimaya; just as *Worldly Young Men* had drawn on and lampooned Ekiken's didactic works, its sequel was a timely response to new developments in the field of didactic print for women. As one might expect, many of the stories in *Worldly Young Women* depict young women who defy these narrow norms: by rejecting humility, displaying too much intelligence, spending their fathers' or husbands' money too freely, making great displays of jealousy, pursuing lovers of their own choosing, marrying repeatedly after successive divorces, cheating on their husbands, and so on. As with the young men depicted in the previous work, few of these women face punishment for their actions beyond the helpless vexation of their relatives.

However, *Worldly Young Women* was more than merely a lampoon of "The Greater Learning for Women." By Kiseki's time, literary depictions of assertive women were not uncommon and lacked the capacity for scandal that they may once have held. Saikaku's *Five Amorous Women* (*Kōshoku gonin onna*, 1686) and *The Life of an Amorous Woman* (*Koshoku ichidai onna*, 1686) had explored in detail the ways in which contemporary young women gleefully flouted conventional gender norms, and Kiseki's writing drew equally on what had become thoroughly familiar and mundane depictions of contemporary feminine mores. Indeed, *A Treasure Chest of Greater Learning for Women* itself may be seen as part of a process by which gender norms were, under the guise of moral didacticism, becoming more flexible and capacious. Despite the long-standing reputation of "The Greater Learning for Women" as a document of Tokugawa patriarchal values, more recent reevaluations have observed that *A Treasure Chest of Greater Learning for Women* as a whole—a massive compendium of 107 folios—presents a much more pragmatic, holistic, and flexible image of the various skills and literacies seen as valuable for women of the time, with elements resembling *chōhōki*, conduct guides, primers on the literary classics, and more.[39] In other words, despite the conservative moralism of its most famous fragment, this text was part of the same renegotiation of the terms of status-based identity—the shift from morality to normality—reflected in the *katagi-mono*. Likewise, Kiseki's aim was less to deconstruct a narrow vision of conservative feminine morality and more to probe the limits of contemporary feminine normality, which in fact already accommodated a range of mundane transgressions.

As with *Worldly Young Men*, Kiseki's female protagonists defy norms of townsman femininity in ever more eccentric ways. In "A Dashing and Extravagant Young Woman of Great Renown" (*Seken ni kakure no nai kankatsuna ogori musume*, vol. 1–2), an exceptionally indulgent young wife, whose every wish is happily entertained by her husband, grows weary of the usual feminine entertainments of flower viewing, theatergoing, and exquisite fashion; she decides that the greatest extravagance would be to cross-dress as a man and experience the pleasures of the brothel districts as a male customer.[40] In "A Poem-Loving Daughter Who Couldn't Count a Hundred Coins" (*Hyaku no zeni yomi-kaneru uta-zuki no musume*, vol. 1–3), a highly intelligent and literate wife, trained in *waka* and the classical literary tradition, supports her incompetent husband by opening a women's calligraphy and letter-writing school, then ends up forging documents for spurious lawsuits; when her husband is appointed as ward elder, she advises on his behalf and ultimately becomes ward elder by proxy.[41] In "Even Managing a Household, She Treasured Neither Money Nor Life: The Daughter of a Samurai" (*Setai motte mo zenikane yori inochi o oshimanu saburai no musume*, vol. 2–1), the beautiful, intelligent, and modest daughter of a *rōnin* is wed to a wealthy merchant, but her warrior upbringing clashes with her husband's townsman values; her conduct becomes ever more extreme as she dedicates herself to practicing swordsmanship and martial strategy while despising her feckless husband for his lack of masculine valor.[42] As these examples suggest, many of the stories probe the boundaries of femininity by depicting young women who, in one way or another, behave like men. But the further Kiseki's narratives push toward the transgression of gender norms, the more they tend to spiral into nonsense. Meanwhile, the more conventional breaches of townsman femininity, like those enumerated so severely in texts such as "The Greater Learning for Women," are normalized as acceptable, harmless, even expected—normative expressions of femininity rather than transgressions thereof.

Regarding Kiseki's reliance on passages poached from Saikaku, it often has been observed that his textual borrowings tend to cluster at the beginning of his stories, whether in the form of a thematic preface (*makura*) or of sketches of setting and character; as the stories progress, they move more toward novel developments that reflect the author's zany sensibility. Kiseki scholar Saeki Takahiro has suggested that this pattern might be taken as a kind of encoded allusion, a hint to the reader that what is to come will represent a new twist on Saikaku, who by Kiseki's time had attained a quasi-canonical status within the emerging field of popular fiction.[43] In a similar vein, Nakajima Takashi has observed that Kiseki's practice of citation has parallels with the compositional tropes of "world" (*sekai*) and "variation" (*shukō*), crystallizing in Kabuki dramaturgy around the same time, that allowed playwrights to rapidly compose novel works based on familiar story worlds. In Nakajima's interpretation, popular prose fiction lacked a familiar repertoire of established forms in the sense of the Kabuki worlds, but was subject to the same commercial pressure to constantly produce new from old; Kiseki solved this problem by borrowing not Saikaku's narrative settings but instead his very language.[44] I find Nakajima's interpretation the more convincing because it does not assume a reader so well versed in Saikaku's writing that they could decode passing references to random stories. I would not, however, go so far as to say that popular prose fiction was lacking in fixed forms. Its forms were merely the emerging norms of contemporary townsman society itself, which Saikaku had deftly rendered into prose descriptions. What Kiseki sought in Saikaku's writing was a normative image of contemporary society, given literary form: renditions of contemporary social mores that would, through their reproduction, become stock descriptions and commonplaces, a familiar ground on which Kiseki's narratives could innovate.

The opening story, "A Girl's Domineering Dowry Gets Her Man Under Her Thumb" (*Otoko o shiri ni shikigane no ikō musume*, vol. 1–1), is exemplary, its extended opening acting as a de facto frame for *Worldly Young Women* as a whole.[45] Over the course of roughly four folios of text (not counting illustrations), Kiseki presents a tongue-clicking commentary on the fallen mores of contemporary women, who give excessive attention to clothing and appearances rather than following the feminine virtues of chastity and humble submission prescribed in the preface. In doing so, Kiseki borrows from Saikaku on at least eight occasions, four passages from *The Life of an Amorous Woman*, two from *Saikaku's Loose Threads Tied Off* (*Saikaku oridome*, 1694), and one each from *The Great Mirror of Myriad Elegance* (*Shoen ōkagami*, 1684), *The Great Mirror of Male Love* (*Nanshoku ōkagami*, 1687), and Yashoku Jibun's *Cure for Love's Ills*; these citations are woven seamlessly into a caricatured image of (supposedly) degenerate femininity. To illuminate the nature of this bricolage, I offer an extended translation, the annotations indicating borrowed prose:

① In the past, the characters of young women were said to be utterly upstanding. In recent years, daughters and wives are ill-behaved, copying the appearances of courtesans and female impersonators from the stage. Like an image of Daughter Lingzhao but without the bamboo basket, they wear their belts high and ① their sleeves wide as men are said to do; assuming the poised posture and affected gait of a courtesan's procession, they restrain their own bodies from moving freely, caring only for how they might appear to others. Those born with birthmarks on the side of their faces hide them, and those with thick ankles cover them up with low hems; those with large mouths are quick to pucker them, and refrain from speaking their mind. Truly the pains taken by today's women defy the imagination. One would think that, as long as their male companions would tolerate them, there should be no need to polish the insides of their nostrils. But no, they despise even the downy hairs that grow along the napes of their necks, plucking out each one with greater care than a priest manicuring the ceremonial sand piles at a shrine. And, ② just as those below imitate the manners they see in their superiors, their attendant handmaidens and servant girls are the same, and ③ even the scullery maid with ladle-calluses on her right hand ② will sharpen the blades she uses to shear off bonito flakes, using them instead to shave her forehead or trim the unruly hair growing in the hollow at the base of her skull; filling old tea bags with rice bran, ④ these young women dawdle in the bath, without the slightest concern for their companions waiting outside, as they polish themselves up to no end, but since they don't know even the basics of a proper toilette, their makeup just ends up looking sickly and grotesque. In the past, there were few women other than courtesans who oiled their hair, but girls these days apply hair oil everywhere down to the curls of their navels; they can use a whole container every morning on their hair alone. In this floating world, if you don't include a budget for hair oil along with food, there's no way you can keep a wife. They say that white skin will mask ten faults, ④ but when a young women with a face that would be perfectly tolerable without makeup insists on smearing it with powder while disregarding anything she deems less visible, the contrast between her face and neck look just like Anrakuan's tea bag: an unsightly patchwork of odds and ends.[46]

Kiseki's tongue-in-cheek critique laments how contemporary women give altogether too much attention and energy to their appearances. The irony of the passage, likely intended, is that Kiseki was writing at a moment when townsman identity had come to be conceived in terms of the performance of externalities of appearance and conduct. This was the predicament the author had confronted in *Worldly Young Men*: a sense of alienation from a polite urban society in which culture had been reduced to a set of signifiers. To be a townsman was to give attention to appearances—to perform the proper *katagi* of townsman-ness—and the hypertrophied self-consciousness of townsman daughters was merely a symptom of a culture of fetishized form in which performed signifiers were prized over substantive signifieds.

The further irony is that Kiseki himself has constructed this passage through a shameless appropriation of signifiers. The numbers and underlining indicate the passages that Kiseki has borrowed—(1) *Amorous Woman* (vol. 3–4), (2) *Great Mirror of Myriad Elegance* (vol. 1–5), (3) *Saikaku's Loose Ends* (vol. 5–2), and (4) *Love's Ills* (vol. 1–2)—but these passages have been thoroughly decontextualized, taken out of narrative contexts that differ drastically from Kiseki's narrative aims. The citations are even of different social types, as some describe sexually precocious daughters; others, sensual young brides; others, aging mothers putting on airs of youth; and others, serving maids and working women aspiring to bourgeois refinement. Although traces of these disparate types remain, the details and distinctions fall away. Through Kiseki's practice of textual bricolage, a stereotyped image of contemporary femininity emerges that readers feel they have surely seen before, though they would likely be unsure precisely where; even the moralizing tongue-clicking is clearly registered here as nothing more than a conventional pose, commenting on mores that any reader would recognize as entirely ordinary. The prose is unmistakably familiar but utterly nondescript. More than a practice of encoded allusion, Kiseki's systematic borrowings suggest a process of breaking down existing prose into raw material for reappropriation and repackaging, of breaking down stories into a reserve of signifiers. Seen from this perspective, Kiseki's work is itself an "unsightly patchwork of odds and ends" (*katami-gawari naru mo migurushikariki*), of characters dressed up and passed off as something slightly different from what they may have once been and fused into a new kind of composite image. This was the nature of the *katagi-mono*—a compilation of disparate cases that together constitute the diverse unity or unitary diversity of contemporary social forms—for which this opening passage acts as a metonym and microcosm.

Following this conspicuously generic description, the story takes a turn for the absurd. A beautiful young daughter has been raised carefully by her parents, kept away from the world so that she will not be tempted by frivolous affairs or passing fashions; on her wedding night, the groom finds that, as a result of her sheltered upbringing, she is not figuratively but literally childlike, unwilling to part with her wet nurse, who speaks to her in baby talk and ultimately suckles her to calm her down. One might read into this story a critique of parenting practices—parents spoil their daughters by babying them—as well as a sardonic commentary on normative femininity in the fashion of "The Greater Learning for Women," a suggestion that the kind of demure chastity demanded of young women was mere degrees away from childish immaturity. But the extreme degree of Kiseki's caricature and the nonsensical nature of the narrative twists that accompany it resist interpretation as satire. Once we have an adult woman suckling at the teat of her wet nurse and babbling like a toddler, we read this not as social commentary but merely as nonsense, a kind of formal play driven by an ever-escalating pursuit of new twists within the combinatorial repackaging of a fixed repertoire of signifiers. Moreover, the symbolic import of such nonsense is not in the norms it seems to deconstruct but in the more mundane transgressions evoked in the opening passage—the materialism, the superficiality, the assumed promiscuity, the attention to appearances over substance—that, in comparison with the nonsensical caricature, have become thoroughly normalized. What was once seen as novel and transgressive is now part of a more flexible norm, indeed one that has nullified any concern with moral substance and replaced it with largely amoral norms of external manner, appearance, form—in short, with *katagi*. In Kiseki's world, young women who wear fine makeup and dress fashionably and wish to flirt with young men and choose their own husbands—these have become so ubiquitous in both social reality and textual representation that they are now the familiar baseline against which more substantive gender and class transgressions might be measured.

As Kiseki's stories progress, they shift away from the ground of generic normality produced through intertextual citation and move toward exaggerated caricatures of eccentric conduct. A ready example may be found in "Even Managing a Household, She Treasured Neither Money Nor Life."[47] The beautiful and upright daughter of a *rōnin* is wed to a wealthy townsman, but her samurai pride and stern demeanor make her a difficult wife, and her husband is persistently frustrated, nonplussed, and even frightened by her bellicose disposition. The story is structured as a series of escalating comic anecdotes, each a brief sketch that allows for the amusing representation of the heroine's samurai character. Following a brief opening that establishes the circumstances of the marriage, the husband offers to take his young wife on an excursion to the Kabuki theater, a form of leisure diversion that many women enthusiastically embraced. The wife, revealing a severe samurai mien, declares that her parents always strictly forbade her from indulging in such vulgar pursuits: "Setting aside moon, snow, and flower viewings, the only outing appropriate for women is the *nō* stage. The modern theatrical spectacle known as Kabuki exists primarily to make a show of indecency and to display immodest conduct, and should not even be spoken about by the daughters of respectable people." The husband, irritated that his generous offer has been declined, responds angrily: "What kind of idiot dislikes going to the Kabuki theater? Cut all that out, and let's get ready to go." His wife answers with a sharp-tongued retort, inflected by the archaic constructions of samurai speech:

> Man though you may be, for the daughter of a respected samurai to be slandered as a fool is to see my pride as a woman disregarded and the honorable name of my ancestors besmirched. I cannot countenance such an affront. Humble as I may be in station, my ancestor was a retainer to the great Uesugi Kenshin.... It is lamentable enough to have fallen to the status of the wife of a mere townsman, but to be derided as a fool and an idiot by some mere peddler is a humiliation to my parents. I may be lacking in practice in recent days, but if you will out of conjugal affection accept me as your opponent, I will be well pleased. Prepare thyself to meet thine end![48]

Saying this, she draws a sword from her storage chest and assumes a dueling posture. When the cowed husband attempts to placate his terrifying wife, she only escalates her tirade, deriding him for his fecklessness, which she takes as a sign of failed masculinity. The narrator proceeds to describe how the wife spends her days practicing martial strategy and, showing no interest in clothing patterns for her New Year kimono, summons a renowned armor dealer to prepare a suit of armor suitable for flower viewing. The anecdotes steadily escalate from plausible satire to overblown stereotype to cartoonish caricature.

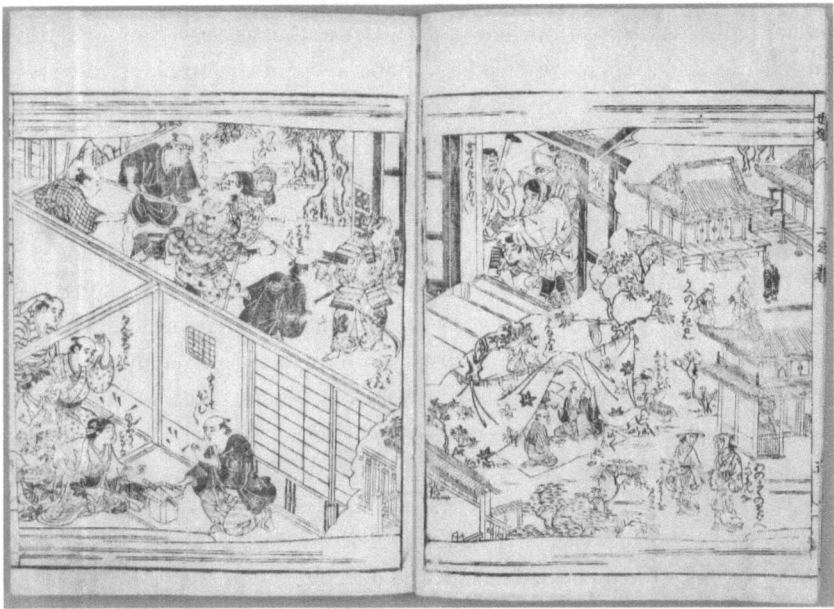

FIGURE 5.1 *Seken musume katagi*. Illustration from "Even Managing a Household, She Treasured Neither Money nor Life" (vol. 2, 5u–6o). Courtesy of Waseda University Library.

From satire to stereotype to caricature and finally to nonsense: The culmination of this character sketch occurs when, one night, the house is invaded by robbers, who tie up the husband and his clerks, but are defeated by the fearsome samurai wife. When the husband expresses his gratitude, she is enraged by his cowardice and demands that he commit ritual suicide to atone for his failures as a man. The wife refuses to stand down, and it is here that the story seems poised to turn away from the toothless humor of the *katagi-mono*, disrupting the surface of the everyday with a grotesquely violent conclusion. But just when all seems lost, the story quickly resolves with an all-too-telling deus ex machina: The robbery was all a dream by the husband! As we move from commonplace violations of conservative feminine norms toward more extreme forms of gender transgression, narrative spirals toward nonsense. The boundary represented by sheer nonsense and marked by the artificial conclusion of the deus ex machina is none other than the limit of normality, a horizon beyond which Kiseki lacked the capacity to imagine. Nevertheless, when the dream ends and we return to the benign space of domestic everyday life, a subtle shift has again taken place. All is well enough, and the husband remains helplessly cowed by his domineering, untownsman-like, and amusingly masculine wife. The townsman's normality consists of a largely amoral set of manners that are deemed ordinary and a wider range of deviations that are marked as eccentric, but eccentricity is constituted as such when more substantive disruptions of the everyday can no longer be imagined or represented.

MERE ECCENTRICITY

The dialectical tension between normativity and eccentricity would emerge into a new and stable balance with *Old Men of the Floating World*. This late work was published by Hachimonjiya following Kiseki's reconciliation with his estranged friend and his functional abandonment of the ambition of making a career as an independent author. The preface lists both Kiseki and Jishō as authors, though the writing is unquestionably Kiseki's. Whether due to the gradual refinement of Kiseki's craft or to his liberation from the daily distractions of running a failing business, *Old Men of the Floating World* is a mature and confident work. The author's penchant for textual appropriation seems to have matured into a looser mode of influence and adaptation: His style of pastiche, which in earlier works had still allowed the attentive reader to glimpse the patchwork of citations behind the text, resolves into the generation of stereotypes as such, familiar and representative but not always clearly rooted in any specific earlier text. Nearly everything in the text, every character and every narrative turn, is familiar, many of them copies of copies of copies. At the same time, the gratuitous eccentricity of Kiseki's characters and the extremity of his narrative progressions, which in earlier works had verged into nonsense, is reined in, transmuted into methodical studies of character. Indeed, this is a work in which the depiction of character comes to displace narrative almost entirely. The reader is presented with a series of largely static sketches of social types that are mildly eccentric yet deeply familiar, a polished and carefully curated distillation of the townsman's literary self-image.

Old Men of the Floating World would be recognized by readers in the following century as a masterwork of the genre and is still celebrated by modern scholars as the author's magnum opus, a work that found within Kiseki's hyperactive comic style an unprecedented plausibility or "sense of reality" (*genjitsukan*).⁴⁹ To an extent, the plausibility of this work was a reflection of its central type. The figure of the retired townsman father contained a set of tensions, not just those that separated older and younger generations, but also those faced by a household head moving into the role of retiree. On retiring, the aging father of the townsman household was expected to withdraw from public life and household management, typically taking Buddhist vows and a Buddhist name and, in the wealthier townsman milieu, moving with his wife to a separate residence to the rear of the property. Such a transition was not always easy for energetic fathers, especially those who had built their fortunes from scratch and were reluctant to pass affairs off to their heirs—in reality, many continued to manage the household in retirement, whether directly or through the mediation of trusted clerks—and many of Kiseki's protagonists are those who refuse to go softly into that good night. More generally, a certain degree of eccentricity was allowed and even expected of aging parents who had retired from public life and were free to pursue their private whims. The figure of the townsman retiree was thus a particularly plausible topos for the humor of incongruity on which the *katagi-mono* was built.

The framework of a generational shift also conceals deeper sociocultural issues, however. In one brilliant reading, Watanabe Kenji finds in *Old Men of the Floating World* a crisis in masculinity brought about by the consolidation of the townsman household as the central institution defining townsman identity. According to Watanabe, the turn to the eighteenth century saw a shift from a strictly Confucian notion of patriarchy based on blood relation, in which the father always demands the respect and love of his children, to an instrumentalized household framework in which the retiree, no longer the household head, has himself become a dependent, formally subordinate to his heir and ultimately a burden on the household. From the latter perspective, the aging protagonists of this work are fools who refuse to relinquish authority and thus lead their households toward ruin, but Watanabe observes that Kiseki nevertheless treats them with an ambivalent empathy that relativizes the ideology of the household and reveals the "falsehood of everyday common sense" (*seken jōshiki no kyoisei*).⁵⁰ In this regard, Watanabe takes the work as an extension of the mode of townsman self-satire developed in *Worldly Young Men*, as discussed in chapter 4. But that work had contained a certain malice; lurking below its sunny outlook, low narrative stakes, and nonsense humor was an unsparing self-indictment both of the household and of the *enfants terribles* who ineffectually rebel against it. That darkness vanishes in *Old Men of the Floating World*, and what is left is a tame and heartwarming comedy of manners. To the extent that it depicts its protagonists' social transgressions as plausible consequences of familiar social realities and generational shifts, it domesticates them, renders them familiar, benign, inevitable, and universal in a sense that remains recognizable today—the tensions and contradictions inherent to the household become stories of eccentric old men set in their ways. As the dialectical tension between household norms and individual eccentrics is made stable and static, normality exerts its power.

Old Men of the Floating World begins with a long episode running over two stories: "A Vigorous Old Man Who Loved to Eat" (*Shoku o tanoshimu tassha oyaji*, vol. 1-1) and "A Brawny Old Man Who Loved Wrestling" (*Sumō o tanoshimu gōriki oyaji*, vol. 1-2).[51] The sequence concerns an aging townsman patriarch, a nouveau riche merchant or "millionaire of the moment" (*ima chōja*), who had risen from rural origins to build his fortune in a single generation. The first story opens with an account of the father's provincial roots: Born in the "humble, weed-thatched hut of a farmer" in Ōmi Province, he was raised by a widowed mother. Although his naturally robust constitution made him suited to field work, a rowdy temperament inclined him to get into scraps with the youths of the neighboring villages; becoming a burden on his mother, he ultimately absconded to Kyoto, where he found work as a servant doing heavy labor for a rice dealer. Saving his earnings over many years, he eventually established his own household, marrying a woman of similar rural background, and, thanks equally to the hard work of husband and wife and to the steady increase in the price of rice, he has by the age of sixty come into a substantial fortune. At this point, he retires and passes the position of household head to his son. However, despite having achieved the financial clout to rub elbows with the finer ranks of Kyoto's townsman elite, he retains the "macho disposition" (*otokodate-katagi*) of his youth. The two stories are structured by a concern with the various amusing ways in which this disposition is materially manifest—in the protagonist's imposing appearance, in his unrefined and aggressive manner of speech, in his distinctly sanguinary set of personal tastes and leisure practices—and with how it contrasts with the norms of manner that had come to define proper townsman society.

The first story centers on the son's marriage to an elite townsman daughter, and on the humorous conduct of the father as revealed in a scenario of meet-the-parents. Kiseki uses the contrast with the son's more refined in-laws to highlight the eccentricities of the retiree's rough-and-tumble disposition. The story first attends to the father's appearance, as the son implores the other members of his father's Buddhist congregation to convince him to remove his myriad tattoos through moxibustion. The father responds that he was planning to get a few more tattoos to commemorate the event—"The bride's parents are from some stuffy old families, and I don't want them lookin' down at my boy like some kind of flash-in-the-pan, so I thought I'd show them what his old man is made of. . . . they won't make no damn fool out of me!"—but eventually relents. On the occasion of the wedding, as the guests are making polite conversation about *nō*, incense, linked verse, tea, *kemari*, and archery, the father boasts loudly of his ability to eat large quantities of food. When the bride's father challenges him to a game of chess, he responds by lifting the heavy chessboard by one corner, a common feat used to demonstrate strength—but, finding that his strength has waned in old age, he drops the chessboard, which gashes his knee. Unfazed, he cauterizes the wound with his tobacco pipe, and the new in-laws are cowed into a horrified silence.

The second story resumes the plot in media res, as the families move on to the wedding banquet. The father is, of course, oblivious to the finer nuances of elite Kyoto cuisine, proudly proclaiming his preference for simple, hearty fare such as whale meat sold by the pound. After dinner, the

FIGURE 5.2 *Ukiyo oyaji katagi*. Illustration from "A Vigorous Old Man Who Loved to Eat" (vol.1, 4u-5o). Courtesy of Waseda University Library.

father of the bride offers a refined performance of *nō* dancing, and the father responds with his own brand of performance, stripping down to give a show of his skill at sumo wrestling and displaying the new throws that he has invented; his son is mortified, and the guests are left aghast. At this point, the narrative of the son's marriage is dropped, and indeed the story loses any sense of a coherent plot, instead presenting a series of micro-narrative vignettes centered on the father's love of sumo wrestling. He forces the servants to spar with him as practice and spends his days eating meat to increase his strength; his family attempts to dissipate his vigor by hiring two young women as mistresses, but he neglects them on the grounds that canoodling with young women will drain his masculine energies. In the end, he is injured and declines because of his injuries, but this is presented neither as a consequence of social or moral transgression nor as a tragic and laughable fate. The tone remains affectionate to the end, and the father dies as he lived, full of the good-natured bluster of his "macho disposition."

These stories present a nuanced and ambivalent humor that pokes good-natured fun at the father's unrefined manners while satirizing the puffed-up, superficial, and pretentious affectations of the merchant elite. Kiseki pointedly deflates the behavior of the latter: At the wedding banquet, as the in-laws are engaging in casual conversational one-upmanship about their respective pedigrees in the leisure arts, the narrator summarizes the scene by saying that "they made a great show of matters of which in their heart they knew nothing" (*nai mo senu hara no naka no tana o kazari*), and similar sardonic asides pepper the narration throughout the collection. We have here a reiteration of the central critique of *Worldly Young Men*: that the townsman is all show, that even the elite are merely representing themselves as such, for this is the nature of the townsman, whose identity is constituted through acts of self-representation. But the critique takes on a different tone here. In *Worldly Young Men*, the suggestion still felt scandalous, all the more so as Kiseki confronted his readers with the ways in which his protagonists' various acts of petty rebellion failed to escape the townsman's logic of self-representation. In *Old Men of the Floating World*, the affected pretensions of the elite are stated as a matter of fact. By now, we know that this is the nature of the townsman elite, and the narrator's casual eye-rolling does not reveal it so much as confirm what we already know. This knowledge does nothing to throw into question the cultural authority of the elite and the ideology of the household, which we know to be a kind of fiction, but one that nevertheless exerts sway over those subject to it. Meanwhile, although the father's absurd behavior is itself posturing and affectation of a different sort: a deployment of signifiers of his own plebeian habitus at the moment that his household has decisively entered the ranks of the elite. He does not want to return to his roots so much as to perform them. Moreover, he is free to act as he wants, for the funds that he brings to the marital exchange remain the same. The protagonist's eccentricities are humored throughout the story, tolerated and even supported by members of his family and community. In this work, the "everyday common sense" of the household may indeed ring hollow, but it remains unquestioned as a norm, one that is all the more deeply entrenched for tolerating certain limited degrees of individual expression and for functioning despite the wide recognition of its hollowness. In sum, these stories find situational humor in the foibles of both the townsman elite and the unrefined nouveau riche, both of whom are marked as eccentric but both in familiar and harmless ways. The space thus established by the tension, now entirely stable, between (provisional, fictional) norm and (moderate, predictable) deviation is the space of normality.

As one might expect, most of the details that Kiseki deploys in the illustration of this character are borrowed—indeed, many of them from Kiseki's earlier rendition of the amateur townsman wrestler in *Worldly Young Men*, which itself had been a pastiche of citations from Saikaku's *Twenty Unfilial Exemplars*. But whereas in Kiseki's earlier work the citations were largely verbatim, *Old Men of the Floating World* rarely reproduces the prose of earlier works. Its relation to those works is emulation and elaboration rather than simple reproduction. Kiseki takes familiar images, fleshes them out, riffs on them, adding telling details and further anecdotes from other sources, and smoothing over the patchwork to produce a multifaceted portrait. For example, in *Worldly Young Men*, Kiseki had written that the young sumo wrestler enjoyed "tossing around the servants," a colorful detail that embellished Saikaku's simple portrait. In *Old Men of the Floating World*, this passing comment is elaborated into its own comic vignette that illustrates the father's character:

> He took unending pleasure in sparring with the servant Kyūshichi and refused to heed no matter how one implored him to stop. His son and wife consulted with each other and decided that, since he showed no signs of

quitting, they might at least save him from injury, so in secret they offered Kyūshichi a raise in exchange for letting him win. But the effect was just the opposite of what they had expected, for he only grew more excited: "Even Kyūshichi, with all the vim and vigor of youth, can't lay a finger on me!"[52]

Through a process of recursive intertextual reproduction, Kiseki's practice of citation transforms Saikaku's idiosyncratic images, scenes, and details into familiar types: images that seem familiar but that need not be traced to a single source or citation.

Along with this shift in the nature of Kiseki's intertextual practice, *Old Men of the Floating World* effects a subtle transformation in narrative form: away from a dynamic plot based on principles of narrative causality—a concern with what happens and why—and toward the episodic depiction of static character. The stories don't go anywhere. Details are elaborated into short vignettes, and vignettes are expanded into subplots that unfold one after another; situations are contrived as a framework for the humorous exemplification of the protagonist's central peccadillo, but plotting as such is minimal and purely instrumental. We might compare this structure with the conventional didactic framework of "promoting virtue and chastising vice" (*kanzen chōaku*) in which characters are witnessed carrying out wicked acts and imminently seen to be punished, and the causal logic of moral karma is thus made to appear self-evident through the causality of narrative. Saikaku's *Twenty Unfilial Exemplars*, despite the ambivalence and complexity of its moral vision, remained within this paradigm: The townsman sumo aficionado refuses to obey his parents and, within a page or two, is crippled by injury. Traces of this logic remain in *Worldly Young Men*, where Kiseki's eccentric young men are occasionally pushed out of their households and to the margins of townsman society. In *Worldly Young Women*, narrative progression is vestigial. In "Even Managing a Household," about the samurai daughter–cum–townsman wife, we simply have a steady escalation of the extremity of caricature, accompanied by an illusion of increasing narrative stakes that disguises a fundamentally static structure, revealed in clear relief by the artificial conclusion—it was all a dream! This structure is perfected in *Old Men of the Floating World*, wherein the dynamism of narrative is abandoned almost entirely in favor of the episodic depiction of character. The first story ends with the protagonist's cauterizing the gash on his knee with his tobacco pipe, followed by the brief and entirely redundant narratorial comment that "all in attendance were utterly aghast" (*zachū shirakete kyō samashinu*). The second story resumes in the middle of the wedding banquet, but after the father begins his sumo demonstration, the wedding is dropped, and the story pivots into a series of sketches that focus on his wrestling habit. Kiseki gives passing attention to the social consequences of eccentricity by describing the reactions of the household or other communities, but this response is of the order of a straight man or a laugh track: cuing the reader's affective response without enforcing any negative narrative consequences for the character. Although it takes inspiration from joke books, most of the stories in *Old Men of the Floating World* lack even the rudimentary telos of the joke—building up to a conclusive punch line. They digest jokes into atomic units, stringing multiple gags into a loosely woven fabric that illustrates the core character from various angles. The anecdotes unfold until a certain length is achieved, or until the author simply runs out of material, and then they abruptly end. The narrative structure of the *katagi-mono* thus functions as a microcosm of the genre's paratextual structure: a collection of anecdotes that variously illustrate the same basic category—old men of the townsman class, all of whom are eccentric in different ways and yet unified in their minor eccentricity—and that thus serve to flesh out the range of amusing novelty contained within the familiar category of old men. The type is constituted as such by the range of individual variations it can contain.

The same logic structures Kiseki's prose style, which, despite his debts to Saikaku, was of an entirely different sort. Where Saikaku's prose is allusive, elliptical, aphoristic, and contradictory, Kiseki's is concrete and logical to the point of redundancy—at its worst plodding and pedantic, at its best smooth and seamless, moving deductively from one point to the next.[53] Kiseki's earlier works retain traces of the dynamism of Saikaku's prose; precisely in their moments of irrationality, nonsense, and abrupt comic turns one can see the structure of Saikaku's energetically shifting narrative vision. But in *Old Men of the Floating World*, that energy is tamed, as the shifts from scene to scene are not those of abrupt tonal inversions or narrative twists, just a steady reiteration and amplification of the same scene, each version of which serves to signify the same underlying character. The narrative pacing is altered as well, as Kiseki takes his time to develop each scene and fill it with telling details and minor comic gags: The story plods forward, unfolding as a steady enumeration of examples. Kiseki often has been described as a writer with a penchant for pedantry or heavy-handed argumentation (*rikutsu*), but perhaps a better description would be to call his writing prosaic, a style that steadily moves from premises to conclusions and carefully guides the reader from one point to the next, leaving little room for interpretation. In part, the development of this prosaic style was driven by the writer's grasp of his audience: Kiseki, who was uniquely sensitive to the needs and literacies of a widening reading public, was careful to adapt Saikaku's language, adding pronouns, conjunctions, and minute details to make the language more concrete, colloquial, and easier to follow for readers without a highly cultivated poetic literacy. But it was also shaped by his evolving attempts to represent the townsman self. Just as Saikaku's dynamic narration was linked to a conception of the mercurial nature of the "hearts of people in the world" (and, ultimately, to the unpredictable movements of money), Kiseki's prosaic style was linked to an increasing sense of the underlying stability and even unchangeability of the self.

Above all, this narrative form was rooted in Kiseki's timely apprehension that different types of people naturally behave in different ways—that such differences are to be expected as a matter of course. Despite the pervasive eccentricity of *Old Men of the Floating World*, everyone behaves precisely according to expectations. Indeed, the most remarkable accomplishment of this work, the social vision that distinguishes it from the author's earlier *katagi-mono* and that lends a "sense of reality" to its eccentricities, is that here Kiseki attributes the "characters" of his protagonists to a sense of ingrained class habitus. The story of the aging wrestler is none other than that of a provincial farmer, absconded from his village to become an urban laborer; he has worked his way up to rub elbows with the urban elite, but his conduct, his sense of taste and distinction, his manner of speech and modes of leisure expression all remain shaped by the habitus formed in his rural upbringing. More than the particular role of retiree and the norms of retirement that faced aging townsman patriarchs, Kiseki's central concern was with the ways in which such social trajectories produced amusing diversity and comic conflict in the ranks of propertied urban society. Many of the hapless protagonists of *Old Men of the Floating World* are those who have made their way into propertied townsman society from origins in other social classes. In "A Pederastic Old Man Who Loved Lads" (*Yarō o tanoshimu nanshoku oyaji*, vol. 1–3), an aging *rōnin*, unable to adapt to the commercial demands of life as a commoner, is supported by his son and daughter-in-law, who run a tea shop. The father's uncompromisingly stern samurai moralism, though, clashes with the flattery, frivolity, and promiscuity inherent in the teahouse trade.[54] In "A High-Interest Old Man Who Loved Money" (*Kane o tanoshimu kōri no oyaji*, vol. 2–1), a stingy moneylender, despite reaching the heights of wealth and retirement age, refuses to adopt the cultural refinement of his peers and instead delights only in the thrift and usury by which he made his way up in the world.[55] In "A Proud Old Man Who Loved to Watch His Child Dance" (*Odori o tanoshimu ko jiman no oyaji*, vol. 3–1), the illiterate proprietor of a humble sundries shop toils his way into wealth but rejects the refinement of his wealthy peers, encouraging his son to learn plebeian forms of street performance rather than literacy and bookkeeping, let alone the polite leisure arts.[56] Through such stories, which pair narrative trajectories of socioeconomic mobility with depictions of habitus rooted in class origins, *Old Men of the Floating World* takes the social heterogeneity that lingered within a normalizing urban society and crystallizes it into a vivid but static tableau.

Old Men of the Floating World is a work of formal perfection. Excising the irrational qualities of Saikaku's prose and, with them, that author's apprehension of the dynamism of townsman society and the townsman self, Kiseki presents a vision of urban society capable of accounting for the diversity of character that the emerging norms of townsman identity—those of the townsman household—tended to repress or exclude. It does so by depicting transgressions of proper townsman habitus as nothing more than vestigial manifestations of the diverse social origins of the townsman class, and by subsuming them within heartwarming and ever so familiar narratives—narratives assumed to be universal and inevitable—of aging men at odds with the younger generation. Paradoxically, it is a profoundly normative work, one that perfects the project of townsman normality by accounting for its exceptions, rendering them harmless, familiar, and indeed entirely predictable, sources of mild amusement and empathetic identification. It normalizes not in the sense of punishing and excluding deviance, but by containing transgressive energy as mere eccentricity. Kiseki created a vision of townsman identity, and a form of townsman prose, that could account for the vast diversity of habitus that persisted in the cities of the early eighteenth century and that any narrowly prescriptive set of didactic mandates could never erase or contain: an image of urban society that was simultaneously normative and diverse.

CONCLUSION

Kiseki was not the only writer of his time to be concerned with how eccentric individuals could or should fit into a normalizing status society. In tandem with the increasing normativity of the Kyōhō era, the eighteenth century saw a rising interest in new identities that might not be bound by such norms. Kiseki's explorations of the quirks and peccadillos of the propertied townsman class in some sense parallel the appearance of the *bunjin* (literatus) and *kijin* (eccentric)—individualistic figures that seem to represent a symbolic surplus to and perhaps reaction against the normative structures of the status order writ large. But these figures, like Kiseki's characters, would quickly become norms in their own ways. The figure of the *bunjin*, as it congealed in early eighteenth-century Japan, was in a sense just that: a figure or idealized self-image, drawn imaginatively through reading and emulation of Chinese textual antecedents, that functioned as a model of social and cultural performance, offering a stable and ultimately normative model of alternative subjectivity to alienated intellectuals.[57] The figure of the *bunjin* was informed by an aesthetics of eccentricity (*ki*) and was closely intertwined with the figure of the *kijin*, but here, too, the deviant, eccentric, or otherwise nonnormative does not simply transgress or defy the norm but instead reconfigures it.[58] W. Puck Brecher has shown that discourses of eccentricity operated in the context of competing claims over the nature of aesthetic orthodoxy, and often (ironically enough) took the form of debates over which forms of eccentricity were proper; through this, the aesthetics of eccentricity, centered on the figure of the *kijin*, "permeated mainstream ethical values to assume an inviolable position within mainstream culture."[59] In sum, just as Tokugawa culture came to fixate on identities and modes of expression that would transgress or situationally transcend otherwise rigid social norms, the paradoxical nature of Tokugawa culture was such that transgressions would become normative in their own ways, their energies contained within stable if flexible forms. The *katagimono* was one exemplary such form, an endlessly eccentric icon of generic normality and keen register of the shifting nature of status identity.

Ejima Kiseki had lived through a moment in which the basic logics of status were shifting. The shift was subtle but fundamental: Social categories that had once been largely objective social structures were progressively incorporated into subjective forms of identity, and universal moral principles such as filiality came to exist alongside class-based social norms of dress, speech, manner, taste, and cultural training. This shift came with the historically new awareness that forms of conduct that would be unremarkable and even obligatory in one milieu would appear strange and even deviant in another—in other words, that people of different social positions were and should be different. For the townsman, this new notion of social normality contained a particularly complex set of tensions. On the one hand, the boundaries of urban society were porous to begin with. Whereas the peasant was, to a degree, bound to his village and the warrior to his household, urban-commoner society included many individuals without connection to such stable communities. To those who managed to work their way up from poverty and marginality into urban property, the norms of townsman identity represented the possibility of inclusion and opportunity within an elite urban milieu. An entrepreneurial class needed standards of culture to define itself. On the other hand, the innate heterogeneity and stratification of urban society meant that different substrata (or regions, or occupations) would, to some degree, develop their own lifestyles, and that many individuals might connect more to the values and norms of their communities of birth (many laboring class or rural) than to the emerging norms that defined the townsman and his milieu. The cultural polishing through which the townsman reproduced himself from generation to generation would always remain incomplete, and urban society would always remain diverse in ways that no unitary norms could fully erase.

Kiseki's *katagi-mono* were the space within which the townsman's repressed origins would endlessly return. The gratuitous eccentricity of Kiseki's protagonists is not always legible in any literal social terms; at times, it appears nonsensical, disrupting narrative expectations with an almost formalist purity. But this compulsion toward formal subversion was none other than a symbolic working out of the tensions within a rapidly but incompletely normalizing urban society: the irreducible alterity of the diverse urban community sublimated into a genre neurotically fixated on troubling social norms and narrative forms. Yet, despite that limitless transgressive energy, Kiseki's works quickly lose their bite. Narrative developments that were once thrillingly novel come to appear as familiar gags; the range of subversion, both social and narrative, becomes familiar, domesticated, safe; and when the impulse to defy norms is pushed too far, it collapses into nonsense before transgressing into the truly abnormal or politically problematic. The causal narrative structure of transgression and its consequences is disarmed and replaced by the description of static character: Minor eccentricities are enumerated endlessly for the reader's amused recognition but elicit no narrative response of punishment, censure, or social consequence. If Kiseki's work was oriented toward the humorous critique of social norms through their transgression, then the development of the *katagi-mono* into a genre in its own right—with its own norms, tropes, and techniques—coincided with the development of a new vision of social normativity that contained a range of acceptable, familiar, and harmless deviation. The irony of the *katagi-mono* is that, in creating a space for the townsman's repressed origins to perpetually return, Kiseki robbed them of their capacity to unsettle and allowed them to merely amuse. This was the dialectical process that the *katagi-mono* ultimately embodied: not to transgress the norms of townsman society, but to map out a space of individual self-expression that could situationally flout those norms without troubling the boundaries of normality. Nowhere were the roiling energies of urban society so effectively contained as in the eminently relatable, heartwarming, domestic comedies of generational conflict in *Old Men of the Floating World*.

Or perhaps they were contained within the act of reading. A generation later, the latter-day *ukiyo-zōshi* writer Nagaidō Kiyū would release a work titled *Characters of Popular Linked Verse Poets* (*Fūzoku haijin katagi*, 1763), but, like most works in the genre, its contents range unpredictably beyond its titular type.[60] One episode depicts a young woman named Fusa soliciting a booklender for works by Kiseki: She describes how she had read one volume of *Old Men of the Floating World* and, "remembering her dearly departed father back in the countryside," shed tears over its pages.[61] In her passing mention of the countryside (*zaisho*), we may almost certainly read a reference to the story of the aging sumo wrestler, whose rough-and-tumble disposition was a product of his provincial and lower-class origins. The story is unlikely to strike a modern reader as a tragic one, but we should take this episode, however fictional, as a testament to the sense of reality that contemporary readers found in Kiseki's works, which may not have elicited mocking or transgressive laughter as much as affectionate recognition and identification. Reading itself of course carried the risk of transgression, whether for young men like the dilettantish scholars and poets of *Worldly Young Men* or for young women like Fusa: Kiseki himself, in *Worldly Young Women*, had depicted a promiscuous daughter who was locked in her room with her sewing, forbidden from reading even *Tales of Ise*, let alone vulgar works like *ukiyo-zōshi*. But young men and women surely did read such works, and through them could safely enjoy a vicarious experience, if only on the printed page, of forms of conduct and social expression that they might only dream of in their daily lives.

EPILOGUE

From the Textual Townsman to Edo Urbanism

At the same time that Ejima Kiseki was using the "space of the collection" to explore the possibilities and pitfalls of alternative townsman selves, another literary culture was forming in the city of Edo, rooted in a different set of social positions and oriented by a different set of textual practices. This was the formally diverse corpus of popular fiction known to posterity as *gesaku* or "playful compositions."[1] From its origins as a form of elevated literary play by literati and students in the Sinitic tradition, *gesaku* came to act as a crucible of high and low literary forms in which the Chinese classics were made contemporary and vulgar through ingenious parodies, while the lowest genres of transcribed street oratory and juvenile illustrated fiction came to be infused with the adult subject matter of the Edo brothel districts and with the intellectual erudition of Sinitic study. Edo *gesaku* also came to incorporate diverse urban identities. Although originally rooted largely in the literary recreation of students and intellectuals (mostly of the warrior class), the hybrid nature of its literary forms attracted readers of all social classes and eventually courted writers of diverse backgrounds, including those of townsman stock. Edo *gesaku* was at the center of a new woodblock-print culture, distinct from that of late seventeenth and early eighteenth-century Kamigata, that incorporated a wider range of reading and writing demographics to mediate an even more diverse urban community. Despite the complexity and diversity of Edo print culture, however, one may find in it traces of the textual townsman.

In 1785, a young townsman illustrator and budding *gesaku* humorist by the pen name of Santō Kyōden (1761–1816) released his comic masterpiece, *Grilled and Basted Edo Playboy (Edo umare uwaki no kabayaki)*.[2] A formative work in the genre of illustrated "yellow-covers" (*kibyōshi*), *Edo Playboy* depicts an impressionable merchant scion named Enjirō who has become intoxicated by images of urban sophistication consumed through popular culture and wishes to remake himself as a proper playboy and fashionably prodigal son. The story unfolds as a series of gags as Enjirō spends his ample inherited wealth to live out a fantasy vision of the degenerate merchant heir: tattooing himself with the names of imaginary courtesan lovers, paying local *geisha* to barge into his household with declarations of love, and hiring rough-and-tumble street toughs to beat him up in public, ostensibly for being so terribly attractive that lowlife thugs like them don't have any chance with the ladies. Enjirō's inspirations are not solely from books—many of the tropes he rehearses are drawn from plays of the kabuki and puppet theaters—but Kyōden gives particular attention to the mediation of print: The text begins with the dreamy Enjirō poring over the printed playscripts of ballads from the puppet theater, and the first fascicle culminates with his commissioning a news-crier to print and distribute broadsheets of fabricated gossip about his supposed romantic exploits. The farce steadily escalates toward the climax of a lovers' double-suicide as Enjirō absconds with his well-paid but increasingly reluctant courtesan costar Ukina. En route to the site of their tragic finale, the two are accosted by bandits who strip them of their clothes and send them slumping home to the accompaniment of a travesty of *jōruri* narration, Enjirō chastened for his flights of fancy and Ukina resentful of his idiotic folly. On their return, they learn that the bandits were none other than his father's loyal clerks, sent to teach the prodigal son a lesson. Following a stern lecture by his father, Enjirō comes to his senses, matures into a responsible adult, and, "to still the frivolous reputation he had cultivated, calls on Kyōden to write up his exploits into a comic book and release it to the world, as an admonition for promiscuous young people."

At first glance, *Edo Playboy* suggests a satire of coddled youth, indulging in preposterous fantasies imagined through the misrecognition of fiction for reality. In this regard, it is not unlike Kiseki's *Characters of Worldly*

Young Men. But Kyōden's comic masterpiece also contains a subtler recognition and indeed an embrace of the virtuality of print. However absurd his conduct seems to onlookers, Enjirō delights at every stage in his capacity to live out a fiction as such, enabled and protected by inherited wealth— "his estate was after all an ample one and would continue to flourish into the future"—and, at the conclusion of the story, Enjirō finally succeeds in his fantasy: entering the fictional world of print in the form of a comic book composed by Kyōden's brush. Enjirō, whose parodic process of townsman self-fashioning was imagined from the beginning through the mediation of the printed page, completes that process by becoming a book himself. It may seem far-fetched that this book would work as a didactic "admonition" (*kyōkun*)— how many young people of the 1780s do we imagine were up to antics like Enjirō's? As we have seen, however, the didactic functions of popular fiction in the Tokugawa Japan were far subtler than simply showing wickedness punished and virtue rewarded. Just as the *katagi-mono* functioned to create a space for harmless transgression within a larger condition of everyday normality, Kyōden's work indicates just how much more normal the urban everyday had become. Transgressive conduct that less than a century earlier had seemed very real—profligate spending, disownment, scandalous conduct with courtesans—now seemed like an outlandish fantasy, safely contained on the stage and within the covers of printed books. Kyōden's admonition seems to be to keep both one's transgressions on the page, where one can indulge freely in one's wildest fantasies, and one's household intact. Kyōden himself seems to have followed this advice: Notwithstanding some scrapes with shogunal authority during the Kansei reforms, he never allowed his textual transgressions to displace his house trade as a purveyor of tobacco products.[3] Avoiding the tragicomic fate of Kiseki and his hapless protagonists, he would achieve his status as the first professional *gesaku* author by finding a symbiosis between the work of his pen and that of his abacus.

By Kyōden's time, it was not only the townsman whose self-image was defined by textual practice. Readers of all kinds cultivated and imagined themselves through an ever-more-complex collection of print genres. This was the guiding premise behind Kyōden's hilarious send-up of Edo publishing, *Those Familiar Bestsellers* (*Gozonji no shōbaimono*, 1782).[4] This work was an ingenious parable of Edo publishing history: Kyōden narrated the rise of Edo *gesaku* through a tropey and madcap story of brothel intrigue, personifying each print genre as a character. The books of Hachimonjiya appear as one of the villains, a stuffy old guard resentful of the rise of flashy new work like Kyōden's own. More important, along with a clever narrative of shifts in the print field, Kyōden also showed a keen awareness of how the sensibilities of his fellow Edo-ites were shaped by print: Each genre is depicted in the form of the type of person who might read or write it. The work thus offers an image of a dense and lively landscape of distinct urban types whose identities are informed by the consumption of commercial print—or conversely, of a richly proliferating print field, diversifying in ever more forms to address the social plurality of urban Edo. Amid this diversity, Kyōden of course gave pride of place to popular genres like those in which he worked, which "delighted the eyes of readers both high and low."

One of the recent maxims of Edo literary studies is that, just as Tokugawa society was compartmentalized into a rigid hierarchy of status groups, books too were subject to the logic of status. As Nakano Mitsutoshi (among others) has observed, early modern Japanese print culture took the form of a complex matrix of print genres and formats, reflecting a hierarchy of cultural value that was loosely homologous to the fixed social hierarchies of the status system.[5] Just as the warrior could be immediately recognized by the swords at his hip, so could the position of a given work in the literary field could be perceived at a glance by its cover and dimensions. To Nakano, this "status system for books" was a figure for a perfectly stable social system, a kind of benevolent feudalism in which the categories of social existence were never meaningfully questioned nor the authority of the high over the low ever truly contested. This harmonious social totality was reflected in a print culture that existed to transmit the values of the ruling class and thus both to reflect and to reproduce the social order. Books, however, do not simply transmit stable values in a top-down fashion. Despite the political hegemony of the warrior class, the woodblock-print culture of Tokugawa Japan was often produced by and for the commoner classes, driven by their economic agency and grounded in their values and lifeworlds. Just as the Tokugawa polity was built on the complex negotiation between top-down administrative frameworks and the bottom-up organization of status communities, Tokugawa print culture was likewise defined by the intersection between hegemonic ideologies and the distinct worldviews of the various communities that made up the dominated classes, and who did not appropriate or resist the language and values of the political elite as much as

EPILOGUE

produce new forms of language, narrative, and media to give shape to their worlds. Moreover, the print genres produced by this bottom-up process did not simply reflect the sensibilities of stable and fixed audiences. Books move across boundaries to figure new publics, and print genres impart to those publics shared values and narratives, producing new communities mediated by the circulation of print. Kyōden's *Familiar Bestsellers* is a testament to the dynamism and plurality of early modern woodblock-print culture, a document of all the diverse ways in which print matter produced new sensibilities and urban types, how genres and their readerships could clash but also overlap and intersect. If we are to take seriously the didactic quality of this print culture, we must consider the "status system for books" not as a passive reflection of the social status system but as one of the constitutive forces behind it: the material and symbolic medium through which status communities were formed and their boundaries negotiated, the medium that gave them a shared sense of identity and models for self-fashioning.

The Edo period was a moment when new forms of subjectivity were made possible by the circulation of print. The woodblock-printed text was not a document or product of a prior social reality but a constitutive part of that reality, part of the communicative and dialogic processes through which social reality was produced and reproduced. Such assertions feel novel for Tokugawa Japan but would feel very uncontroversial in the modern era: As in Anderson's classic formulation, moveable type mediates the imagined community of the nation. In light of the familiarity of such narratives, it is natural that we would be tempted to treat the print culture of "early modern" Japan as a prototype for modern print capitalism and the imagined communities of the woodblock print as incipient forms of modern national consciousness. However, even setting aside the teleological premises of such an approach, it fails to grasp the distinguishing characteristics of the social and media systems of Tokugawa Japan. In terms of social structure, it misses the ways in which the logic of status functioned to bring together and integrate disparate populations and status communities without dissolving the boundaries between them: not a nation built on shared (national) identity but a status polity predicated on public recognition of social and political difference. In terms of media, the comparison with modern print may obscure the ways in which those disparate but interrelated subjectivities evolved in relation to the articulations of different media cultures, genres, and distribution systems. The woodblock-printed text could cross boundaries but could also reaffirm them. The status system was not a set of artificial and arbitrary containers that it was the fate and function of print to overcome: It was a guiding structure of early modern selfhood—defining the nature of the self, its relationship to other selves, its place in a larger polity—that would both define the structures of print culture and evolve through the ongoing mediation of print. Understanding the logic of this system requires grappling with the essential if sometimes subtle differences between status communities and their media cultures, and doing so without recourse to grand narratives that would relegate such differences to mere footnotes in the prehistory of the modern nation.

Giving attention to the particularities of distinct status communities and their media cultures also allows us a more nuanced view of the politics of popular culture. We can recognize the simultaneous existence of multiple, distinct forms of social power, formed through bottom-up social processes and expressed in the textual self-fashioning of different status groups. Social power is constituted through the "stratified and composite" relationships between status communities, constantly renegotiated both through lived social and spatial practice and through a cultural imaginary, mediated by texts, that aids in defining the boundaries of the community, policing its relationship to other groups, and establishing hierarchies of relative authority within the community. Thus I have argued that Saikaku's *Eternal Storehouse* imagines a new townsman community based on shared values but predicated on the drawing of selective boundaries between city and countryside, on the systematic exclusion of the marginalized classes of beggars and hereditary outcasts, and on the legitimation of economic hierarchies within townsman society—the legitimation of wealth and property as a product of individual, entrepreneurial merit. These negotiations had little to do with contesting or resisting the hegemonic authority of the shogunate (or the values of the warrior class generally) but much to do with the active construction of new forms of status power, inextricably linked both to new forms of domination and to new forms of writing (literal inscription of texts and figural inscription of townsman property on urban space), and sustained through a symbiosis with governmental authority and the existing structures of the status polity. The townsman subject formed through this process was centered on the household, which, paradoxically but also tellingly, exerted its power over its own members. Accordingly, the more subversive elements of the townsman's literary voice—the cutting

EPILOGUE

self-satire of Ejima Kiseki—were directed not at the authority of the shogunate, the warrior class, or the status system writ large, but at the townsman's own sense of self. Nevertheless, even Kiseki's most paranoid satire was part of a process of social normalization, producing a sense of everyday urban normality that contained the lingering transgressive energies of townsman society in safe and familiar forms, or else redirected them toward virtual experience on the printed page.

The print cultures mediating the self-formation processes of distinct status communities were never fully autonomous, of course, and would intersect with increasing frequency as the period progressed. Whereas the *ukiyo-zōshi* of late seventeenth- and early eighteenth-century Kamigata was firmly grounded in the identity of the townsman, Edo *gesaku* was a textual space through which townspeople interacted with warrior-intellectuals, with cultural professionals of various class backgrounds, with the women of the demimonde (whose voices were almost always filtered through the brushes of male writers but who inarguably exerted a profound influence on Edo urban culture), and with the urban laboring classes, who in eighteenth- and nineteenth-century Edo came to wield their own forms of cultural authority, develop their own literary voices, and ultimately produce their own textual cultures. This intersection has sometimes been treated as a carnivalesque space that functioned to relativize shogunal authority.[6] I would suggest, however, that the dialogic negotiations playing out in the pages of *gesaku* were less focused on throwing into question the ideological hegemony of the shogunate and more with constructing and contesting relative hierarchies of social and cultural authority within Edo urban society.

For example, one exemplary work of early *gesaku* is *The Biography of Lady Seki* (*Seki fujin den*, 1753), by the warrior-intellectual Yamaoka Matsuake (1726–1780).[7] Like most of the early *gesaku* writers, Matsuake was of the warrior class (a shogunal vassal) and was a minor intellectual—a student of nativist learning (*kokugaku*) under Kamo no Mabuchi—and composed the work as a form of erudite literary play. The text is an elaborate parody of Zhuangzi: of the parable of Robber Zhi, who chastises Confucius for pursuing political ambition under the guise of offering high-handed social philosophy. Matsuake transposes the scenario to Edo and to the topos of prostitution: Zhi becomes Seki the "night hawk" (*yotaka*), the lowest rank of street prostitute. Seki's sister is a high-ranking courtesan and enlists her esteemed colleagues to entreat Seki to join their elite ranks and embrace the supposed comfort and prestige of work in the glamorous brothels of the Yoshiwara district. Seki responds with a vulgar tirade, at once denouncing the Yoshiwara courtesans for their elitism while exposing the variously exploitative systems that conspire to make keep even the highest-ranking courtesans perpetually in debt. At the heart of her invective is a critique of the Yoshiwara's systems of prestige. In her view, the purpose of the Yoshiwara district and its esteemed institutions is to surround the trade of prostitution with an aesthetic aura that justifies all manner of inflated charges; the working woman, of course, receives none of this surplus. As an alternative, Seki argues that the street prostitute offers a simple service for a fair price: "For twenty-four *mon* you make twenty-four *mon* of nookey . . . no lies from the customer, and no need to play hard to get."[8]

Because of its imaginative criticism of hierarchies of prestige, Matsuake's hilarious parody has been read as a tongue-in-cheek critique of social hierarchies of rank and status—in other words, of the Tokugawa status system.[9] But closer examination reveals that the main target of Seki's tirade is the commodification of the mainstream sex trade, which uses various aesthetic pretenses to justify exorbitant prices and results in a displacement of the honest truth (*jitsu*) of sexual pleasure with the dissembling lies (*uso*) of commercial exchange. In other words, it is a critique of the merchant belief in exchange value—sex is worth as much as you can get someone to pay for it—from the perspective of a warrior's belief in use value; indeed, Seki's lecture concludes with her denouncing the most famous merchant playboys of Saikaku's era. From this perspective, Matsuake's text is less a satire of social hierarchy writ large than a warrior-intellectual's humorous broadside against merchant values that were becoming dominant in the space of culture: in particular, the merchant embrace of fictional dissembling, the roots of which we have seen in the "wit" of Saikaku's entrepreneurs and in the culture of "repute" deconstructed by Kiseki's townsman deviants. This critique had a philosophical side, grounded in intellectual discourses of economic value and truth and fictionality, but it also carried significance in the context of Edo brothel culture, where warrior-intellectuals competed with wealthy merchants for cultural capital. This sublimation of social tensions into aesthetic and sartorial debates would play out in the pages of eighteenth-century *gesaku* through the ambiguous figure of the *tsū* (sophisticate).[10]

EPILOGUE

At the other end of the social spectrum, consider Shikitei Sanba, best known for his sketches of Edo's commoner districts: *The Floating World Bathhouse* (*Ukiyoburo*, 1809–1813) and *The Floating World Barbershop* (*Ukiyodoko*, 1813–1814).[11] In these works, Sanba depicted the everyday publics of downtown Edo, finding humor in the interactions between various urban types, sketched with an exquisite attention to sociolinguistic detail. Sanba has long been associated with the townsman class and is one of the main figures through which the interpretive framework of "townsman literature" has been extended to Edo *gesaku*.[12] At the same time, his dialogic masterworks have also been read as a symbolic form embodying total ideological relativism, not asserting the authority of any specific class but through their very relativism serving to decenter hegemonic values.[13] However, despite the loose and plotless form of Sanba's works, one can find relative centers within them: Sanba, whose work was inspired in part by influences from Kiseki's *katagi-mono*, used dialogue to create a new permutation of the "space of the collection" that allowed him to represent a range of social positions while orienting them around certain voices that asserted social and cultural authority.

Who were these voices? Despite his formal status as a townsman of mid-ranking stature, Sanba was the son of a working craftsman (woodblock carver) and had a strong cultural affinity for the plebeian strata of craftsmen, laborers, and street peddlers, to the degree that his literary archrival, the highly elitist (declassed warrior) Takizawa Bakin, described him as having "not the character of a literatus, nor that of a merchant, but something more like a street thug."[14] His *Bathhouse* and *Barbershop*, likewise, are centered on the local communities of tenement residents and oriented by the voices of plebeian figures, whose performances of confrontational and distempered bluster subtly function to police the use of shared space: reaching out to engage strangers in dialogue, ejecting the drunk and unruly, and enforcing the norms of everyday etiquette necessary for diverse populations to get along in close quarters.[15] Moreover, these works push the propertied townspeople to the margins of what are clearly represented as plebeian publics: Wealthy merchants are viewed with suspicion, for lacking community spirit and, indeed, for their tendency to dissemble and to put on airs—the very qualities that Kiseki had identified as central to the textually mediated performance of the townsman self. Sanba was an artist of the written word, but his approach to writing was grounded in the oral culture of Edo's laboring classes—the vaudeville theater (*yose*) and the arts of oral performance that took place on its stages—which allowed him to inflect the forms of *gesaku* to represent and advocate for the cultural authority of the lower urban strata.

These are merely two examples of the range of social positions within the *gesaku* corpus as it evolved from a form of erudite literary play in the mid-eighteenth century to something approaching mass entertainment in the nineteenth, but they should suffice to illustrate the points I have suggested about Tokugawa print culture. First is that these works cannot be understood in terms of a rubric of resistance to shogunal hegemony or subversion of the status order as such. This does not mean that *gesaku* was without politics, only that its politics was of the order of the everyday, concerned with negotiating the relative standing of and mutual relationships between different subjectivities within a larger urban community. Second is that the community mediated by Edo print culture was not that of the modern nation, predicated on a posited identity shared across various local communities and readerships. These texts draw explicit attention to the differences between different social categories and make competing claims of social and cultural authority, predicated on a vision of the urban community as heterogeneous in a constitutive sense. Notably absent from this community is the countryside: One premise that most *gesaku* authors shared, regardless of social background, is that hicks were hicks, and provincial audiences would only be slowly and haphazardly integrated into the *gesaku* readership in the nineteenth century. The urban imaginary of *gesaku* was not one in which distinct identities dissolved into a community of shared values, but one in which those identities emerged into mutual relation despite never quite agreeing on the terms of that relation. In this regard, Edo *gesaku*, like Tokugawa print culture writ large, was both an extension and an agent of the early modern urban process: the integration of distinct status communities into heterogeneous composites, and the ongoing and open-ended negotiation of the relationships between those communities. This urban process played out both in the lived spaces of the city and in the textual spaces of the printed page.

This book has traced such urban processes on a smaller scale, but one that illuminates more clearly the essential intertwining of the status order with the dynamics of woodblock-print culture. The case of the textual townsman reveals that the woodblock print not only functioned to cross

EPILOGUE

boundaries of status and figure cross-status urban publics (however complex and contested) like that of Edo *gesaku*, but also formed the material (media) basis through which the very categories of status were imagined as identities. The urban world of seventeenth-century Japan was still to a large degree a local one, a patchwork of atomized and semi-autonomous communities (*chō*) in various cities and towns, including innumerable trades with their own lifestyles and social networks, and comprising multiple socioeconomic strata that were often in practice at odds with one another. Through the circulation of woodblock-printed texts, the local was transfigured into the universal: urban commoners came to be provisionally unified by a sense of shared values or lifestyles (as in Saikaku's work), and ultimately by a body of shared social forms and norms of conduct (as in Kiseki's work). This normalization was enforced in part by didactic and informational texts, such as the get-rich guides and the *chōhōki*, that explicitly prescribed basic values, practices, social norms, and forms of cultural literacy as a baseline qualification for participating in upwardly mobile urban society. More subtly, it was also accomplished by literary narrative: by new forms of writing that offered models for identification and mythic modes of making meaning out of the townsman's various social trajectories.

These forms of townsman narrative offer a revised and richer understanding of the nature of literary didacticism in Tokugawa Japan. They reveal how literary narrative, even when not obviously didactic in the form of moralistic tales of "promoting virtue and chastising vice" (*kanzen chōaku*), can communicate and reinforce emergent social norms—even when those norms are shown to be incomplete or contradictory, or when they are gleefully flouted. The new modes of townsman writing, which were both built on and disseminated through the mediation of print, came with their own politics, centered on the construction of the townsman community as a locus of status power: one that included certain social positions and excluded others, that arranged its members in certain hierarchies that were posited as natural and merited, that formed alliances with other status communities, and that policed the conduct of individuals.

The paradox and the crux of the "space of the collection" of the *ukiyo-zōshi* is that it exerted a profound normalizing force but retained and represented the irreducible particularism of status society and of the Tokugawa urban community. In Saikaku's *Eternal Storehouse*, differences of trade or commercial regime—the differences between old "privileged townsmen" and new entrepreneurial merchants and street peddlers—are not effaced so much as set in relation to a unifying set of norms and values. It is the obligation of each individual to find, within their trade and their social position, a way of realizing the maximum potential for capital accumulation. Nor are contingencies of place or history completely erased: Saikaku found the genesis of townsman property in the ethos of "wit," which was based on the capacity to recognize and instrumentalize such contingencies, a practice of reading the urban text for significant details that have gone unnoticed but that may become the basis for new entrepreneurial trajectories and new modes of spatial inscription. And where that ethos fails, Saikaku was still happy to represent and even to celebrate the contingency of "fortune" as an object of sublime beauty, always holding out the possibility that further scrutiny might reveal its secrets and allow yet another aspiring merchant to join the community of the marketplace; such exceptions did not weaken the didactic rationalism of the space of the collection as much as supply an endlessly replenished energy to drive the didactic impulse.

Kiseki's character pieces likewise attend to the exceptions to the norms of the townsman household—its deviants and dropouts—and, at their most transgressive, almost suggest a realization of the centrifugal force of the collection as a space of ideological critique, through satire that verges into nonsense and the collapse of didactic form. As I have argued, however, the ultimate symbolic function of the character piece was, through recursive processes of textual reproduction, to subject these social and textual eccentricities to the centripetal pull of a generic image of urban normality, one made flexible and all the more robust for containing a range of individual expressions and circumscribing the limits of imaginable transgressions. Norms are produced not by the erasure of particularity but by the representation of particularity. Specificities of place and time and trade, the constitutive specificities of a still-local status society, become tokens or instances or examples of shared norms.

Despite and through this emphasis on representing particularity, I have also traced the emergence of a generic sense of townsman identity, unmarked by place or trade: splendidly blank signifiers of nothing but exemplary townsman-ness. Indeed, one of the tendencies to emerge subtly but persistently in the townsman's textual culture, before any description of values, norms, or politics, is the premise that the townsman self was constituted

EPILOGUE

through acts of signification—of self-representation. To be a townsman was to represent oneself as such: to become a primer or copybook (*tehon*). Through acts of self-representation that were also acts of self-formation, the particular was transfigured into the universal. To a certain degree, this logic was shared with other identities, as a product of the transformation of status into habitus—into social forms to be per-formed. The warrior, of course, was even in the seventeenth century exhorted to become a mirror (*kagami*), whether modeling moral substance to the commoner classes or performing acts of martial virtue to demonstrate his merit as a warrior. But the difference between the warrior and the townsman should be clear. The warrior's performance of moral or martial merit was based on a belief in underlying moral substance to be signified; the townsman, in contrast, was constituted as a pure signifier. The capacity for performative self-representation, which occasionally appears as virtuosic dissembling, becomes the townsman's core competency: whether in the sense of Saikaku's entrepreneurial protagonists, who dissemble the origins of their wealth and property while borrowing didactic language to represent their estates as virtuously and honestly made and refashioning themselves as talismanic models for the merchant community; or in the sense of the rigidly normalized households of Kiseki's time, which sought to instrumentalize even the act of leisure as a signifier of repute. Kiseki's works reveal just how deeply this logic ran, to the point that transgression of the townsman self was conceived only as the phantasmal signification of alternative status selves. The townsman self was a self as signifier.

I have suggested that this quality of the townsman self as signifier was at some level related to the constitutive role played by textual practice, in particular by print, in processes of social becoming and self-fashioning. It was the medium of the woodblock print that created images, narratives, and norms that circulated freely across boundaries to address readers regardless of background—readers who were unified only by the signifiers that they shared through the mediation of print—and that suggested that to be a townsman was to refashion oneself according to such signifiers. This quality of print media was surely related to other dimensions of the townsman's social being as well. It was related to his ambivalent relationship to place and to community. Whereas the warrior was bound in principle to the household of his lord (a community of a larger scale than the townsman household) and the peasant to his village, the entrepreneurial townsman quickly left behind the community of the *chō*, and though he embraced stable property in the form of the household, this was a much more flexible and portable form of property than those of other status groups, one that could ultimately be abstracted into the quantitative form of the estate (*shindai*). The townsman's textual existence was a quantitative existence, detached to a degree from the land and from the more stable socio-spatial structures of the Tokugawa polity. In this regard, it was also related to the townsman's economic character and measures of value. Whereas the economic activities of the warrior and peasant classes remained grounded, to varying degrees, in agricultural production and in conceptions of use value (Matsuake's "twenty-four *mon* of nookey"), the townsman's economic existence was centered on forms of quantitative and symbolic exchange—between goods and money, between the differing currencies of rice, gold, silver, and copper—in which reckoning with use value could, to a significant if never total extent, be deferred through the clever play of signifiers. Further exploration of this intersection between the textual and the economic, as through the lenses of economic criticism, would further illuminate the interplay between the social and the literary in Tokugawa Japan.

Such exploration would also shed light on how the habitus of different status groups, as inflected in economic belief or practice and manifest in narrative economies and signifying systems, came to structure different literary forms: how the logic of *gesaku* in the hands of a townsman such as Kyōden differed from that of a warrior-intellectual such as Matsuake or a plebeian spokesman such as Sanba, and how the ambivalent tension, negotiation, intersection, and fusion between these urban subjectivities played out at the level of literary form. The free play of signifiers that I have attributed to the textual townsman should not be taken as a general characteristic of Tokugawa popular culture or of Edo *gesaku*, as has occasionally been suggested by imaginative theorizations of "postmodern Edo," but instead as a distinctive characteristic of the townsman and of the textual and literary cultures he produced, one that interacted in the space of culture with the signifying practices of other communities and status groups.[16] Indeed, the identification of this semiotic logic with the habitus of the townsman in particular, grounded in his economic activities and media cultures, points toward a reinterpretation of the political significance of the forms of literary play carried out in the pages of the *gesaku* corpus: not as a total detachment of signifiers from signifieds and thus a complete relativization of cultural authority, but instead as a negotiation of such authority carried out through symbolic contest between semiotic regimes and literary forms.

The most striking characteristic of Tokugawa woodblock-print culture is that it could represent the internal differentiation and essential particularism of early modern status society, placing disparate communities in ongoing processes of social, spatial, and textual negotiation without dissolving the distinctions separating them. This was as true of *gesaku* as it was of the *ukiyo-zōshi*. Although the mediation of the woodblock print worked partially to transform the townsman into a signifier, this print culture could contain but not erase the particularities of place, trade, circumstance, individual disposition, the diversity of the urban community and the irreducible heterogeneity of status society that persists throughout the *ukiyo-zōshi*. The "space of the collection" is most striking for how it both retains and contains the traces of particularity that both complicated and constituted the status community. The significance of this form was not for giving expression to a coherent and homogenous merchant culture, into which it might be so readily flattened in a grand historical narrative or in a comparative study driven by top-down theory, but in producing an image of a nominally unified culture through the symbolic configuration of diverse communities. Understanding the social logics and cultural politics of Tokugawa popular culture requires a sensitivity to this tension between particularism and generality, between empirical specificity and theoretical generalization, between the capacity of the category and the diversity of token cases that it renders commensurable and yet still distinct—and at the level of method, a sustained attention to the tension between theoretical models and particular materials, a tension that persistently renders visible the stakes of resolving particular examples into general theories. When viewed from this perspective, we gain a new view of the Tokugawa status system: not as a feudalistic social hierarchy (whether harmonious or oppressive) but as a system characterized by a constitutive balance between social distinction and cultural integration. What better figure for such a system than the woodblock print, which retains the particularism of manuscript culture—the idiosyncratic hand of the calligrapher, the material affordances of distinct printing formats, the integration of text and image—while transforming those particularities into norms through their very reproduction?

ACKNOWLEDGMENTS

It is sometimes said that academic research is a labor of love. This book was a labor of paranoia.

I first felt this paranoia in the early stages of research, when, on a break from reading Ihara Saikaku's tales of entrepreneurial wit, I was browsing a news site about San Francisco, a city for which I hold a great deal of love, and found an article on *homeless tours*: informational tours of the living habits of the city's growing unhoused population, whose ingenious tactics of urban survival (the tours claimed) offered various lifestyle lessons for aspiring entrepreneurs. Such tours were merely one particularly ghoulish manifestation of the hustle culture of Silicon Valley in one of its more mercenary incarnations, but they existed alongside any number of blog posts narrating how living out of your car could be an effective way of bootstrapping, or indeed a productivity hack—rise with the sun, after all. Clearly, these didactic blog posts were tactical acts of self-representation by still-nameless entrepreneurs, meant to fashion their authors as paragons of start-up spirit. But how could the cultural figure of the entrepreneur so effectively obscure the real class tensions playing out every day in the very fabric of the city? My grasp of this problem would evolve over the years, as I began to think through how the social imaginary used to fashion the entrepreneurial self is (or is not) related to social class—how it comes to stand in for a consciousness of class—and how these ways of imagining the self are made possible by new uses of media (whether digital or woodblock print), new ways of writing that cross the line between the practical and the literary, and new forms of narrative.

This paranoia would take different forms as it came to illuminate other sides of my research and writing. I felt it again many years later while composing this monograph under the ever-urgent imperatives of the neoliberal academy, when I began to feel that academic writing was itself an act of entrepreneurial self-representation: that so much of scholarship is in the capacity to assume the voice of a scholar and to master the rhetorical tactics that enable such self-representation, and that such tactics are often brazenly appropriative, a matter of taking one's sources and alchemically spinning them into something else that may be deployed in service of the writer's self-fashioning while obscuring their nature and provenance—their conscientious citation in form so often disguising an opportunistic repurposing in spirit. And I felt it yet again as I was pushing forward with the manuscript amid the isolation of the COVID-19 pandemic, under pressure that had ceased to crush and begun to seem an ambient condition, as for the strange creatures that float through the darkness of the ocean trenches; when, in the depths of imposter syndrome, I began to feel that my own writing had come to follow the same entrepreneurial logic and would amount to nothing more than a less practiced act of self-fashioning, the romantic hobbyist moonlighting as an intellectual, doomed to produce a travesty of scholarship and to fall into obscurity.

As much as any intellectual agenda, it is this paranoia that has given shape to this book, and these anecdotes, just a few among many possible, chart some of its chapters. This is to say that the book contains as its seed a core of critical consciousness with respect to our current moment, as well as some measure of personal autobiography. It remains beyond my comparative capacity to make the imaginative historical leaps that would elaborate such critical consciousness into a proper methodology, so I have left this paranoia as merely a guiding intuition and have worked to subject that intuition to the most exacting scrutiny through dialogue with my materials and with the scholars whose work has informed my *mondai ishiki* in a more proper sense. But I begin these acknowledgments by acknowledging the personal perspective that informs the work and that drives its unapologetically paranoid treatment of its materials. I add that this paranoia is merely one expression of the profound respect I have for the authors who

ACKNOWLEDGMENTS

have allowed me to spar with them for these years and over these pages, and who through that sparring have deepened my understanding of my world, my moment, and myself.

Despite this paranoia, I have only love for the many mentors, colleagues, friends, and family who have guided me in this labor and helped me complete it. I owe debts both material and immaterial to more individuals than I can name here, and the naming will count little against the debt. I hope that all those who have supported me, both named and unnamed, will allow me to repay those debts in other ways in time.

I must begin with my graduate mentors at Columbia University. Haruo Shirane and Tomi Suzuki took much on faith when they accepted me as a PhD student, despite my superlatively spotty background in the field, and worked patiently to instill in me the methods of reading and thinking that have allowed me to produce this book. They humble me with their truly limitless support, generosity, encouragement, and blessedly unfiltered advice. I was fortunate also to work with Paul Anderer, who offered intellectual support both in and out of the classroom, and David Lurie, whose offhand comments and marginalia have continued to spark moments of insight years later—to say nothing for the advice and feedback given on this project throughout its early development. I also thank Indra Levy, to whom I owe my very beginnings in Japanese literature and who continues to inspire me as a scholar and a person. Of my classmates, there are too many to list, and I am grateful to all for years of encouragement and companionship, but I name a few whose support helped shape this book more directly. Ariel Stilerman was a voice of support and sanity throughout the project, especially in the difficult last months of writing. Tyler Walker offered much-needed encouragement and critical feedback on parts of the manuscript. Nan Ma Hartmann helped center me during the final crunch and pulled me across the finish line. My very sincere thanks go to David Atherton, a fellow traveler on the paths of Edo literature and brother-in-arms. This book has evolved through near-constant conversations with David, and owes much to his contributions as a *senpai*, reader, interlocutor, and friend, and to his voice of earnest encouragement and solidarity at times when the way forward was less than clear.

The ideas developed in this book are shaped by the thought of many Japanese scholars, both those I have met and those I have not: There is no better list of acknowledgments than a bibliography. Although my work

ACKNOWLEDGMENTS

unfolds as a critical dialogue with some of these scholars, I hope it will be clear that whatever criticisms I have made are meant as an intellectual tribute to the forebears who have, through the medium of the written word, shaped my thinking as much as any of my personal mentors; I have endeavored not to instrumentalize their work and dissolve their voices into mine but to engage each in genuine dialogue on their own terms. I express my sincere gratitude to Nakajima Takashi for years of inspiring and exacting mentorship. My work owes much to his relentless rigor and uncompromising sense of *mondai ishiki*, but not just that. Through his many reflections on the history of Edo studies, whether in writing or in the classroom or in the watering holes of Waseda, he instilled in me a sense that the lived experiences and political beliefs behind the work of every scholar need not be dismissed as obstacles to objectivity, but that they might be embraced for what they allow us to perceive about the texts we read. I also owe much to the generosity of Toeda Hirokazu, who sponsored me for multiple terms as a visiting researcher at Waseda University, and to Tanaka Yukari, whose encouragement and support have taken many forms over the years.

Much of this book was written with the support of a fellowship from the Reischauer Institute for Japanese Studies at Harvard University. The fellowship year was devastated by the COVID-19 pandemic, but the faculty of Harvard made every effort to make a rocky stay in Boston into a productive one. Karen Thornber, David Howell, and Shigehisa Kuriyama were particularly welcoming despite the existential disruptions of the pandemic, as were the indefatigable staff of the Reischauer Institute, especially Stacie Matsumoto. I also enjoyed the support and (virtual) camaraderie of a wonderful cohort of Reischauer Fellows: Michaela Kelly, Daniele Lauro, and Mattias Van Ommen, who offered their insightful commentaries on my work and entertained my unqualified ruminations on theirs. In addition, parts of chapters 1 and 4 draw on dissertation research supported by the Fulbright program, the Japan Society for the Promotion of Science, and Waseda University. The manuscript benefited greatly from a workshop sponsored by the Northwestern University Weinberg College of Arts and Sciences.

A few individuals have contributed to the shape of the manuscript in both direct and indirect ways. Laura Moretti has been a voice of warm encouragement, insight, and much-needed criticism, and has inspired me in her work, her curiosity, and her tireless commitment to the field. Our

ACKNOWLEDGMENTS

conversations about the nitty-gritty of Edo literature are as inspiring as they are centering, and perennially renew my excitement for this work. Satoko Shimazaki has also been a source of advice at many stages and in innumerable ways. I owe much to her individual support, mentoring, and selfless advocacy. Amy Stanley has over the years generously offered her perspective "as a historian," informing me of my blind spots and helping me to think across the gaps between disciplines. Dani Botsman and Anne Walthall have also offered encouragement and advice at various stages. Irene Pavitt reviewed and edited the full manuscript, and offered many perceptive suggestions that strengthened the project in its final stages. And I am delighted to be able to thank Melania Shipton for the wonderful cover design.

At Columbia University Press, Christine Dunbar went above and beyond in offering her support throughout the publication process, in addition to important words of interest and encouragement when the project was still in its early stages. I am grateful also to Kathryn Jorge and Helen Glenn Court for their meticulous editing, and to Fred Leise for the index.

An early and fragmentary version of chapter 4 was published as "The Household and its Discontents: Ejima Kiseki's *Seken musuko katagi*," *Japanese Language and Literature* 59, no. 1. Select translations from chapters 2 and 3 appear in "Distribution Poetics: Ihara Saikaku and the Literature of the Marketplace," *East Asian Publishing and Society* 16, no. 1. I thank Waseda University Library for generously granting permission to reproduce images from its collections.

The community at Northwestern has shaped this project in ways that are difficult to put into words. I thank my colleagues in the Department of Asian Languages and Cultures—Paola Zamperini, Laura Brueck, Corey Byrnes, Patrick Noonan, Daniel Majchrowicz, Dahye Kim, Annabel We, as well as Andrew Leong, Mi-Ryong Shim, and David Boyk—for giving me the *shūnen* necessary to see this work through. Corey Byrnes has provided solidarity at moments of institutional chaos; his work has also inspired me to pursue my own vision of scholarship, even in the face of trends in my field. Dahye Kim has offered camaraderie, commiseration, and accountability, supporting me through co-writing during some difficult roadblocks and through conversation and perambulation when I was lost in my head. Her friendship has meant much in the book's final stages. Phyllis Lyons has been a voice of encouragement, and an occasionally necessary reminder of why we do what we do. Laura Hein has offered moral support while inspiring me with her good humor, her unsparing honesty, her lucid grasp of the big picture, and her love of the work. And I owe much to Jean Deven, who has always helped to begin the day with a friendly voice.

Words of mere gratitude are not enough to express the appreciation and admiration I feel for my wonderful colleagues Junko Sato, Yumi Shiojima, and Noriko Taira Yasohama, who have shown me what it means to turn a department into a community, and who humble me every week with their boundless energy, warmth, and loyalty. I could not have hoped to be working side-by-side with better people. I reserve my most profound thanks for Patrick Noonan, who has supported this work and its author in too many ways to describe. He read nearly every piece of my manuscript at every stage of its development, and his comments both on and off the page have enriched my thinking immeasurably. This book would likely not exist without his contributions to my writing and my thinking and my well-being. I am honored to call him a mentor and a friend.

Finally, I thank my family—Mom, Dad, Gwyn, Matt, Jane, Willa, Sonya, Conrad—who have believed in me in ways that I may sometimes take for granted but that I never doubt, and who support me simply by being there; Matilda, Mary, and Jason, whose friendship is a daily source of strength, courage, and clarity; and Em, who helps me believe that I have the power to create, and to whom I dedicate this book.

NOTES

INTRODUCTION: WRITING URBAN IDENTITY

1. Nakamura Yukihiko, ed., *Kinsei chōnin shisō*, Nihon shisō taikei 59 (Iwanami Shoten, 1975), 88–89.
2. Nakamura, *Kinsei chōnin shisō*, 87.
3. Regarding the birth of commercial woodblock printing in Japan, see Peter Kornicki, *The Book in Japan: A Cultural History from the Beginnings to the Nineteenth Century* (University of Hawaii Press, 2001), chap. 5; Laura Moretti, *Pleasure in Profit: Popular Prose in Seventeenth-Century Japan* (Columbia University Press, 2020), chaps. 1, 2; Konta Yōzō, *Edo no hon'ya-san: kinsei bunkashi no sokumen* (Heibonsha, 2009), chaps. 1, 2.
4. Kornicki, *Book in Japan*, 26–30.
5. Kornicki, *Book in Japan*, 192–207.
6. The analogy between the structure of the publishing field (organized by a hierarchy of book formats) and that of the social field (organized as a matrix of status groups) is developed at length by Nakano Mitsutoshi. See *Edo no hanpon* (Iwanami Shoten, 1995), 11–18; *Wahon no susume: Edo o yomitoku tame ni* (Iwanami Shoten, 2011), 73–120.
7. The most characteristic work in this vein is Teruoka Yasutaka's paradigm-defining study of Ihara Saikaku, which synthesized Marxian methods of historical sociology and prewar proletarian literary theory with a conception of literature drawn from the Japanese naturalists. See Teruoka Yasutaka, *Saikaku: hyōron to kenkyū*, 2 vols. (Chūō Kōronsha, 1950), esp. 1:1–7, 2:205–21. Second to Saikaku, the trope of townsman literature has been used to interpret the popular fiction of early nineteenth-century Edo, as in the work of Mizuno Minoru and Jinbō Kazuya. See Mizuno Minoru and Uzuki Hiroshi, eds., *Edo chōnin bungaku*, Iwanami kōza Nihon

bungakushi 7 (Iwanami Shoten, 1959). This work on Edo fiction evolved in symbiosis with Nishiyama Matsunosuke's pioneering studies of Edo townsman culture, which explicitly sought in the literary and cultural expression of the Edo townspeople a spirit of resistance to warrior hegemony. For a comprehensive synthesis, see Nishiyama Matsunosuke, ed., *Edo chōnin no kenkyū*, vol. 1 (Yoshikawa Kōbunkan, 1972); in English, see Nishiyama Matsunosuke, *Edo Culture: Daily Life and Diversions in Urban Japan, 1600–1868*, trans. and ed. Gerald Groemer (University of Hawaii Press, 1997).

8. For example, see Katsuya Hirano, *The Politics of Dialogic Imagination: Power and Popular Culture in Early Modern Japan* (University of Chicago Press, 2013), 26. For characteristic textbook treatments, see E. Taylor Atkins, *A History of Popular Culture in Japan: From the Seventeenth Century to the Present* (Bloomsbury, 2017), chaps. 2, 3; Nancy K. Stalker, *Japan: History and Culture from Classical to Cool* (University of California Press, 2018), chap. 7.

9. Nakano Mitsutoshi, "Saikaku gesakusha setsu saikō: Edo no me to gendai no me no motsu imi," *Bungaku* 15, no. 1 (2014): 143–49; "Jūhasseiki no Edo bunka," in *Jūhasseiki no Edo bungei: ga to zoku no seijuku* (Iwanami Shoten, 1999), 2–4. Nakano originally developed this model as a theory of the popular fiction or "frivolous compositions" (*gesaku*) of eighteenth- and nineteenth-century Edo, but he would ultimately propose to extend these premises a unified theory of early modern Japanese literature in toto. It is telling that Nakano developed many of these premises through a highly polemical "theory of Saikaku-as-*gesaku*-writer" (*Saikaku gesakusha setsu*), strategically replacing Teruoka's Marxist-naturalist vision of Saikaku (the townsman author whose humanistic realism saw beyond the hierarchies of feudal society) with a new portrait of Saikaku as an apolitical stylist. See Nakano, "Saikaku gesakusha setsu saikō," 149–54. For further discussion of Nakano's interventions in Edo literary studies, see Moretti, *Pleasure in Profit*, 12–15; David C. Atherton, *Writing Violence: The Politics of Form in Early Modern Japanese Literature* (Columbia University Press, 2023), 3–4.

10. Nakano Mitsutoshi, "The Role of Traditional Aesthetics," trans. Maria Flutsch, in *Eighteenth Century Japan: Culture & Society*, ed. C. Andrew Gerstle (Allen & Unwin, 1989), 125. Nakano's critique echoes comments made by Nakamura Yukihiko in "Kinsei bungaku no tokuchō: shogen ni kaete," in *Kinsei shōsetsu yōshiki shikō*, Nakamura Yukihiko chojutsushū 5 (Chūō Kōronsha, 1982), 10.

11. Atherton, *Writing Violence*, 8.

12. Jacques Rancière, *The Politics of Aesthetics: The Distribution of the Sensible*, ed. and trans. Gabriel Rockhill (Continuum, 2006), 8.

13. This approach takes inspiration from a few recent studies. Satoko Shimazaki's groundbreaking study of Edo kabuki argues against the notion that the kabuki theater was a "theater of the townspeople" that represented a symbolic threat to warrior authority: to the contrary, at least in the city of Edo, the kabuki theater served a function of constructing "regional community" and a sense of shared urban (Edo) identity that included both warriors and commoners. See Satoko Shimazaki, *Edo Kabuki in Transition: From the Worlds of the Samurai to the Vengeful Ghost* (Columbia University Press, 2016), 17–24, 29–31; regarding regional community, see also chap. 1. Similarly, Laura Moretti's monumental survey of the seventeenth-century print culture explores how the commercialization of vernacular print created a

INTRODUCTION

productive circuit between low and high culture and between dominant and dominated classes: she shows that popular print culture disseminated ethical and social norms meant to be shared across status communities. See Moretti, *Pleasure in Profit*, 15–19. Other treatments of Tokugawa print culture in relation to (national) community are discussed later.

14. Regarding the relationship between the concept of the four estates and Tokugawa social structure, see Asao Naohiro, "Kinsei no mibun to sono hen'yō," in *Mibun to kakushiki*, Nihon no kinsei 7, ed. Asao Naohiro (Chūō Kōronsha, 1992), 14–24. For detailed discussion of the four estates as an intellectual construction and the parameters of its adaptation in Tokugawa thought, see Watanabe Hiroshi, *Kinsei Nihon shakai to Sōgaku* (Tōkyō Daigaku Shuppankai, 1985), 43–49; Uematsu Tadahiro, *Shinōkōshō: Jukyō shisō to kanryō shihai* (Dōbunkan, 1997), 17–50.

15. For the most concise introductions to this body of work in English, see Daniel Botsman, "Recovering Japan's Urban Past: Yoshida Nobuyuki, Tsukada Takashi, and the Cities of the Tokugawa Period," *City, Culture and Society*, no. 3 (2012): 9–14; David Howell, *Geographies of Identity in Nineteenth-Century Japan* (University of California Press, 2005). See also Daniel Botsman, *Punishment and Power in the Making of Modern Japan* (Princeton University Press, 2005), esp. chaps. 2, 3; Maren A. Ehlers, *Give and Take: Poverty and the Status Order in Early Modern Japan* (Harvard University Asia Center, 2018); Amy Stanley, *Selling Women: Prostitution, Markets, and the Household in Early Modern Japan* (University of California Press, 2012), esp. chap. 2; Gerald Groemer, *Street Performers and Society in Urban Japan, 1600–1900: The Beggar's Gift* (Routledge, 2016), esp. chaps. 1, 2. One of the earliest and most important English-language contributions to this body of work remains the pioneering study of rural social politics by Herman Ooms. See *Tokugawa Village Practice: Class, Status, Power, Law* (University of California Press, 1996).

16. Yoshida Nobuyuki's scholarship is voluminous and eclectic, ranging from highly technical analysis of different forms of merchant practice in his early work to holistic synthesis of urban society and culture in his late work. Many of his later collections contain concise and highly lucid historiographical exposition and description of his program of research; see, for example, *Dentō toshi, Edo* (Tōkyō Daigaku Shuppankai, 2012), 1–34, as well as the introductory essays in Yoshida Nobuyuki and Itō Takeshi, eds., *Dentō toshi*, 4 vols. (Tōkyō Daigaku Shuppankai, 2010). For further historiographical and critical reflection, see Tsukada Takashi, "Kinsei mibunsei kenkyū no tenkai," in *Nihon kinsei no toshi, shakai, mibun* (Kadensha, 2019), 18–43. Regarding "the geography of status," see Howell, *Geographies of Identity*, chap. 2.

17. For a concise treatment, see Yoshida, *Dentō toshi, Edo*, 139–45.

18. Tsukada Takashi, "Shakai shūdan o megutte," *Rekishi-gaku kenkyū*, no. 548 (1985): 58–66. For further elaboration, see Tsukada, *Nihon kinsei no toshi, shakai, mibun*.

19. The memorable characterization of Tokugawa Japan as a "container" society is by John W. Hall. See "Rule by Status in Tokugawa Japan," *Journal of Japanese Studies* 1, no. 1 (1974): 39–49.

20. Henri Lefebvre, *The Production of Space*, trans. Donald Nicholson-Smith (Blackwell, 1991), 26. For a discussion of the early modern Japanese spatial imaginary in roughly Lefebvrian terms, see Marcia Yonemoto, *Mapping Early Modern Japan:*

INTRODUCTION

Space, Place, and Culture in the Tokugawa Period, 1603–1868 (University of California Press, 2003).

21. This formulation is originally that of Asao Naohiro. See "Kinsei no mibunsei to senmin," in *Asao Naohiro chosakushū* (Iwanami Shoten, 2004), 7:38–47. For a detailed discussion, see Yoshida Nobuyuki, "Chōnin to chō," in *Kinsei toshi shakai no mibun kōzō* (Tōkyō Daigaku Shuppankai, 1998), 45–55.
22. Regarding the roots of the *chō* in medieval Kyoto, see Suzanne Gay, *The Moneylenders of Late Medieval Kyoto* (University of Hawaii Press, 2001), 24–26; Matthew Stavros, *Kyoto: An Urban History of Japan's Premodern Capital* (University of Hawaii Press, 2014), 11–13, 32–36. Regarding shifts in the affiliational structure of urban Kyoto in late medieval Japan, see also Mary Elizabeth Berry, *The Culture of Civil War in Kyoto* (University of California Press, 1994), 210–41. In Japanese, see Akiyama Kunizō and Nakamura Ken, *Kyōto "machi" no kenkyū* (Hōsei Daigaku Shuppankyoku, 1975), esp. 88–167.
23. Tamai Tetsuo, "Kinsei toshi kūkan no tokushitsu," in *Toshi no jidai*, Nihon no kinsei 9, ed. Yoshida Nobuyuki (Chūō Kōronsha, 1992), 40–44.
24. Howell, *Geographies of Identity*, chap. 2.
25. Regarding the system of population registration and its relationship to the status group system, see, for example, Yokota Fuyuhiko, "Kinsei no mibunsei," in *Kinsei 1*, Iwanami kōza Nihon rekishi 10, ed. Ōtsu Tōru, Sakurai Eiji, Fujii Jōji, Yoshida Yutaka, and I Keifan (Iwanami Shoten, 2014), 275–312; Yokota Fuyuhiko, "Kinsei-teki mibun seido no seiritsu," in *Mibun to kakushiki*, 41–78.
26. Regarding the interface between *chō* and the Tokugawa state, see Yoshida Nobuyuki, "Kōgi to chōnin mibun," in *Kinsei toshi shakai no mibun kōzō*, 3–44.
27. Later work by Yoshida and Tsukada has extended to the problem of urban culture: Yoshida Nobuyuki, *Mibun-teki shūen to shakai-bunka kōzō* (Buraku Mondai Kenkūjo, 2003); Tsukada Takashi, "Nihon kinsei no shakai-teki ketsugō," in *Nihon kinsei no toshi shakai mibun: mibun-teki shūen o megutte* (Kadensha, 2019), 72–76.
28. For a study of comparable shifts in France, see David Garrioch, *The Formation of the Parisian Bourgeoisie, 1690–1830* (Harvard University Press, 1996).
29. Sarah Maza, *The Myth of the French Bourgeoisie: An Essay on the Social Imaginary, 1750–1850* (Harvard University Press, 2003), 12. For a comparable study of the category of "middle class," see Dror Wahrman, *Imagining the Middle Class: The Political Representation of Class in Britain, c. 1780–1840* (Cambridge University Press, 1995). Both Maza and Wahrman are focused on the production of images (or myths) of the given classes in the context of political representation and of a totalizing social imaginary, whereas my study is focused on the problem of the (literary) self-image of the townsman class in a context that largely excludes the proper sphere of the political, but Maza and Wahrman nevertheless provide inspiration in understanding the symbolic logics surrounding classes that may be more image (or myth) than social substance.
30. More broadly, my treatment of class identity as a form of consciousness that is cultural as much as social draws inspiration from E. P. Thompson's classic study. See *The Making of the English Working Class* (Vintage, 1966), 9–11.
31. Pierre Bourdieu, "Social Space and the Genesis of 'Classes,'" in *Language and Symbolic Power*, trans. Gino Raymond and Matthew Adamson, ed. John B. Thompson (Polity Press, 1991), 236.

INTRODUCTION

32. Amino Yoshihiko, "Nihon no moji shakai no tokushitsu," in *Rettō shakai no tayōsei*, Amino Yoshihiko chosakushū 15 (Iwanami Shoten, 2007), 389–429. The following draws also from Tsujimoto Masashi, "Kyōiku shakai no seiritsu," in *Kinsei 4*, Iwanami kōza Nihon rekishi 13, ed. Ōtsu Tōru, Sakurai Eiji, Fujii Jōji, Yoshida Yutaka, and I Keifan (Iwanami Shoten, 2015), 253–86; "Moji shakai no seiritsu to shuppan media," in *Kyōiku shakaishi*, Shin taikei nihonshi 16, ed. Tsujimoto Masashi and Okita Yukuji (Yamakawa Shuppansha, 2002), 121–46.
33. Regarding the development of literacy in rural communities, see Yakuwa Tomohiro, "Kinsei minshū no ningen keisei to bunka," in Tsujimoto and Okita, *Kyōiku shakaishi*, 171–244.
34. Yakuwa, "Kinsei minshū no ningen keisei to bunka," 208. For detailed studies in English, see Richard Rubinger, *Popular Literacy in Early Modern Japan* (University of Hawaii Press, 2007); R. P. Dore, *Education in Tokugawa Japan* (Center for Japanese Studies, University of Michigan, 1984).
35. Nakai Nobuhiko, *Chōnin*, Nihon no rekishi 21 (Shōgakkan, 1975), 236.
36. For transcriptions of the Shimai and Kōnoike documents, see Yamamoto Shinkō, ed., *Kakunshū* (Heibonsha, 2001); Nakamura, *Kinsei chōnin shisō*, 377–91. For English translations and basic exposition, see J. Mark Ramseyer, "Thrift and Diligence: House Codes of Tokugawa Merchant Families," *Monumenta Nipponica* 43, no. 2 (1979): 209–30. For a thorough but outdated treatment, see Miyamoto Mataji, *Kinsei shōnin ishiki no kenkyū*, Miyamoto Mataji chosakushū 2 (Kōdansha, 1977); however, it must be kept in mind that Miyamoto's analysis is of its time, and remains defined by frameworks of feudal authority and an implicit politics of merchant resistance or complicity with such a system. For a more recent descriptive treatment, see Irie Hiroshi, *Kinsei shomin kakun no kenkyū: "Ie" no keiei to kyōiku* (Taga Shuppan, 1996).
37. Yoshida, "Chōnin to chō," 164–69.
38. Quoted in Asao, "Kinsei no mibunsei to senmin," 39. For a full transcription of regulations released at this juncture, see Kyōto-shi Rekishi Shiryōkan, eds., *Kyōto machi shikimoku shūsei*, Sōsho Kyōto no shiryō 3 (Kyōto-shi Rekishi Shiryōkan, 1999), 164–65.
39. Mary Elizabeth Berry, *Japan in Print: Information and Nation in the Early Modern Period* (University of California Press, 2006), 17.
40. Eiko Ikegami, *Bonds of Civility: Aesthetic Networks and the Political Origins of Japanese Culture* (Cambridge University Press, 2005), chap. 2; regarding print, see chap. 11.
41. Moretti, *Pleasure in Profit*, 4.
42. A concise survey of early Osaka publishing is Nagatomo Chiyoji, "Saikaku no sakusha kankyō, shuppan shoshi, dokusha," in *Saikaku o manabu hito no tame ni*, ed. Taniwaki Masachika and Nishijima Atsuya (Sekai Shisōsha, 1993), 70–91. For further detail, see Nagatomo Chiyoji, "Edo jidai no hon'ya," in *Edo jidai no tosho ryūtsū* (Shibunkaku Shuppan, 2002), 27–40.
43. Regarding the readership of the Osaka publishing field, see Konta Yōzō, "Genroku Kyōhō-ki ni okeru shuppan shihon no keisei to sono rekishi-teki igi ni tsuite," *Hisutoria* 19 (1957): 59–62; Noma Kōshin, "Ukiyo-zōshi no dokushasō," in *Kinsei sakkaden kō* (Chūō Kōronsha, 1985), 148–66.
44. The following draws from Kornicki, *The Book in Japan*, 197–99; Nagatomo, "Saikaku no sakusha kankyō"; Konta, *Edo no hon'ya-san*, 45–98; Nakajima Takashi, *Saikaku*

to Genroku media: sono senryaku to tenkai (Nippon Hōsō Shuppan Kyōkai, 1994), 55–62, 99–125.

45. Very little is known about the author's biography beyond what can be gleaned from his major works, a few surviving pieces of correspondence, and brief mentions in select writings by his contemporaries. For discussion in English, see Schalow, "Ihara Saikaku and Ejima Kiseki," 416–21; Ihara Saikaku, *The Japanese Family Storehouse or the Millionaires' Gospel Modernised, Nippon eitai-gura or Daifuku shin chōja kyō 1688*, trans. G. W. Sargent (Cambridge University Press, 1959), xiii–xxix. The voluminous scholarship in Japanese offers many entry points. See, for example, Taniwaki Masachika, "Genroku bunka to Saikaku," in Taniwaki and Nishijima, *Saikaku o manabu hito no tame ni*, 61–69. The authoritative chronological reference is Noma Kōshin, *Saikaku nenpu kōshō*, rev. ed. (Chūō Kōronsha, 1983).
46. Regarding the relationship between Ihara Saikaku and the Osaka publishing community, Hanyū Noriko offers a a series of exceptionally detailed and illuminating case studies in *Saikaku to shuppan media no kenkyū* (Izumi Shoin, 2000), 103–262.
47. Ichiko Natsuo, "Nito-ban, santo-ban no hassei to sono imi: Saikaku-bon ni sokushite," in *Kinsei shoki bungaku to shuppan bunka* (Wakakusa Shobō, 1998), 305–20.
48. Regarding the increasing readership of the late seventeenth and early eighteenth century, see Nishijima Atsuya, "Katagi-mono no seiritsu: Dokusha no zōka to teizokuka," in *Saikaku to ukiyo-zōshi* (Ōfūsha, 1989), 360–37.
49. The term *ukiyo-zōshi*, as defining a specific corpus that is clearly delineated from the seventeenth-century *kana-zōshi*, is to a certain degree a modern extrapolation (early modern sources do not use the term systematically), but I am following the standard scholarly terminology, as I believe it reflects a loose but nevertheless coherent shift in textuality. For a detailed discussion of the term, see Hasegawa Tsuyoshi, *Ukiyo-zōshi no kenkyū: Hachimonjiya-bon o chūshin ni* (Ōfūsha, 1969), 7–36. Hasegawa's monumental work is the standard survey of post-Saikaku *ukiyo-zōshi* but focuses primarily on the works of Hachimonjiya; for a more comprehensive reference, see Hasegawa Tsuyoshi, ed., *Ukiyo-zōshi daijiten* (Kasama Shoin, 2017). For a more concise narrative introduction, see Nakajima Takashi, "Ukiyo-zōshi kai to Saikaku," in Taniwaki and Nishijima, *Saikaku o manabu hito no tame ni*, 265–76.
50. Moretti, *Pleasure in Profit*, 21; Laura Moretti, "*Kanazōshi* Revisited: The Beginnings of Japanese Popular Literature in Print," *Monumenta Nipponica* 65, no. 2 (2010): 301–13.
51. For the classic treatments of the relationship between Saikaku's fiction and seventeenth-century courtesan reviews, see Teruoka, *Saikaku*, 2:427–66; Noma Kōshin, "Ukiyo-zōshi no seiritsu," in *Saikaku shin shinkō* (Iwanami Shoten, 1981), 1–31. For a concise summary in English, see Teruoka Yasutaka, "The Pleasure Quarters and Tokugawa Culture," trans. C. Andrew Gerstle, in *Eighteenth Century Japan*, 16–19.
52. Regarding the later evolution of the courtesan review and related genres of erotic guidebooks, see Nakano Mitsutoshi, "Yūjo hyōbanki to yūri annai," *Kokubungaku* 9, no. 2 (1964): 59–67; for Nakano's treatment of the genre's influence on Saikaku, see "Yūjo hyōbanki kenkyū: Saikaku bungaku no hito kihan," *Kinsei bungaku*, no. 8 (1962): 21–33.
53. For characteristic treatments, see Paul Schalow, "Ihara Saikaku and Ejima Kiseki: the literature of urban townspeople," in *The Cambridge History of Japanese*

1. THE COMMUNITY OF THE MARKETPLACE

Literature, ed. Haruo Shirane and Tomi Suzuki, with David Lurie (Cambridge University Press, 2016), 415–23; Howard Hibbet's classic study, *The Floating World in Japanese Fiction* (Oxford University Press, 1959).
54. Regarding this narrative form, see David J. Gundry, *Parody, Irony and Ideology in the Fiction of Ihara Saikaku* (Brill, 2017), 14–26; Jeffrey Johnson, "Saikaku and the Narrative Turnabout," *Journal of Japanese Studies* 27, no. 2 (2001): 323–45.
55. Gundry, *Parody, Irony and Ideology*, 19. See also David J. Gundry, "Hierarchy, Hubris, and Parody in Ihara Saikaku's *Kōshoku ichidai otoko*," *Journal of Japanese Studies* 43, no. 2 (2017): 355–87.
56. Hirosue Tamotsu, *Saikaku no shōsetsu: Jikū ishiki no tenkan o megutte* (Heibonsha, 1982), 36–50.
57. See, for example, Hirano, *Politics of Dialogic Imagination*, 26–27; Harry Harootunian, "Late Tokugawa Culture and Thought," in *The Cambridge History of Japan*, vol. 5, *The Nineteenth Century*, ed. Marius B. Jansen (Cambridge University Press, 1989), 174; Johnson, "Saikaku and the Narrative Turnabout." David Gundry is more ambivalent in his treatment of Bakhtin: on the one hand, he stresses that Saikaku's writing does not aim to subvert, but on the other, he views its ideological content primarily in terms of its relationship to elite culture and warrior authority: see *Parody, Irony and Ideology*, 18–19, 25–26.
58. M. M. Bakhtin, *The Dialogic Imagination: Four Essays*, ed. Michael Holquist, trans. Caryl Emerson and Michael Holquist (University of Texas Press, 1981), 270.

1. THE COMMUNITY OF THE MARKETPLACE

1. For Bakhtin's discussion of the language of the marketplace in Rabelais, see Mikhail Bakhtin, *Rabelais and his World*, trans. Hélène Iswolsky (Indiana University Press, 1984), 181–87.
2. Benedict Anderson, *Imagined Communities: Reflections on the Origin and Spread of Nationalism*, rev. ed. (Verso, 1991), 5–7.
3. Mary Elizabeth Berry, *Japan in Print: Information and Nation in the Early Modern Period* (University of California Press, 2006), 209–51.
4. My analysis is particularly indebted to Noma Kōshin's extraordinarily rich annotation: Noma Kōshin, ed., *Saikaku shū 2*, Nihon koten bungaku taikei 48 (Iwanami Shoten, 1960). Citations that follow refer to this edition, abbreviated as NKBT 48. Although my interpretations of Saikaku's stories are my own, they have been informed by the diverse and often dissonant commentarial tradition surrounding this text. For readers interested in exploring further, an accessible and orthodox introduction to *Eitaigura*, with annotation by Taniwaki Masachika, is in Taniwaki Masachika, Jinbō Kazuya, and Teruoka Yasutaka, eds., *Ihara Saikaku shū 3*, Nihon koten bungaku zenshū 40 (Shōgakukan, 1972). Murata Atsushi's annotation provides stimulating and unorthodox oppositional readings: Murata Atsushi, ed., *Nippon eitaigura*, Shinchō Nihon koten shūsei 9 (Shinchōsha, 1977). A capable English translation and introduction is *The Japanese Family Storehouse, or, The Millionaires' Gospel Modernised. Nippon eitai-gura, or Daifuku shin chōja kyō (1688)*, trans. G. W. Sargent (Cambridge University Press, 1959). All translations here are my own. Although many scholars have produced cultural histories of the Genroku

1. THE COMMUNITY OF THE MARKETPLACE

townsman based on Saikaku's work (see chapter 3), few have approached the text with the granular attention to details of social and economic history attempted here. One exception is Matsumoto Shirō, *Saikaku to Genroku jidai* (Shin Nihon Shuppansha, 2001).

5. Yoshida Nobuyuki, "Chōnin to chō," in *Kinsei toshi shakai no mibun kōzō* (Tōkyō Daigaku Shuppankyoku, 1985), 47–58.
6. NKBT 48, 50–54. To avoid cluttering the text with citations, I indicate page numbers for each story on its introduction but forgo citation of short passages and phrases; transliterations of Japanese text are given where it is deemed necessary or illuminating, but as a rule are omitted for longer quotations. The numbers indicate the volume and story: for example, vol. 1–5 is the fifth story of the first volume.
7. Regarding wages for serving maids, see Ono Takeo, *Edo bukka jiten* (Tenbōsha, 1983), 215; Gary P. Leupp, *Servants, Shophands, and Laborers in the Cities of Tokugawa Japan* (Princeton University Press, 1992), 100–5.
8. Nihon Fūzokushi Gakkai, ed., *Nihon fūzokushi jiten* (Kōbundō, 1979), 399. See also Harashima Yōichi, "Tanomoshi," in *Nihon rekishi taikei* (Yamakawa Shuppansha, 1988), 3:1005–6.
9. Tetsuo Najita, *Ordinary Economies in Japan: A Historical Perspective, 1750–1950* (University of California Press, 2009), 60–103.
10. Najita, *Ordinary Economies in Japan*, 71–76. Najita notes some exceptions to this stigmatization: thinkers like Kaiho Seiryō who saw even the more speculative appropriation of the *mujin* lottery as a rational economic tactic, and, from the perspective of ruling authorities, a potential alternative to taxation for domainal income (77–79).
11. Regarding the succession of townsman property to female heirs, see Nakano Setsuko, "Kinsei shomin no jendā," in *Jendā shi*, Shintaikei Nihonshi 9, ed. Ōguchi Yūjirō, Narita Ryūichi, and Fukutō Sanae (Yamakawa Shuppansha, 2014), 252–54; Makita Rieko, "Kinsei Kyōto ni okeru josei no kasan shoyū," in *Kinsei joseishi*, ed. Kinsei Joseishi Kenkyūkai (Yoshikawa Kōbunkan, 1986), 219–55; Katakura Hisako, "Edo machikata ni okeru sōzoku," in *Kinsei joseishi*, 177–218.
12. Tsukada Takashi, "Mibunsei no kōzō," in *Kinsei* 2, Iwanami kōza Nihon tsūshi 12, ed. Asao Naohiro et al. (Iwanami Shoten, 1994), 111–35.
13. NKBT 48, 77–81,
14. NKBT 48, 77–78.
15. NKBT 48, 484n127.
16. NKBT 48, 80.
17. NKBT 48, 80.
18. NKBT 48, 79.
19. For characteristic treatments, see, for example, Moriya Takeshi, *Genroku bunka: yūgei, akusho, shibai* (Kōbundō, 1987), 9–20; Nakada Yasunao, "Saikaku to shinkō chōnin," *Kokubungaku: Kaishaku to kanshō* 22, no. 6 (1957): 50–54. For historical treatments of shifting commercial regimes, see Hayashi Reiko, "Shinkyū shōnin no kōtai," in *Shōnin no katsudō*, Nihon no kinsei 5, ed. Hayashi Reiko (Chūō Kōronsha, 1992), 43–88; E. S. Crawcour, "Changes in Japanese Commerce in the Tokugawa Period," *Journal of Asian Studies* 22, no. 4 (1963): 387–400. Literary scholars are less consistent in terminology, but a parallel articulation in literary history may be found in Teruoka Yasutaka's paradigm-defining narrative of Saikaku as *chōnin* author:

1. THE COMMUNITY OF THE MARKETPLACE

Teruoka Yasutaka, "Saikaku bannen no tēma to hōhō," in *Saikaku shinron* (Chūō Kōronsha, 1981), 199–215.
20. NKBT 48, 49.
21. Nakada Yasunao, *Mitsui Takatoshi* (Yoshikawa Kōbunkan, 1959), 16–70.
22. Wakita Haruko, "The Japanese Woman in the Premodern Merchant Household," *Women's History Review* 19, no. 2 (2010): 270–72.
23. Yoshida Nobuyuki, *Seijuku suru Edo*, Nihon no rekishi 17 (Kōdansha, 2009), 61–102. See also Thomas Gaubatz, "The Early Modern City in Japan," in *The New Cambridge History of Japan*, vol. 2, ed. David Howell (Cambridge University Press, 2024), 639–46.
24. Regarding Mitsui's early Hon-chō locations, see Mitsui Bunko, ed., *Mitsui jigyō-shi: hon-pen dai 1-kan* (Mitsui Bunko, 1980), 18–30. For further detail regarding Mitsui's business models and its appropriation of the store-front space, see Yoshida Nobuyuki, "Furi-uri," in *Nihon toshi-shi nyūmon 3: Hito*, ed. Takahashi Yasuo and Yoshida Nobuyuki (Tōkyō Daigaku Shuppankai, 1990), 125–37; *Seijuku suru Edo*, 79–82.
25. Mitsui Bunko, *Mitsui jigyō-shi*, 31–38.
26. Yoshida, "Chōnin to chō," 63–69.
27. NKBT 48, 49.
28. Quoted in Nakada, *Mitsui Takatoshi*, 110–11.
29. David Harvey, *The Urban Experience* (Johns Hopkins University Press, 1989), 166–70. I also draw inspiration from Harvey's treatment of community as part of his five-tiered schema (along with individualism, class, state, and family) in describing what he refers to as "the urbanization of consciousness" (233–35). But there he means community in a somewhat more concrete though flexible sense, like that of a local neighborhood or of a city. What I mean by the community of the marketplace is somewhere between this and the theoretical abstraction of the community of money, an imagined community that cannot be reduced to any concrete set of individuals, social relations, or spatial locus.
30. NKBT 48, 103–7.
31. NKBT 48, 67–73.
32. NKBT 48, 125–29.
33. NKBT 48, 145–51.
34. Harvey, *Urban Experience*, 168–69.
35. NKBT 48, 121–25.
36. NKBT 48, 95–99.
37. NKBT 48, 96.
38. NKBT 48, 43–44.
39. NKBT 48, 113–17.
40. NKBT 48, 115.
41. NKBT 48, 73–77.
42. NKBT 48, 75.
43. Nakada, "Saikaku to shinkō chōnin," 54.
44. NKBT 48, 91–94.
45. Henri Lefebvre, *The Urban Revolution*, trans. Robert Bononno (University of Minnesota Press, 2003), 4–5.
46. NKBT 48, 160–63.

1. THE COMMUNITY OF THE MARKETPLACE

47. Regarding women's roles in urban commoner society, see Nakano, "Kinsei no jendā," 244–54; Hayashi Reiko, "Machiya josei to kagyō," in *Nihon joseishi*, ed. Wakita Haruko, Hayashi Reiko, and Nagahara Kazuko (Yoshikawa Kōbunkan, 1987), 155–159; Hayashi Reiko, "Edo jidai no chōka josei-tachi," in *Edo Kamigata Ōdana to machiya josei* (Yoshikawa Kōbunkan, 2001), 284–96. In English, see Kathleen S. Uno, "Women and Changes in the Household Division of Labor," in *Recreating Japanese Women, 1600–1945*, ed. Gail Lee Bernstein (University of California Press, 1991), 17–41; Amy Stanley, *Stranger in the Shogun's City: A Japanese Woman and Her World* (Scribner, 2020).
48. Nakano, "Kinsei no jendā," 254–58. There were also, as early as the seventeenth century, exceptional cases of women assuming the public responsibilities of household head, but these remained rare. See Hayashi Reiko, "Kyōto no Kashiwabara Riyo," in *Edo Kamigata Ōdana to chōka josei*, 297–326.
49. NKBT 48, 41–46.
50. For example, see NKBT 48, 389.
51. NKBT 48, 59–63. For a detailed analysis of this story in relation to the institution of the *chō*, see Horikiri Minoru, "'Sekai no kashiya-daishō' no jōkyō settei: Kyō no machibure ni miru kyōdōtai ishiki no shiten kara," in *Yomikaerareru Saikaku* (Perikansha, 2001), 81–114.
52. The most reliable biographical information surrounding Fuji-ichi comes from Mitsui Takafusa's *Chōnin kōkenroku*: see Nakamura Yukihiko, *Kinsei chōnin shisō* (Iwanami Shoten, 1975), 208–9. Incidentally, many representations of this legendary figure after the publication of *Eitaigura* were directly indebted to Saikaku's rendition, but prior to *Eitaigura*, the image of Fuji-ichi was of an inhuman miser; Saikaku's rendition was a revisionist rehabilitation in service of entrepreneurial mythmaking. For detailed discussion of this figure and the documentary sources surrounding him, see NKBT 48, 485–86n130; Fuji Akio, "Bannen no Saikaku no sekai," in *Saikaku e no shōtai*, ed. Teruoka Yasutaka et al. (Iwanami Shoten, 1995), 230–33.
53. NKBT 48, 59.
54. NKBT 48, 60.

2. THE POETICS AND POLITICS OF TOWNSMAN PROPERTY

1. Noma Kōshin, ed., *Saikaku shū 2*, Nihon koten bungaku taikei 48 (Iwanami Shoten, 1960), 185. Citations that follow refer to this edition, abbreviated as NKBT 48.
2. Yokota Fuyuhiko, "Kinsei-teki mibun seido no seiritsu," in *Mibun to kakushiki*, Nihon no kinsei 7, ed. Asao Naohiro (Chūō Kōronsha, 1992), 65–78.
3. Michel de Certeau, *The Practice of Everyday Life*, trans. Steven Rendall (University of California Press, 1984), 29–42.
4. For a constructive synthesis of critiques on Certeau's work, see Brian Morris, "What We Talk About When We Talk About 'Walking in the City,'" *Cultural Studies* 18, no. 5 (2004): 675–97.
5. Certeau, *Practice of Everyday Life*, 37.
6. Regarding the distinction between occupation and livelihood, see David L. Howell, *Geographies of Identity in Nineteenth-Century Japan* (University of California

2. THE POETICS AND POLITICS OF TOWNSMAN PROPERTY

Press, 2005), chap. 3; Hiraishi Naoaki, "Kinsei Nihon no 'shokugyō' kan," in *Rekishi-teki zentei*, Gendai Nihon shakai 4, ed. Tōkyō Daigaku Shakaigakka Kenkyūsho (Tokyo Daigaku Shuppankai, 1991), 47–52.

7. Nakamura, *Kinsei chōnin shisō*, Nihon shisō taikei 59 (Iwanami Shoten, 1975), 89.
8. Tetsuo Najita, *Visions of Virtue in Tokugawa Japan: The Kaitokudō Merchant Academy of Osaka* (University of Chicago Press, 1987), 48–56. Regarding circulation and the public quality of money, see also Shigehisa Kuriyama, "The Historical Origins of *Katakori*," *Japan Review*, no. 9 (1997): 134.
9. Nakamura, *Kinsei chōnin shisō*, 101.
10. Howell, *Geographies of Identity*, 45.
11. Yokota Fuyuhiko, "'Heijin mibun' no shakai ishiki," in *Nihon shakai no shi-teki kōzō: Kinsei, kindai*, ed. Asao Naohiro Kyōju Taikan Kinenkai (Shibunkaku Shuppan, 1995), 125–50.
12. NKBT 48, 33–36. For a lucid synthesis of approaches to this notoriously challenging passage, see Yano Kimio, "Jo: mondai no shozai," in *Kyokō to shite no "Nippon eitaigura"* (Kasama Shoin, 2002), 3–12. The analysis I develop here builds on the discussion of reading practices in Thomas Gaubatz, "Distribution Poetics: Ihara Saikaku and the Literature of the Marketplace," *East Asian Publishing and Society* 16, no. 1 (2026): 28–30.
13. NKBT 48, 33.
14. Hirosue Tamotsu, *Saikaku no shōsetsu: Jikū ishiki no tenkan o megutte* (Heibonsha, 1982), 45–50.
15. Fabio Rambelli, "The Mystery of Wealth and the Role of Divinities: The Economy in Pre-Modern Japanese Fiction and Practice," *Hualin International Journal of Buddhist Studies* 2, no. 2 (2019): 169–73.
16. Certeau, *Practice of Everyday Life*, 37.
17. Yano Kimio, "Hatsumuma wa notte kuru shiawase," in *Kyokō to shite no "Nippon eitaigura*," 24–43.
18. Certeau, *Practice of Everyday Life*, 37.
19. Certeau, *Practice of Everyday Life*, 91–110.
20. NKBT 48, 87–91. The title parodies the instructions conventionally found on bags of medicine: "Boil in the normal fashion, with one slice of ginger" (*senjiyō tsune no gotoshi, shōga hitohira*). The standard method of preparing medicine was to add the medicine to a cup and a half of water along with one slice of ginger and boil the contents down to one cup. My analysis of this story develops a reading briefly sketched in Gaubatz, "Distribution Poetics," 31–34.
21. NKBT 48, 88–89.
22. The most concise survey of the castle-town paradigm is Yoshida Nobuyuki, *Toshi: Edo ni ikiru* (Iwanami Shoten, 2015), 1–50. See also Yoshida Nobuyuki, "Jōkamachi no kōzō to tenkai," in *Toshi shakai-shi*, Shin taikei Nihon-shi 6, ed. Satō Makoto and Yoshida Nobuyuki (Yamakawa Shuppansha, 2001), 87–120; Itō Hirohisa, "Toshi kūkan no bunsetsu haaku," in *Bunsetsu kōzō*, Dentō toshi 4, ed. Yoshida Nobuyuki and Itō Takeshi (Tōkyō Daigaku Shuppankai, 2010), 73–107; Itō Takeshi, "Kinsei toshi no seiritsu," in *Kinsei 1*, Iwanami kōza Nihon rekishi 10, ed. Ōtsu Tōru, Sakurai Eiji, Fujii Jōji, Yoshida Yutaka, and I Keifan (Iwanami Shoten, 2014), 241–76; Matsumoto Shirō, *Jōkamachi* (Yoshikawa Kōbunkan, 2013); James L. McClain, *Kanazawa: A Seventeenth-Century Japanese Castle Town* (Yale University Press, 1982).

2. THE POETICS AND POLITICS OF TOWNSMAN PROPERTY

23. Ronald P. Toby, "Spatial Visions of Status," in *Cartographic Japan: A History in Maps*, ed. Kären Wigen, Sugimoto Fumiko, and Cary Karacas (University of Chicago Press, 2016), 78–80. See also Marcia Yonemoto, *Mapping Early Modern Japan: Space, Place, and Culture in the Tokugawa Period* (University of California Press), 17–26.
24. Marcia Yonemoto, "Nihonbashi: Edo's Contested Center," *East Asian History*, nos. 17–18 (1999): 49–70.
25. Jinnai Hidenobu, *Tokyo: A Spatial Anthropology* (University of California Press, 1995), chap. 2.
26. Matsuda Osamu, "Neko no toshigaku," in *Edo itan bungaku nōto* (Seidosha, 1993), 62. For the passage in *Eitaigura*, see NKBT 48, 41–42.
27. Certeau, *Practice of Everyday Life*, 93.
28. NKBT 48, 89.
29. NKBT 48, 89–90.
30. Mayama Seika, "Saikaku to Edo chiri," in *Mayama Seika zuihitsu senshū* (Dai-Nihon Yūbenkai Kōdansha, 1952), 2:88–89.
31. Certeau, *Practice of Everyday Life*, 98, see also 133–39.
32. NKBT 48, 67–73.
33. Asakura Haruhiko, ed., *Jinrin kinmōzui* (Tōyō Bunko, 1990), 110.
34. Nakamura, *Kinsei chōnin shisō*, 89.
35. NKBT 48, 69.
36. NKBT 48, 487n154.
37. Shiomura Kō, "Saikaku no anji-teki shuhō," in *Kinsei zenki bungaku kenkyū: Denki, shoshi, shuppan* (Wakakusa Shobō, 2004), 208–13. See also Rambelli, "Mystery of Wealth," 179.
38. Nakamura, *Kinsei chōnin shisō*, 88–89.
39. Howell, *Geographies of Identity*, 36–41.
40. Regarding unregistered beggars and their relationship to the institutions of the Edo outcast order, see Howell, *Geographies of Identity*, 30–31.
41. Regarding *gōmune*, see Gerald Groemer, *Street Performers and Society in Urban Japan, 1600–1900* (Routledge, 2016), chap. 4.
42. I owe my reading of the economic logic of Shinroku's decision to lectures by Nakajima Takashi.
43. The following draws from Yokota, "Heijin mibun no shakai ishiki," 144–47.
44. Robert N. Bellah, *Tokugawa Religion: The Cultural Roots of Modern Japan* (Free Press, 1985); Najita, *Visions of Virtue*. For a more recent synthesis of the "way of the merchant," see Richard Bowring, *In Search of the Way: Thought and Religion in Early-Modern Japan, 1582–1860* (Oxford University Press, 2017), 156–65.
45. Hiraishi, "Kinsei Nihon no 'shokugyō' kan," 52–58.
46. Amy Borovoy argues that Robert Bellah's interest in Baigan's heart learning was not merely an analogical extension of Weber's Protestant ethic; rather, Bellah sought in the non-West a communitarian alternative, rooted in religious tradition, that might constrain the more rapacious tendencies of modern capitalism under the regime of American liberal individualism. Amy Borovoy, "Robert Bellah's Search for Community and Ethical Modernity in Japan Studies," *Journal of Asian Studies* 75, no. 2 (2016): 467–94.

3. FROM TOWNSMAN CULTURE TO TOWNSMAN NARRATIVE

1. For example, see Takao Kazuhiko, *Kinsei no shomin bunka* (Iwanami Shoten, 1968), 110–257; Nakai Nobuhiko, *Chōnin*, Nihon no rekishi 21 (Shōgakkan, 1975), 211–49; Miyamoto Mataji, *Kinsei shōnin ishiki no kenkyū*, Miyamoto Mataji chosakushū 2 (Kōdansha, 1977), 34–42; Moriya Takeshi, *Genroku bunka: yūgei, akusho, shibai* (Kōdansha, 2011), 9–21. In English, see Donald Shively, "Popular Culture," in *The Cambridge History of Japan, vol. 4: Early Modern Japan*, ed. John Whitney Hall (Cambridge University Press, 1991), 761–69.
2. Noma Kōshin, ed., *Saikaku shū 2*, Nihon koten bungaku taikei 48 (Iwanami Shoten, 1960), 33, 43, 117. Citations that follow refer to this edition, abbreviated as NKBT 48.
3. NKBT 48, 72, 101, 148.
4. The most complete articulation of this reading is Teruoka Yasutaka, "Saikaku bannen no tēma to hōhō," in *Saikaku shinron* (Chūō Kōronsha, 1981), 197–247, esp. 208–18.
5. Jeffrey Johnson, "Saikaku and the Narrative Turnabout," *Journal of Japanese Studies* 27, no. 2 (2001): 323–45.
6. David J. Gundry, *Parody, Irony and Ideology in the Fiction of Ihara Saikaku* (Brill, 2017), 19. See also David J. Gundry, "Hierarchy, Hubris, and Parody in Ihara Saikaku's *Kōshoku ichidai otoko*," *Journal of Japanese Studies* 43, no. 2 (2017): 378–83.
7. Gundry, *Parody, Irony, and Ideology*, 45–53.
8. Gundry, *Parody, Irony, and Ideology*, 30–37.
9. The narrative of early, middle, and late works, historically emerged out of (and in turn authorizes) attempts to theorize Saikaku's development as an author, this in the face of extremely limited documentary sources outside of the texts themselves. The most influential such account is that of Teruoka Yasutaka. See *Saikaku: hyōron to kenkyū*, 2 vols. (Chūō Kōronsha, 1948–1950).
10. Nakamura Yukihiko, "Saikaku no sōsaku ishiki to sono suii," in *Kinsei shōsetsu yōshiki kō*, Nakamura Yukihiko chojutsushū 5 (Chūō Kōronsha, 1982), 112–43.
11. Regarding the relationship between plot and didactic narration in medieval *setsuwa* collections, see, for example, D. E. Mills, *A Collection of Tales from Uji: A Study and Translation of Uji Shūi Monogatari* (Cambridge University Press, 1970), 33–36; Marian Ury, *Tales of Times Now Past: Sixty-Two Stories from a Medieval Japanese Collection* (University of California Press, 1979), 7–9.
12. Haruo Shirane, "Setsuwa (anecdotal) literature: *Nihon ryōiki* to *Kokon chomonjū*," in *The Cambridge History of Japanese Literature*, ed. Haruo Shirane and Tomi Suzuki, with David Lurie (Cambridge University Press, 2016), 281.
13. Charlotte Eubanks, *Miracles of Book and Body: Buddhist Textual Culture & Medieval Japan* (University of California Press, 2011), 7–12.
14. For an introductory overview of the various forms of early modern *setsuwa*, see Fuji Akio, "Kinsei setsuwa no shosō," in *Saikaku to kana-zōshi* (Chikuma Shoin, 2011), 54–72.
15. Regarding the influence of medieval *setsuwa* collections on Saikaku's work, see Taniwaki Masachika, "Saikaku shōsetsu no setsuwa-teki kihan: *Uji shūi, Senjūshō* no yakuwari," in *Saikaku kenkyū josetsu* (Shintensha, 1981), 238–253.

3. FROM TOWNSMAN CULTURE TO TOWNSMAN NARRATIVE

16. Laura Moretti, *Pleasure in Profit: Popular Prose in Seventeenth-Century Japan* (Columbia University Press, 2020), esp. chaps 3, 7.
17. Teruoka Yasutaka, "Kana-zōshi no tenbō," in *Saikaku shinron* (Chūō Kōronsha, 1981), 9–54.
18. Regarding the naming of *Saikaku shokoku-banashi*, see Teruoka Yasutaka, "Saikaku to shuppan jānarizumu," in *Saikaku shinron*, 382–83.
19. Nakamura Yukihiko, "Saikaku ni okeru setsuwa-sei han-setsuwa-sei," *Kokubungaku kaishaku to kanshō* 38, no. 4 (1973): 13–16. See also Teruoka Yasutaka, "Saikaku bungaku no setsuwa-sei to hi-setsuwa-sei," in *Saikaku shinron*, 102–15. A separate strain of scholarship sees the legacy of *setsuwa* in terms of an interplay between written narrative and forms of oral storytelling. See Nakamura Yukihiko, "Kana-zōshi no setsuwa-sei," in *Kinsei shōsetsu-shi no kenkyū* (Nan'undō Shuppan, 1961), 34–48; Noma Kōshin, "Saikaku no hōhō," and "Saikaku itsutsu no hōhō," both in *Saikaku shin shinkō* (Iwanami Shoten, 1981), 75–100, 101–21; Fuji Akio, "Saikaku no setsuwa-sei," in *Saikaku to kana-zōshi* (Kasama Shoin, 2011), 204–22.
20. NKBT 48, 41–46.
21. Hirosue Tamotsu, *Saikaku no shōsetsu: Jikū ishiki no tenkan o megutte* (Heibonsha, 1982), 36–50.
22. Noma Kōshin, "*Chōjakyō* kō," in *Saikaku shinkō* (Chikuma Shobō, 1948), 380–81.
23. *Kingin mannōgan* was in fact a repackaged reprint of a text called *Jinkyōron* (*The Mirror of Man*), published at some point earlier in the same decade; Morita would reprint it again in 1694 with the title *Kanemochi chōhōki* (*A Record of Great Treasures for the Wealthy*). The text consists of an extended debate between representatives of the major philosophical traditions—a Confucian, a Buddhist, and a Shintoist—over which is the best mirror for the people, but the text is punctuated with an extended soliloquy by a fourth character advocating for the supreme authority of money over all things. For detailed discussion of this text and its relationship with Saikaku's work, see Nagatomo Chiyoji, "*Kingin mannōgan* to *Nippon eitaigura*," in *Edo jidai no shomotsu to dokusho* (Tōkyōdō Shuppan, 2001), 127–45.
24. Fujiwara Noboru, "*Chōjakyō* kara *Nippon eitaigura* e: Ie ishiki o chūshin ni," *Nōtorudamu seishin joshi daigaku kokubungaku-ka kiyō* 7 (1974), 25–48.
25. Moretti, *Pleasure in Profit*, 233.
26. Tanaka Shin, "Saikaku no egaita kinsen: *Nippon eitaigura* kō," in *Kinsei shōsetsu ronkō* (Ōfūsha, 1985), 147–56.
27. Nakamura Yukihiko, *Kinsei chōnin shisō*, Nihon shisō taikei 59 (Iwanami Shoten, 1975), 9.
28. Nakamura, *Kinsei chōnin shisō*, 10–11.
29. Andrew Hui, "Aphorism," *New Literary History* 50, no. 3 (2019): 419.
30. Gary Saul Morson, "The Aphorism: Fragments from the Breakdown of Reason," *New Literary History* 34, no. 3 (2003): 415–19. Morson juxtaposes the dictum with what he refers to as "aphorism," but his aphorism is closer to a riddle without a fixed answer: an enigmatic turn of phrase that seems to contain worlds of meaning but refuses to disclose them directly (his archetypal aphorist is Laozi). But I take inspiration from his Bakhtinian approach to how such genres of short expression give form to ideology, reflecting both worldviews and patterns of thought, in Gary Saul Morson, "Bakhtin, the Genres of Quotation, and the Aphoristic Consciousness," *Slavic and East European Journal* 50, no. 1 (2006): 213–27.

3. FROM TOWNSMAN CULTURE TO TOWNSMAN NARRATIVE

31. Noma, "Chōjakyō kō," 380–81.
32. Kanda Hideo, Nagazumi Yasuaki, and Yasuraoka Kōsaku, eds., *Hōjōki, Tsurezuregusa, Shōbō genzō zuimonki, Tannishō*, Nihon koten bungaku zenshū 27 (Shōgakkan, 1971), 261–62.
33. Regarding the early modern reception of *Tsurezuregusa*, see Linda Chance, "Constructing the Classic: *Tsurezuregusa* in Tokugawa Readings," *Journal of the American Oriental Society* 117, no. 1 (1997): 39–56; Nakamura Yukihiko, "Tsurezuregusa juyō-shi," *Kokubungaku: Kaishaku to kanshō* 22, no. 12 (1957): 62–67.
34. Regarding the influence of *Tsurezuregusa* on Saikaku's work, see, for example, Danieru Sutoryūbu, "Saikaku ni okeru kane to iro no ronri: *Tsurezuregusa* to no kanren o chūshin ni shite," *Saikaku to ukiyo-zōshi kenkyū* 3 (2010): 61–74; Taniwaki Masachika, "*Tsurezuregusa* to Saikaku no chōnin-mono," in *Kinsei bungei e no shiza: Saikaku o jiku to shite* (Shintensha, 1999), 269–79.
35. Nakamura, *Kinsei chōnin shisō*, 15.
36. NKBT 48, 101.
37. NKBT 48, 144.
38. NKBT 48, 157.
39. Teruoka, "Saikaku bannen no tēma to hōhō," 199–215.
40. Teruoka Yasutaka, "*Nippon eitaigura* no seiritsu," and "*Nippon eitaigura* ni okeru Shisō no hen'yō: shokō to tsuikakō ni tsuite," in *Saikaku shinron*, 329–52, 353–74.
41. For a brief synopsis, see Hamada Yasuhiko, "*Nippon eitaigura*," in *Saikaku to ukiyo-zōshi no kenkyū*, ed. Taniwaki Masachika et al. (Kasama Shoin, 2010), 3:188–92. The most influential oppositional position was that of Taniwaki Masachika, who argued that the last two volumes were fragments of an unsophisticated early draft, appended to bolster the length of the text: see the various essays compiled in *Saikaku kenkyū josetsu* (Shintensha, 1981), and *"Nippon eitaigura" seiritsu dangi: Kaisō, hihan, tenbō* (Seibundō Shuppan, 2006). Despite Taniwaki's polemic, more recent scholarship is generally closer to Teruoka's position. See Nishijima Atsuya, "*Nippon eitaigura* no seiritsu: Shokō to tsuikakō no ginmi," in *Saikaku to ukiyo-zōshi* (Ōfūsha, 1989), 295–340; Hiroshima Susumu, "*Nippon eitaigura* ni okeru 'daifuku' to shoshō no hen'yō: Seiritsu no mondai o megutte," in *Saikaku tankyū: Chōnin-mono no sekai* (Perikansha, 2004), 32–55. In my view, the most compelling approaches explore the possible influence of Saikaku's publisher, Morita Shōtarō. See Hanyū Noriko, "*Nippon eitaigura* no shuppan jijō: Santo no shoshi to Saikaku" and "*Nippon eitaigura* no kōzō: Sōsaku shisei to kyōkun no arikata," in *Saikaku to shuppan media no kenkyū* (Izumi Shoin, 2000), 223–62, 426–50; Nagatomo, "*Kingin mannōgan* to *Nippon eitaigura*."
42. NKBT 48, 87–88.
43. Roland Barthes, *Mythologies*, trans. Annette Lavers (Noonday Press, 1972), 117–27, 150–55.
44. NKBT 48, 63–67.
45. NKBT 48, 64.
46. Teruoka Yasutaka, "Saikaku bungaku ni okeru warai," in *Saikaku shinron*, 119–34.
47. NKBT 48, 184–88.
48. NKBT 48, 184–86.
49. NKBT 48, 188.
50. NKBT 48, 316.

3. FROM TOWNSMAN CULTURE TO TOWNSMAN NARRATIVE

51. Regarding *Risshin daifukuchō*, see Nagao Michio, "*Risshin daifukuchō* no shisei: *Nippon eitaigura* no juyō to hihan," *Kinsei bungei: kenkyū to hyōron*, no. 22 (1982): 24–37.
52. Noma Kōshin and Yoshida Kōichi, eds., *Hōjō Dansui shū, sōshi hen* 3 (Koten Bunko, 1980), 191.
53. Emoto Hiroshi, "Hōei Shōtoku-ki ni okeru chifutan no kenkyū: *Nippon shin eitaigura, Shison daikoku-bashira* o chūshin to shite," in *Kinsei zenki shōsetsu no kenkyū* (Wakakusa Shobō, 2000), 182–95.

4. THE MISFORTUNE OF BEING SAVED BY ONE'S ARTS

1. For an illuminating discussion of this text and other documents of the Mitsui house, see Mary Elizabeth Berry, "Family Trouble: Views from the Stage and a Merchant Archive," in *What Is a Family: Answers from Early Modern Japan*, ed. Mary Elizabeth Berry and Marcia Yonemoto (University of California Press, 2019), 224–29. See also E. S. Crawcour, "Some Observations on Merchants: A Translation of Mitsui Takafusa's *Chōnin Kōken Roku*, with an Introduction and Notes," *Transactions of the Asiatic Society of Japan*, 3rd ser., no. 8 (1962): 1–139.
2. Nakamura Yukihiko, *Kinsei chōnin shisō*, Nihon shisō taikei 59 (Iwanami Shoten, 1975), 176,
3. I opt for "household" (or occasionally "house") as a heuristic translation for *ie* rather than the more technical and comparatively oriented "stem family," which suggests the existence of a more universal and normative family structure. To the average resident of early modern Japan, the *ie* was the family—a normative and universal (though also flexible and diverse) unit of social organization, one that was above all taken for granted. Regarding terminology, see Mary Elizabeth Berry and Marcia Yonemoto, introduction to *What Is a Family?*, 4–7.
4. For a statistical study of the spread of the *ie* as institution in the late seventeenth century, albeit one focused primarily on rural households, see Fabian Drixler, "Imagined Communities of the Living and the Dead: The Spread of the Ancestor-Venerating Stem Family in Tokugawa Japan," in *What Is a Family?*, 68–107.
5. These three components were typically sustained across successive generations by a principle of sole transmission: usually to the eldest son, but often (in the case that the eldest was deemed to lack the proper disposition of heir) to a younger son, or, in the absence of sons, to an adoptive son-in-law; other sons were sent into apprenticeship, married as adoptive sons-in-law to households lacking their own heirs, or, in the case of the most well-off households, placed in charge of branch houses. Regarding the problem of succession and its relationship to the townsman concept of house trade, see Nakai Nobuhiko, *Chōnin*, Nihon no rekishi 21 (Shōgakukan, 1975), 250–94.
6. For an accounting of the rationales for such a system, and its costs, see Berry, "Family Trouble," 229–33.
7. The standard biographical treatments in English are Hibbett and Fox. See Howard Hibbett, *The Floating World in Japanese Fiction* (Oxford University Press, 1959), 50–64; Charles E. Fox, "Old Stories, New Mode: Ejima Kiseki's *Ukiyo Oyaji Katagi*," *Monumenta Nipponica* 43, no. 1 (1988): 63–77.

4. THE MISFORTUNE OF BEING SAVED BY ONE'S ARTS

8. For detailed biographical background, see Noma Kōshin, "Daibutsu-mochi raiyūsho," and "Ejima Kiseki to sono ichizoku," in *Kinsei sakkaden kō* (Chūō Kōronsha, 1985), 259–97.
9. Kiseki may have written or been involved with Hachimonjiya's illustrated playbooks (*eiri kyōgen-bon*) prior to undertaking the writing of actor reviews, according to Ishikawa Junjirō: see "*Yakusha kuchi jamisen* seiritsu zengo: Ejima Kiseki no shūsaku jidai," *Kokubungaku kenkyū* 20, no. 10 (1960): 33–45.
10. Regarding the actor-review genre as a training ground for Kiseki's fiction, see Saeki Takahiro, "Kiseki no shūsakuki no yakusha hyōbanki: *Yakusha kuchi jamisen* o chūshin ni," *Kokugo to kokubungaku* 954 (2003): 34–46; Kawai Masumi, "Yakusha hyōbanki no kaikōbu: Saikaku sakuhin no riyō o megutte," *Kokugo kokubun* 50 (1981): 27–42; Kurakazu Masae, "Ejima Kiseki no yakusha hyōbanki to genroku makki no ukiyo-zōshi," *Edo bungaku* 23 (2001): 108–19.
11. Berry, "Family Trouble," 218. See also J. Mark Ramseyer, "Thrift and Diligence: House Codes of Tokugawa Merchant Families," *Monumenta Nipponica* 43, no. 2 (1979): 209–20.
12. Citations for Kiseki's works refer are taken from Hachimonjiyabon Kenkyūkai, eds., *Hachimonjiyabon zenshū*, 23 vols. (Kyūko Shoin, 1992–2013) [HZS, followed by the volume and page numbers]. As with Saikaku's works, I indicate a page range for the given story and otherwise avoid granular citations of scenes except for extended quotations. The story in question may be found in HZS 6:4–9.
13. Tsutsumi Kunihiko, "*Seken musuko katagi* to Ekiken kyōkunsho: Chōnin rinri no bungeika," in *Edo no kaiitan: chika suimyaku no keifu* (Perikansha, 2004), 230–37.
14. HZS 6:8.
15. The most concise introduction to Moriya Takeshi's wide-ranging work is *Genroku bunka: yūgei, akusho, shibai* (Kōbundō, 1987). See also Moriya Takeshi, "Kinsei no chōnin to yūgei," in *Kinsei geinō bunkashi no kenkyū* (Kōbundō, 1992), 59–82; and Moriya Takeshi, "*Yūgei* and *Chōnin* Society in the Edo Period," *Acta Asiatica* 33 (1977): 32–54.
16. Fuji Akio, Inoue Toshiyuki, and Satake Akihiro, eds., *Kōshoku nidai otoko, Saikaku shokoku banashi, Honchō nijū fukō*, Shin Nihon koten bungaku taikei 76 (Iwanami Shoten, 1991), 187.
17. Nakai, *Chōnin*, 246–49.
18. Nakamura, *Kinsei chōnin shisō*, 199–200.
19. Moriya, *Genroku bunka*, 36–42.
20. Eiko Ikegami, *Bonds of Civility: Aesthetic Networks and the Political Origins of Japanese Culture* (Cambridge University Press, 2005), 43.
21. Nishiyama Matsunosuke, "Edo bunka ni okeru kyozō to jitsuzō," in *Kinsei bunka no kenkyū*, Nishiyama Matsunosuke chosakushū 4 (Yoshikawa Kōbunkan, 1983), 20–24.
22. Pierre Bourdieu, *Distinction: A Social Critique of the Judgement of Taste*, trans. Richard Nice (Harvard University Press, 1979), 466–67.
23. Here I take inspiration from Judith Butler's critique of Bourdieu in "Performativity's Social Magic," in *Bourdieu: A Critical Reader*, ed. Richard Shusterman (Blackwell, 1999), 113–28.
24. Nakamura, *Kinsei chōnin shisō*, 378–83; Yamamoto Shinkō, *Kakun shū* (Heibonsha, 2001), 236–50. For an English translation, see Ramseyer, "Thrift and Diligence," 221–26.

4. THE MISFORTUNE OF BEING SAVED BY ONE'S ARTS

25. Noma Kōshin, ed., *Saikaku shū 2*, Nihon koten bungaku taikei 48 (Iwanami Shoten, 1960), 72. Citations that follow refer to this edition, abbreviated as NKBT 48. For a detailed analysis of Saikaku's treatments of the leisure arts, see Ku Tefun, "Genroku no chōnin shakai to yūgei: Saikaku no yūgei kan o chūshin to shite," in *Yūgei bunka to dentō*, ed. Kumakura Isao (Yoshikawa Kōbunkan, 2003), 124–47.
26. Moriya, *Genroku bunka*, 38–39.
27. Henri Lefebvre, *Critique of Everyday Life*, vol. 1 (Verso, 2008), 30.
28. Regarding the place of the leisure arts in this text, see Kumakura Isao, "Kinsei ni okeru geinō no tenkai," in *Dentō geinō no tenkai*, Nihon no kinsei 11 (Chūō Kōronsha, 1993), 42–52.
29. NKBT 48, 43.
30. HZS 6:28–31. For an English translation, see Howard Hibbett, *Floating World in Japanese Fiction*, 145–51.
31. HZS 6:30. Some of this is borrowed from Saikaku's *Honchō nijū fukō* (see chap. 5).
32. HZS 11:76–81.
33. The most influential authorial sketch is in the miscellany *At the Eastern Window* (*Tōyūshi*, 1803), written by the minor Osaka-based scholar Tamiya Nakanobu. For his account of Kiseki, see Nihon Zuihitsu Taisei Henshūbu, ed., *Tōyūshi, Okotarigusa*, Nihon zuihitsu taisei, dai 1-ki 19 (Yoshikawa Kōbunkan, 1976), 186. Noma Kōshin speculates that the decline of the Murase household was less a matter of Kiseki's individual comportment and more a symptom of larger economic shifts: Kiseki's household suffered the consequences of dealing with the circles of moneylenders who financed their loans to *daimyō* by borrowing from commoners. In addition, Kiseki likely spent large portions of his fortune in negotiating marriage and adoption arrangements for his many children. See Noma, "Ejima Kiseki to sono ichizoku," 289–94.
34. Noma, "Daibutsu-mochi raiyūsho," 264–72.
35. Moriya, *Genroku bunka*, 42–43; Ikegami, *Bonds of Civility*, 153–60.
36. For a discussion of this text, see Reiko Tanimura and David Chart, "The Record of Women's Great Treasures: Pregnancy and Childbirth in the Edo Period: A Translation of Volume Three of *Onna chōhōki*," *Asiatische Studien* 71, no. 2 (2017): 545–66.
37. Regarding the emotional labor of the townsman wife in managing relationships on behalf of the household, see, for example, Nakano Setsuko, *Onna wa itsu kara yasashiku natta ka: Edo no josei-shi* (Heibonsha, 2014), esp. 29–50.
38. HZS 6:490–94.
39. Sugano Noriko, Hayashi Reiko, and Mega Atsuko, "Shomin josei no seikatsu to rōdō," in *Nihon joseishi*, ed. Wakita Haruko, Hayashi Reiko, and Nagahara Kazuko (Yoshikawa Kōbunkan, 1987), 150–55.
40. Teruoka Yasutaka and Higashi Akimasa, eds., *Ihara Saikaku shū 1*, Nihon koten bungaku zenshū 38 (Shōgakkan, 1971), 478–82. For an English translation, see Ihara Saikaku, *The Life of an Amorous Woman and Other Writings*, trans. Ivan Morris (New Directions, 1969), 153–58.
41. Yokota Fuyuhiko, "Imagining Working Women in Early Modern Japan," in *Women and Class in Japanese History*, ed. Hitomi Tonomura, Anne Walthall, and Wakita Haruko (Center for Japanese Studies, University of Michigan, 1999), 163–66.
42. Regarding women in the early modern household, see Wakita Haruko, "The Japanese Woman in the Premodern Merchant Household," trans. by G. G. Rowley,

4. THE MISFORTUNE OF BEING SAVED BY ONE'S ARTS

Women's History Review 19, no. 2 (2010): 259–82; Wakita Haruko, "Women and the Creation of the *Ie* in Japan: An Overview from the Medieval Period to the Present," trans. David P. Phillips, *U.S.-Japan Women's Journal, English Supplement* 1993, no. 4 (1993): 83–105; Hayashi Reiko, "Edo jidai no chōka josei-tachi," in *Edo Kamigata no ōdana to chōka josei* (Yoshikawa Kōbunkan, 2001), 284–96; Kathleen S. Uno, "Women and Changes in the Household Division of Labor," in *Recreating Japanese Women, 1600–1945*, ed. Gail Lee Bernstein (University of California Press, 1991), 17–41.

43. Kaibara Ekiken, *Yōjōkun, Wazoku dōjikun*, ed. Ishikawa Ken (Iwanami Shoten, 1961), 237.
44. HZS 6:19–22. For an English translation, see Hibbett, *Floating World in Japanese Fiction*, 132–38.
45. Laura Moretti, *Pleasure in Profit: Popular Prose in Seventeenth-Century Japan* (Columbia University Press, 2020), 51.
46. Moretti, *Pleasure in Profit*, 64.
47. For the original, see Fuji Akio and Hiroshima Susumu, eds., *Ihara Saikaku shū 4*, Shinpen Nihon koten bungaku zenshū 69 (Shōgakkan, 2000), 521–27.
48. Kaibara, *Yōjōkun, Wazoku dōjikun*, 215.
49. Takahashi Akihiko, "Gujintan o meguru shōsetsu no keifu: Katagi-mono no yōshiki to hōhō," *Nihon bungaku* 38, no. 8 (1989): 15–16, 18–19.
50. HZS 6:33–36.
51. HZS 6:34–35.
52. HZS 6:35–36.
53. Nakamura, *Kinsei chōnin shisō*, 88.
54. For example, see Saeki Takahiro, "Katagi-mono no sōshutsu," in *Ejima Kiseki to katagimono* (Wakakusa Shobō, 2004), 45–46; Tsutsumi, "Seken musuko katagi to Ekiken kyōkunsho," 243–44; Ishikawa Junjirō, "Ejima Kiseki katagi-mono josetsu," *Kokubungaku kenkyū*, no. 17 (1958): 123–24.
55. Pierre Bourdieu, "Field of Power, Literary Field and Habitus," in *The Field of Cultural Production: Essays on Art and Literature*, ed. Randal Johnson (Columbia University Press, 1993), 163.
56. Bourdieu, "Field of Power," 174.
57. For example, see Hibbett, *Floating World in Japanese Fiction*, 58; Fox, "Old Stories, New Mode," 68.
58. Linked to the physical possession of the printing blocks, copyright represented the right to portions of profits derived from printing and selling works produced from the blocks, and the only way writers could retain such rights and control over works they produced was by holding the blocks themselves. Moreover, most documented disputes over copyright were concerned with more serious books (*shomotsu*); the less prestigious category of *sōshi* was likely understood as a space where anything goes. See Peter Kornicki, *The Book in Japan: A Cultural History from the Beginnings to the Nineteenth Century* (University of Hawaii Press, 2001), 242–51; Ichiko Natsuo, "Kinsei ni okeru jūhan ruihan no shomondai," *Edo bungaku* 16 (1996): 26–39.
59. HZS 2:455.
60. The standard treatments of this period of rivalry are Nakamura Yukihiko, "Jishō Kiseki kakushitsu jidai," in *Kinsei shōsetsu-shi no kenkyū* (San'ichi Shobō, 1961), 101–26; Hasegawa Tsuyoshi, *Ukiyo-zōshi no kenkyū: Hachimonjiya-bon o chūshin to*

4. THE MISFORTUNE OF BEING SAVED BY ONE'S ARTS

suru (Ōfūsha, 1969), 285–324; Fujii Otoo, ed., *Ukiyo-zōshi meisaku shū* (Dai-Nihon Yūbenkai Kōdansha, 1937), 90–113. The most economical introduction is Nakamura Yukihiko, "Hachimonjiya-bon no tenmatsu," in *Kinsei shōsetsu shi*, Nakamura Yukihiko chojutsushū 4 (Chūō Kōronsha, 1987), 123–27.

61. Here I am simplifying a complex set of conflicting interests that also relate to the relative claims of each publisher over the two genres of *yakusha hyōbanki* and *ukiyo-zōshi*, the relationship between those genres, and the respective markets and business models they represent. Roughly, the *hyōbanki*, as an annual serial with a stable readership of theater fans, was reliably profitable but likely had higher production costs because it was subject to the demand that its reviews be current, comprehensive, and reasonably accurate. The *ukiyo-zōshi*, which depended largely on the creativity of the writer and his ability to predict or respond to the fickle tastes of the reading public, was easier (in theory) to produce and had the potential to become a smash hit, but also risked flopping. More work must be done to clarify how these two markets interacted and the respective stakes of Hachimonjiya and Ejimaya in each. For a relevant discussion, see Nakamura, "Jishō Kiseki kakushitsu jidai," 104–8; Shinohara Susumu, "Kōsōki no Kiseki," *Kinsei bungei* 34 (1981): 47–48.
62. Regarding Miren, see Shinohara Susumu, "Miren to Hachimonjiya," *Hirosaki Gakuin Daigaku Hirosaki Gakuin Tanki Daigaku kiyō*, no. 17 (1981): 23–43.
63. Regarding the evolution of Kiseki's writing during this period, see Shinohara, "Kōsōki no Kiseki," 51–62.
64. Most scholars share the consensus that Kiseki's decision to pass on his family shop, which likely was accompanied by a substantial injection of capital, was at least partially motivated by financial urgency as well. For example, see Noma, "Daibutsu-mochi raiyūsho," 272–76; Nakamura, "Hachimonjiya-bon no tenmatsu," 124–25.
65. Nakamura, "Jishō Kiseki kakushitsu jidai," 180–81. Nakamura speculates that this reconciliation may have been prompted by the shogunal recognition of publishing guilds in 1716; it also seems to anticipate the articulation of clearer publishing laws amid the Kyōhō Reforms. Nakamura only goes so far as to suggest a general atmosphere of reconciliation and consolidation of relationships, but one might observe that one of the stipulations of the reform edicts was that all publications must include the names of both writer and publisher, a policy that would have curtailed, at risk of shogunal intervention, disputes over credit and thus acted as a de facto recognition of authorship. For a discussion of the content of the reforms in relation to issues of intellectual property, see, for example, Nakano Mitsutoshi, "Jūhasseiki no Edo bunka," in *Jūhasseiki no Edo bungei: Ga to zoku no seijuku* (Iwanami Shoten, 1999), 39–49.
66. Noma, "Ejima Kiseki to sono ichizoku," 292–95.
67. Bourdieu, "Field of Power," 175.

5. REPRESENTING NORMALITY

1. In the modern era, amid the literary reforms of 1880s, Tsubouchi Shōyō would unearth the trope for his *Characters of Contemporary Students* (*Tōsei shosei katagi*, 1885–1886), though the work had more in common with Tamenaga Shunsui's *ninjōbon* than with the Kamigata-based *ukiyo-zōshi* tradition exemplified by

5. REPRESENTING NORMALITY

Kiseki's works. Regarding the afterlife of the genre, see Charles E. Fox, "Old Stories, New Mode: Ejima Kiseki's Oyaji Katagi," *Monumenta Nipponica* 43, no. 1 (Spring 1988): 77; Hasegawa Tsuyoshi, *Ukiyo-zōshi no kenkyū: Hachimonjiya-bon o chūshin to suru* (Ōfūsha, 1969), 543-47.

2. For detailed discussion of the defining characteristics of the *katagi-mono*, see Saeki Takahiro, "Katagi-mono no sōshutsu," in *Ejima Kiseki to katagi-mono* (Wakakusa Shobō, 2004), 19-26; Hasegawa, *Ukiyo-zōshi no kenkyū*, 353-66.
3. Regarding comparisons between the *katagi-mono* and the Theophrastan character, see Howard S. Hibbett, "Ejima Kiseki (1667-1736) and His *Katagi-Mono*," *Harvard Journal of Asiatic Studies* 14, no. 3 (1951): 424; Takayama Hiroshi, "Zattsu kyarakutarisutikku: Katagi bungaku tōzai," *Bungaku* 10, no. 1 (2009): 204-6.
4. For characteristic treatments, see Donald Keene, *World Within Walls: Japanese Literature of the Pre-Modern Era, 1600-1867* (Holt, Rinehart and Winston, 1978), 225-26; Tanaka Shin, "Katagi-mono no hōhō to sono genkai," *Kinsei bungei*, no. 1 (1954): 48-56. This critique rings true, to a degree: especially in the work of later writers, the term *katagi* was little more than a form of effective branding that could be relied on to package and sell fiction of diverse form and content. Kiseki himself had no qualms about applying the *katagi* title to works of that diverged in form and content: *Characters of Intrepid Actors* (*Kankatsu yakusha katagi*, 1712) and *Characters of Courtesans from Japan and China* (*Wakan yūjo katagi*, 1718) bear little resemblance to Kiseki's other works and are generally excluded from the *katagi-mono* proper despite their titles.
5. For recent treatments of Kiseki's intertextual practice, see Saeki Takahiro, "Kiseki katagi-mono no hōhō: Saikaku riyō no ito," in *Ejima Kiseki to katagi-mono* (Wakakusa Shobō, 2004), 54-96; Nakajima Takashi, "Saikaku to Kiseki: 'Mohō' no bigaku," *Kokugo to kokubungaku* 80, no. 5 (2003): 23-33.
6. For detailed discussion, see Pierre Bourdieu, *Outline of a Theory of Practice*, trans. Richard Nice (Cambridge University Press, 1977), 72-95; *Distinction: A Social Critique of the Judgement of Taste* (Harvard University Press, 1984), 467-70.
7. David Atherton, *Writing Violence: The Politics of Form in Early Modern Japanese Literature* (Columbia University Press, 2023), 13. See also Herman Ooms, "Forms and Norms in Edo Arts and Society," in *Edo Art in Japan, 1615-1868*, ed. Robert T. Singer (National Gallery of Art, 1998).
8. Laura Moretti, *Pleasure in Profit: Popular Prose in Seventeenth-Century Japan* (Columbia University Press, 2020), 19.
9. Here I am informed by Herman Ooms's rich work on the problem of ideology in Tokugawa Japan and the place of Song Confucian thought in it. See "Neo-Confucianism and the Formation of Early Tokugawa Ideology: Contours of a Problem," in *Confucianism and Tokugawa Culture*, ed. Peter Nosco (Princeton University Press, 1984), 27-61; *Tokugawa Ideology: Early Constructs, 1570-1680* (Princeton University Press, 1985), esp. chap. 1.
10. Peter Flueckiger, "Literary Thought in Confucian Ancient Learning and Kokugaku," in *The Cambridge History of Japanese Literature*, ed. Haruo Shirane and Tomi Suzuki, with David Lurie (Cambridge University Press, 2016), 479-80.
11. Nakamura Yukihiko, "Bakusho Sōgakusha-tachi no bungakukan," in *Kinsei bungei shichō ron*, Nakamura Yukihiko chojutsushū 1 (Iwanami Shoten, 1975), 7-30. See also

5. REPRESENTING NORMALITY

Daniel Poch, *Licentious Fictions: Ninjō and the Nineteenth-Century Japanese Novel* (Columbia University Press, 2020), 33–35.
12. Nakamura, "Bungaku wa 'ninjō o iu' no setsu," in *Kinsei bungei shichō ron*, 61–64.
13. Fuji Akio and Hiroshima Susumu, eds., *Ihara Saikaku shū 4*, Shinpen Nihon koten bungaku zenshū 69 (Shōgakkan, 2000), 319.
14. The following discussion draws from Saeki Takahiro, "Katagi: kinsei shōsetsu no jinbutsu keizō," *Edo bungaku*, no. 34 (2006): 169–75; Ishikawa Junjirō, "Ejima Kiseki katagi-mono josetsu," *Kokubungaku kenkyū*, no. 17 (1958): 109–27; Nishijima Atsuya, "Ukiyo-zōshi shi no zahyōjiku: Kinsei shōsetsu to shite no tokuchō," in *Saikaku to ukiyo-zōshi* (Ōfūsha, 1989), 343–59.
15. Shinmura, "Nihon katagi," 140–43; Takayama, "Zattsu kyarakutarisutikku," 206–10.
16. Noma Kōshin, ed., *Saikaku shū 2*, Nihon koten bungaku taikei 48 (Iwanami Shoten, 1960), 48, 79. Citations that follow refer to this edition, abbreviated as NKBT 48. For a discussion of the story, see chapter 1.
17. Nakamura Yukihiko, *Kinsei chōnin shisō*, Nihon shisō taikei 59 (Iwanami Shoten, 1975), 89.
18. Asao Naohiro, "Jūhasseiki no shakai hendō to mibun-teki chūkansō," in *Kindai e no shidō*, Nihon no kinsei 10, ed. Tsuji Tatsuya (Chūō Kōronsha, 1993), 52–60.
19. See, for example, Donald Shively, "Sumptuary Regulation and Status in Early Tokugawa Japan," *Harvard Journal of Asiatic Studies* 25 (1964–1965): 123–64.
20. Ishikawa Ken, ed. *Yamato zokkun* (Iwanami Shoten, 1938), 53; for other examples of Ekiken's use of *kishitsu*, see, for example, 90, 118, 148, 181. In his philosophical works, Ekiken gave voice to reservations about Song Confucian metaphysics, but such qualms are largely absent from his popular didactic works. Regarding Kaibara Ekiken's skeptical response to Song Confucianism, see Masao Maruyama, *Studies in the Intellectual History of Tokugawa Japan*, trans. Mikiso Hane (Princeton University Press, 1974), 61–67. For broader background on Ekiken's thought and publications, see, for example, Tetsuo Najita, "Intellectual Change in Early Eighteenth-Century Tokugawa Confucianism," *Journal of Asian Studies* 34, no. 4 (1975): 931–44; Mary Evelyn Tucker, *Moral and Spiritual Cultivation in Japanese Neo-Confucianism: The Life and Thought of Kaibara Ekken (1630–1714)* (State University of New York Press, 1989).
21. Kaibara Ekiken, *Yōjōkun, Wazoku dōjikun*, ed. Ishikawa Ken (Iwanami Shoten, 1961), 237.
22. Tsutsumi Kunihiko, "Seken musuko katagi to Ekiken kyōkunsho: Chōnin rinri no bungeika," in *Edo no kaiitan* (Perikansha, 2004), 226–47.
23. Citations for Kiseki's works refer are taken from Hachimonjiyabon Kenkyūkai, eds., *Hachimonjiyabon zenshū*, 23 vols. (Kyūko Shoin, 1992–2013) [HZS, followed by the volume and page numbers]. HZS 6:3.
24. David Gundry notes that this text (like much of Saikaku's writing) contains an ideological ambivalence and complexity that at times seem to relativize its more serious didactic claims. See *Parody, Irony and Ideology in the Fiction of Ihara Saikaku* (Brill, 2017), 159–96. I follow Gundry's observation that the text is "morally ambiguous rather than amoral" (196) and situate it generally within the author's affirmative exploration of the didactic tradition as discussed in chapter 3.
25. HZS 6:28–31. For a discussion of the story, see chapter 4.

5. REPRESENTING NORMALITY

26. Fuji Akio, Inoue Toshiyuki, and Satake Akihiro, eds., *Kōshoku nidai otoko, Saikaku shokoku banashi, Honchō nijū fukō*, Shin Nihon koten bungaku taikei 76 (Iwanami Shoten, 1991), 489–93. For analysis, see Gundry, *Parody, Irony and Ideology*, 190–96.
27. Regarding the light and humorous quality of Kiseki's *katagi-mono*, see, for example, Saeki, "Katagi-mono no sōshutsu," 36–45; Shinohara Susumu, "Seken musume katagi ron," *Hirosaki Gakuin Daigaku, Hirosaki Gakuin Tanki Daigaku Kiyō* 16 (1980): 12–14.
28. HZS 6:22. For a discussion of the story, see chapter 4.
29. On the expansion of the readership for popular fiction at this time, see, for example, Nishijima Atsuya, "Katagi-mono no seiritsu: Dokusha no zōka to teizokuka," in *Saikaku to ukiyo-zōshi*, 361–68.
30. Regarding the influence of joke-telling and jest books on Kiseki's writing, see Saeki Takahiro, "Kiseki katagi-mono to hanashi-bon," in *Ejima Kiseki to katagi-mono*, 128–152; Shinohara Susumu, "Seken musuko katagi ron," *Hirosaki Gakuin Daigaku, Hirosaki Gakuin Tanki Daigaku Kiyō* 15 (1979): 40–43.
31. HZS 6:64.
32. Hasegawa Tsuyoshi, ed., *Ukiyo-zōshi shū*, Shinpen Nihon koten bungaku zenshū 65 (Shōgakkan, 2000), 84–89.
33. Shinohara, "Seken musuko katagi ron," 38.
34. Georg Simmel, "The Metropolis and Mental Life," in *Simmel on Culture: Selected Writings*, ed. David Frisby and Mike Featherstone (Sage Publications, 1998), 174–85.
35. Fuji, Inoue, and Satake, eds., *Kōshoku nidai otoko*, 264.
36. Saeki, "Katagi-mono no sōshutsu," 19–26.
37. My characterization of the evolution of Kiseki's style in *Seken musume katagi* draws partial inspiration from Hasegawa, *Ukiyo-zōshi no kenkyū*, 363–65; Shinohara, "Seken musume katagi ron," 1–23.
38. HZS 6:479.
39. For discussion of *Onna daigaku takarabako*, see Yabuta Yutaka, "Kinsei josei no saihakken," in *Nihon kinsei-shi no kanōsei* (Azekura Shobō, 2005), 143–51; Martha C. Tocco, "Norms and Texts for Women's Education in Tokugawa Japan," in *Women and Confucian Cultures in Premodern China, Korea, and Japan*, ed. Dorothy Ko, JaHyun Kim Haboush, and Joan R. Piggott (University of California Press, 2003), 199–200.
40. HZS 6:485–89.
41. HZS 6:490–94. For a discussion of the story, see chapter 4.
42. HZS 6:496–501.
43. Saeki, "Kiseki katagi-mono no hōhō," 65–70. See also Emoto Hiroshi, "Ejima Kiseki no hōhō josetsu: Saikaku hyōsetsu o tōshite," *Kokugo to kokubungaku* 80, no. 5 (2003): 12–22.
44. Nakajima, "Saikaku to Kiseki."
45. HZS 6:481–85. The title turns on a pun of "get someone under one's thumb" (*shiri ni shiku*, literally "lay down under one's buttocks") and *shikigane* (dowry).
46. HZS 6:481.
47. HZS 6:496–501.
48. HZS 6:497.
49. The term "sense of reality" was coined by Hasegawa, in *Ukiyo-zōshi no kenkyū*, 477. For a further discussion, see Saeki Takahiro, "*Ukiyo oyaji katagi* no genjitsukan,"

5. REPRESENTING NORMALITY

in *Ejima Kiseki to katagi-mono*, 179–207; Shinohara Susumu, "*Ukiyo oyaji katagi* ron," *Hirosaki Gakuin Daigaku, Hirosaki Gakuin Tanki Daigaku kiyō* 19 (1983): 43–58.

50. Watanabe Kenji, "Ukiyo-zōshi no bakamono-tachi: *Ukiyo oyaji katagi* o chūshin ni," in *Bungaku ni okeru chichi to ko*, ed. Satō Yasumasa (Kasama Shoin, 1983), 61–64, 71–78.
51. HZS 7:451–57.
52. HZS 7:456.
53. Regarding Kiseki's prose style, see Saeki, "Kiseki katagi-mono no bunshō," in *Ejima Kiseki to katagi-mono*, 153–78; Shinohara, "*Ukiyo oyaji katagi* ron," 53–54; Hamada Keisuke, "Saikaku-ryū no buntai ni tsuite: Sono sōsei to taitō," in *Kinsei shōsetsu: keii to yōshiki ni kan suru shiken* (Kyoto Daigaku Gakujutsu Shuppankai, 1993), 108–10.
54. HZS 7:457–61.
55. HZS 7:463–66.
56. HZS 7:475–78.
57. Peter Flueckiger, *Imagining Harmony: Poetry, Empathy, and Community in Mid-Tokugawa Confucianism and Nativism* (Stanford University Press, 2001), 127.
58. Lawrence E. Marceau, "Bunjin (Literati) and Early Yomihon: Nankaku, Nankai, Buson, Gennai, Teishō, Ayatari, and Akinari," in Shirane, Suzuki, and Lurie, *Cambridge History of Japanese Literature*, 488–92.
59. W. Puck Brecher, *The Aesthetics of Strangeness: Eccentricity and Madness in Early Modern Japan* (University of Hawaii Press, 2013), 5. See also Patti Kameya, "When Eccentricity Is Virtue: Virtuous Deeds in *Kinsei kijinden* (*Eccentrics of Our Times*, 1790)," *Early Modern Japan* 17 (2009): 7–21.
60. Regarding Nagaidō Kiyū, see Nishijima Atsuya, "Nagaidō Kiyū no denki: makki sakusha no tenkei," in *Saikaku to ukiyo-zōshi*, 491–512.
61. Shinohara, "*Ukiyo oyaji katagi* ron," 43.

EPILOGUE: FROM THE TEXTUAL TOWNSMAN TO EDO URBANISM

1. The authoritative treatment of Edo *gesaku* remains Nakamura Yukihiko, *Gesaku-ron*, Nakamura Yukihiko chojutsushū 8 (Iwanami Shoten, 1982). In English, see Adam L Kern, *Manga from the Floating World: Comicbook Culture and the Kibyōshi of Edo Japan* (Harvard University Asia Center, 2006), chap. 2; Sumie Jones with Kenji Watanabe, eds., *An Edo Anthology: Literature from Japan's Mega-City, 1750–1850* (University of Hawaii Press, 2013), 1–38.
2. Hamada Gi'ichirō, Suzuki Katsutada, and Mizuno Minoru, eds., *Kibyōshi senryū kyōka*, Nihon koten bungaku zenshū 46 (Shōgakkan, 1971), 117–37. For English translations, see Jones, *An Edo Anthology*, 185–218; Kern, *Manga from the Floating World*, 339–426.
3. Regarding Kyōden's brush with shogunal censorship, see Peter F. Kornicki, "Nishiki no Ura: An Instance of Censorship and the Structure of a Sharebon," *Monumenta Nipponica* 32, no. 2 (1977): 153–62.

EPILOGUE

4. Mizuno Minoru, ed., *Kibyōshi sharebon shū*, NKBT 59 (Iwanami Shoten, 1958), 86–105; for an English translation, see Kern, *Manga from the Floating World*, 263–38.
5. See, for example, Nakano Mitsutoshi, *Edo no hanpon* (Iwanami Shoten, 1995), 11–18; *Wahon no susume: Edo o yomitoku tame ni* (Iwanami Shoten, 2011), 73–120.
6. Katsuya Hirano, *The Politics of Dialogic Imagination: Power and Popular Culture in Early Modern Japan* (University of Chicago Press, 2014), esp. chap. 3.
7. Nakano Mitsutoshi, Jinbō Kazuya, and Maeda Ai, eds., *Sharebon kokkeibon ninjōbon*, Nihon koten bungaku zenshū 47 (Shōgakkan, 1971), 33–51. For an English translation, see Jones, *An Edo Anthology*, 45–60.
8. I have borrowed this memorable translation from Jones, *An Edo Anthology*, 53.
9. Jones, *An Edo Anthology*, 46; a similar reading is suggested by Nakamura Yukihiko in *Gesakuron*, 80–81. Nakano Mitsutoshi, in contrast, argues that the text expresses no sense of social critique other than a "wholesome" (*kenzen*) playfulness. See "Bunjin to zenki gesaku," in *Jūhasseiki no Edo bungei: Ga to zoku no seijuku* (Iwanami Shoten, 1999), 210–17.
10. I have developed this point at length in "Urban Fictions of Early Modern Japan: Identity, Media, Genre" (PhD diss., Columbia University, 2016), chap. 3.
11. Jinbō Kazuya, ed., *Ukiyoburo, Gejō suigen maku no soto, Daisen sekai gakuyasagashi*, Shin Nihon koten bungaku taikei 86 (Iwanami Shoten, 1989); Nakano, Jinbō, and Ai, *Sharebon kokkeibon ninjōbon*, 255–369.
12. Regarding Sanba as a townsman author, see, for example, Robert W. Leutner, *Shikitei Sanba and the Comic Tradition in Edo Fiction* (Council on East Asian Studies, Harvard University, and the Harvard-Yenching Institute, 1985), 49–51.
13. Hirano, *Politics of Dialogic Imagination*, 95–97.
14. Kyokutei Bakin, *Kinsei mono no hon Edo sakusha burui*, ed. Tokuda Takeshi (Iwanami Shoten, 2014), 55. Regarding Sanba's biography, see Tanahashi Masahiro, *Shikitei Sanba: Edo no gesakusha* (Perikansha, 1994), 1–34; Honda Yasuo, *Shikitei Sanba no bungei* (Kasama Shoin, 1973), chap. 1.
15. I have developed this point in "The Early Modern City in Japan," in *The New Cambridge History of Japan*, vol. 2, ed. David Howell (Cambridge University Press, 2024), 654–56.
16. For commentary on treatments of "postmodern Edo," see Christopher Smith, "The Always Already (But Maybe Not Quite) Pre-Postmodern Edo," in *Interdisciplinary Edo: Toward an Integrated Approach to Early Modern Japan*, ed. Joshua Schlachet and William C. Hedberg (Routledge, 2024), 232–47.

BIBLIOGRAPHY

Akiyama Kunizō, and Nakamura Ken. *Kyōto "machi" no kenkyū*. Hōsei Daigaku Shuppankyoku, 1975.

Amino Yoshihiko. "Nihon no moji shakai no tokushitsu." In *Rettō shakai no tayōsei*, Amino Yoshihiko chosakushū 15. Iwanami Shoten, 2007.

Anderson, Benedict. *Imagined Communities: Reflections on the Origin and Spread of Nationalism*, rev. ed. Verso, 1991.

Asakura Haruhiko. *Chōjakyō*. Koten Bunko, 1954.

———, ed. *Jinrin kinmōzui*. Heibonsha, 1990.

———, ed. *Kana-zōshi shūsei* 5. Tōkyōdō Shuppan, 1984.

Asakura Haruhiko, and Ōkubo Junko, eds. *Kana-zōshi shūsei* 28. Tōkyōdō Shuppan, 2000.

Asao Naohiro. "Jūhasseiki no shakai hendō to mibun-teki chūkansō." In *Kindai e no shidō*, Nihon no kinsei 10, edited by Tsuji Tatsuya. Chūō Kōronsha, 1993.

———. "Kinsei no mibun to sono hen'yō." In *Mibun to kakushiki*, Nihon no kinsei 7, edited by Asao Naohiro. Chūō Kōronsha, 1992.

———. "Kinsei no mibunsei to senmin." In *Asao Naohiro chosakushū* 7. Iwanami Shoten, 2004.

Atherton, David C. *Writing Violence: The Politics of Form in Early Modern Japanese Literature*. Columbia University Press, 2023.

Atkins, E. Taylor. *A History of Popular Culture in Japan: From the Seventeenth Century to the Present*. Bloomsbury, 2017.

Bakhtin, M. M. *The Dialogic Imagination: Four Essays*. Edited by Michael Holquist. Translated by Caryl Emerson and Michael Holquist. University of Texas Press, 1981.

Bakhtin, Mikhail. *Rabelais and His World*. Translated by Hélène Iswolsky. Indiana University Press, 1984.

Barthes, Roland. *Mythologies*. Translated by Annette Lavers. Noonday Press, 1972.
Befu, Ben. *Worldly Mental Calculations: An Annotated Translation of Ihara Saikaku's Seken munezan'yō*. University of California Press, 1976.
Bellah, Robert N. *Tokugawa Religion: The Cultural Roots of Modern Japan*. Free Press, 1985.
Berry, Mary Elizabeth. *The Culture of Civil War in Kyoto*. University of California Press, 1994.
———. "Family Trouble: Views from the Stage and a Merchant Archive." In *What Is a Family: Answers from Early Modern Japan*, edited by Mary Elizabeth Berry and Marcia Yonemoto. University of California Press, 2019.
———. *Japan in Print: Information and Nation in the Early Modern Period*. University of California Press, 2006.
Berry, Mary Elizabeth, and Marcia Yonemoto. Introduction to Berry and Yonemoto, *What Is a Family*.
Borovoy, Amy. "Robert Bellah's Search for Community and Ethical Modernity in Japan Studies." *Journal of Asian Studies* 75, no. 2 (2016): 467–94.
Botsman, Daniel V. *Punishment and Power in the Making of Modern Japan*. Princeton University Press, 2005.
———. "Recovering Japan's Urban Past: Yoshida Nobuyuki, Tsukada Takashi, and the Cities of the Tokugawa Period." *City, Culture and Society*, no. 3 (2012): 9–14.
Bourdieu, Pierre. *Distinction: A Social Critique of the Judgement of Taste*. Translated by Richard Nice. Harvard University Press, 1984.
———. "Field of Power, Literary Field and Habitus." In *The Field of Cultural Production: Essays on Art and Literature*, edited by Randal Johnson. Columbia University Press, 1993.
———. "Is the Structure of *Sentimental Education* an Instance of Social Self-Analysis?" In Johnson, *Field of Cultural Production*.
———. *Outline of a Theory of Practice*. Translated by Richard Nice. Cambridge University Press, 1977.
———. "Social Space and the Genesis of 'Classes.'" Translated by Gino Raymond and Matthew Adamson. In *Language and Symbolic Power*, edited by John B. Thompson. Polity Press, 1991.
Bowring, Richard. *In Search of the Way: Thought and Religion in Early-Modern Japan, 1582–1860*. Oxford University Press, 2017.
Brecher, W. Puck. *The Aesthetics of Strangeness: Eccentricity and Madness in Early Modern Japan*. University of Hawaii Press, 2013.
Butler, Judith. "Performativity's Social Magic." In *Bourdieu: A Critical Reader*, edited by Richard Shusterman. Blackwell Publishers, 1999.
Certeau, Michel de. *The Practice of Everyday Life*. Translated by Steven Rendall. University of California Press, 1984.
Chance, Linda H. "Constructing the Classic: Tsurezuregusa in Tokugawa Readings." *Journal of the American Oriental Society* 117, no. 1 (1997): 39–56.
———. *Formless in Form: Kenkō, Tsurezuregusa, and the Rhetoric of Japanese Fragmentary Prose*. Stanford University Press, 1997.
Crawcour, E. S. "Changes in Japanese Commerce in the Tokugawa Period." *The Journal of Asian Studies* 22, no. 4 (1963): 387–400.

BIBLIOGRAPHY

———. "Some Observations on Merchants: A Translation of Mitsui Takafusa's Chōnin Kōken Roku, with an Introduction and Notes." *Transactions of the Asiatic Society of Japan*, 3rd ser., no. 8 (1962): 1–139.

Danieru Sutoryūbu. "Saikaku ni okeru kane to iro no ronri: *Tsurezuregusa* to no kanren o chūshin ni shite." *Saikaku to ukiyo-zōshi kenkyū* 3 (2010): 61–74.

Dore, R. P. *Education in Tokugawa Japan*. Center for Japanese Studies, University of Michigan, 1984.

Drixler, Fabian. "Imagined Communities of the Living and the Dead: The Spread of the Ancestor-Venerating Stem Family in Tokugawa Japan." In Berry and Yonemoto, *What Is a Family*.

Ehlers, Maren A. *Give and Take: Poverty and the Status Order in Early Modern Japan*. Harvard University Asia Center, 2018.

Eubanks, Charlotte. *Miracles of Book and Body: Buddhist Textual Culture & Medieval Japan*. University of California Press, 2011.

Emoto Hiroshi. "Ejima Kiseki no hōhō josetsu: Saikaku hyōsetsu o tōshite." *Kokugo to kokubungaku* 80, no. 5 (2003): 12–22.

———. "Hōei Shōtoku-ki ni okeru chifutan no kenkyū: *Nippon shin-eitaigura*, *Shison daikoku-bashira* o chūshin to shite." In *Kinsei zenki shōsetsu no kenkyū*. Wakakusa Shobō, 2000.

Flueckiger, Peter. *Imagining Harmony: Poetry, Empathy, and Community in Mid-Tokugawa Confucianism and Nativism*. Stanford University Press, 2001.

———. "Literary Thought in Confucian Ancient Learning and Kokugaku." In Shirane, Suzuki, and Lurie, *Cambridge History of Japanese Literature*.

Fox, Charles E. "Old Stories, New Mode: Ejima Kiseki's *Oyaji Katagi*." *Monumenta Nipponica* 43, no. 1 (1988): 63–77.

Fuji Akio. "Bannen no Saikaku no sekai." In *Saikaku e no shōtai*, edited by Teruoka Yasutaka, Asano Akira, Fuji Akio, Emoto Hiroshi, and Taniwaki Masachika. Iwanami Shoten, 1995.

———. "Kinsei setsuwa no shosō." In *Saikaku to kana-zōshi*. Chikuma Shoin, 2011.

———. "Saikaku no setsuwa-sei." In *Saikaku to kana-zōshi*.

Fuji Akio, Inoue Toshiyuki, and Satake Akihiro, eds. *Kōshoku nidai otoko, Saikaku shokoku banashi, Honchō nijū fukō*, Shin Nihon koten bungaku taikei 76. Iwanami Shoten, 1991.

Fuji Akio, and Hiroshima Susumu, eds. *Ihara Saikaku shū 4*. Shinpen Nihon koten bungaku zenshū 69. Shōgakkan, 2000.

Fujii Otoo, ed. *Ukiyo-zōshi meisaku shū*. Dai-Nihon Yūbenkai Kōdansha, 1937.

Fujiwara Noboru. "*Chōjakyō* kara *Nippon eitaigura* e: Ie ishiki o chūshin ni." *Nōtorudamu seishin joshi daigaku kokubungaku-ka kiyō* 7 (1974): 25–48.

Garrioch, David. *The Formation of the Parisian Bourgeoisie, 1690–1830*. Harvard University Press, 1996.

Gaubatz, Thomas. "Distribution Poetics: Ihara Saikaku and the Literature of the Marketplace." *East Asian Publishing and Society* 16, no. 1 (2026): 1–47.

———. "The Early Modern City in Japan." In *The New Cambridge History of Japan*, vol. 2, edited by David Howell. Cambridge University Press, 2024.

———. "Urban Fictions of Early Modern Japan: Identity, Media, Genre." PhD diss., Columbia University, 2016.

BIBLIOGRAPHY

Gay, Suzanne. *The Moneylenders of Late Medieval Kyoto.* University of Hawaii Press, 2001.
Gluck, Carol. "The Invention of Edo." In *Mirror of Modernity: Invented Traditions of Modern Japan*, edited by Stephen Vlastos. University of California Press, 1998.
Groemer, Gerald. *Street Performers and Society in Urban Japan, 1600–1900: The Beggar's Gift.* Routledge, 2016.
Gundry, David J. "Hierarchy, Hubris, and Parody in Ihara Saikaku's *Kōshoku ichidai otoko*." *Journal of Japanese Studies* 43, no. 2 (2017): 355–87.
———. *Parody, Irony and Ideology in the Fiction of Ihara Saikaku.* Brill, 2017.
Hachimonjiyabon Kenkyūkai, ed. *Hachimonjiyabon zenshū.* 23 vols. Kyūko Shoin, 1992–2013.
Hall, John W. "Rule by Status in Tokugawa Japan." *Journal of Japanese Studies* 1, no. 1 (1974): 39–49.
Hamada Gi'ichirō, Suzuki Katsutada, and Mizuno Minoru, eds. *Kibyōshi senryū kyōka.* Nihon koten bungaku zenshū 46. Shōgakkan, 1971.
Hamada Keisuke. "Saikaku-ryū no buntai ni tsuite: Sono sōsei to taitō." In *Kinsei shōsetsu: eii to yōshiki ni kansuru shiken.* Kyōto Daigaku Gakujutsu Shuppankai, 1993.
Hamada Yasuhiko. "*Nippon eitaigura*." In *Saikaku to ukiyo-zōshi no kenkyū*, edited by Taniwaki Masachika et al. Kasama Shoin, 2010.
Hanyū Noriko. "Honya Morita Shōtarō no katsudō: Santo o mezashite." In *Saikaku to shuppan media no kenkyū.* Izumi Shoin, 2000.
———. "Ihara Saikaku to shuppan shoshi: Okuda, Morita to no sōkan. In *Saikaku to shuppan media no kenkyū.*
———. "*Nippon eitaigura* no kōzō: Sōsaku shisei to kyōkun no arikata." In *Saikaku to shuppan media no kenkyū.*
———. "*Nippon eitaigura* no shuppan jijō: Santo no shoshi to Saikaku." In *Saikaku to shuppan media no kenkyū.*
———. "Shuppan bunka to sakusha: Jōkyō-ki no Saikaku o chūshin ni." In *Saikaku to shuppan media no kenkyū.*
Harashima Yōichi, "Tanomoshi." In *Nihon rekishi taikei* 3. Yamakawa Shuppansha, 1988.
Harootunian, Harry. "Late Tokugawa Culture and Thought." In *The Cambridge History of Japan*, vol. 5, *The Nineteenth Century*, edited by Marius B. Jansen. Cambridge University Press, 1989.
Harvey, David. *The Urban Experience.* Johns Hopkins University Press, 1989.
Hasegawa Tsuyoshi, ed. *Keisei iro jamisen, Keisei denju kamiko, Seken musume katagi.* Shin Nihon koten bungaku taikei 78. Iwanami Shoten, 1989.
———. "Kiseki no hōhō ippan: Tsūzoku e no michi." *Kokugo to kokubungaku* 80, no. 5 (2003): 1–11.
———, ed. *Ukiyo-zōshi daijiten.* Kasama Shoin, 2017.
———. *Ukiyo-zōshi koshō nenpyō: Hōei ikō.* Nihon shoshigaku taikei 42. Seishōdō, 1984.
———. *Ukiyo-zōshi no kenkyū: Hachimonjiya-bon o chūshin to suru.* Ōfūsha, 1969.
Hayashi Reiko. "Edo-dana no seikatsu: Shiragiya Nihonbashi-ten o chūshin to shite." In *Edo chōnin no kenkyū* 2, edited by Nishiyama Matsunosuke. Yoshikawa Kōbunkan, 1973.

BIBLIOGRAPHY

———. "Edo jidai no chōka josei-tachi." In *Edo Kamigata no ōdana to chōka josei.* Yoshikawa Kōbunkan, 2001.
———. *Edo ton'ya nakama no kenkyū: Bakufu taisei ka no toshi shōgyō shihon.* Ochanomizu Shobō, 1978.
———. "Kyōto no Kashiwabara Riyo." In *Edo Kamigata Ōdana to chōka josei.* Yoshikawa Kōbunkan, 2001.
———. "Shinkyū shōnin no kōtai." In *Shōnin no katsudō,* Nihon no kinsei 5, edited by Hayashi Reiko. Chūō Kōronsha, 1992.
Hayashiya Tatsusaburō. *Machishū: Kyōto ni okeru "shimin" keiseishi.* Chūō Kōronsha, 1964.
Hibbett, Howard. "Ejima Kiseki (1667–1736) and His Katagi-Mono." *Harvard Journal of Asiatic Studies* 14, no. 3 (1951): 404–32.
———. *The Floating World in Japanese Fiction.* Oxford University Press, 1959.
Hiraishi Naoaki. "Kinsei Nihon no 'shokugyō' kan." In *Rekishi-teki zentei,* Gendai Nihon shakai 4, edited by Tōkyō Daigaku Shakaigakka Kenkyūsho. Tokyo Daigaku Shuppankai, 1991.
Hirano, Katsuya. *The Politics of Dialogic Imagination: Power and Popular Culture in Early Modern Japan.* University of Chicago Press, 2013.
Hiroshima Susumu. "*Nippon eitaigura* ni okeru 'daifuku' to shoshō no hen'yō: Seiritsu no mondai o megutte." In *Saikaku tankyū: Chōnin-mono no sekai.* Perikansha, 2004.
Hirosue Tamotsu. *Henkai no akusho.* Heibonsha, 1973.
———. *Saikaku no shōsetsu: Jikū ishiki no tenkan o megutte.* Heibonsha, 1982.
Honda Yasuo. *Shikitei Sanba no bungei.* Kasama Shoin, 1973.
Horikiri Minoru. "'Sekai no kashiya-daishō' no jōkyō settei: Kyō no machibure ni miru kyōdōtai ishiki no shiten kara." In *Yomikaerareru Saikaku.* Perikansha, 2001.
Howell, David. *Geographies of Identity in Nineteenth-Century Japan.* University of California Press, 2005.
Hui, Andrew. "Aphorism." *New Literary History* 50, no. 3 (2019): 417–21.
———. *A Theory of the Aphorism: From Confucius to Twitter.* Princeton University Press, 2019.
Ichiko Natsuo. "Kinsei ni okeru jūhan ruihan no sho mondai." *Edo bungaku,* no. 16 (1996): 26–39.
———. "Nito-ban, santo-ban no hassei to sono imi: Saikaku-bon ni soku-shite." In *Kinsei shoki bungaku to shuppan bunka.* Wakakusa Shobō, 1998.
Ihara Saikaku. *The Life of an Amorous Woman and Other Writings.* Translated by Ivan Morris. New Directions, 1969.
Ikegami, Eiko. *Bonds of Civility: Aesthetic Networks and the Political Origins of Japanese Culture.* Cambridge University Press, 2005.
Inui Hiromi. "Ōsaka chōnin shakai to Saikaku." In *Saikaku shin tenbō.* Benseisha, 1993.
Irie Hiroshi. *Kinsei shomin kakun no kenkyū: "Ie" no keiei to kyōiku.* Taga Shuppan, 1996.
Ishikawa Junjirō. "Ejima Kiseki katagimono josetsu." *Kokubungaku kenkyū,* no. 17 (1958): 109–127.
———. "*Yakusha kuchi jamisen* seiritsu zengo: Ejima Kiseki no shūsaku jidai." *Kokubungaku kenkyū* 20, no. 10 (1960): 33–45.
Ishikawa Ken, ed. *Yamato zokkun.* Iwanami Shoten, 1938.

BIBLIOGRAPHY

Itō Hirohisa. "Toshi kūkan no bunsetsu haaku." In *Bunsetsu kōzō*, Dentō toshi 4, edited by Yoshida Nobuyuki and Itō Takeshi. Tōkyō Daigaku Shuppankai, 2010.

Itō Takeshi. "Kinsei toshi no seiritsu." In *Kinsei 1*, Iwanami kōza Nihon rekishi 10, edited by Ōtsu Tōru, Sakurai Eiji, Fujii Jōji, Yoshida Yutaka, and I Keifan. Iwanami Shoten, 2014.

Jinbō Kazuya, ed. *Ukiyoburo, Gejō suigen maku no soto, Daisen sekai gakuya-sagashi*. Shin Nihon koten bungaku taikei 86. Iwanami Shoten, 1989.

Jinbō Kazuya, Aoyama Tadakazu, Kishi Tokuzō, Taniwaki Masachika, and Hasegawa Tsuyoshi, eds. *Kanazōshi shū, ukiyozōshi shū*. Nihon koten bungaku zenshū 37. Shōgakkan, 1971.

Jinnai Hidenobu. *Tokyo: A Spatial Anthropology*. University of California Press, 1995.

Johnson, Jeffrey. "Saikaku and the Narrative Turnabout." *Journal of Japanese Studies* 27, no. 2 (2001): 323–45.

Jones, Sumie, with Kenji Watanabe, eds. *An Edo Anthology: Literature from Japan's Mega-City, 1750–1850*. University of Hawaii Press, 2013.

Kaibara Ekiken. *Yōjōkun, Wazoku dōjikun*. Edited by Ishikawa Ken. Iwanami Shoten, 1961.

Kameya, Patti. "When Eccentricity Is Virtue: Virtuous Deeds in *Kinsei kijinden* (*Eccentrics of Our Times*, 1790)." *Early Modern Japan*, no. 17 (2009): 7–21.

Kanda Hideo, Nagazumi Yasuaki, and Yasuraoka Kōsaku, eds. *Hōjōki, Tsurezuregusa, Shōbō genzō zuimonki, Tannishō*. Nihon koten bungaku zenshū 27. Shōgakkan, 1971.

Katakura Hisako. "Edo machikata ni okeru sōzoku." In *Kinsei joseishi*, edited by Kinsei Joseishi Kenkyūkai, 177–218. Yoshikawa Kōbunkan, 1986.

Kawaguchi Hiroshi. "Economic Thought Concerning Freedom and Control." In *Economic Thought in Early Modern Japan*, edited by Bettina Gramlich-Oka and Gregory Smits. Brill, 2010.

Kawai Masumi. "Yakusha hyōbanki no kaikōbu: Saikaku sakuhin no riyō o megutte." *Kokugo kokubun* 50 (1981): 27–42.

Keene, Donald. *Essays in Idleness: The Tsurezuregusa of Kenkō*. Columbia University Press, 1967.

——. *World Within Walls: Japanese Literature of the Pre-Modern Era, 1600–1867*. Holt, Rinehart and Winston, 1978.

Kern, Adam L. *Manga from the Floating World: Comicbook Culture and the Kibyōshi of Edo Japan*. Harvard University Asia Center, 2006.

Konta Yōzō. "Genroku Kyōhō-ki ni okeru shuppan shihon no keisei to sono rekishiteki igi ni tsuite." *Hisutoria* 19 (1957): 59–62.

——. *Edo no hon'ya-san: kinsei bunkashi no sokumen*. Heibonsha, 2009.

Konta Yōzō, Nakano Mitsutoshi, Munemasa Isoo, and Ogata Tsutomu. "Zadankai: Kinsei no shuppan." *Bungaku* 49, no. 11 (1981): 1–31.

Ku Tefun. "Genroku no chōnin shakai to yūgei: Saikaku no yūgeikan o chūshin to shite." In *Yūgei bunka to dentō*, edited by Kumakura Isao. Yoshikawa Kōbunkan, 2003.

Kumakura Isao. "Kinsei ni okeru geinō no tenkai." In *Dentō geinō no tenkai*, Nihon no kinsei 11, edited by Kumakura Isao. Chūō Kōronsha, 1993.

——. "Nihon yūgeishi jokō." In *Yūgei bunka to dentō*, edited by Kumaura Isao. Yoshikawa Kōbunkan, 2003.

BIBLIOGRAPHY

Kurakazu Masae. "Ejima Kiseki no yakusha hyōbanki to genroku makki no ukiyo-zōshi." *Edo bungaku*, no. 23 (2001): 108–19.

———. "Saikaku to Kiseki: Ukiyo-zōshi shi no ichi sokumen." *Kinsei bungei kenkyū to hyōron*, no. 22 (1982): 14–23.

Kuriyama, Shigehisa. "The Historical Origins of Katakori." *Japan Review* 9 (1997): 127–49.

Kyokutei Bakin. *Kinsei mono no hon Edo sakusha burui*. Edited by Tokuda Takeshi. Iwanami Shoten, 2014.

Kyōto-shi Rekishi Shiryōkan, ed. *Kyōto machi shikimoku shūsei*. Sōsho Kyōto no shiryō 3. Kyōto-shi Rekishi Shiryōkan, 1999.

Kornicki, Peter F. *The Book in Japan: A Cultural History from the Beginnings to the Nineteenth Century*. University of Hawaii Press, 2001.

———. "Nishiki no Ura: An Instance of Censorship and the Structure of a Sharebon." *Monumenta Nipponica* 32, no. 2 (1977): 153–62.

———. "Women, Education, and Literacy." In *The Female as Subject: Reading and Writing in Early Modern Japan*, edited by Peter F. Kornicki, Mara Patessio, and G. G. Rowley. Center for Japanese Studies, University of Michigan, 2010.

Lefebvre, Henri. *Critique of Everyday Life*, vol. 1. Verso, 2008.

———. *The Production of Space*. Translated by Donald Nicholson-Smith. Blackwell, 1991.

———. *The Urban Revolution*. Translated by Robert Bononno. University of Minnesota Press, 2003.

Leupp, Gary P. *Servants, Shophands, and Laborers in the Cities of Tokugawa Japan*. Princeton University Press, 1992.

Leutner, Robert W. *Shikitei Sanba and the Comic Tradition in Edo Fiction*. Council on East Asian Studies, Harvard University, and the Harvard-Yenching Institute, 1985.

Maeda Kingorō, ed. *Saikaku oridome*. Kadokawa Shoten, 1973.

———, ed. *Seken munazan'yō*. Kadokawa Shoten, 1972.

———, ed. *Shinchū Nippon eitaigura*. Taishūkan Shoten, 1968.

Makita Rieko. "Kinsei Kyōto ni okeru josei no kasan shoyū." In *Kinsei joseishi*, edited by Kinsei Joseishi Kenkyūkai. Yoshikawa Kōbunkan, 1986.

———. "Shōka josei no rōdō: Shufu to hōkōnin." In *Josei rōdō no Nihonshi: kodai kara gendai made*, edited by Sōgō Joseishi Kenkyūkai. Bensei Shuppan, 2019.

Marceau, Lawrence E. "Bunjin (Literati) and Early Yomihon: Nankaku, Nankai, Buson, Gennai, Teishō, Ayatari, and Akinari." In Shirane, Suzuki, and Lurie, *Cambridge History of Japanese Literature*.

Matsuda Osamu. "Neko no toshigaku." In *Edo itan bungaku nōto*. Seidosha, 1993.

Matsumoto Shirō. *Jōkamachi*. Yoshikawa Kōbunkan, 2013.

———. *Saikaku to Genroku jidai*. Shin Nihon Shuppansha, 2001.

Maruyama, Masao. *Studies in the Intellectual History of Tokugawa Japan*. Translated by Mikiso Hane. Princeton University Press, 1974.

Mayama Seika. "Saikaku to Edo chiri." In *Mayama Seika zuihitsu senshū* 2. Dai-Nihon Yūbenkai Kōdansha, 1952.

Maza, Sarah. *The Myth of the French Bourgeoisie: An Essay on the Social Imaginary, 1750–1850*. Harvard University Press, 2003.

McClain, James L. *Kanazawa: A Seventeenth-Century Japanese Castle Town*. Yale University Press, 1982.

Mills, D. E. *A Collection of Tales from Uji: A Study and Translation of Uji Shūi Monogatari*. Cambridge University Press, 1970.
Mitsui Bunko, ed. *Mitsui jigyō-shi: hon-pen dai 1-kan*. Mitsui Bunko, 1980.
Miyamoto Mataji. *Kinsei shōnin ishiki no kenkyū*. Miyamoto Mataji chosakushū 2. Kōdansha, 1977.
Mizuno Minoru, ed. *Kibyōshi sharebon shū*, NKBT 59. Iwanami Shoten, 1958.
Mizuno Minoru, and Uzuki Hiroshi, eds. *Edo chōnin bungaku*. Iwanami kōza Nihon bungakushi 7. Iwanami Shoten, 1959.
Moretti, Laura. "Kanazōshi Revisited: The Beginnings of Japanese Popular Literature in Print." *Monumenta Nipponica* 65, no. 2 (2010): 297–356.
———. *Pleasure in Profit: Popular Prose in Seventeenth-Century Japan*. Columbia University Press, 2020.
Moriya Takeshi. *Genroku bunka: yūgei, akusho, shibai*. Kōdansha, 2011.
———. "Kinsei no chōnin to yūgei." In *Kinsei geinō bunkashi no kenkyū*. Kōbundō, 1992.
———. "*Yūgei* and *Chōnin* Society in the Edo Period." *Acta Asiatica* 33 (1977): 32–54.
Morris, Brian. "What We Talk About When We Talk About 'Walking in the City.'" *Cultural Studies* 18, no. 5 (2004): 675–97.
Morson, Gary Saul. "The Aphorism: Fragments from the Breakdown of Reason." *New Literary History* 34, no. 3 (2003): 409–29.
———. "Bakhtin, the Genres of Quotation, and the Aphoristic Consciousness." *Slavic and East European Journal* 50, no. 1 (2006): 213–27.
Murata Atsushi, ed. *Nippon eitaigura*. Shinchō Nihon koten shūsei 9. Shinchōsha, 1977.
Nagao Michio. "*Risshin daifukuchō* no shisei: *Nippon eitaigura* no juyō to hihan." *Kinsei bungei: kenkyū to hyōron* 22 (1982): 24–37.
Nagatomo Chiyoji. *Chōhōki no chōhōki: Seikatsushi hyakka jiten hakkutsu*. Rinsen Shoten, 2005.
———. "Chōhōki no genryū: *Kenai chōhōki* to *Chūya chōhōki*." In *Edo jidai no tosho ryūtsū*. Shibunkaku Shuppan, 2002.
———. "Edo jidai no hon'ya." In *Edo jidai no tosho ryūtsū*. Shibunkaku Shuppan, 2002.
———. "*Kingin mannōgan* to *Nippon eitaigura*." In *Edo jidai no shomotsu to dokusho*. Tōkyōdō Shuppan, 2001.
———, ed. *Onna chōhōki, Nan chōhōki: Genroku wakamono kokoroeshū*. Shakai Shisōsha, 1993.
———. "Saikaku no sakusha kankyō, shuppan shoshi, dokusha." In *Saikaku o manabu hito no tame ni*, edited by Taniwaki Masachika and Nishijima Atsuya. Sekai Shisōsha, 1993.
———. "Saikaku to shoshi to dokusha." In *Genroku bungaku no kaika 1: Saikaku to Genroku no shōsetsu*, Kōza Genroku no bungaku 2, edited by Asano Akira et al. Benseisha, 1992.
Najita, Tetsuo. "Intellectual Change in Early Eighteenth-Century Tokugawa Confucianism." *Journal of Asian Studies* 34, no. 4 (1975): 931–44.
———. *Ordinary Economies in Japan: A Historical Perspective, 1750–1950*. University of California Press, 2009.
———. *Visions of Virtue in Tokugawa Japan: The Kaitokudō Merchant Academy of Osaka*. University of Chicago Press, 1987.

BIBLIOGRAPHY

Nakada Yasunao. *Mitsui Takatoshi*. Yoshikawa Kōbunkan, 1959.
——. "Saikaku to shinkō chōnin." *Kokubungaku: Kaishaku to kanshō* 22, no. 6 (1957): 50–54.
Nakai Nobuhiko. *Chōnin*. Nihon no rekishi 21. Shōgakkan, 1975.
——. "Commercial change and urban growth in early modern Japan." In *The Cambridge History of Japan*, vol. 4, *Early Modern Japan*, edited by John Whitney Hall. Cambridge University Press, 1991.
Nakajima Takashi. *Saikaku to Genroku media: sono senryaku to tenkai*. Nippon Hōsō Shuppan Kyōkai, 1994.
——. "Saikaku to Kiseki: 'Mohō' no bigaku." *Kokugo to kokubungaku* 80, no. 5 (2003): 23–33.
——. "Saikaku to media: *Nippon eitaigura* ihan o meguru shuppan jōkyō." In *Saikaku to Genroku bungei*. Wakakusa Shobō, 2003.
——, ed. *Seken musuko katagi, Seken musume katagi*. Shakai Shisōsha, 1990.
——. "Ukiyo-zōshi kai to Saikaku." In *Saikaku o manabu hito no tame ni*, edited by Taniwaki Masachika and Nishijima Atsuya. Sekai Shisōsha, 1993.
Nakamura Yukihiko. "Bakusho Sōgakusha-tachi no bungakukan." In *Kinsei bungei shichō ron*, Nakamura Yukihiko chojutsushū 1. Iwanami Shoten, 1982.
——. "Bungaku wa 'ninjō o iu' no setsu." In *Kinsei bungei shichō ron*, Nakamura Yukihiko chojutsushū 1. Iwanami Shoten, 1982.
——. *Gesakuron*. Nakamura Yukihiko chojutsushū 8. Iwanami Shoten, 1982.
——. "Hachimonjiya-bon no tenmatsu." In *Kinsei shōsetsu shi*, Nakamura Yukihiko chojutsushū 4. Chūō Kōronsha, 1987.
——. "Jishō Kiseki kakushitsu jidai." In *Kinsei shōsetsu-shi no kenkyū*. Ōfūsha Shuppan, 1961.
——. "Kana-zōshi no setsuwa-sei." In *Kinsei shōsetsu-shi no kenkyū*. Ōfūsha Shuppan, 1961.
——. "Kinsei bungaku no tokuchō: shogen ni kaete." In *Kinsei shōsetsu yōshiki shikō*, Nakamura Yukihiko chojutsushū 5. Chūō Kōronsha, 1982.
——, ed. *Kinsei chōnin shisō*. Nihon shisō taikei 59. Iwanami Shoten, 1975.
——. "Saikaku ni okeru setsuwa-sei han-setsuwa-sei." *Kokubungaku kaishaku to kanshō* 38, no. 4 (1973): 13–20.
——. "Saikaku no sōsaku ishiki to sono suii." In *Kinsei shōsetsu yōshiki kō*, Nakamura Yukihiko chojutsushū 5. Chūō Kōronsha, 1982.
——. "Tsurezuregusa juyō-shi." *Kokubungaku kaishaku to kanshō* 22, no. 12 (December, 1957): 62–67.
Nakano Mitsutoshi. "Bunjin to zenki gesaku." In *Jūhasseiki no Edo bungei: Ga to zoku no seijuku*. Iwanami Shoten, 1999.
——. *Edo no hanpon*. Iwanami Shoten, 1995.
——. "Gesaku kenkyū josetsu." In *Gesaku kenkyū*. Chūō Kōronsha, 1981.
——. "Jūhasseiki no Edo bunka." In *Jūhasseiki no Edo bungei: Ga to zoku no seijuku*. Iwanami Shoten, 1999.
——. "Saikaku gesakusha setsu saikō: Edo no me to gendai no me no motsu imi." *Bungaku* 15, no. 1 (2014): 140–58.
——. "The Role of Traditional Aesthetics." Translated by Maria Flutsch. In *Eighteenth Century Japan: Culture & Society*, edited by C. Andrew Gerstle. Allen & Unwin, 1989.

BIBLIOGRAPHY

———. *Wahon no susume: Edo o yomitoku tame ni*. Iwanami Shoten, 2011.
———. "Yūjo hyōbanki kenkyū: Saikaku bungaku no hito kihan." *Kinsei bungaku* 8 (1962): 21–33.
———. "Yūjo hyōbanki to yūri annai." *Kokubungaku* 9, no. 2 (1964): 59–67.
Nakano Mitsutoshi, Jinbō Kazuya, and Maeda Ai, eds. *Sharebon kokkeibon ninjōbon*. Nihon koten bungaku zenshū 47. Shōgakkan, 1971.
Nakano Setsuko. "Kinsei shomin no jendā," in *Jendā shi*, Shintaikei Nihonshi 9, edited by Ōguchi Yūjirō, Narita Ryūichi, and Fukutō Sanae. Yamakawa Shuppansha, 2014.
———. *Onna wa itsu kara yasashiku natta ka: Edo no josei-shi*. Heibonsha, 2014.
Nihon Fūzokushi Gakkai, ed. *Nihon fūzokushi jiten*. Kōbundō, 1979.
Nihon Zuihitsu Taisei Henshūbu, ed. *Tōyūshi, Okotarigusa*. Nihon zuihitsu taisei, dai 1-ki 19. Yoshikawa Kōbunkan, 1976.
Nishijima Atsuya. "Katagi-mono no seiritsu: Dokusha no zōka to teizokuka." In *Saikaku to ukiyo-zōshi*. Ōfūsha, 1989.
———. "Kaidai shuppan no ryūkō: Ukiyo-zōshi no shūen." In *Saikaku to ukiyo-zōshi*.
———. "Makki katagi-mono no hōhō: Sōgō, seiri to kyokutanka." In *Saikaku to ukiyo-zōshi*.
———. "Nagaidō Kiyū no denki: Makki sakusha no tenkei." In *Saikaku to ukiyo-zōshi*.
———. "*Nippon eitaigura* no seiritsu: Shokō to tsuikakō no ginmi." In *Saikaku to ukiyo-zōshi*.
———. "Ukiyo-zōshi shi no zahyōjiku: Kinsei shōsetsu to shite no tokushitsu." In *Saikaku to ukiyo-zōshi*.
Nishiyama Matsunosuke. "Edo bunka ni okeru kyozō to jitsuzō." In *Kinsei bunka no kenkyū*, Nishiyama Matsunosuke chosakushū 4. Yoshikawa Kōbunkan, 1983.
———, ed. *Edo chōnin no kenkyū*. 6 vols. Yoshikawa Kōbunkan, 1972–2006.
Nishiyama, Matsunosuke. *Edo Culture: Daily Life and Diversions in Urban Japan, 1600–1868*. Translated and edited by Gerald Groemer. University of Hawaii Press, 1997.
Noma Kōshin. "*Chōjakyō* kō." In *Saikaku shinkō*. Chikuma Shobō, 1948.
———. "Daibutsu-mochi raiyūsho." In *Kinsei sakka denkō*. Chūō Kōronsha, 1985.
———. "Ejima Kiseki to sono ichizoku." In *Kinsei sakka denkō*. Chūō Kōronsha, 1985.
———. "Saikaku no hōhō." In *Saikaku shin shinkō*. Iwanami Shoten, 1981.
———. "Saikaku itsutsu no hōhō." In *Saikaku shin shinkō*. Iwanami Shoten, 1981.
———. *Saikaku nenpu kōshō*, rev. ed. Chūō Kōronsha, 1983.
———, ed. *Saikaku shū 2*. Nihon koten bungaku taikei 48. Iwanami Shoten, 1960.
———. "Ukiyo-zōshi no dokushasō." In *Kinsei sakkaden kō*. Chūō Kōronsha, 1985.
———. "Ukiyo-zōshi no seiritsu." In *Saikaku shin shinkō*. Iwanami Shoten, 1981.
Noma Kōshin and Yoshida Kōichi, eds. *Hōjō Dansui shū, sōshi hen*. 4 vols. Koten Bunko, 1980.
Ōguchi Yūjirō. *Josei no iru kinseishi*. Keisō Shobō, 1995.
Ono Takeo. *Edo bukka jiten*. Tenbōsha, 1983.
Ooms, Herman. "Forms and Norms in Edo Arts and Society." In *Edo Art in Japan, 1615–1868*, edited by Robert T. Singer. National Gallery of Art, 1998.
———. "Neo-Confucianism and the Formation of Early Tokugawa Ideology: Contours of a Problem." In *Confucianism and Tokugawa Culture*, edited by Peter Nosco. Princeton University Press, 1984.
———. *Tokugawa Ideology: Early Constructs, 1570–1680*. Princeton University Press, 1985.

BIBLIOGRAPHY

———. *Tokugawa Village Practice: Class, Status, Power, Law*. University of California Press, 1996.
Poch, Daniel. *Licentious Fictions: Ninjō and the Nineteenth-Century Japanese Novel*. Columbia University Press, 2020.
Rambelli, Fabio. "The Mystery of Wealth and the Role of Divinities: The Economy in Pre-Modern Japanese Fiction and Practice." *Hualin International Journal of Buddhist Studies* 2, no. 2 (2019): 163–201.
Ramseyer, J. Mark. "Thrift and Diligence: House Codes of Tokugawa Merchant Families." *Monumenta Nipponica* 43, no. 2 (1979): 209–30.
Rancière, Jacques. *The Politics of Aesthetics: The Distribution of the Sensible*. Edited and translated by Gabriel Rockhill. Continuum, 2006.
Rubinger, Richard. *Popular Literacy in Early Modern Japan*. University of Hawaii Press, 2007.
Saeki Takahiro. "Katagi: kinsei shōsetsu no jinbutsu keizō." *Edo bungaku*, no. 34 (2006): 169–75.
———. "Kiseki katagi-mono no bunshō." In *Ejima Kiseki to katagi-mono*. Wakakusa Shobō, 2004.
———. "Katagi-mono no sōshutsu." In *Ejima Kiseki to katagi-mono*.
———. "Kiseki katagi-mono no hōhō: Saikaku riyō no ito." In *Ejima Kiseki to katagi-mono*.
———. "Kiseki katagi-mono to hanashi-bon." In *Ejima Kiseki to katagi-mono*.
———. "Kiseki no shūsakuki no yakusha hyōbanki: *Yakusha kuchi jamisen* o chūshin ni." *Kokugo to kokubungaku* 80, no. 5 (2003): 34–46.
———. "*Ukiyo oyaji katagi* no genjitsukan." In *Ejima Kiseki to katagi-mono*.
Saikaku, Ihara. *The Japanese Family Storehouse, or, The Millionaires' Gospel Modernised. Nippon eitai-gura, or Daifuku shin chōja kyō (1688)*. Translated by G. W. Sargent. Cambridge University Press, 1959.
Schalow, Paul. "Ihara Saikaku and Ejima Kiseki: The Literature of Urban Townspeople." In Shirane, Suzuki, and Lurie, *Cambridge History of Japanese Literature*.
Satoko Shimazaki. *Edo Kabuki in Transition: From the Worlds of the Samurai to the Vengeful Ghost*. Columbia University Press, 2016.
Shinohara Susumu. "Deforumashon to shite no shikake: Wakan yūjo katagi no shuhō." *Nihon bungaku* 31, no. 7 (1982): 11–24.
———, ed. *Hachimonjiya shū*. Sōsho Edo bunko 8. Kokusho Kankōkai, 1988.
———. "Kōsōki no Kiseki." *Kinsei bungei* 34 (1981): 44–64.
———. "Miren to Hachimonjiya." *Hirosaki Gakuin Daigaku Hirosaki Gakuin Tanki Daigaku kiyō* 17 (1981): 23–43.
———. "*Seken musuko katagi* ron." *Hirosaki Gakuin Daigaku, Hirosaki Gakuin Tanki Daigaku Kiyō* 15 (1979): 22–45.
———. "*Seken musume katagi* ron." *Hirosaki Gakuin Daigaku, Hirosaki Gakuin Tanki Daigaku Kiyō* 16 (1980): 1–23.
———. "*Ukiyo oyaji katagi* ron." *Hirosaki Gakuin Daigaku, Hirosaki Gakuin Tanki Daigaku Kiyō* 19 (1983): 43–58.
Shinmura Izuru. "Nihon katagi." In *Nihon no kotoba*. Sōgensha, 1940.
Shiomura Kō. "Saikaku no anji-teki shuhō." In *Kinsei zenki bungaku kenkyū: Denki, shoshi, shuppan*. Wakakusa Shobō, 2004.

Shirane, Haruo. "Setsuwa (Anecdotal) Literature: *Nihon ryōiki* to *Kokon chomonjū*." In Shirane, Suzuki, and Lurie, *Cambridge History of Japanese Literature*.
Shirane, Haruo, Tomi Suzuki, with David Lurie, eds. *The Cambridge History of Japanese Literature*. Cambridge University Press, 2016.
Shively, Donald. "Bakufu Versus Kabuki." *Harvard Journal of Asiatic Studies*, no. 18 (1955): 326–56.
———. "Popular Culture." In *The Cambridge History of Japan, vol. 4: Early Modern Japan*, edited by John Whitney Hall. Cambridge University Press, 1991.
———. "Sumptuary Regulation and Status in Early Tokugawa Japan." *Harvard Journal of Asiatic Studies* 25 (1964–1965): 123–64.
Simmel, Georg. "The Metropolis and Mental Life." In *Simmel on Culture: Selected Writings*, edited by David Frisby and Mike Featherstone. Sage Publications, 1998.
Smith, Christopher. "The Always Already (But Maybe Not Quite) Pre-Postmodern Edo." In *Interdisciplinary Edo: Toward an Integrated Approach to Early Modern Japan*, edited by Joshua Schlachet and William C. Hedberg. Routledge, 2024.
Someya Tomoyuki. "Saikaku shōsetsu to jūnana-seiki no keizai jōkyō: Kanbun-Genroku-ki no kōdo keizai seichō to shōka ni okeru ie no kakuritsu o haikei ni." In *Saikaku shōsetsu ron: taishō-teki kōzō to 'higashi Ajia' e no shikai*. Kanrin Shobō, 2005.
Stalker, Nancy K. *Japan: History and Culture from Classical to Cool*. University of California Press, 2018.
Stanley, Amy. *Selling Women: Prostitution, Markets, and the Household in Early Modern Japan*. University of California Press, 2012.
———. *Stranger in the Shogun's City: A Japanese Woman and Her World*. Scribner, 2020.
Stavros, Matthew. *An Urban History of Japan's Premodern Capital*. University of Hawaii Press, 2014.
Sugano Noriko, Hayashi Reiko, and Mega Atsuko. "Shomin josei no seikatsu to rōdō." In *Nihon joseishi*, edited by Wakita Haruko, Hayashi Reiko, and Nagahara Kazuko. Yoshikawa Kōbunkan, 1987.
Sugimoto Kazuhiro. "Hōei Shōtoku ki no chōnin-mono ukiyo-zōshi: 'tedai-mono' seiritsu no haikei." *Kokugo to kokubungaku* 71, no. 4 (1994): 36–47.
Takagi Shōsaku. "Bakuhan shoki no mibun to kuniyaku." In *Nihon kinsei kokka-shi no kenkyū*. Iwanami Shoten, 1990.
———. "Kinsei no mibun to heinō bunri." In *Nihon kinsei kokka-shi no kenkyū*. Iwanami Shoten, 1990.
Takahashi Akihiko. "Gujintan o meguru shōsetsu no keifu: Katagi-mono no yōshiki to hōhō." *Nihon bungaku* 38, no. 8 (1989): 10–21.
Takao Kazuhiko. *Kinsei no shomin bunka*. Iwanami Shoten, 1968.
Takayama Hiroshi. "Zattsu kyarakutarisutikku: Katagi bungaku tōzai." *Bungaku* 10, no. 1 (2009): 204–11.
Tamai Tetsuo. *Edo: ushinawareta toshi kūkan o yomu*. Heibonsha, 1986.
———. "Kinsei toshi kūkan no tokushitsu." In *Toshi no jidai*, Nihon no kinsei 9, ed. Yoshida Nobuyuki. Chūō Kōronsha, 1992.
Tanahashi Masahiro. *Shikitei Sanba: Edo no gesakusha*. Perikansha, 1994.
Tanaka Shin. "Katagi-mono no hōhō to sono genkai." *Kinsei bungei* 1 (1954): 48–56.

BIBLIOGRAPHY

——. "Saikaku no egaita kinsen: *Nippon eitaigura* kō." In *Kinsei shōsetsu ronkō*. Ōfūsha, 1985.
Tanimura, Reiko, and David Chart. "The Record of Women's Great Treasures—Pregnancy and Childbirth in the Edo Period: A Translation of Volume Three of *Onna Chōhōki*." *Asiatische Studien* 17, no. 2 (2017): 545–66.
Taniwaki Masachika. "Genroku bunka to Saikaku." In *Saikaku o manabu hito no tame ni*, edited by Taniwaki and Nishijima. Sekai Shisōsha, 1993.
——. "*Nippon eitaigura* no hito-sokumen: Inpei, kyokuhitsu, fūshi no hōhō." In *Saikaku: Kenkyū to hihyō*. Wakakusa Shobō, 1995.
——. *Nippon eitaigura seiritsu dangi: Kaisō, hihan, tenbō*. Seibundō Shuppan, 2006.
——. *Saikaku kenkyū josetsu*. Kasama Shoin, 1981.
——. "Saikaku shōsetsu no setsuwa-teki kihan: *Uji shūi*, *Senjūshō* no yakuwari." In *Saikaku kenkyū josetsu*. Shintensha, 1981.
——. "*Tsurezuregusa* to Saikaku no chōnin-mono." In *Kinsei bungei e no shiza: Saikaku o jiku to shite*. Shintensha, 1999.
Taniwaki Masachika, Jinbō Kazuya, and Teruoka Yasutaka, eds. *Ihara Saikaku shū 3*. Nihon koten bungaku zenshū 40. Shōgakkan, 1972.
Teruoka Yasutaka. "Kana-zōshi no tenbō." In *Saikaku shinron*. Chūō Kōronsha, 1981.
——. "*Nippon eitaigura* ni okeru shisō no henyō: Shokō to tsuika kō ni tsuite," In *Saikaku shinron*.
——. "*Nippon eitaigura* no seiritsu." In *Saikaku shinron*.
——. "Saikaku bannen no tēma to hōhō." In *Saikaku shinron*.
——. "Saikaku bungaku ni okeru warai." In *Saikaku shinron*.
——. "Saikaku bungaku no setsuwa-sei to hi-setsuwa-sei." In *Saikaku shinron*.
——. *Saikaku: hyōron to kenkyū*. 2 vols. Chūō Kōronsha, 1948–1950.
——. "The Pleasure Quarters and Tokugawa Culture." Translated by C. Andrew Gerstle. In *18th Century Japan: Culture and Society*, edited by C. Andrew Gerstle. Allen & Unwin, 1989.
Teruoka Yasutaka, and Higashi Akimasa, eds. *Ihara Saikaku shū 1*. Nihon koten bungaku zenshū 38. Shōgakkan, 1971.
Teruoka Yasutaka, and Noma Kōshin, eds. *Saikaku*. Kokugo kokubungaku kenkyūshi taisei 11, rev. ed. Sanseidō, 1978.
Thompson, E. P. *The Making of the English Working Class*. Vintage, 1966.
Toby, Ronald P. "Spatial Visions of Status." In *Cartographic Japan: A History in Maps*, edited by Kären Wigen, Sugimoto Fumiko, and Cary Karacas. University of Chicago Press, 2016.
Tocco, Martha C. "Norms and Texts for Women's Education in Tokugawa Japan." In *Women and Confucian Cultures in Premodern China, Korea, and Japan*, edited by Dorothy Ko, Jahyun Kim Haboush, and Joan R. Piggott. University of California Press, 2003.
Tsubouchi Shōyō, and Mizutani Futō. *Retsudentai shōsetsushi*. Shunyōdō, 1897.
Tsujimoto Masashi. "Kyōiku shakai no seiritsu." In *Kinsei 4*, Iwanami kōza Nihon rekishi 13, edited by Ōtsu Tōru, Sakurai Eiji, Fujii Jōji, Yoshida Yutaka, and I Keifan. Iwanami Shoten, 2015.
——. "Moji shakai no seiritsu to shuppan media." In *Kyōiku shakaishi*, edited by Tsujimoto Masashi and Okita Yukuji, Shin taikei nihonshi 16. Yamakawa Shuppansha, 2002.

BIBLIOGRAPHY

Tsukada Takashi. "Mibunsei no kōzō." In *Kinsei 2*, Iwanami kōza Nihon tsūshi 12, edited by Asao Naohiro, Amino Yoshihiko, Ishii Susumu, Kano Masanao, Hayakawa Shōhachi, and Yasumaru Yoshio. Iwanami Shoten, 1994.

———. "Kinsei mibunsei kenkyū no tenkai." In *Nihon kinsei no toshi, shakai, mibun*.

———. "Nihon kinsei no shakai-teki ketsugō." In *Nihon kinsei no toshi, shakai, mibun*.

———. *Nihon kinsei no toshi, shakai, mibun: Mibun-teki shūen o megutte*. Kadensha, 2019.

———. "Shakai shūdan o megutte." *Rekishi-gaku kenkyū* 548 (1985): 58–66.

———. "Toshi shakai no bunsetsu-teki haaku: Yoshiwara o jirei ni." In *Kinsei mibun-sei to shūen shakai*. Tōkyō Daigaku Shuppankai, 1997.

Tsutsumi Kunihiko. "Seken musuko katagi to Ekiken kyōkunsho: Chōnin rinri no bungeika." In *Edo no kaiitan*. Perikansha, 2004.

Tucker, Mary Evelyn. *Moral and Spiritual Cultivation in Japanese Neo-Confucianism: The Life and Thought of Kaibara Ekken (1630–1714)*. State University of New York Press, 1989.

Uematsu Tadahiro. *Shinōkōshō: Jukyō shisō to kanryō shihai*. Dōbunkan, 1997.

Uno, Kathleen S. "Women and Changes in the Household Division of Labor." In *Recreating Japanese Women, 1600–1945*, edited by Gail Lee Bernstein. University of California Press, 1991.

Ury, Marian. *Tales of Times Now Past: Sixty-Two Stories from a Medieval Japanese Collection*. University of California Press, 1979.

Vaporis, Constantine Nomikos. *Breaking Barriers: Travel and the State in Early Modern Japan*. Council on East Asian Studies, Harvard University, 1994.

Wahrman, Dror. *Imagining the Middle Class: The Political Representation of Class in Britain, c. 1780–1840*. Cambridge University Press, 1995.

Wakita Haruko. "The Japanese Woman in the Premodern Merchant Household." Translated by G. G. Rowley. *Women's History Review* 19, no. 2 (2010): 259–82.

———. "Women and the Creation of the *Ie* in Japan: An Overview from the Medieval Period to the Present." Translated by David P. Phillips. *U.S.-Japan Women's Journal*. English Supplement 4 (1993): 83–105.

Wakita Haruko, Hayashi Reiko, and Nagahara Kazuko, eds. *Nihon joseishi*. Yoshikawa Kōbunkan, 1987.

———. *Nihon kinsei toshi-shi no kenkyū*. Tōkyō Daigaku Shuppankai, 1994.

Watanabe Hiroshi. *Kinsei Nihon shakai to Sōgaku*. Tōkyō Daigaku Shuppankai, 1985.

Watanabe Kenji. "Ukiyo-zōshi no bakamono-tachi: *Ukiyo oyaji katagi* o chūshin ni." In *Bungaku ni okeru chichi to ko*, edited by Satō Yasumasa. Kasama Shoin, 1983.

Yabuta Yutaka. "Kinsei josei no saihakken." In *Nihon kinseishi no kanōsei*. Azekura Shobō, 2005.

———. "Moji to josei." In *Nihon kinseishi no kanōsei*. Azekura Shobō, 2005.

Yakuwa Tomohiro. "Kinsei minshū no ningen keisei to bunka." In *Kyōiku shakaishi*, Shin taikei nihonshi 16, edited by Tsujimoto Masashi and Okita Yukuji. Yamakawa Shuppansha, 2002.

Yamamoto Shinkō, ed. *Kakun shū*. Heibonsha, 2001.

Yano Kimio. "'Hatsumuma wa notte kuru shiawase.'" In *Kyokō to shite no Nippon eitaigura*. Kasama Shoin, 2002.

———. "Jo: mondai no shozai." In *Kyokō to shite no Nippon eitaigura*.

———. "*Nippon eitaigura* ni okeru Mujun to kurikaeshi." In *Kyokō to shite no Nippon eitaigura*.

BIBLIOGRAPHY

——. "Saikaku." In *Kyokō to shite no Nippon eitaigura*.
Yasumaru Yoshio. *Nihon no kindaika to minshū shisō*. Aoki Shoten, 1974.
Yokota Fuyuhiko. "'Heijin mibun' no shakai ishiki." In *Nihon shakai no shi-teki kōzō: Kinsei, kindai*, edited by Asao Naohiro Kyōju Taikan Kinenkai. Shibunkaku Shuppan, 1995.
——. "Imagining Working Women in Early Modern Japan." In *Women and Class in Japanese History*, edited by Hitomi Tonomura, Anne Walthall, and Wakita Haruko. Center for Japanese Studies, University of Michigan, 1999.
——. "Kinsei no mibunsei." In *Kinsei 1*, Iwanami kōza Nihon rekishi 10, edited by Ōtsu Tōru, Sakurai Eiji, Fujii Jōji, Yoshida Yutaka, and I Keifan. Iwanami Shoten, 2014.
——. "Kinsei-teki mibun seido no seiritsu." In *Mibun to kakushiki*, Nihon no kinsei 7, edited by Asao Naohiro. Chūō Kōronsha, 1992.
Yonemoto, Marcia. *Mapping Early Modern Japan: Space, Place, and Culture in the Tokugawa Period, 1603–1868*. University of California Press, 2003.
——. "Nihonbashi: Edo's Contested Center." *East Asian History* 17/18 (1999): 49–70.
——. *The Problem of Women in Early Modern Japan*. University of California Press, 2016.
Yoshida Nobuyuki. "Chōnin to chō." In *Kinsei toshi shakai no mibun kōzō*. Tōkyō Daigaku Shuppankai, 1998.
——. *Dentō toshi, Edo*. Tōkyō Daigaku Shuppankai, 2012.
——. "Furi-uri." In *Nihon toshi-shi nyūmon 3: Hito*, edited by Takahashi Yasuo and Yoshida Nobuyuki. Tōkyō Daigaku Shuppankai, 1990.
——. "Jōkamachi no kōzō to tenkai." In *Toshi shakaishi*, Shin taikei Nihonshi 6, edited by Satō Makoto and Yoshida Nobuyuki. Yamakawa Shuppansha, 2001.
——. "Kōgi to chōnin mibun." In *Kinsei toshi shakai no mibun kōzō*. Tōkyō Daigaku Shuppankai, 1998.
——. *Mibun-teki shūen to shakai-bunka kōzō*. Buraku Mondai Kenkūjo, 2003.
——. *Seijuku suru Edo*. Nihon no rekishi 17. Kōdansha, 2009.
——. *Toshi: Edo ni ikiru*. Iwanami Shoten, 2015.
Yoshida Nobuyuki, and Itō Takeshi, eds. *Dentō toshi*, 4 vols. Tōkyō Daigaku Shuppankai, 2010.

INDEX

Figures are indicated by "*f*" after the page number.

Abumiya Sōzaemon, 63–65, 76, 223
Actor's Vocal Shamisen, The (*Yakusha kuchi jamisen*, Kiseki), 175
aesthetic practice, social identity and, 184
aesthetic publics, 183
agricultural production, impact of interregional markets on, 80
akusho. *See* prostitution
alienation. *See* townsman households
Amino Yoshihiko, 22
Amiya (fict.), 103–108, 109, 117, 124
amusement (*kokkei*), 8
Analects, 197–198
Anderson, Benedict, 52, 87, 259
anecdotal narratives (*setsuwa*): characteristics of, 140–141; description of, 137–139; diversity of narrative content in, 144; early modern legacy of, 290n19; Nakamura on, 140; *setsuwa*-esque narrative, 166, 167
aphorisms: aphoristic rationalism, 145–152, 156, 157, 165; aphoristic rhetoric, in *Eternal Storehouse*, 163–164; dictums, aphorisms versus, 149; Joken's use of, 2; Morson on, 290n30; precious sayings (*kingen*), 152; proverbs, 158; Saikaku's use of, 85; in "A Winter Thunderbolt Brings Injury," 160–161
Aratoya Magobei, 29
arts. *See* leisure arts
Atherton, David, 9–10, 219
authorship: Bourdieu on, 211; cultural illegibility of, 207–208

Baigan. *See* Ishida Baigan
Bakhtin, Mikhail, 36, 136
Barthes, Roland, 157
"Bathtub Tycoon for the Provinces, A" (*Kuni ni utsushite furogama no daijin*, Saikaku), 81
beggars, 128
Bellah, Robert, 288n46
Berry, Mary Elizabeth, 25, 26, 52
Biography of Lady Seki, The (*Seki fujin den*, Matsuake), 261–262
books: boundaries and, 26; status system for, 258
Borovoy, Amy, 288n46

INDEX

boundaries: books and, 26; between commoners and outcasts, 128; of community of the marketplace, 120

Bourdieu, Pierre, 21, 171, 183, 184, 207, 211, 217

"Brawny Old Man Who Loved Wrestling, A" (*Sumō o tanoshimu gōriki oyaji*, Kiseki), 243, 244–246

Brecher, W. Puck, 251

brokers: broker millionaires (*toiya chōja*), 62, 64–65, 76; great brokers (*ōdoiya*), 63; lesser brokers (*kotoiya*), 63; purchasing brokers (*kai-toiya*), 61–62; *toiya* (purchasing broker), 62, 63, 65

brothel districts. See prostitution

Buddhism: conceptions of origins of wealth, 104; scholarship, as leisure art, 191; temples, lending by, 103–104, 106–107

bunbu ryōdō. See two paths of martial and literary arts

bunjin (literatus), 251

"Burial Mound for Debts on Mount Kōya, A" (*Kōya-san shakusen-zuka no seshu*, Saikaku), 153

calligraphy, 194

castle towns (*jōkamachi*), 3, 112, 114

Certeau, Michel de: on narrative, 118; on sense of vision, 113; on strategies versus tactics, 91; on tactics, 93-94, 108, 129; on urban walking, 108–109

"Chanting His Way into His Clients' Pockets, *Jōruri* Became Business Capital" (*Tokuigata o kataritsukeru jōruri wa akinai no motode*, Kiseki), 190–191

character pieces. See *katagi-mono*

Characters of Contemporary Students (*Tōsei shosei katagi*, Tsubouchi Shōyō), 296–297n1

Characters of Drunkards (*Namaei katagi*, Shikitei Sanba), 214

Characters of Old Men of the Floating World (*Ukiyo oyaji katagi*, Kiseki), 176, 214, 241–251, 244f; borrowings and elaborations in, 246–247; characters in, 249, 250; narrative structure of, 247–248; on pretensions of the elite, 245; prose style of, 248; reception of, 241–242; summary of, 253

Characters of Popular Linked Verse Poets (*Fūzoku haijin katagi*, Nagaidō Kiyū), 253

Characters of Worldly Clerks (*Seken tedai katagi*, Kiseki), 190–191, 214

Characters of Worldly Young Men (*Seken musuko katagi*, Kiseki): borrowings and elaborations in, 246; causal logic of moral karma in, 247; humor in, 188; *katagi*, use of term, 214; leisure arts in, 193; mentioned, 41, 256–257; possible autobiographical reading of, 206–207; publication of, 226–227; subjects of, 176–177; *Worldly Young Women*, comparison with, 232

Characters of Worldly Young Women (*Seken musume katagi*, Kiseki), 41, 176, 214, 232–233, 247

Cheng Yi (Tei I), 220

Chikamatsu Monzaemon, 29, 174

chō (urban blocks or wards): changing status of, 18; community of, 14, 56-57; description of, 14; in *Eternal Storehouse*, 55–56, 86; declining influence of, 69–72; origins of, 15; regulations of, 24–25, 56–57; socio-spatial landscape of, 51; two-sided *chō* (*ryōgawa-chō*), 14

chōhōki (records of great treasures), 32, 225, 265

Chōjakyō (*The Millionaires' Teachings*), 145–146, 147–150, 151–152, 155–156

chōnin (social category): as category, ambiguities within, 17; *chōnin* identity, shift in spatial locus of, 39–40; *chōnin* status group, internal hierarchies of, 66; impact of woodblock-print capitalism on, 27; question of definition of, 225; Saikaku's use of term, 81–82; scholarly treatments of emerging subjectivity of, 94; as term, use of, 16–17, 25; See also four estates

chōnin no michi. See way of the townsman

INDEX

cities: early modern, nature of, 38; growth of, 93; as spaces of flux and ephemerality, 111–112; *See also* castle towns

class(es): class consciousness, use of term, 20–21; internal class structure of townsman status group, 20; of Kiseki's protagonists, 249; leisure class, 182; markers of, 183–184; social classes, nature of, 21–22; townsman identity and, 16. *See also* four estates

"Clockmaker's Hands Move Slowly, A" (*Mawari-dōki wa tokei-zaikaku*, Saikaku), 153–154

clothiers, 67–70

commerce: circulation of merchant capital as new form of, 75; commercial enterprise, stigmatization of, 12; ethical commerce, ethos of, 130; as livelihood, 123; Saikaku on, 40

commoners: arts practiced by, 180; as audience for Osaka textual culture, 29; commoner households, impact on *chō*, 72; poetry of, 202–203; question of political significance of cultural production by, 7–8; warriors, separation from, 93. *See also* peasants

community of money, 76, 78

community of the marketplace, 49–90; basis in social mobility, 91; characteristics of, 76; collective nature of, 85; description of, 53; entrepreneurial ethos of, 78, 84; as reflection of community of readers, 90; as term, meaning of, 285n29; women's absence from, 82–83

Compilation of Ten Precepts (*Jikkinshō*), 138

conspicuous consumption, 56, 82

contingency, 153–164, 162f

contradictions: in *Eternal Storehouse*, 164–166; representation of, in *ukiyo-zōshi*, 37

copper wheel. *See* lending

copyright, 208, 295n58

countryside (*zaisho*), 253, 264

Courtesan's Amorous Shamisen, The (*Keisei iro jamisen*, Kiseki), 175

craftsmen, 54, 79, 80, 213

culture: commercial marketplace for, 180; cultural literacy, roles of, 265; manuscript culture, 25; merchant values, 262; mobility of, 187. *See also* woodblock-print culture

Cure for Love's Ills (*Kōshoku haidokusan*, Yashoku Jibun), 230

"Daikoku, Who Wore Wit as His Shelter" (*Saikaku o kasa ni kiru Daikoku*, Saikaku), 76–77, 120–128, 186

"Daikokumai" ("The Dance of the God Daikokuten"), 123

Danrin school, 28

Dansui. *See* Hōjō Dansui

"Dashing and Extravagant Young Woman of Great Renown, A" (*Seken ni kakure no nai kankatsuna ogori musume*, Kiseki), 233–234

dictums. *See* aphorisms

didactic literature: entrepreneurial handbooks, 51; *Eternal Storehouse* as, 153; *setsuwa*, 138

didacticism (*kyōkun*): amusement and, 8; of *kana-zōshi*, 139; in Saikaku's works, 35, 135–145, 165–166; of Tokugawa popular fiction, 10–11

disownment, legal, 120–121

Dōtetsu (fict.), 202–203

duties (*yaku*), 97

eccentricity, 241–251; of aging parents, 242; deviation from townsman's normality, 241; discourses of, 251; *katagi-mono*'s fixation on, 214, 215, 217; in Kiseki's works, 229, 230, 246; nature of, 214; tension with normativity, 218; social consequences of, 248; transgressive energy as, 250

Echigoya. *See* Mitsui

economy: domestic, transformation of, 17–18; domestic consumer economy, 66; economic activities of warrior and peasant classes, 268; economic

economy (*continued*)
  activity, discursive constructions of, 98–99; economic causality, 142, 156, 159–160; interregional economic system, later seventeenth century, 3
edicts of compassion for living beings (*shōrui awaremi rei*), 128
Edo: beggar community of, 125; brothel culture, 262; as city of water, 113; city planning for, 112; Commoner Edo, nature of, 112; Edo kabuki, 278n13; everyday publics of downtown, 263–264; *gesaku* from, description of, 261; Hon-chō community, narrative of, 73–74; Hon-chō district clothiers, 69–70; Kanda district, 115; laboring classes, oral culture of, 264; print culture of 29–31; urbanism, formation of, 255–269
Edo Playboy. See *Grilled and Basted Edo Playboy*
education, Tokugawa shogunate's promotion of, 23
Eiko Ikegami, 25, 26; on leisure arts, 82–183
Ejima Genkichi, 211
Ejima Kiseki (Murase Gonnojō): career, 174–175, 191–192, 207, 210; dilettantism, 211; Hachimonjiya, relationship with, 210, 226, 241; Hachimonjiya's illustrated playbooks and, 293n9; as humorist, 187, 190, 261; *katagi*, use of term, 214, 297n4; *kishitsu*, use of term, 226; knowledge of townsman ideologies, 205–206; mentioned, 30, 167; Murase house, 174, 294n33; as publisher, 209; readership, relationship with, 229; Saikaku's influence on, 34, 194; social commentary of, 196; use of pen name, 210; verbal play of, 204
Ejima Kiseki, views of: on artistic literacy, 200; on fall of households, 179; on merchant elite, 245; on repute, 184–185; on townsman households, 212; on townsman's others, 190; on women's literacy, 195
Ejima Kiseki, works of: anonymous publication of early works, 207; borrowings and elaborations in, 246–247; character pieces, 5–6, 41, 252, 263, 266; eccentricity in, 230; fool's tales, 201; formal qualities of, 229; frequency of release of, 210; generic nature of characters of, 231; humorous exploration of the townsman's social norms in, 226–227; importance of, 33–34; influence of, 253–254; narrative pacing of, 248–249; nonsense in, 239–241; prose style of, 248–249; protagonists in, 228, 252; Saikaku, borrowings from, 215–216, 226–227, 234–235; as self-satire, 261; shift in concepts in, 226–229; spatial settings of, 231; subjects of, 190; townsman antiheroes in, 185; transformation of narrative forms in, 247
Ejimaya Ichirōzaemon, 209
Ejimaya imprint, 211
Ekiken. See Kaibara Ekiken
Elixir of Wealth, The (*Kingin mannōgan*, Morita Shōtarō), 146, 290n23
Enjirō (fict.), 256–257
entrepreneurialism: entrepreneurial class, requirements for self-definition of, 252; entrepreneurial endeavor, goal of, 119; entrepreneurial ethos, 40, 84, 89, 90, 133–134; entrepreneurial handbooks, 51; entrepreneurial self-fashioning, 224; entrepreneurship as self-representation, 90, 129; entrepreneurship as virtue, 126; entrepreneurial wit, 92
Essays in Idleness (*Tsurezuregusa*, Kenkō), 150–151
eta. See hereditary outcasts
Eternal Storehouse. See *Japan's Eternal Storehouse*
"Etiquette and Calligraphy for Women" (*Shorei onna yūhitsu*, Saikaku), 194–195
Eubanks, Charlotte, 138
"Even Managing a Household, She Treasured Neither Money Nor Life: The Daughter of a Samurai" (*Setai motte mo zenikane yori inochi o*

INDEX

oshimanu saburai no musume, Kiseki), 234, 238–241, 240f, 247
extemporaneous solo composition (*yakazu haikai*), 29

Familiar Bestsellers. See *Those Familiar Bestsellers*
fiction. *See* popular fiction
Five Amorous Women (*Kōshoku gonin onna*, Saikaku), 233
floating world (*ukiyo*), 98
Floating World Barbershop, The (Ukiyodoko, Sanba), 263–264
Floating World Bathhouse, The (Ukiyoburo, Sanba), 263–264
floating world booklets. See *ukiyo-zōshi*
Flueckiger, Peter, 221
folktales, 122–123
fool's tales (*gujintan*), 201
forms: conventional didactic framework, 247; in metaphysics of Song Confucian tradition, 223; of popular prose fiction, 235; of Saikaku's writings, 5; transformation of narrative forms in Kiseki's works, 247
fortune (*shiawase*), 153, 155, 158, 161, 266
"Fortune Comes Riding on the First Horse Day of Spring" (*Hatsumuma wa notte kuru shiawase*, Saikaku), 99–108, 105f, 123
four estates (*shimin*), 12, 97, 171
French bourgeoisie, 20–21
Fujiwara Noboru, 146
Fujiya Ichibei (Fuji-ichi), 88–90, 286n52
Fun'ya no Yasuhide, 202–203
furi-uri. See street peddling

gaibun. See repute
gekokujō. See low overcoming the high
gender: and the arts, 192–196; of *chōnin*, 15; class and norms for, 16; gender norms, transgressions of, 234; in *Japan's Eternal Storehouse*, 53. *See also* women
Genroku culture (*Genroku bunka*), 3, 11, 132
"Gentle Trade Winds for the Good Ship Jinzū" (*Namikaze shizuka ni Jinzū-maru*, Saikaku), 79, 83–84, 142–145

geography of status, 13
gesaku (frivolous books): of Edo, description of, 261; formation of, 255–269; political significance of the forms of literary play in, 268–269; range of social positions within, 264; Shingaku thought and, 43; urban imaginary of, 264
get-rich guides, 145–147, 265
"Girl's Domineering Dowry Gets Her Man Under Her Thumb, A" (*Otoko o shiri ni shikigane no ikō musume*, Kiseki), 235–238
gōmune. See street performers
Great Buddha rice-cake shop, 174
Great Meireki Fire, 126, 157
Great Mirror of Myriad Elegance, The (*Shoen ōkagami*, Saikaku), 32, 180
"Greater Learning for Women, The" (*Onna daigaku*), 232, 233
"Greatest Among the World's Renters" (*Sekai no kashiya-daishō*, Saikaku), 88–90
Grilled and Basted Edo Playboy (*Edo umare uwaki no kabayaki*, Kyōden), 256–257
gujintan. See fool's tales
Gundry, David, 34, 136, 283n57, 298n24

habitus, 217–218, 219, 249–250, 268
Hachimonjiya Hachizaemon (Jishō): efforts to expand readership, 228–229; Kiseki, relationship with, 208–210, 226, 241; publications from, 175; as publisher-writer, 208; rise of, 30
hanashi. See joke-telling
hanashi-bon. See jest books
Hanyū Noriko, 282n46
Harvey, David, 76, 78, 285n29
Hasegawa Tsuyoshi, 282n49
Hashiya Jinbei (fict.), 116–118, 124, 155–158
hereditary outcasts (*eta*), 128
heteroglossia, 36
"High-Interest Old Man Who Loved Money, A" (*Kane o tanoshimu kōri no oyaji*, Kiseki), 250
hinashi. See lending

Hiraishi Naoaki, 99
Hirosue Tamotsu, 35–36, 38, 101–102, 144–145
Hishikawa Moronobu, 29
history, myth's relationship to, 157–158
Hōjō Dansui, 166–167
house trade (*kagyō* or *kashoku*), 41, 172
households. *See* townsman households
Howell, David, 13, 99
Hui, Andrew, 149
hunters, 121

Ibarakiya Ryūshiken, 1, 5
identity: early modern, nature of, 26–27; meaning of, 19–20. *See also* townsman identity
ie. See townsman households
Ihara Saikaku: aphorisms, use of, 85; as apolitical stylist, 278n9; humanism of, 163; importance of, 29, 33–34; *katagi*, use of term, 222, 223; life of, 29; literacy of, 151; market economy, shifting understanding of, 154; as professional poet, 205; Saikaku-as-*gesaku*-writer, theory of, 278n9; status of, 235; writing career, major pivots in, 137–138
Ihara Saikaku, views of: on accumulation of wealth, 91; on contemporary world, 230; on great merchants, model of, 224; on influence of individual merchant houses, 75; on leisure arts, 186–187; on livelihood, 101; on measures of value, 102; on social mobility, 99; on townsman property, genesis of, 99; on urban communities, 52, 55, 75; on urban imaginary, 55–56
Ihara Saikaku, works by: characteristics of, 31, 34, 144; comic narrative forms, development of, 32; contradictory narratives in, 134, 144; didactic frameworks in fiction of, 140–141, 145; erotic prose fiction of, 29, 32; fiction of, as model, 30; interpretative incompleteness of, 141; keywords in, 133; Kiseki, influence on, 194; Kiseki's borrowings from, 215, 234–235; later works, focus of, 222; miscellaneous pieces (*zatsuwa-mono*), 137; narrative form and style of, 34–35, 135–136; prose style of, 248; protagonists of, 173; question of time periods for, 289n9; readings of, 132–133; social mobility as topic of, 131; space of the collection in, 35; spatial settings of, 231; subjects of, 5; tonal pivots in, 110–111; townsman pieces, 5, 33; urban spaces in, 113; wit in, 266. *See also Japan's Eternal Storehouse*
Illustrated Encyclopedia of Humanity (*Jinrin kinmōzui*), 121, 128
ima chōja. See millionaire of the moment
impermanence (*mujō*), 151, 161
"In the Past on Credit, Now Money Down" (*Mukashi wa kakezan ima wa tōzagin*, Saikaku), 67–74
individuals: material nature of, 221; relationship to households, 173
interregional economic system, 3, 6, 40, 56, 80
Ippū. *See* Nishizawa Tahei (Ippū)
Ishida Baigan, 130, 131
Ishikawa Tomonobu, 30
Itō Jinsai, 132

Japan: early-modern, as society of forms, 218–219; spatial dimensions of identity and community in early modern, 37; urban world of seventeenth-century Japan, 265. *See also* Edo; Tokugawa Japan
Japan's Eternal Storehouse (*Nippon eitaigura*, Saikaku), 49–90, 132–167; about, 38–39; architectural space of the *chō* in, 50f, 57; characteristics of, 33, 136–137, 140; conclusions on, 260; content versus form of, 137; contents of, 51; contradictions in, 134–137, 164–166; countryside locales in, 80; dialectic between the tactical and the strategic in, 96–97; didacticism of, 145, 154; gender in, 53; get-rich guides,

INDEX

relationship to, 147; historical figures in, 66–67; laughter in, 163; on mobility within domestic money-based economy, 76; narrative form of, 153; order of composition of stories in, 154–155; publication of, 30; social and spacial mobility in, 93; status in, 52–53; structure of, 141; subjects of, 75, 165–166; Teruoka on, 135; traces of local community in, 55–65, 59f; as turning point in Saikaku's works, 137–138; urban community in, 53
jest books (*hanashi-bon*), 229
Jinnai Hidenobu, 112–113
Jishō. *See* Hachimonjiya Hachizaemon
Johnson, Jeffrey, 135–136
jōkamachi. *See* castle towns
joke-telling (*hanashi*), 163, 229
Joken. *See* Nishikawa Joken
jōruri (puppet theater): *jōruri* chanting, 190–191; *jōruri* librettos, 28; *jōruri* puppetry, 188

kabuki: Edo kabuki, 278n13; Hachimonjiya's illustrated playbooks, 293n9
kagami. *See* mirrors
kagyō. *See* house trade
Kaibara Ekiken: Joken, comparison with, 1; Kiseki and, 226; on literacy, 199; mentioned, 32; shift in didactic tracts of, 225; on Song Confucian metaphysics, 298n20; on townsman norms, 225–226; *Vernacular Precepts for Children*, 178, 197
kaitoiya. *See* brokers
Kamakuraya Jinbei, 117, 157, 158
Kamigata region: print culture in, 31; woodblock-print cultures of, 255–256
Kamiya Jihei (fict.), 174
Kamo no Mabuchi, 261
kana-zōshi (vernacular booklets), 27, 31, 139, 144, 219-220
Kan'eiji temple, 126–127
Kaneya Chōhei, 30
kanzen chōaku. *See* promoting virtue and chastising vice

Karakaneya (fict.), 142
kashoku. *See* house trade
katagi (character): as concept, 223–224; definitions and meanings of, 222–224; meaning of, 213–214; use of term, 297n4
katagi-mono (character piece): components of, 176–177; as genre, development of, 253; Kiseki's, 266; narrative structure of, 248; regime of normality of, 216; as space of the collection, 215; spatial settings of, 231; Takahashi on, 201
Kenkō. *See* Yoshida no Kenkō
Ki no Tsurayuki, 202–203
kibyōshi. *See* yellow-covers
Kiheiji (fict.), 158–163
kijin (eccentric), 251
kingen. *See* aphorisms
Kiseki. *See* Ejima Kiseki
kishitsu: Ekiken's adaptation of, 225; Kiseki's use of term, 226; place in thought of Zhu Xi school, 221; as term, 220
kōeki. *See* trade
Kokin wakashū (*Collection of Ancient and Modern Poems*), 202–203
kokkei. *See* amusement
kokugaku. *See* nativist learning
kotoiya. *See* brokers
kuruma-gashi. *See* lending
kuruma-sen. *See* lending
Kyōden. *See* Santō Kyōden
Kyōhō era: characteristics of, 5; Kyōhō Reforms, 40
kyōkun. *See* didacticism
Kyoto: diverse demographics in, 28; as early center of print production, 28; popular fiction in, 30; textual culture of, comparison with Osaka, 29

large shops (*ōdana*), 72
laughter, 162–163, 205
Lefebvre, Henri, 13, 81, 186
leisure: disruptive potentialities of, 176; labor and, gendered forms of, 192–193; Lefebvre on, 186; role played by, 41

leisure arts (*yūgei*), 171–212; contradictory attitudes toward, 41–42; culture of, 184; deleterious influences of, 185–186; description of, 179–180; examples of, 77; gender and, 192–196; impact on the newly wealthy, 187; nature of, 207; of old urban elite, 181–182; overview of, 41–42; as signifiers of status, 182–183; townsman status and, 197; townsman's others and, 187–192, 189*f*

lending: copper wheel (*kuruma-sen*), 107; dailies (*hinashi*), 107; wheel lending (*kuruma-gashi*), 107; by temples, 103–104, 106–107; microfinance, 78; moneylenders, 78, 294n33; pawnbrokers, 78–79

Life of an Amorous Man, The (*Kōshoku ichidai otoko*, Saikaku), 29, 32

Life of an Amorous Woman, The (*Koshoku ichidai onna*, Saikaku), 82, 194–195, 233

lime ash, 126

literacy, 22–23, 196–201, 198*f*

livelihood (*nariwai*), 98; amoral nature of, 120–121; commerce as, 123; moral ambiguities of, 127; nature of, 122, 123, 129–130; Saikaku on, 99–100, 101; tactical quality of, 96–108, 105*f*

local communities, 15, 55–65, 59*f*, 75

lotteries (*tanomoshi, mujin*), 58–60

Love Suicides at Amijima (*Shinjū ten no Amijima*, Monzaemon), 174

low city (*shitamachi*), 112

low overcoming the high (*gekokujō*), 92

"Lucky Bid from the World of Greed, A" (*Yo wa yoku no irefuda ni shiawase*, Saikaku), 57–62, 59*f*, 83

lumber trade, 116–117

Magojirō (fict.), 188
Magosaburō (fict.), 188
Magotarō (fict.), 188
"Making a Living by Yodo Carp" (*Yowatari wa yodo-goi no hataraki*, Saikaku), 77–78
manual labor, 114, 120
marketplace: language of the, 49, 51. *See also* community of the marketplace

masculinity, crisis in, 242
Matsuake. *See* Yamaoka Matsuake
Matsuda Osamu, 113, 114
Matsumoto Jidayū, 175
Matsuo Bashō, 132
Matsuya (textile broker), 61, 76
Maza, Sarah, 20–21, 280n29
"Measure of Wisdom from a Rice Ladle at Eighty-Eight, A" (*Chie o hakaru hachijū-hachi no masukaki*, Saikaku), 163
"Medicine Prepared in Abnormal Fashion" (*Senjiyō tsune to wa kawaru toigusuri*, Saikaku), 109–118, 111*f*, 155–158, 161
merchants: fictional dissembling by, 262; great, model of, 224; merchant capital, 75, 86; merchant class, 44, 64; merchant households, 87; marketplace and, 65–74; merchant entrepreneur, ideal of, 54; nature of, 123
Merchant's Ledger of Worldly Success, The (*Risshin daifukuchō*, Yuirakuken), 166
metaphysics, Song Confucian, 221
mibun. *See* status
microfinance. *See* lending
millionaire of the moment (*ima chōja*), 243
Millionaires' Teachings, The (*Chōjakyō*), 145–146, 147–150, 151–152, 155–156
Miren (ghost writer), 209–210
mirrors (*kagami*), 33
mise. *See* shop fronts
Mitsui house: characteristics of, 75; Echigoya department store, 67, 70–74, 172; historical privilege of, 68; Hon-chō clothier shop, 70; as outsider in Hon-chō, 72; properties owned by, 71
Mitsui Hachirōemon, 69, 74
Mitsui Jusan, 69
Mitsui Kurōemon (fict.), 68, 69, 73, 90
Mitsui Norihei, 68–69, 181–182
Mitsui Shuhō, 69
Mitsui Takafusa, 171–172, 174, 212
Mitsui Takahira, 69, 171
Mitsui Takatomi, 69
Mitsui Takatoshi, 69, 71–72, 74, 171

INDEX

Mitsui Toshitsugu, 69, 181
Miyako no Nishiki, 208, 215
Miyamoto Mataji, 281n36
Mizuma Temple, 103–108, 109
mobility, in Tokugawa society, 92–93
moji shakai. *See* textual society
monbatsu chōnin. *See* privileged townsmen
money, in Saikaku's stories, 85
moneylenders. *See* lending
Monzaemon. *See* Chikamatsu Monzaemon
morality: coexistence with wealth, 102; moral karma, 247; moral transgression, 228; morally ambiguous practices in service of entrepreneurial success, 2, 78, 101–102, 107, 119, 120–121, 122, 127; shift to normality, 233
Moretti, Laura, 27, 31, 139, 146, 199, 278–279n13
Morita Shōtarō, 30, 49, 146, 290n23
Moriya Takeshi, 180
Moriyama Genkō (fict.), 160
Morson, Gary Saul, 149, 290n30
moveable type, 259
mujō. *See* impermanence
Murase Gonnojō. *See* Ejima Kiseki
Murase Shōzaemon, 210
myth, 157–158
Mythologies (Barthes), 157

Nagaidō Kiyū, 253
nagaya. *See* tenements
Nakai Nobuhiko, 24
Nakajima Takashi, 235
Nakamura Yukihiko, 138, 140, 222, 278n10, 296n65, 301n9
Nakano Mitsutoshi, 8–9, 258, 278n9
Naniwa Bridge, 113
nariwai. *See* livelihood
narrative: Certeau on, 118; as legitimating strategy of entrepreneurial townsman property, 118; literary narrative, 265; narrating the details (*shisai o katarite*), 106; narrative art, townsman's lifeworlds as, 129–130; omnibus narrative form, 141. *See also* reading
nativist learning (*kokugaku*), 261

New Eternal Storehouse of Japan, The (*Nippon shin eitaigura*, Dansui), 166
New Laughable Record (*Shin kashōki*, Saikaku), 200
Nihonbashi bridge, 112, 113, 114
ninbetsuchō. *See* population registration
Nishikawa Joken: on commerce, 97–98, 123, 130; Ekiken, comparison with, 1; on leisure arts, 205; on morality, 121, 130; *The Townsman's Satchel*, 1–5, 205; on townsmen, 1, 224
Nishikawa Sukenobu, 175
Nishimura Baifūken (Hanbei), 30
Nishimura Ichirōemon, 30, 140, 208
Nishiyama Matsunosuke, 183, 278n7
Nishiyama Sōin, 28
Nishizawa Ippu (Kyūzaemon), 208
Nishizawa Tahei (Ippū), 30
nō drumming, 183
Noma Kōshin, 149–150, 294n33
nonsense, in Kiseki's works, 239–241
normality: regime of normality, of *katagi-mono*, 216–217; of townsman society, 232; of urban everyday, 257. *See also* norms
norms: emerging norms of townsman identity, 250; everyday common sense as, 246; in Kiseki's works, 229; literatus and eccentrics as, 251; production of, 266; social normativity, development of new vision of, 253; of townsman society, 217–218; universal moral norms, 220. *See also* normality
nouveau riche, 187, 246
novels, 36

occupation (*shokubun*), 96–97
ochi. *See* punch lines
ōdana. *See* large shops
ōdoiya. *See* brokers
Ogawa Hikokurō, 232
Ooms, Herman, 297n9
Osaka: entrepreneurial environment of publishing field in, 31; as publishing center, 4; publishing in, 28–29; in Saikaku's works, 113

others, 53, 187–192, 189f, 190
outcasts, 124–125, 128

paradoxes: in *Eternal Storehouse*, 164; paradoxical tension between normativity and eccentricity, 218
particularity, norms and, 266–267
pawnbrokers. *See* lending
peasants: literacy among, 23–24; migration to cities, 18; urban commoners, differences from, 81. *See also* commoners
"Pederastic Old Man Who Loved Lads, A" (*Yarō o tanoshimu nanshoku oyaji*, Kiseki), 249–250
"Plucking Out the Very Eye of the Boddhisattva Kannon" (*Yo wa nukidori no Kan'on no manako*, Saikaku), 78–79
"Poem-Loving Daughter Who Couldn't Count a Hundred Coins, A" (*Hyaku no zeni yomi-kaneru uta-zuki no musume*, Kiseki), 193–194, 196, 234
polite arts. *See* leisure arts
politics: of form, 9–10; of *gesaku*, 264; nature of, 10; of townsman writing, 265
popular fiction: as commercial print, 228–229, fiction writing, perceptions of, 191–192; as ideologically productive medium, 7, 11; Nakano on, 8–9; nature of authorship of, 208
popular print, influence of, 173
population registration (*ninbetsuchō*), 15, 92
poverty, god of, 151–152
power: socio-spatial structure and, 14; status communities and, 10
primers (*tehon*), 33
print culture. *See* woodblock-print culture
privileged townsmen (*monbatsu chōnin*), 65–66, 180–181
promoting virtue and chastising vice (*kanzen chōaku*), 247
the proper, 94–95
proper conduct, 89–90
property, 56–57. *See also* urban property
prostitution: bad places (*akusho*), 176; brothel districts, 176, 188, 229; commercialization of Edo sex trade, 262; courtesan reviews (*yūjo hyōbanki*), 31–32; street prostitutes, 261
"Proud Old Man Who Loved to Watch His Child Dance, A" (*Odori o tanoshimu ko jiman no oyaji*, Kiseki), 250
proverbs. *See* aphorisms
publishing field, 21–22, 28
punch lines (*ochi*), 163

quacks, 121–123

rags-to-riches stories, 38, 77, 126, 143, 166
Rambelli, Fabio, 104
Rancière, Jacques, 10
rationalism, aphoristic, 145–152
reading: active reading, 111; appropriative reading, 109–110; influences on, 253–254; reading public, growth of, 228–229; stories of, 109
realism, 8
Record of Great Treasures for Men, A (*Nan chōhōki*), 186, 200
Record of Great Treasures for Women, A (*Onna chōhōki*), 192
Record of Observations on Townsmen, A (*Chōnin kōken roku*, Mitsui Takafusa), 171–172, 174, 181
renters, 16, 18
repute (*gaibun*), 180
rice stalk millionaires (*warashibe chōja*), 122–123
Right Action for All (*Banmin tokuyō*, Suzuki Shōsan), 220
Robber Zhi (fict.), 261
rōnin. *See* warriors
rural districts (*zaikata*), 17
ryōgawa-chō. *See chō*

Saeki Takahiro, 234
saikaku. *See* wit
Saikaku. *See* Ihara Saikaku
Saikaku's Loose Threads Tied Off (*Saikaku oridome*, Saikaku), 166
Saikaku's Stories from the Provinces (*Saikaku shokoku banashi*, Saikaku), 137, 140, 230

INDEX

Sakamotoya Jinbei (fict.), 160
Sanba. *See* Shikitei Sanba
Santō Kyōden, 256–258
santoban. *See* three-city editions
Satoko Shimazaki, 278n13
Satomura Shōtaku, 192
"Scattering Coins Like Seeds of Good Fortune" (*Shiawase no tane o makisen*, Saikaku), 78
scholarship: as leisure art, 191, 197–199; relationship to literacy, 199
Seki (fict.), 261–262
self: early modern selfhood, 259–260; material individuality of, 221–222; representations of selfhood, 215; townsman self, composition of, 266–267
"Selling Scouring Rushes to Scrub the Heart Clean: The Character of an Honest Peasant" (*Tokusa-uri wa kokoro o migaku shōjikina hyakushō katagi*, Kiseki), 177–179
setsuwa. *See* anecdotal narratives
Shikitei Sanba, 263–264
Shimai Sōshitsu, 24, 185
shimin. *See* four estates
shimotaya (*shimōtaya*, closed-up shop), 181
Shingaku (heart learning) movement, 42–43
Shinohara Susumu, 230
Shinroku (fict.), 120–128, 186
"Shippers and Packhorses in the Courtyard of Abumiya" (*Funabito umakata Abumiya no niwa*, Saikaku), 62–65, 82, 223
shitamachi. *See* low city
shokoku-banashi. *See* stories from the provinces
shokubun. *See* occupation
shokunin katagi (character of the craftsman), 213
shop fronts (*mise*), 192–193
shōrui awaremi rei. *See* edicts of compassion for living beings
shū no kūkan. *See* space of the collection
signifiers, 201–206, 237, 267, 268–269
Simmel, Georg, 76, 230

society: mobility of, 22; polite urban society, culture of, 237; social boundaries, 119; social difference, 123; social distinctions, 217; social forms, 222; social identity, 184; social imaginary, 18; social improvement, 228; social mobility, 17, 51, 91, 134; social networks, 14; social normality, 252; social norms, 217; social power, 60; urban, 11, 56, 60
society of writing. *See* textual society
socio-spatial structure, 13, 14
Sōgi's Tales from the Provinces (*Sōgi shokoku monogatari*, Nishimura Ichirōemon), 140
Sōkyū (Kiseki's grandfather), 192
sole transmission principle, 292n5
Song Confucianism, 139, 221, 223, 225, 227, 298n20
space of the collection (*shū no kūkan*): characteristics of, 269; description of, 144; as device of ideological consolidation, 37; interpretation of, 33–42; in Sanba's works, 263; as term, use of, 35; of *ukiyo-zōshi*, 265–266
space(s): conflictual, 95; social systems and, 13–15; spatial itineraries of collecting and selling, 115–116; spatial reading, appropriative acts of, 109; spatiality of *ukiyo-zōshi*, 38; of urban leisure, 113; use of shared, 263
status: Atherton on, 219; as fundamental framework of social distinction, 220; geography of, 13; impact of woodblock-print capitalism on, 27–28; in *Japan's Eternal Storehouse*, 52–53; shifts in logic of, 252; leisure arts and, 192; status in Tokugawa urban world, 12–22; status display, 183; status group (*mibun*), 8, 12, 13–14, 215, 224–225, 259–260, 264–265; status system for books, 258–259; of townsman, markers of, 184–185
storefront sales, 68, 70
storefronts, images of, 49, 50f
stories: as products, 49; of reading, 109
stories from the provinces (*shokoku-banashi*), 137, 139–140

INDEX

strategies, 94, 126. *See also* tactics
street peddlers, 70, 74, 86
street peddling (*furi-uri*), 77
street performers (*gōmune*), 125
"Strung Along by Those Better Versed in the Ways of the World: The Character of a Poet" (*Seken no hito ni hanage o yomaruru kajin katagi*, Kiseki), 202–205
sui (elegance, connoisseurship), 32
Sukenobu. *See* Nishikawa Sukenobu
Suketarō (fict.), 202–205
sumo wrestling, 188, 227
sumptuary regulations, 225
Suruga-chō, 71
Suzuki Shōsan, 220

tactics: Certeau on, 108; of livelihood, 96–108, 105*f*; pivot to strategy, 126; in Saikaku's works, 118; spatial, 93–94; strategies, relationship to, 94, 126
Takahashi Akihiko, 201
"Taking Inventory" (*Tana-oroshi*, Yashoku Jibun), 230
Takizawa Bakin, 263
Tales of Samurai Honor (*Buke giri monogatari*, Saikaku), 222
Tamenaga Shunsui, 296n1
Tamiya Nakanobu, 294n33
Taniwaki Masachika, 291n41
taste (discernment), 183
tehon. *See* primers
temples. *See* Buddhism
"Ten Virtues of Tea, Gone in an Instant, The" (*Cha no jittoku mo ichido ni mina*, Saikaku), 77
tenarai (reading and writing), 199
tenements (*nagaya*), 16, 263
"Tengu by Name, with a Windflower Crest" (*Tengu wa iena no kazaguruma*, Saikaku), 80–81
Teruoka Yasutaka, 135, 137, 154, 162–163, 278n9, 289n9
Tetsuo Najita, 59
textual society (*moji shakai*, society of writing), 22–23
Theophrastan characters, 215

Those Familiar Bestsellers (*Gozonji no shōbaimono*, Kyōden), 257–258, 259
"Three *monme* and five *bun* at New Year" (*San-monme go-fun akebono no kane*, Saikaku), 82
three-city editions (*santoban*), 30
toiya. *See* brokers
toiya chōja. *See* brokers
Tokugawa Ieyasu, 219
Tokugawa Japan: literacy in, 22–23; polity, 26, 92; popular culture, 269; print culture, 4, 264; shogunate, premise of, 8; social and media systems of, 259; society in, 92–93, 172, 218–219; urban society, 13–14; woodblock-print culture of, audience for, 258
Tokugawa Tsunayoshi, 128
Tokugawa Yoshimune, 171
tosei (making a way through the world), 98
townsman/townsmen: as cultural professionals, 205; early modern, scholarly treatments of emerging subjectivity of, 94; economic existence of, 268; in *Eternal Storehouse*, 76–77; house trade of, 172; identity of, 14–16; literacy of, 23–24; literary voice of, 260–261; markers of successful, 212; narration of identity of, 44; performative self-representation, 267; power of, 95; self-made townsman, 67; shift to merchant class, 54; as signifiers, 45; as text, approach to, 86–90; townsman authorship, 206–212; townsman conduct, 224; townsman culture, 18, 185–186; townsman entrepreneur, 129; townsman femininity, 232; townsman leisure, 188; townsman norms, 226, 246; townsman retirees, 242; townsman self, 218–226, 266–267; townsman society, 179, 217, 230, 231; warriors, comparison with, 267. *See also* urbanism
townsman households: aging father of, 242; alienation within; 173, 174, 206; components of, 173; contradictions within ideology of, 41; establishment

INDEX

of, 172–173; fictionality of, 211–212; house codes of, 24; leisure arts and, 179, 184–185; as locus for behavioral norms, 41; nature of, 206; norms of, 201; as target of Kiseki's writings, 176; as unit of townsman society, 24

townsman identity: characteristics of, 6; components of, 245; constructions of, and woodblock-print culture, 25; emerging norms of, 250; entrepreneurial ethos and, 133–134; generic sense of, 266; literacy's role in, 22; Mitsui Takafusa on, 212; shared sense of, 37

townsman literature: critics of narratives of, 8; politics of, 7–12; townsman prose, birth of, 164–167; trope of, 277–278n7; as voice of popular resistance to warrior authority, 7–8

Townsman's Satchel, The (*Chōnin bukuro*, Joken), 1–5, 205

trade (*kōeki*), 97, 147

transgressions: in community of the marketplace, 78; *katagi-mono*'s fixation on, 214–215; minor, in Kiseki's works, 229

transportation networks, 140

Travel Baskets of Lads and Ladies (*Yakei tabi tsuzura*, Kiseki), 208

Treasure Chest of Greater Learning for Women, A (*Onna daigaku takarabako*), 232, 233–234

trickster heroes, 94–95

tsū (sophisticate), 262

Tsubouchi Shōyō, 296–297n1

Tsukada Takashi, 13, 62

Twenty Unfilial Exemplars of Japan (*Honchō nijū fukō*, Saikaku) 175, 179, 226–228, 246, 247

two paths of martial and literary arts (*bunbu ryōdō*), 23

Ukina (fict), 256

ukiyo. *See* floating world

ukiyo-zōshi (floating world booklets): birth of, 31; contradictions in, 44; form of, 32, 214; function of, 37;

paratextual structure of, 35; reading of, 254; social and spatial positions of, 38; space of the collection of, 265; as term, 282n49; *yakusha hyōbanki*, comparison with, 296n61

Unfilial Exemplars. *See Twenty Unfilial Exemplars of Japan*

"Unheeded Advice Makes for Ineffective Medicine: The Character of a Doctor Who Wouldn't Mend His Own Ways" (*Iken wa kikanu kusuri kokoro o naosanu isha katagi*, Kiseki), 197–201, 198f, 228

urbanism: interregional urban communities, 39; urban centers, 3, 6; urban commerce, 75, 182–183; urban commoners, 16, 81; urban community(ies), 52, 53, 55, 86, 87; urban consumer markets, 56; urban districts (*machikata*), 15, 17; urban economy, 161; urban entrepreneurship, 109; urban identity, 3, 6, 11–12, 39, 86, 91; urban imaginary, 55–56, 231; urban laboring classes, 261; urban leisure class, 66; urban life, contingent ephemerality of, 118; urban maps, 112; urban property, 19, 60; urban riots, 16; urban social imaginary, 73; urban society, 11, 56, 60, 252–253; urban spaces, 113; urban spatiality, 38, 72; urban walking, 108–109

"Useless Show of Strength, A" (*Muyō no chikara-jiman*, Saikaku), 227–228

various arts (*shogei*). *See* leisure arts

Veblen, Thorsten, 182

Vernacular Precepts for Children (*Wazoku dōjikun*, Ekiken), 178, 197

"Vigorous Old Man Who Loved to Eat, A" (*Shoku o tanoshimu tassha oyaji*, Kiseki), 243–244, 244f, 245–246

"Votive Mat, a Sign of Prayers Answered, A" (*Inoru shirushi no kami no oshiki*, Saikaku), 79–80

Wahrman, Dror, 280n29

warashibe chōja. *See* rice-stalk millionaire

warriors: commoners, separation from, 93; leisure arts, pursuit of, 225–226; as mirrors, 267; *rōnin*, administrative policies surrounding, 224–225; warrior authority, 15, 101, 128; warrior households, 66–68

Watanabe Kenji, 242

way of the townsman (*chōnin no michi*), 130

wealth: coexistence with morality, 102; contingency of, 164; importance of, in new urban identity, 91; Joken on accumulation of, 98; locus of origins of, 123; logic of distribution of, 159–160; means of accumulation of, 96, 104, 126–127, 128, 130, 142–145, 146–147; paths to, 77, 154; worldly, Buddhist conceptions of origins of, 104

"Weary of Leisure: The Character of a Retiree Laid Up to Recover" (*Yūkyō ni kutabirete yōjō ni hikikomu inja katagi*, Kiseki), 229–230

"When a Paper Fortune Falls in Tatters" (*Kamiko shindai no yabure-doki*, Saikaku), 76

"Winter Thunderbolt Brings Injury, A" (*Kega no fuyu-gaminari*, Saikaku), 158–161, 162f

wit (*saikaku*): entrepreneurial, 108; in *Eternal Storehouse*, 92; ethos of, 129; of millionaires, 103; nature of, 105–106, 120; Saikaku on, 61, 129; as spatial tactics, in *Eternal Storehouse*, 93–94; spatiality of, 104–10

women: and community of the marketplace, 82–83; accomplishments of, 193–194; agency of, 83, 84; assertive, literary depictions of, 233; of the Edo demimonde, 261; as household heads, 15, 286n48; Kiseki's female protagonists, 233–241; in leisure arts, 192; married women, leisure arts and, 192; property ownership by, 60–61; roles in townsman household, 82; woman's pen (*nyohitsu*), 193–194; women's labor, social agency of, 195–196; women's literacy, 195; Yoshiwara courtesans, 262

woodblock-print culture: characteristics of, 269; commercialization of, 3; didacticism of, 219, 225; distinct status communities and, 261; emergence of, 18, 26; *gesaku* and, 255; influence of, 267; status order and, 264–265; as normalizing force, 4, 33

Worldly Young Men. See *Characters of Worldly Young Men*

"Wounded by His Own Strength: The Character of a Sumo Wrestler Who Tossed His Own Estate" (*Dairiki wa mi no kizu shindai nageta sumō-tori katagi*, Kiseki), 188-190, 189f, 227–228

yakazu haikai. See extemporaneous solo composition

yaku. See duties

yakusha hyōbanki, ukiyo-zōshi, comparison with, 296n61

Yama no Yatsu (Yamamoto Hachizaemon), 208

Yamaoka Matsuake, 261–262

Yano Kimio, 107

Yashoku Jibun, 215, 230, 235

yellow-covers (*kibyōshi*), 256

Yokota Fuyuhiko, 99, 195

Yoshida no Kenkō, 150–151

Yoshida Nobuyuki, 13, 56, 71, 279n16

Yuirakuken (writer), 166

yūgei. See leisure arts

yūjo hyōbanki. See prostitution

zaikata. See rural districts

zaisho. See countryside

zatsuwa-mono. See Ihara Saikaku, works by

Zhu Xi, 220–221, 225, 227

GPSR Authorized Representative: Easy Access System Europe, Mustamäe tee 50, 10621 Tallinn, Estonia, gpsr.requests@easproject.com

www.ingramcontent.com/pod-product-compliance
Lightning Source LLC
Chambersburg PA
CBHW022030290426
44109CB00014B/813